Researching Chinese Learners

Researching Chinese Learners

Skills, Perceptions and Intercultural Adaptations

Edited by

Lixian Jin
Reader in Linguistics and Health Communication, De Montfort University, UK

and

Martin Cortazzi
Visiting Professor, University of Warwick, UK

First published 2011 by
PALGRAVE MACMILLAN

Palgrave Macmillan in the UK is an imprint of Macmillan Publishers Limited,
registered in England, company number 785998, of Houndmills, Basingstoke,
Hampshire RG21 6XS.

Palgrave Macmillan in the US is a division of St Martin's Press LLC,
175 Fifth Avenue, New York, NY 10010.

Palgrave Macmillan is the global academic imprint of the above companies
and has companies and representatives throughout the world.

Palgrave® and Macmillan® are registered trademarks in the United States,
the United Kingdom, Europe and other countries.

ISBN 978–0–230–24388–0   hardback

This book is printed on paper suitable for recycling and made from fully
managed and sustained forest sources. Logging, pulping and manufacturing
processes are expected to conform to the environmental regulations of the
country of origin.

A catalogue record for this book is available from the British Library.

A catalog record for this book is available from the Library of Congress.

10   9   8   7   6   5   4   3   2   1
20   19   18   17   16   15   14   13   12   11

Printed and bound in the United States of America

Contents

v

List of Figures

List of Tables

Acknowledgements

The editors and all the authors would like to acknowledge the help of the many hundreds or, rather, thousands of Chinese students in China, Hong Kong, the UK, Australia, New Zealand and Canada who took part in the research projects which are featured in each chapter of this book. Many thanks also to the Chinese teachers and teachers from the West in China and in universities in the above countries/areas who participated in these projects.

We are grateful for their cooperation and assistance in this research and we hope that the results will be of direct or indirect assistance to their learning and that of future cohorts of Chinese learners and their teachers in China and around the world. No doubt some will in their turn continue to research aspects of the learning of Chinese students and teachers.

Lixian Jin and Martin Cortazzi

Notes on Contributors

Dr Jenny Barnett is a Senior Lecturer and key researcher in the Centre for Studies in Literacy, Policy and Learning Cultures at the University of South Australia where she has been working since 1987. Much of Dr Barnett's current teaching lies in supervising doctoral students on diverse topics in TESOL, literacy education and Indigenous education, which are also the main areas of her own research.

Dr Jonathan G. Bayley is an Associate Professor in the Faculty of Education, University of Windsor, Canada. He co-supervises Yi Zhou's dissertation with Dr Shijing Xu. In addition to performing, teaching, adjudicating and music workshop activities, Dr Bayley has published numerous articles, arrangements and original works. His research interests focus on music and arts education, survey research and design, interviewing as qualitative research, and historical research with a curriculum focus.

Prof. Jill Bourne was Professor and Dean of the Faculty of Education at the University of Strathclyde, Glasgow. She was previously a Vice President of AILA and Chair of the British Association for Applied Linguistics. Prof. Bourne specializes in the detailed analysis of classroom interaction, with a particular interest in multilingual classrooms and in raising the attainment of students from disadvantaged backgrounds. With her husband, Euan Reid, she edited the 2003 *World Yearbook on Language Education* (London: Routledge Falmer).

Prof. Martin Cortazzi is a Visiting Professor in the Centre of Applied Linguistics at Warwick University, UK and at a number of key universities in China. He is also Academic Advisor for English at the Polytechnic University of Hong Kong and at the University of Science in Malaysia. He has taught applied linguistics courses for English teachers in Britain, China, Turkey, Lebanon, Malaysia, Singapore, Iran, Brunei, Norway, Cyprus and elsewhere. He has extensive experience of teaching and serving as external examiner for MA courses and supervising and examining for PhD degrees in Britain and internationally. He has published books and articles on narrative analysis, the application of metaphor analysis, issues in language and education such as literacy, vocabulary learning, and cultures of learning. His current research examines narratives and students' metaphors as a way to explore issues in intercultural experience, identity and cultures of learning.

Dr Peter Crisp has lived and taught in China and Hong Kong for the past 25 years, at the Chinese University of Hong Kong for 22 of those years. Prof. Crisp has recently begun to divide his time mainly between Hong Kong and Dublin, Ireland. He was originally trained as a literary scholar but in the context of 1970s literary 'theory' turned to a more serious approach to literary studies by drawing on linguistics and stylistics. He has been largely involved in the areas of semantics and pragmatics and for the past 15 years has concentrated on the study of metaphor and metonymy. Most recently he has been involved in the study of allegory and has had a large number of articles published in this area. Despite his continuing literary focus, he has supervised a number of PhDs in Applied Linguistics, most of which have involved issues of metaphor and metonymy and cross-cultural/linguistic issues between Chinese and English.

Dr Joan Cutting is a Senior Lecturer in TESOL at the University of Edinburgh, specializing in EFL methodology, and text and discourse for TESOL. She researches spoken English, with an interest in vague language and in-group code and applications to TESOL. One of Dr Cutting's main research areas is the needs of Chinese students in UK universities: she has studied the grammar of Chinese students speaking English, and requirements of EAP design for Chinese students, focusing in particular on their interactions in seminars and tutorials, and their adaptation to the UK university system. She considers the implications for non-language-specialist-staff development. She is the author of *Analysing the Language of Discourse Communities* (2000), *Vague Language Explored* (2007) and *Pragmatics and Discourse* (2008), and co-editor of the Edinburgh Textbooks in TESOL series.

Dr Kathy Durkin is a Senior Lecturer at the Media School, Bournemouth University where, for the past ten years, she has taught research methodology, cross-cultural communication, study skills and critical thinking. She has conducted research in China, Israel and Australia, as well as in the United Kingdom, investigating how international students adapt to the norms of academic critical thinking and argumentation in different cultures. Her current research interest is the marketization of education and its effect on critical thinking as an important component of higher education.

Dr Qing Gu is an Associate Professor in the School of Education, University of Nottingham, UK. She is a member of the Executive Committee of the British Association for International and Comparative Education (BAICE), a member of the *Compare* Editorial Board and Reviews Editor of the *International Journal of Educational Development*. Her research interests are teacher professional development, school improvement and the internationalization of higher education. Dr Gu is the author of *Teacher Development: Knowledge and Context* (2007), co-author of *Teachers Matter* (2007) and *New Lives of Teachers* (2010), and Guest Editor of the Special Issue of *Language and Intercultural Communication* on 'The role of culture in English as an international language' (2009). Her articles on Chinese learners have been published in academic journals including *Compare, European Journal of Education, Language and Intercultural Communication* and *Language, Culture and Curriculum*.

Prof. Jane Jackson (PhD, OISE, University of Toronto) is Professor in the English Department at the Chinese University of Hong Kong. Her research interests include intercultural communication/pragmatics, reticence and anxiety in L2 learners, identity (re)construction and student residence abroad. With the support of competitive research grants, she is investigating the learning of study-abroad students. Prof. Jackson serves on the editorial board or manuscript review panels of several applied linguistics and intercultural communication journals. She has published numerous articles and book chapters in peer-reviewed applied linguistics, intercultural communication/education, and study-abroad journals. Recent monographs include *Language, Identity, and Study Abroad: Sociocultural Perspectives* (2008) and *Intercultural Journeys: From Study to Residence Abroad* (2010). She is currently editing the *Routledge Handbook of Intercultural Communication*.

Dr Lixian Jin is Reader in Linguistics & Health Communication at De Montfort University, UK and a Visiting Professor at a number of key universities in China. She is the Director for the Centre of Intercultural Research in Communication and Learning (CIRCL) at De Montfort University. Internationally, she is an Executive editorial board member for *International Journal of Language & Communication Disorders*, UK and USA; the Review Editor for *Asian Journal of English Language Teaching* (*AJELT*), Hong Kong; and a board member for other international journals. She has taught applied linguistics courses and trained English teachers and speech and language therapists at universities in China, Cyprus, Turkey, Hong Kong and Britain and supervised research students from different countries. She is regularly invited to give public lectures, keynote speeches and workshops to international and professional audiences, for example by British universities, the Royal Colleges of Speech and Language

Therapists, Nursing, and General Practitioners, by the British Council and by universities in China, Taiwan, Hong Kong and in Middle Eastern and European countries. Her research interests and publications are in the areas of cultures of learning, bilingual language assessments, narrative analysis, metaphor analysis, academic intercultural communication and Chinese learners of English.

Dr Divya Jindal-Snape is a senior lecturer in the School of Education, Social Work and Community Education at the University of Dundee, UK. She has experience of working in primary and secondary schools, and higher education in different countries. Dr Jindal-Snape's research interests lie in the field of educational transitions and inclusion. A significant proportion of her work has been with children and young people with additional support needs, especially children and young people with visual impairment, autism, learning difficulties, and emotional and behavioural needs This has also involved developing social interaction through drama techniques and other forms of creative arts education.

Dr Danny Chung-hong Leung received his PhD degree in applied English linguistics from the Chinese University of Hong Kong (CUHK) in 2008. In the same year, he joined the Department of English at CUHK, where he is currently assistant professor and director of the MA Programme in Applied English Linguistics. Having been teaching in the ESL context in Hong Kong as well as conducting applied cognitive linguistics research for nearly a decade, Dr Leung understands both the linguistic and conceptual difficulties facing L2 learners of English when learning L2 figurative language. His research interests encompass a wide range of education-oriented issues in applied cognitive linguistics such as L2 figurative language teaching and learning, L2 metaphoric and metonymic competence, and cross-linguistic/cultural analysis of idioms.

Dr Xiuping Li holds several posts related to Chinese as a Second Language (L2) and Foreign Language (CFL), including Language Instructor at the Faculty of Oriental Studies, University of Oxford; Lecturer at Newcastle College; Adviser at Open Access Centre (OAC), School of Modern Languages, Newcastle University; Head of Chinese Language Content Writers Team for Routes into Languages, North East, UK; Exam Moderator with a university and a leading awarding body in the UK; Associate Editor of *Asian EFL Journal*. She has nearly 30 years' experience of teaching English and Chinese in a variety of contexts in

China and the UK, covering primary, secondary and higher education with interest in applied linguistics, cross-cultural communications and bilingual education skills teacher training. Dr Li's latest research focuses on *Chinese Community Language in Newcastle*; her latest publications are as a joint author of textbooks and teacher resource books, *Edexcel Chinese for AS* (2008) and *Edexcel Chinese for A2* (2009).

Dr Meihua Liu is associate professor of English at the Department of Foreign Languages, Tsinghua University, China. Her research interests mainly include second/foreign language teaching and learning in Chinese contexts, reticence and anxiety in EFL classrooms, individual differences, and second language writing. Dr Liu is a reviewer for such journals as *The Journal of Asia TEFL*, *Indonesian Journal of English Language Teaching* and *China EFL Journal*. She has published in a number of journals such as *Modern Language Journal*, *TESL Canada Journal*, *TESL Reporter*, *System*, *ITL: International Journal of Applied Linguistics*, *Asian Journal of English Language Teaching*, *Indonesian Journal of English Language Teaching*, *The Journal of Asia TEFL* and *Asian EFL Journal*. Her recent monograph is *Reticence and Anxiety in Oral English Lessons* (2009).

Heather Parris-Kidd is a teacher of English as a Second Language with over 15 years' experience throughout Asia, Europe and Australia. She completed her Master's of Education by research on 'Cultures of learning and student participation: a study in two multicultural classrooms for English as an Additional Language' at UniSA in July 2007 under the Supervision of Dr Jenny Barnett. She is working as the Director of Studies and International Office Manager for Southern Cross University, Coffs Harbour Campus in New South Wales, Australia.

Dr Nick Pilcher is a lecturer in In-sessional English for Academic Purposes at Edinburgh Napier University, Edinburgh, UK. He taught EAP at Heriot Watt University, Edinburgh, from 2001 to 2009, where he also received his doctorate in 2007. He is interested in EAP teaching, qualitative research, experiences and perceptions of learning, and the dissemination and usage of qualifications framework.

Dr Gillian Skyrme is a lecturer in linguistics, second language teaching and English for Academic Purposes in the School of Language Studies at Massey University, New Zealand. She completed her PhD in 2008, investigating the experiences of Chinese international undergraduate students studying in a New Zealand university from a socio-cultural perspective. She was winner of the Applied Linguistics Association of New Zealand Best PhD Thesis award for that year. Articles from this research have appeared in *Studies in Higher Education*, *New Zealand Studies in Applied Linguistics* and *Journal of English for Academic Purposes*. Dr Skyrme is co-editor of *New Zealand Journal of Applied Linguistics*. Other research interests include the learning of English by migrants in community settings.

Dr Phiona Stanley is a lecturer in Academic Development at the University of South Australia. She holds master's degrees in Education and Politics and for her PhD she investigated the training needs, roles and identities of Western English language teachers at a university in China. Since 1993, she has worked in TESOL in six countries including China, where she worked as an educational consultant for a multinational company that conducts language-teaching operations in 60+ Chinese cities. Since arriving in Australia in 2004, she has trained English language teachers on Cambridge CELTA courses and has taught on master's programmes in Applied Linguistics and Education at the Universities of Adelaide, South Australia and Sydney, the latter including teaching on offshore master's courses at Fudan University, China. Her research interests include the internationalization of higher education, transnationalism, interculturality, identity and gender.

Prof. Keith Topping is Professor of Educational and Social Research in the School of Education at the University of Dundee. His main research interest is peer learning, in many contexts and subject areas. Other interests include parents as educators, problematic behaviour and social competence, and computer-assisted learning and assessment. Prof. Topping has published 140 peer-reviewed journal papers, 44 chapters and 19 books, including *Peer-Assisted Learning* (1998), *Thinking Reading Writing* (2001), *Inclusive Education* (2005) and *Cultural and Educational Adaptation of Chinese Students in the UK* (2009). He has consulted with national government and large organizations in several countries and his work has been translated into 11 languages.

Prof. Cynthia White is Professor of Applied Linguistics in the School of Language Studies, Massey University, New Zealand. She has research interests in language-learning strategies, learner autonomy, distance learning environments, e-learning and language, and settlement issues among migrants and refugees In 2004 Prof. White received the International TESOL Virginia French Allen Award for Scholarship and Service. In 2003 her book *Language Learning in Distance Education* was published, and a co-edited book entitled *Languages and Distance Education: Evolution and Change* appeared in 2005. Prof. White's articles appear in *System, TESOLANZ Journal, Distance Education, Open Learning, Journal of Distance Learning, Hong Kong Journal of Applied Linguistics* and *Innovation in Language Learning and Teaching*. She serves on the editorial boards of seven international journals and two national journals. In 2008 she was invited presenter at the Bertelsmann Foundation, Berlin, on language, settlement and social cohesion among immigrant youth.

Dr Shijing Xu is an Affiliated Research Associate at the National Research Centre for Foreign Language Education, Beijing Foreign Studies University, China, and Assistant Professor, Faculty of Education, University of Windsor, Canada. She was formerly Associate Professor of English as a Foreign Language (EFL) and Associate Dean of Humanities and Social Sciences, University of Science and Technology Beijing. Dr Xu's research interests focus on narrative approaches to intergenerational, bilingual and multicultural educational issues and school–family–community connections in cross-cultural curriculum studies and teacher education. Her current research is on the reciprocal adaptation and learning of new-comers and the Canadian society. She is concerned about international and intercultural communication of values in education.

Dr Tianshu Zhao is an Associate Professor of the School of Foreign Languages at Shenyang Normal University, China. She recieved her PhD (Applied Linguistics for Language Teaching) in the School of Education, University of Southampton, UK in 2007. Dr Zhao's research interest is in classroom interaction and intercultural communication, especially intercultural adaptation. In June 2008, she attended the 8th CAFIC (China Association for Intercultural Communication) and ACCS (Association for Chinese Communication Studies) International Conference, and her paper entitled 'An ethnographic study of the two-way intercultural adaptation process between Chinese students and British lecturers in the UK' has been included in the volume entitled *Intercultural Communication between China and the World: Interpersonal, Organizational and Mediated Perspectives*, published in China (2010).

Yi Zhou is a PhD Candidate at the Faculty of Education, University of Windsor, Canada. She holds master's degrees in Linguistics and Education. She used to teach English as a Foreign Language (EFL) at a Chinese university. Her research interests include intercultural language teaching and learning, EFL teacher education and language-learning motivation. Her doctoral research focuses on Chinese EFL teachers and their intercultural competence teaching.

Dr Yuefang Zhou is a Research Fellow in the Bute Medical School, University of St Andrews. She was awarded an MSc with distinction in applied research methods in 2003 and a PhD on 'Processes of cultural pedagogical shock and adaptation of Chinese postgraduate students in the UK' in 2006, both by the University of Dundee. Her main research interest lies in the field of intercultural communication and cultural and educational adaptation. Dr Zhou's main publications include 'Chinese students in the UK: a two-way reciprocal adaptation' (2008), 'Patterns of adaptation of Chinese students in the United Kingdom' (2009) and 'Cultural and educational adaptation during transition from Chinese to UK universities' (2010). She is the co-author of the book *Cultural and Educational Adaptation of Chinese Students in the UK* (with Keith Topping and Divya Jindal-Snape, 2009).

Introduction: Contexts for Researching Chinese Learners

Lixian Jin and Martin Cortazzi

This book has a broad focus on three themes related to Chinese learners: teaching and learning in classrooms in China, the intercultural adaptation of Chinese learners in international contexts of education, and the application of a range of research approaches and methodologies. These themes are discussed and illustrated below. The book should be of interest to those concerned with issues in teaching and learning in higher education, specifically in education in China and of Chinese students internationally; to students and teachers in applied linguistics and language learning, to those concerned with intercultural adaptation and how internationalization affects learners and teachers; and to researchers and students involved in the application and combination of different research approaches and methods, including some more innovative methods, to studies of learners. The book is also relevant to those with an interest in comparative education, since teaching and learning in China is implicitly compared with that found in other countries in many chapters.

The next sections here look briefly at the Chinese context of education and internationalization, at how this book fits into the current movement of literature about Chinese learners and at the title of this book, before we give a thematic overview of the chapters of the book.

1.1   Chinese education and internationalization

There are several important reasons why Chinese learners should be of interest to researchers, teachers and learners elsewhere. A first reason concerns the scale: education in China is easily characterized by statistical superlatives. Compared to other countries, China has the largest education system. In terms of quantity, this means China has more teachers, awards more degrees, teaches the largest number of learners, circulates more books, teaches the most learners of English as a foreign language, and China is the originating country of the single largest group of international students to many other education systems. Since the pace of development is rapid, and education in China is expanding and undergoing reforms in a context of social change, many specific figures will be outdated as soon as they are published.

However, it is much less easy to make similar qualitative statements about the learners in such a huge system: one reason is that education in China includes a range of diversity and differences in development, geographically and socially, and therefore necessarily includes a range of excellent features, other facets which are fast developing and other aspects as yet relatively undeveloped. Thus, a second reason to take an interest in Chinese learners is the changing context. In recent years China has officially emphasized 'quality education'. This implies that quality aspects are still developing and hence that there is a continuing need to research underlying issues surrounding the quality of the social and educational development of Chinese learners. Since 'quality education' in China includes a turn to more modern approaches to teaching and learning – including learner-centred ones – it is appropriate and timely to collect research reports of recent studies of Chinese learners, especially those which include Chinese perspectives. In this collection of research studies, most were conducted collaboratively by Chinese academics working with Western scholars. We hope this affords a double vision of 'inside' and 'outside' views and interpretations of research.

Apart from the aspects of statistical superlatives and the changing quality of learner-centred education of Chinese learners, there are further reasons why researchers or teachers and learners inside and outside China should take an interest in Chinese learners. A third set of reasons involves international perspectives. The rapid economic development and significant international status of China mean that studies of Chinese learners may inform us of the students' ways of learning, knowing that as future professionals and perhaps as later leaders in many fields they will have an important role in China and the world tomorrow. The internationalization of universities in the West has meant, among other aspects, that in many places Chinese students often form the largest or at least a major group of international learners, so the more teachers and others know or are aware of regarding their backgrounds, contexts and learning, the better these institutions may be able to meet their needs and help them to be successful in their studies and future life (which of course also benefits these institutions). China is also concerned with international education, as shown in the establishment of Confucius Institutes in many countries and the rising number of international students who go to Chinese universities to study the Chinese language and other subjects. Chinese universities are therefore also becoming internationalized. Increasingly they enter into collaborative arrangements and partnerships for research and study, which means that many Western visitors, scholars, teachers and students go to Chinese universities (which again benefits both the sojourners and the hosts).

A fourth reason is that Chinese education has interesting features which demand study to identify reasons for students' success and to draw implications for teaching and learning elsewhere: the significant traditional respect for education and learning, the willingness of parents and students to invest a great deal of time and finance to support students' studies in secondary and tertiary education, the sense of optimism and confidence in the future combined with a belief in success through hard work in education that characterizes many Chinese students.

For these kinds of reasons both Chinese educators and others worldwide can learn from these investigations. There is an array of knowledge, insights and applications which can be drawn from them for the teaching and learning of anyone anywhere. Thus there is a fifth reason which combines some of the ones listed above: Chinese learners can be anywhere. There is an obvious transnational or multicultural dimension now in most of the world's education systems, so studies of Chinese learners are among those of which educational professionals and researchers need to be informed. Through migration, heritage, travel for visits and exchanges, study and employment sojourns, Chinese learners are represented almost everywhere. Comparative education is not something far away; it is now at home in everyone's school, college or university. Such points of comparison are highlighted here by the theme of intercultural adaptation which is a notable feature of many chapters (see below).

1.2 Literature on Chinese learners

Considering the international interest in China and that education in China serves 1.3 billion people, one might expect a substantial literature and long research tradition concerned with Chinese learners. Actually, there is rather little, given the size and significance of the enterprise of Chinese learning. However, there is a growing movement in this direction in which the present book may have a role. The following might be consulted in conjunction with this book (together with the additional references given in each chapter here).

A series of oft-quoted books about 'the Chinese learner' (Watkins & Biggs, 1996, 2001; Chan & Rao, 2010) have drawn on psychological and educational perspectives to look at a range of issues relating to the 'Confucian heritage' (e.g. rote learning), the learning of English and maths, teachers' and students' beliefs, and changes and initiatives in classroom practices and teacher development, but these studies largely relate to Hong Kong where education is hardly representative of China as a whole (though a few chapters in each book are about Mainland China). The standard references on the psychology of the Chinese (Bond 1986, 1996) contain a few sections related to learning but understandably these are not written from educational or applied linguistics viewpoints. More recent collections of papers have begun to examine 'the Chinese learner' in international education contexts within China (Ryan, 2010b) and of Chinese students in the West (Coverdale-Jones & Rastall, 2006, 2009) and in international schools and cross-cultural exchanges (Ryan & Slethaug, 2010), but while these essential collections pay attention to students' needs they do not attend to intercultural adaptation and issues of research methodology. There is also a series of useful studies of higher education in China, largely from historical, modernizing and reform or policy perspectives (Hayhoe, 1989, 1999; Angelasto & Adamson, 1998; Li, 2004; Ryan, 2010a) and with some attention to cross-cultural dialogue (Hayhoe & Pan, 2001) and to the stories of university leadership (Hayhoe, 2006) and feminist accounts of educators' lives (Zheng, 1999), which fit into some of the intercultural and narrative concerns of the present book. However, these do not always give full attention to the actual learners or teachers in classrooms and would need to be supplemented by studies of practical initiatives and new developments (Spencer-Oatey, 2007) and monograph research studies of small groups of language teachers in China (Ouyang, 2004; Wu, 2005; Gu, 2007; Zheng & Davison, 2008) to get a feel for classroom realities. Other short accounts of the personal experience of teachers and learners in China – which originally appeared as newspaper interviews and are related to the narratives and episodes in this book – can be found among collected memoirs (Liu & Xiong, 1990; Anon., 2008a, 2008b). The subtitle of the latter two books, *Bitter-Sweet Portraits*, indicates a mixture of joy and achievement with suffering and sacrifice which emerges from the present book. There are also accounts of personal experiences of Western teachers in China (Muehl & Muehl, 1993;

Hill, 1997; Hessler, 2001), which relate to one chapter here, but given recent changes these are now of historical interest.

From the language perspective, there are reviews of issues and mass developments in English Language Teaching (ELT) in China (Cortazzi & Jin, 1996; Jin & Cortazzi, 2004) and a small number of key collections of papers about ELT (Feng, 2007; Liu, 2007) and identity issues (Lo Bianco, 2009), but some contributions are not research-based and their frame of reference does not include intercultural adaptation. Within the range of literature about language and intercultural communication with Chinese speakers (Hartzell, 1988; Kulich *et al.*, 2007) there are Chinese–American comparisons (Hu & Grove, 1999), and among the studies from a linguistics or social psychological perspective (Bond, 1991; Young, 1994; Kasper, 1995; Gao & Ting-Toomey, 1998; Pan, 2000; Jia, 2001) there are detailed considerations of how to communicate with Chinese people with regard to discourse and topic management, politeness, face, identity and face-to-face interaction. These are related to the present collection with its themes as interaction in classrooms and intercultural adaptation, but none of them give consideration to educational angles or to classroom matters. Nevertheless, the extent of the detail in these studies underlines that specialists have reason to believe that Chinese communication can have features which are distinct from those in Europe or North America and that these need to be taken into account in studies of classroom interaction in China or internationally with Chinese learners.

From the above brief outline review, it should be clear that studies of Chinese learners range across several fields and so there is a need to adopt a number of perspectives (educational, social, cultural, linguistic, psychological, historical, professional, personal, practical and so on). There seems to be no collection of research-based papers which considers Chinese learners from teaching and learning perspectives in classrooms in China and internationally and also examines issues of intercultural adaptation. *Researching Chinese Learners* brings together papers on these themes. The title merits a brief discussion.

1.3   Researching Chinese learners

The title of the book, *Researching Chinese Learners: Skills, Perceptions and Intercultural Adaptations*, could well have had more plural elements ('Researches', 'Researchings', 'Research studies' or 'Chineses') but these would be grammatically odd and stylistically clumsy. However, there are underlying pluralities and it is worth explaining some of these pluralities right at the beginning.

'Research' reflects the fact that these chapters are soundly based on empirical research studies; most of them were originally successfully completed doctoral theses and are written here in their present form with the supervisors (hence the plural of 'researchers' or the authorial 'we' in some chapters). 'Researching' indicates a deliberate selection of a range of research approaches and methods: broadly both quantitative and qualitative, chronologically shorter or broader synchronic studies and longitudinal studies, and more particularly combinations of the use of questionnaire surveys, semi-structured interviews, focus group and group interviews, case studies, controlled experiments, classroom observations, the use of learners' journals, and applications of metaphor analysis, narrative enquiry and episode analysis, and the use of newer visual techniques to represent learners' perceptions and experiences of their learning and study journeys. There is a similar range of theoretical orientations behind these approaches and methods and the book title could have included the understandable but maybe misleading terms of 'researches' or 'researchings'.

'Chinese' refers here to learners and sometimes teachers from Mainland China. As several chapters point out, this general label is not intended to mean, and should not be interpreted as, some kind of reduction to a homogeneous group or an essentialist, simplistic national label. 'Chinese' here means 'Chineses', plural: an identifiable ethnic and linguistic grouping, self-identified as 'Chinese', known to embrace – and appreciated as – a range of diversity. This diversity includes minorities (some 55 officially, but of course many more in different senses of social and cultural minorities); regional, provincial and local communities; cultures (in most cases pluralized, as in 'Chinese cultures of learning'); and educational institutions and social practices of learning within them. The authors here would not like to see Chinese learners in 'deficit' terms, as 'lacking' something educational that the West is presumed to have or as having problems and needs that other students are thought not to have. This immense caution about such views could well include 'deficit' ideas about language, say with reference to the use of English for study purposes, since it is our experience in many Western, Middle Eastern, and South and East Asian contexts that most students have some or other language need, including those who are regarded as native speakers: is anybody really a 'native speaker' of academic or professional English or of postgraduate-thesis-English? Everybody, including Chinese learners, needs to develop advanced or professional language skills. So, rather than think of a deficit view, the authors here prefer to think about what we can learn from Chinese learners and about how our educational and professional understanding can be enhanced and better applied through studies of Chinese learners. This is a positive view: saying that we can learn something does not mean a deficit, even in ourselves; it just means we are committed to developing learning and that we are learning ourselves. Often we are learning about ourselves: through the study of others, other cultures, other learners and intercultural adaptation, we reflect on and learn about our own contexts and cultures, so we learn about ourselves. This does not need to mean an 'us–them', 'we–other' polarization. We are all human, hopefully humane, and destined in some sense to become world citizens or members of a world ecology of education. The balance between what is held in common and what may be varied or different is an aspect that emerges in several chapters here which discuss intercultural adaptation.

 'Learners' refers mostly to undergraduate or postgraduate students in contexts of educational institutions in China or those from China who study abroad. This term has a relationship with learners from other significant Chinese communities, such as those in Taiwan, Singapore or Malaysia, or the large diaspora communities and families of a Chinese heritage around the world, but our focus here is on learners specifically from China. As will be clear from some chapters, some of the learners here are in fact Chinese teachers (who are of course learning, too) and (in the other sense of 'Chinese learners') some of those learning about Chinese learners are Western teachers, either in China or in Western colleges and universities. Further, the group of those learning about Chinese learners includes the present authors and researchers. 'Chinese learners' thus has multiple meanings and is definitely plural. Several of the researchers here explicitly avoid, quote or give some critique of the term '*the* Chinese learner', though they understand why the term has appeared in several book titles referred to earlier.

1.4   Outline of the chapters in this book

The chapters are organized around three main themes of researching Chinese learners, which are interwoven throughout the sequence of chapters. The first theme relates to *teaching and learning* in classrooms and to the development of Chinese learners' language skills in English and their academic knowledge and skills for university study at undergraduate and postgraduate levels. The second theme concerns *intercultural adaptation* and in general this relates to how Chinese students adapt in Western university contexts academically, socially and culturally.

A third theme is to explore the application of a variety of *research approaches and methods* in the focus on Chinese learners, including some more innovative methods. The following brief outline of the chapters highlights these themes. The chapters are arranged so that in the early chapters (1–6) the context is broadly the teaching and learning of skills in China, while in later chapters (7–13) the contexts are in Australia, New Zealand and the UK and the focus is more on the intercultural adaptation of learners – and also of teachers – in academic contexts.

In **Chapter 1**, Li and Cutting investigate what Chinese students believe about *rote-learning* methods in their study of English vocabulary and how this relates to their measured performance of learning new words. This is an important question for three reasons: first, the learning of vocabulary has been central in Chinese approaches to learning English for many years and remains important in current curricula reforms and innovations; second, Chinese students are often said to use rote learning as a strategy to memorize words and phrases (and as a general approach to learning other subjects, beside English) although many other learning strategies are available; and, third, any rote learning is often said to stem from the traditions of a Confucian heritage, which is supposed to have encouraged such memorization. Li and Cutting give a clear account of their survey questionnaires and interviews with 100 students, together with a survey of 42 teachers. Their statistical results confirm participants' preferences for rote learning and a correlation between students' beliefs about Chinese educational and cultural backgrounds and their vocabulary test scores: the stronger these beliefs, the higher the scores. However, 'rote learning' is shown to be not a singular concept for these Chinese learners, but multifaceted; it is not just repetition and memorization but also includes an active approach to understanding, practising and reviewing. Li and Cutting suggest this package of practices should be called 'Active Confucian-Based Memory Strategies'; this term may help to counter any stereotype about 'passive' or 'parrot' memorization and, of course, memory and remembering one way or another is a key feature of language learning and use.

The topic of vocabulary learning is taken up further in **Chapter 2** where Leung and Crisp focus on the more innovative possibility of teaching vocabulary through explicitly informing students of a cognitive analysis of specific idioms. They conduct an *applied linguistics experiment* in several phases with 106 students in Hong Kong to investigate whether the teaching and learning of a set of idioms in English which use body terms might be improved by focusing explicit attention on the analysis of *metonyms* and *metaphors*, together with the application of a contrastive analysis between Cantonese and English idioms. The authors show how, in many cases, the contrastive analysis involves a cross-cultural comparison. This comparison is made in order to raise learners' awareness of the conceptual system underlying the idioms, rather than to treat them simply and more arbitrarily as isolated phrases to be learnt, say by memorizing (as is common with the learners studied in Chapter 1). Cantonese is the major language of Hong Kong and the province of Guangdong with perhaps 70 million speakers (including many Chinese people living around the world), and it uses the standard Chinese writing system, so there is enough in common with Mandarin (*putonghua*) structurally and in writing to suppose that Leung and Crisp's results may broadly apply to other Chinese groups. These results show that, compared to control groups, applying a cognitive linguistic analysis to the classroom teaching of idioms is statistically effective, particularly when the metonym and metaphor analysis is applied with Cantonese–English contrasts; it raises the learners' awareness of contrasts and gives underlying principles behind these particular idioms.

Where Chapter 2 treats metonyms and metaphors in terms of the language and cognitive systems and presents the analysis to students to help them learn vocabulary, in **Chapter 3** Jin and Cortazzi take an opposite approach in order to investigate the learners' perceptions of two defining features of classrooms in China (or of classrooms elsewhere): learning and teachers. Their approach is to elicit the learner's own self-generated *metaphors* in English or Chinese about 'learning' and 'teachers'; collecting thousands of metaphors from over 1000 students in China, they analyse this large database in an original cultural application of the cognitive linguistic approach taken in Chapter 2 to build up a *network cultural model* of 'learning as a journey' with features of a model of Chinese teachers. Jin and Cortazzi's analysis and brief comparisons with other cultures show that the Chinese metaphors have features which may be universal; however, they also combine innovative metaphors with traditional cultural and educational features which are regionally or culturally specific and which can be interpreted as continuing Chinese traditions of education and learning. Their results give a rich picture of how students in China view teachers and learning – a picture which has thought-provoking insights for the study and application of education elsewhere. Their work also counters some stereotypes of Chinese learners by showing the huge range and diversity of metaphors and how many students can be creative in both Chinese and English with metaphors, rather than simply reproducing what they have heard or read.

This picture of Chinese teachers, broadly positive but with some mixed and negative elements, is complemented by Stanley's close look in **Chapter 4** at the meanings given to the classroom interaction in oral English classes in China when the teachers are Westerners from the UK, USA or Canada. Stanley employs a theoretical framework of *symbolic interactionism*: this is familiar in the sociology of education but rarely applied to analyse the intercultural interaction of classrooms in China. She draws on 200 hours of recorded interviews, focus group discussions and classroom observations to analyse some key episodes in which the actions of the small group of Western teachers under study are interpreted differently – and, in fact, negatively – by their Chinese students in oral English classes. Stanley shows that this gap of expectations and interpretations of behaviour sets up a vicious cycle of negative views on both sides which stems from different implicit theories about teaching, learning and language education and a process of cultural 'othering'. Since many universities and schools in China employ Western teachers of English, very often to help to develop learners' oral skills and perhaps provide intercultural opportunities, these results have strong implications about the need for informed inter-cultural adaptation and, as other chapters suggest, more 'cultural synergy' (Jin & Cortazzi, 1993) so that both teachers and learners learn about each other's expectations and approaches to education, language learning or the development of knowledge and skills. Stanley's chapter shows, as Chapters 10, 11, 12 and 13 confirm, that 'meeting in the middle' cannot be taken for granted, it does not necessarily take place at all and that it warrants further research.

Chapter 5 also examines the context of oral English classes, with the more usual situation in China that the teacher of English is Chinese. Liu and Jackson focus on investigating empirically the common observation (illustrated also in other chapters here) that many Chinese learners show *reticence* and *anxiety* in answering teachers' questions or in offering comments in discussion. Often students are observed to give short or minimal replies and only give more extended utterances when they have preparation time. Liu and Jackson use a combination of research methods to analyse classroom video recordings of interaction, the journals of 93 learners and interviews with 20 students to show that anxiety is a major reason for reluctance to speak. Reticence and anxiety stem from lack of confidence, fear of making mistakes, perceived low proficiency, and other personal, educational and cultural factors identi-fied in this chapter. Apparently these factors set up a negative cycle of nervousness which may inhibit further expression in English even on relatively easy topics, especially when students speak in front of the whole class (notably less so when they engage in paired interaction). Liu and Jackson's findings may well be a surprise, given that the site of their study is a major prestigious university in Beijing which recruits students with high entry scores in English. Possibly these highly successful students are 'high-anxious' and more risk-averse (and feel they may have more face to lose in speaking publicly in class) than some less able students in provincial universities who can be observed to speak up more easily and confidently. Since Liu and Jackson's research is carefully supported with wide-ranging references, this is a thought-provoking chapter with clearly drawn implications for teaching Chinese students.

Chapter 6, still in the context of teaching and learning skills in English in China, looks again at Chinese teachers and how well they feel they are culturally prepared by training and experience to teach cultural topics. This is a matter of current concern because cultural elements and using English in intercultural contexts are highlighted in the recent curriculum reforms for College English in China, which are aimed at learners' active use and application of the knowledge of language and making international connections. Zhou, Xu and Bayley, based in Canada, take a research approach of *narrative enquiry*: this approach is known in studies of the education and development of teachers, particularly in North America, but has until now hardly been used in contexts of research in China. The approach allows the researchers to be participants by drawing on their own episodes of lived experience – and of course those of the teacher participants – as well as their knowledge and opinions. Within this approach Zhou *et al.* use questionnaires and interviews by phone and email to investigate the nature and extent of 20 experienced and highly qualified Chinese teachers' intercultural competence and their perceptions and experience of teaching culture in their English classes. They show why it is difficult for English teachers in China to 'teach' culture and how classroom comparisons with Chinese cultures are not so common, even with this skilled group of teachers. *Teachers' knowledge* (this is contrasted with knowledge for teachers such as may be found in reference books) and perceptions do not necessarily match up with those found in current frameworks of intercultural competence and the cultures of 'world Englishes' which are found in the language-teaching literature. The importance of personal and preferably international experience for Chinese teachers of English is underlined here (perhaps raising questions about the roles of vicarious experience, say through the media and literature).

From Chapter 7 onwards, the settings of the research move to international ones to focus on learners from China who are studying abroad. Many Chinese students take language courses in a country where they intend to study, essentially to improve their academic language skills and to pass relevant university language requirements prior to registering for degree programmes. In **Chapter 7** Parris-Kidd and Barnett in Australia follow the learning experiences of three such learners in a private college. This is a common context for many Chinese students but one which is rarely researched, perhaps because access for researchers is not easy and because the classes are transitional with dynamic membership in the sense that courses are comparatively short and students come and go every few weeks. Through data from classroom observation and interviews, Parris-Kidd and Barnett analyse episodes of asking questions (a theme in Chapters 5, 9 and 11), sharing information which entails embarrassment and potential loss of face (elements of Chapter 5), and the use of humour and uncomfortable discussion topics. This is explored within a framework of academic and social distances between *cultures of learning*. In some ways this chapter illustrates the reticence and anxiety examined in Chapter 5, showing how this may feature in international contexts of multicultural classrooms. The Australian teacher's 'dialogic' approach is much more learner-centred and 'democratic' than the Chinese learners are used to, and the teacher's expectations about learner independence are realized in ways which are unfamiliar to the Chinese learners (though many Chinese students are well used to self-study outside the classroom as preparation for classroom work, and current school and college reforms emphasize more learner-centred approaches).

In **Chapter 8**, within a socio-cultural framework of *communities of practice* which closely informs their interviewing, Skyrme and White conduct an intensive longitudinal study of 12 Chinese students who are undergraduates in a university in New Zealand. Each learner was interviewed iteratively up to six times, allowing for repeated 'member validation' in which the participants can confirm or modify whatever they said in preceding interviews. The longitudinal element here is between one semester and three years. Skyrme and White focus on intercultural adaptation to a new academic culture and on identity issues using *visual methods* in their interviews to trace the progressive movement of the students from 'peripheral participation' to a more central membership of the academic community. These visual methods include the use of photographs, 'feelings graphs' to record affective aspects of learning over several weeks, and the researcher's construction in diagram or map format (a 'big picture') of the trajectory of each student's *journey of learning*, confirmed (and in fact treasured) by the learners. The up-and-down nature, the affective dimension and the power of this metaphor of learning for students from China are evident and detailed also in Chapters 3 and 9. Chapter 8 also raises issues about affective aspects of identity and learners' agency, which are also key elements of Chapter 9.

The journey metaphor continues as an organizing concept in **Chapter 9**, where the research context moves to the UK. Chapter 9 gives a background to the role of Chinese students in the internationalization of British universities. Here Gu shows how the intercultural experiences of these students need to be reconceptualized to be careful of the term 'culture' and to include ideas about *agency* of the learners themselves and their *maturation*, that is, students are developing over time and thus some changes, challenges and learning shocks are to be expected in the adaptation to any higher education context. Drawing on a sequence of studies involving questionnaires, individual and group interviews, and narrative interviews, Gu shows how the emotional journey includes loneliness and networks and patterns of friendship (both of which can be either productive or constraining for acculturation as demonstrated in Chapter 10) but also personal growth and maturation in intercultural contexts. Like the metaphors of Chapter 3, the emotional journey has 'ups and downs': Gu and her colleagues call the visual representation of this 'Managing the Ups and Downs of Living and Studying' (MUDLS), which may be compared to the 'Feelings Graphs' and 'Big Pictures' of students in New Zealand in Chapter 8. All of this means, as other chapters imply, that culture is one element among a range of others but one that can be affected or overridden by learners' agency in their 'personal expansion'. Gu's argument is that a more *holistic* vision of Chinese learners is necessary and that culture is not a single determining factor in their intercultural adaptation in international contexts of study.

Intercultural adaptation and the possibility of *cultural synergy* in mutual adaptation in behaviour between Chinese postgraduate students in the UK and their university teachers is investigated longitudinally in **Chapter 10** by Zhou, Topping and Jindal-Snape. They employ questionnaires administered to 45 students at the three stages of pre-departure from China, soon after arrival in the UK, and six months later, together with interviews and focus groups, plus interviews with staff who taught the students and who also completed questionnaires. One focus is on the 'manner of coming': to investigate whether the students who came *in groups* from partner universities or came *individually* may have had different experiences. This question is important because internationalization from the Chinese perspective includes a growing number of international partnerships and programmes of collaboration involving universities in China with those in other countries. One statistical finding here is that the students in groups help each other in the process of initial adjustment but because those in groups tend to use Chinese with each other they use less English overall and thus reduce their opportunities to learn about other cultures in the UK, compared to the 'individual' students who develop advanced language skills more quickly and may acculturate better despite initial difficulties. Like other chapters here, the findings are illustrated with comments from students and staff; this presents an inside view and gives a better idea of the adaptation experience.

From the chapter titles concerning intercultural adaptation and postgraduate learners in Britain, Chapter 11 may seem similar to Chapter 10, but here in **Chapter 11** Zhao and Bourne use a more *ethnographic approach*. Their longitudinal study focuses on 36 students who were involved in participant observation, repeated interviews and also web-based questionnaires, together with other data from British students, staff and other international students. Through an examination of three stages of the adaptation process of learners' initial familiarity and frustration, gradual adaptation with more frustration, and better adaptation and relaxation, Zhao and Bourne show that both the students and the staff need – and develop – intercultural sensitivity in their orientation to and support of 'others'. Like Chapter 10, this chapter takes the concept of *cultural synergy* further, in this case towards a model of *intercultural adaptation competence*. Like Chapters 4 and 7, Zhao and Bourne investigate key episodes experienced by the Chinese learners in their study and, further, they employ the methodologi-cal device of an *artificial dialogue* – juxtaposed quotes from data – to exemplify legitimate pedagogic culture (recognized as 'on record' or official by teachers and contrasted with unrecognized or inappropriate illegitimate pedagogic culture).

In **Chapter 12**, Durkin investigates how Chinese postgraduate students in the UK adapt to a key aspect of writing, which is the expectation that academic writing should demonstrate features of critical argumentation. Durkin discusses views of critical thinking and features of multiple view-points, the problematization of knowledge and the nature of debate expected of postgraduates in the UK, posing views of 'Western' argumen-tation as assertive or 'masculine' (a 'wrestling debate') with a critique suggesting alternative more 'feminine', conciliatory or nurturing views (in the light of Chapters 2 and 3 some terms here may be viewed as metaphors). She draws on interviews with 24 Chinese students in Britain and 18 Chinese undergraduates in China, plus other interviews with British staff and students to discuss the students' academic adaptation and to propose a 'middle way', as described by some Chinese learners; this model intended for Chinese students is not a simple compromise but a more transcendent or harmonized view which she shows is more aligned to some Eastern philosophies and also close to the more 'feminine' view discussed earlier.

In **Chapter 13**, Pilcher, Cortazzi and Jin consider the process of Chinese postgraduates completing dissertations. Such dissertations or projects are generally a lengthy and significant piece of writing, usually based on research, and are the culmination of many master's programmes. The process often involves several or many months' work and includes interaction with academic supervisors through a number of tutorial meetings. Pilcher *et al.* focus on both the students' and dissertation supervisors' perspectives and experiences through a longitudinal study of 45 learners who were interviewed iteratively four times, together with interviews with 31 of the students' supervisors. Like the studies featured in Chapters 8, 10 and 11 this allows the participants ample opportunity to confirm, modify or develop statements made in prior interviews. Pilcher *et al.* propose that studies of postgraduate dissertations (and of Chinese learners in general) may be seen as circling two complementary hubs of *commonality* across groups and *variation* or exceptions within groups; this is illustrated through this study. Within this proposed concept, the findings are further organized around *metaphors* of learners as 'waves' which 'crash' onto different 'coastlines' (of the supervisors). This variant of 'cultural synergy', derived from representative quotes from the data, shows a dynamic aspect of conflicting ideas and experiences which are modified over the dissertation process: the learners' adaptation may be smooth or not, a common or exceptional experience, while the academic supervisors both shape the learners' experience and are, slowly, shaped by it, as 'coastlines' change over time. The metaphor of waves and coastlines may be linked with other metaphors of Chapter 2 and the journey metaphors of Chapters 3, 8 and 9. This metaphor may be readily extended from the data by considering 'currents' and 'wind' which affect learners and conditions of academic 'climate' and 'weather' which affect all participants.

In their conclusions, Jin and Cortazzi present some critical reflections on the book as a whole by drawing out several implications and making comments on some of the key themes of discussions about 'Chinese learners', the Confucian and other heritages, intercultural adaptation and cultures of learning, and what we have learnt through these research studies about learning and teaching.

Note

The whole book uses a system to present quotations which are generally numbered and coded to identify different participants: students are identified with S, while teachers are identified with T, together with an abbreviation to indicate which country they are from. Thus CS 1 refers to a Chinese student, CS 2 refers to a different student, CT is a Chinese teacher, BS is a British student, BT is a British teacher, AT is an Australian teacher, NZT is a teacher in New Zealand, and so on.

References

Angelasto, M. & Adamson, B. (eds) (1998) *Higher Education in Post-Mao China*. Hong Kong: Hong Kong University Press.

Anon. (2008a) *Chinese Life: Bitter-Sweet Portraits, 1978–1990*. Beijing: Foreign Languages Press.

Anon. (2008b) *Chinese Life: Bitter-Sweet Portraits, 1991–2008*. Beijing: Foreign Languages Press.

Bond, M. H. (ed.) (1986) *The Psychology of the Chinese People*. Hong Kong: Oxford University Press.

Bond, M. H. (1991) *Beyond the Chinese Face: Insights from Psychology*. Hong Kong: Oxford University Press.

Bond, M. H. (ed.) (1996) *The Handbook of Chinese Psychology*. Hong Kong: Oxford University Press.

Chan, C. K. K. & Rao, N. (eds) (2010) *Revisiting the Chinese Learner: Changing Contexts, Changing Education*. Hong Kong: Comparative Education Research Centre, the University of Hong Kong.

Cortazzi, M. & Jin, L. (1996) English teaching and learning in China, *Language Teaching*, 29(2), 61–80.

Coverdale-Jones, T. & Rastall, P. (eds) (2006) *The Chinese Learner*, Special issue of *Language, Culture and Curriculum*, 19, 1.

Coverdale-Jones, T. & Rastall, P. (eds) (2009) *Internationalizing the University: The Chinese Context*. London: Palgrave Macmillan.

Feng, A. (ed.) (2007) *Bilingual Education in China: Practices, Policies and Concepts*. Clevedon: Multilingual Matters.

Gao, G. & Ting-Toomey, S. (1998) *Communicating Effectively with the Chinese*. Thousand Oaks, CA: Sage.

Gu, Q. (2007) *Teacher Development: Knowledge and Context*. London: Continuum.

Hartzell, R. W. (1988) *Harmony in Conflict: Active Adaptation to Life in Present-Day Chinese Society*. Taipei: Caves Books.

Hayhoe, R. (1989) *China's Universities and the Open Door*. New York: M. E. Sharpe.

Hayhoe, R. (1999) *China's Universities, 1895–1995: A Century of Cultural Conflict*. Hong Kong: Comparative Education Research Centre, the University of Hong Kong.

Hayhoe, R. (2006) *Portraits of Influential Chinese Educators*. Hong Kong: Comparative Education Research Centre, the University of Hong Kong.

Hayhoe, R. & Pan, J. (eds) *Knowledge across Cultures: A Contribution to Dialogue among Civilizations*. Hong Kong: Comparative Education Research Centre, the University of Hong Kong.

Hessler, P. (2001) *River Town: Two Years on the Yangtze*. London: John Murray.

Hill, J. (1997) *A Bend in the Yellow River*. London: Phoenix.

Hu, W. & Grove, C. (1999) *Encountering the Chinese: A Guide for Americans*. Yarmouth, MA: Intercultural Press.

Jia, W. (2001) *The Remaking of the Chinese Character and Identity in the 21st Century*. Westport, CT: Ablex Publishing.

Jin, L. & Cortazzi, M. (1993) Cultural orientation and academic language use. In D. Graddol, L. Thompson & M. Byram (eds) *Language and Culture*. Clevedon: Multilingual Matters, pp. 84–97.

Jin, L. & Cortazzi, M. (2004) English language teaching in China: a bridge to the future. In W. K. Ho & R. Y. L. Wong (eds) *English Language Teaching in East Asia Today*. Singapore: Eastern Universities Press, pp. 119–134.

Kasper, G. (ed.) (1995) *Pragmatics of Chinese as Native and Target Language*. Honolulu, HA: Second Language Teaching and Curriculum Center, University of Hawaii.

Kulich, S., Prosser, M. H., Zhang, H. & Wang, Z. (eds) *Intercultural Perspectives on Chinese Communication*. Shanghai: Shanghai Foreign Language Education Press.

Li, L. (2004) *Education for 1.3 Billion*. Beijing: Foreign Language Teaching and Research Press.

Liu, B. & Xiong, L. (1990) *Portraits of Ordinary Chinese*. Beijing: Foreign Languages Press.

Liu, J. (2007) *English Language Teaching in China: New Approaches, Perspectives and Standards*. London: Continuum.

Lo Bianco, J. (ed.) (2009) *China and English: Globalization and Dilemmas of Identity*. Clevedon: Multilingual Matters.

Muehl, L. & Muehl, S. (1993) *Trading Cultures in the Classroom: Two American Teachers in China*. Honolulu: University of Hawaii Press.

Ouyang, H. H. (2004) *Remaking of Face and Community Practices: An Ethnography of Local and Expatriate English Teachers' Reform Stories in Today's China*. Beijing: Peking University Press.

Pan, Y. (2000) *Politeness in Chinese Face-to-Face Interaction*. Stamford, CT: Ablex Publishing.

Ryan, J. (ed.) (2010a) *China's Higher Education Reform*. London: Routledge.

Ryan, J. (ed.) (2010b) *Education Reform in China*. London: Routledge.

Ryan, J. & Slethaug, G. (eds) (2010) *International Education and the Chinese Learner*. Hong Kong: Hong Kong University Press.

Spencer-Oatey, H. (ed.) (2007) *e-Learning Initiatives in China: Pedagogy, Policy and Culture*. Hong Kong: Hong Kong University Press.

Watkins, D. A. & Biggs, J. B. (eds) (1996) *The Chinese Learner: Cultural, Psychological and Contextual Influences*. Hong Kong: Comparative Education Research Centre, the University of Hong Kong.

Watkins, D. A. & Biggs, J. B. (eds) (2001) *Teaching the Chinese Learner: Psychological and Pedagogical Perspectives*. Hong Kong: Comparative Education Research Centre, the University of Hong Kong.

Wu, Z. (2005) *Teacher's Knowing in Curriculum Change: A Critical Discourse Study of Language Teaching.* Beijing: Foreign Language Teaching and Research Press.

Young, L. W. L. (1994) *Crosstalk and Culture in Sino-American Communication.* Cambridge: Cambridge University Press.

Zheng, W. (1999) *Women in the Chinese Enlightenment: Oral and Textual Histories.* Berkeley, CA: University of California Press.

Zheng, X.-M. & Davison, C. (2008) *Changing Pedagogy: Analysing ELT Teachers in China.* London: Continuum.

Part I

Developing Teaching and Learning in China

1
Rote Learning in Chinese Culture: Reflecting Active Confucian-Based Memory Strategies

Xiuping Li and Joan Cutting

1.1 Introduction

1.1.1 Opposing views of rote learning

In studies of the language-learning strategies used by Chinese learners, rote learning (RL) is often the main subject, linked to the legacy of Confucianism, which has been influential for 2500 years. In both Western and Eastern cultures RL is seen as mechanical repetition (Biggs, 1997; Parry & Su, 1998):

> (*usually disapproving*) memory or habit, rather than understanding. To learn something by rote, or rote learning, means learning something in order to be able to repeat it from memory rather than learning it in order to understand it. (*Cambridge International Dictionary of English*, 1995: 1235)

The Confucian Heritage Cultures (CHC) have been proposed as the key reason for learners using RL, and the explanation for their engaging in 'passive' learning in general (Bond & Hwang, 1986; Chang, 2001; Bond, 1996; Rao, 1996) and behaving like 'tape recorders' (Biggs, 1996: 47). Some writers ask how Chinese learners can be so successful academically when their teaching and learning methods seem so oriented to mindless memorization (Watkins & Biggs, 1996); others even label RL as a 'foolish' learning strategy (Luk & Lin, 2007: 17). This view of RL, the researchers in the present study call 'the common concept'.

On the other hand, there is a body of literature (Bond, 1996; Kember, 1998; Li, 2001; Kennedy, 2002; Luk & Lin, 2007; Jiang & Smith, 2009) that acknowledges that the use of memory promoted by CHC is in fact memorization *with* understanding and very much 'active' learning. These writers are aware that CHC education advocates a strong relationship between studying and reflecting on what one has learnt: 'To learn without thinking is unavailing' (*Analects* 2.15, in De Bary & Bloom, 1999: 47). Bell (2009: 1) points out that the Analects is

> a collection of anecdotes of how [Confucius] engaged his students, almost in dialogue form … he comes off as a very charming, humorous figure, not at all dogmatic and very modern … that is partly why he has been so influential.

Gardner explains the tight relationship between RL and understanding for Chinese learners: 'If we recite it but don't think it over, we still won't appreciate its meaning. If we think it over but don't recite it, even though we might understand it, our understanding will be precarious' (1990: 138). Some writers (Gu & Johnson, 1996; Biggs, 1996, 1998) say that Chinese learners believe that RL is not just repetition, which they see as shallow and generally ineffective, but also memorization, understanding, practising and reviewing, which they believe leads to deep understanding. This concept of RL is viewed by the researchers in the study as 'the CHC concept'; RL is viewed positively within Confucian traditions.

There is evidently a certain amount of contradiction in the literature, which points to the need to conduct a systematic study of how RL is perceived in the context of CHC. Since language-learning strategies are shaped by learners' beliefs, and learners' beliefs are shaped by their cultural backgrounds (Wenden, 1987; Horwitz, 1987; Biggs, 1999; Horwitz, 1999), these beliefs should be taken into account if we want to understand why Chinese learners of English as a Foreign Language (EFL) use RL.

1.1.2 Rote learning as a memory strategy

The researchers in this study examined both the common and the CHC concepts of RL, and then explored it in the context of other memory strategies to discover whether more was involved. They began therefore by adapting Gairns and Redman's (1986: 93) model, which is limited to defining RL as 'repetition' (see the 'common concept' subcategories in Table 1.1).

A survey of the literature showed that there is no consensus as to which memory strategy category RL comes under. The researchers chose Oxford's model, agreeing with Schmitt that 'of the more established systems, the one developed by Oxford (1990) seemed best able to capture and

Table 1.1 Working definitions of memory strategies for vocabulary learning

Strategies	Description
Rote learning	
The CHC concept	
1. Repetition	Reading, speaking or writing what is learnt in the course again and again.
2. Memorization	Committing any useful vocabulary to memory.
3. Understanding	Giving priority to understanding when learning.
4. Practising	Doing varieties of exercises repeatedly to strengthen memory.
5. Reviewing	Going over old materials many times for a solid basis to learn new.
The common concept	
1. Reading silently or aloud	Reading words aloud or silently again and again.
2. Writing down the items	Writing words again and again.
3. Learning in list/card forms	Repeating lists of words.
4. Using typical examples	Using fixed or idiomatic expressions repeatedly.
5. Finding translation equivalents	Translating lists of words back and forth.
6. Finding definitions	Writing and rewriting definitions of words.
7. Grouping paired items	Repeating paired words, such as synonyms or antonyms as pairs.
8. Memorizing irregular verbs	Reciting irregular verb tables.
Creating mental linkages	
9. Grouping	Classifying or reclassifying language material into meaningful units.
10. Associating/elaborating	Relating new language information to concepts already in memory.
11. Placing new words into a context	Placing a word or phrase in a meaningful sentence, conversation or story, to remember it.
Applying images and sounds	
12. Using imagery	Relating new language information to concepts in memory by means of meaningful visual imagery, either in the mind or in a drawing.

(*Continued*)

Table 1.1 Continued

Strategies	Description
13. Using semantic mapping	Making arrangement of words into a diagram, which has a key concept at the centre or at the top, and related words and concepts linked to the key concept by means of a line or arrows.
14. Using keywords	Remembering a new word by using auditory and visual links. Identifying a word in one's mother tongue that sounds like the new word – this is the 'auditory link'. Generating an image of a relationship between the mother tongue and target language words – this is the 'visual link'.
15. Representing sounds in memory	Remembering new language information according to its sound. This involves linking the new word with familiar words or sounds from any language: the target language, mother tongue, or any other.
Reviewing well	
16. Doing structured reviewing	Reviewing in carefully spaced intervals, gradually increasing the length of time between reviews.

organize the wide variety of vocabulary learning strategies identified' (Schmitt, 1997: 205). Oxford (1990: 17–21) suggests two classes of vocabulary-learning strategies: direct ones, which include 'memory', 'cognitive' and 'compensation' strategies, and indirect ones, which include 'metacognitive', 'affective' and 'social' strategies. Oxford divides the 'memory' strategies into four subcategories: 'creating mental linkages', 'applying images and sounds', 'reviewing well' and 'employing actions' (see Table 1.1 for subcategories of these and definitions).

The researchers adapted Oxford's model for their purposes. They renamed her 'employing action' category as 'RL' because she defined 'employing action' as using mechanical techniques – using creative but tangible techniques such as writing words on cards, the new word written on one side and the definition on the other. Oxford includes 'repetition', which she defines as saying something over and over, listening to something several times, rehearsing and imitating, in her list of 'cognitive' strategies. For the researchers, 'repetition' is a 'memory' strategy, because they understand that, if it is mindless and passive, it is more at home in the 'employing action' category of the 'memory' strategies.

In the researchers' model, 'reviewing' and 'reviewing well' are distinct categories. 'Reviewing' is a subcategory of the CHC concept RL strategy, described as going over old materials many times for a solid basis to learn new; 'Reviewing well' is a 'memory' strategy, described as reviewing in carefully spaced intervals, gradually increasing the length of time between reviews.

1.1.3 Purpose of the study

This study investigates Chinese EFL learners' beliefs and preferences vis-à-vis RL strategies in vocabulary learning, and the extent of their usage. It aims to examine the relationship between RL and other memory strategies (henceforth MS) in the minds of Chinese EFL learners, and the extent to which any commitment to RL strategies is a reflection of traditional Chinese culture and values, and has any effect on their performance on the English vocabulary test.

The study's hypotheses were:

1 Chinese EFL learners state that they prefer RL strategies to other MS and that they use more RL strategies than other MS.
2 Chinese EFL learners believe that RL works better for memorizing vocabulary than other MS.
3 Those who believe in the effectiveness of RL perform better in vocabulary tests than those who do not.
4 Chinese EFL learners believe that RL is effective in both the initial stages and the higher stages of language learning.
5 Chinese EFL learners believe that RL conveys the basic knowledge to develop other MS.
6 RL is believed to be of Confucian cultural value in China.

1.2 Methods

The hypotheses were tested by quantitative and qualitative research methods. The data were obtained through three instruments: questionnaires, interviews and an English vocabulary test, each administered to 100 Chinese learners in the English Department at a large university in the north-east of China, 25 from each of the four stages of the degree. To triangulate the results of the study and to examine their generalizability across China, open-ended questionnaires were also administered to 42 Chinese university teachers from different parts of China. The data were analysed using descriptive analysis, Condorcet's method, Kendall's *W*, content analysis and factor analysis, and confirmed with chi-square test.

1.2.1   Student questionnaire

A questionnaire was designed to elicit learners' beliefs about MS and their self-reported preference for MS in vocabulary learning. Most of the questions were adapted from questions relating to MS in Oxford's (1990: 277–300) *Strategy Inventory for Language Learning* (SILL), and Gu & Johnson's (1996: 673–679) *Vocabulary Learning Strategies Questionnaire* (VLSQ). Horwitz's (1987: 127–128) *Beliefs About Language Learning Inventory* (BALLI) also informed the research design. Some questions were devised specifically for the present study. See Li (2005) for a full copy of the questionnaire.

The questionnaire consisted of three parts. Parts 1 and 2 contained statements: Part 1 had 12 relating to learners' beliefs about the value of MS in vocabulary learning, and Part 2 had 28 relating to learners' preferred MS. Participants rated each item by circling the response on a five-point Likert scale, with (1) indicating 'strongly agree' and (5) 'strongly disagree'. Part 3 was an open-ended section, with three questions prompting them to express themselves freely. Table 1.2 shows examples of questions in the three parts.

1.2.2   Student interview

In order to prompt the students to verbalize their beliefs about their MS in vocabulary learning, the researchers used a two-part semi-structured

Table 1.2   Examples from the student questionnaire

Part 1					
1. Vocabulary should be learnt through repetition.	1	2	3	4	5
2. Rote learning is an effective way to memorize words.	1	2	3	4	5
3. English words have fixed meanings.	1	2	3	4	5
Part 2					
13. I make vocabulary lists of new words that I meet.	1	2	3	4	5
14. I write the new words on one side of a card and their explanations on the other side.	1	2	3	4	5
15. I keep the vocabulary lists of new words that I make.	1	2	3	4	5
Part 3					
1. What are the most effective strategies that you believe produce the better results when you are learning vocabulary?					
2. What do you think of rote learning for Chinese learners in vocabulary-learning strategies?					
3. Do you have any other strategies for either learning or memorizing vocabulary?					

interview. The interviews were conducted in Chinese to ensure subjects' understanding. The first part of the interview was designed to triangulate information acquired from the questionnaire. It asked respondents to rate their agreement with each of ten statements about MS on a scale of 1 to 10. See Li (2005) for a full copy of the interview schedule.

The second part allowed them to express their opinions freely in response to these questions:

1 Which English vocabulary-learning strategies do you think Chinese learners use the most and why?
2 Have you ever thought of getting rid of RL? Why?
3 Which kinds of strategies can help you personally become a better English learner?
4 What do you think of the relationship between RL and the other three large MS categories?
5 Which kinds of strategies do you think are all useful for learners at different levels of English?

Content analysis (Wenden, 1987) was carried out to identify the factors which the subjects believed affected the choice of strategy for EFL vocabulary learning, and to categorize respondents in three belief groups: those who gave 'full support' to RL, those who gave 'partial support' and those who gave 'no support'.

1.2.3 Student test

The students were administered a vocabulary test, to investigate hypothesis 3. The test was designed to divide the subjects into three groups according to their scores: 'high achievers', 'borderline' and 'low achievers': this facilitated chi-square analysis to see if there was a significant association between the belief group and scores.

The words and phrases tested were based on the subjects' university 6000-word EFL vocabulary list (Ministry of Education, 2007), and the question formats came from the framework by Watcyn-Jones (1990) and Thomas (1991). Devising a new test in this way was felt to be preferable to using ready-published test papers in China, as it ensured that the test was new to the subjects and avoided diligent preparation for the test by Chinese students. Using the subjects' university 6000-word vocabulary list allowed the researchers to avoid the possibility that some participants might not know the words on which this test was based: students have copies of this list and know they should learn the items in it.

Parts 1 (Definitions), 2 (Complete Proverbs) and 3 (Collocation) were used to test the understanding of the meaning of the selected words, and collocation for idioms and fixed phrases in some recognizable group or pattern. See Table 1.3 for examples from the vocabulary test. The test targeted words from the list that would constitute receptive knowledge; the researchers checked whether subjects had got to the posited 'repetition' and 'memorization' stages of RL as it tested the

Table 1.3   Examples from the vocabulary test

Part 1
Match up the definitions on the left (1–10) with the correct idiom on the right (a–j).

1. clever, intelligent	a. all thumbs
2. inquisitive, curious	b. brainy
3. rich, wealthy	c. cheeky

Part 2
Complete the following proverbs by choosing an ending from those marked a–j.

1. Absence ...	a. ... begins at home
2. Beauty...	b. ... spoil the broth
3. When the cat's away ...	c. ... is the mother of invention

Part 3
Please put each word from the following list in its correct space in the sentences below.

all-out	pitch	dog	dire	blank	rock
wide	paper	flat	crystal		

1. I was —— tired after such a hard day's work.
2. It was —— dark. I couldn't see a thing.
3. The sea near those rocks is —— clear.

Part 4
Fill each space in the sentences below with the correct form of the word in bold print above it.

1. beauty
   They're going to —— the town with more trees and parks.
2. pay
   Please make your cheque —— to John Watson.
3. receive
   I made several suggestions to improve production, but the management was not very —— to my ideas.

Part 5
Choose the correct word for each space.

1. misused/disused
   An airport —— since its closure ten years before was used for car-racing.
2. unreadable/illegible
   His handwriting is so bad it's ——
3. story/storey
   The basic —— of the novel is rather weak but it's amusing and well written.

meaning of words and phrases in isolation, not taking into account the grammar, the co-text or the context.

Part 4 (Word Formation) was used to find out if students could use grammatical inflections, including prefixes and suffixes. These questions reflected both receptive and productive knowledge. They required an understanding of the form and function of each word in context, so taking into account the grammar, co-text or context. This part checked whether subjects had gone on to the 'understanding' and 'practice' stages of RL.

Part 5 (Word Discrimination) aimed to see if the respondents could appreciate which shade of meaning was most suitable for the context, and make associations with related words in context. It assessed both receptive and productive knowledge, and whether subjects had gone on to the 'understanding' and 'practice' stages.

1.2.4   Teacher questionnaire

Another semi-structured questionnaire was designed for Chinese EFL teachers, in order to seek their views on the students' use of RL. These were not the teachers of the particular students in the study since they came from different parts of China. They were asked the following questions:

1   Chinese EFL learners are believed to use more rote learning than any other memory strategies. Is this true? Why?
2   Rote learning suits Chinese learners best to memorize vocabulary. What do you think?
3   Rote learning works better than other memory strategies in China. Do you agree?
4   Could you talk about your attitudes towards rote learning for Chinese EFL learners in China? Support your argument with examples and evidence.

The responses were coded as 'Agree', 'Disagree' and 'Other'.

1.3   Results and discussion

1.3.1   Rote learning is preferred to other memory strategies

The analysis of the student questionnaire Parts 1 and 2 confirmed very clearly the hypotheses that Chinese EFL learners prefer RL to other MS, use more RL than other MS, and believe that RL works better than other MS.

Table 1.4 presents Part 1 of the student questionnaire, which focused on beliefs about the value of MS. Nine of the 12 MS (75%) had mean values exceeding 3.57 (High usage) and the other three MS (25%) were

Table 1.4 Student questionnaire Part 1 results – students' beliefs about MS *n* = 100

Categories and abbreviated statements	Rank	Mean	SD
High usage (M = 3.5 or above)			
RL English words have fixed meanings (3)	1	4.30	0.67
RL Vocabulary should be learnt through repetition (1)	2	4.23	0.93
RL RL is an effective way to remember words (2)	3	4.18	1.04
RL The translation equivalents are helpful (5)	4	4.08	1.01
CML Words should be acquired in context (6)	5	3.98	1.12
RW Structured reviewing is only useful for exams (12)	6	3.97	1.31
RW Reviewing regularly is very helpful (11)	7	3.90	1.10
AIS Semantic mapping is valuable for memory (9)	8	3.76	0.878
RL Word list/cards are very helpful (4)	9	3.57	1.01
Medium usage (M = 2.5 to 3.4)			
CML Organized material is easier to memorize (7)	10	3.47	1.11
AIS Mentally picturing can quicken memorization (8)	11	3.32	1.14
AIS Keyword method should be used (10)	12	2.78	0.89
Low usage (M = 2.4 or lower)			

AIS = Applying Images and Sounds
CML = Creating Mental Linkages
MS = Memory Strategies
RL = Rote Learning
RW = Reviewing Well

in the Medium usage level; the overall mean for the sample was 3.80, indicating overall High usage of the strategies listed. The mean of the RL is the highest of the three MS categories.

Analysis of Part 2 (see Table 1.5), which focused on the subjects' beliefs about the preferred MS that they used in vocabulary learning, showed that the overall mean was 3.27, indicating overall Medium usage of the strategies listed, even though half of the strategies had High, and half Medium usage category. The mean of the RL was again the highest.

The responses to the open-ended part of the student questionnaire revealed that they believed that RL and reviewing were the most effective strategies for learning vocabulary. Significantly, they cited repetition as a main feature of RL and the most effective strategy for memorizing vocabulary. Importantly, in answer to the question 'Do you have any other strategies for either learning or memorizing vocabulary?' 95% of the subjects answered 'no'. They made it clear that by 'RL', they meant a combination of many ways such as repetition, memorization, understanding and practice. In addition to this, they saw reviewing and using the vocabulary in interaction or other communication as part of RL. 'Reviewing' was evidently an activity that could be used to encourage

Table 1.5 Student questionnaire Part 2 results – students' preferred MS *n* = 100

Categories and abbreviated statements		Rank	Mean	SD
High usage (M = 3.5 or above)				
RL	Memorize English words and Chinese equivalents (22)	1	4.10	1.38
RL	Memorize set phrases and collocations (39)	2	4.08	1.11
RL	Use after memorizing the words (27)	3	4.02	0.97
RL	Make vocabulary lists of new words (13)	4	3.88	1.27
RL	Do vocabulary exercises many times (23)	5	3.83	1.28
RL	Use rote learning all the time (40)	6	3.78	1.35
CML	Remember words by grouping into categories (34)	7	3.69	1.02
RW	Do regular and structured reviews of new words (18)	7	3.69	0.94
RL	Do oral spelling exercises of words with others (21)	8	3.68	1.25
RL	Write words repeatedly to remember the words (20)	9	3.67	1.30
RL	Repeat words aloud to oneself for memorizing (19)	10	3.65	1.32
RL	Seek accurate keys for the test (38)	11	3.58	1.43
RL	Use cards with two sides of words and meaning (14)	12	3.53	1.37
RL	Remember dictionary definitions for words (37)	13	3.50	1.27
Medium usage (M = 2.5 to 3.4)				
RL	Keep the vocabulary list of new words (15)	14	3.47	1.3
RL	Go through the lists repeatedly to understand (16)	15	3.42	1.3
RL	Take the vocabulary cards wherever going (17)	16	3.34	1.39
RW	Recall words by pair checking with someone (25)	17	3.28	1.40
CML	Compose sentences with the words being learnt (24)	18	3.25	1.23
CML	Search synonyms and antonyms for new words (35)	19	3.23	1.45
CML	Read related topic to be exposed to vocabulary (32)	20	3.08	1.33
CML	Remember words that share similar letters (29)	21	2.99	1.17
AIS	Associate sounds of words with similar English (30)	22	2.96	1.18
CML	Remember words by roots or affixes (33)	23	2.91	1.22
CML	Group words by grammatical class (26)	24	2.87	1.13
CML	Remember examples of word use in a context (28)	25	2.79	1.10
AIS	Associate words with similar Chinese sound (31)	26	2.60	1.1

AIS = Applying Images and Sounds
CML = Creating Mental Linkages
MS = Memory Strategies
RL = Rote Learning
RW = Reviewing Well

individuals to reflect, describe, analyse and communicate what they have recently experienced, and thus strengthen memory. As Greenaway puts it (2002: 1), 'Reviewing processes can include reflecting on experience, analysing experience, making sense of experience, communicating experience, reframing experience and learning from experience.'

The interviews with the 100 students showed that a variety of MS were preferred. The results of the first part were analysed using Condorcet's method (ranking) and Kendall's *W*. The 100 respondents

Table 1.6   Student interview – rank orderings of preferred MS *n = 100*

Categories	Strategies	Rank
RL	5. Reading and writing words many times.	1
RW	10. Remembering words by reviewing often.	2
AIS	3. Remembering a new word by a combination of sounds and images.	3
CML	6. Guessing the meanings of words in context.	4
RL	4. Getting definitions from a dictionary for accuracy.	5
AIS	8. Using keywords for memorization.	6
RL	1. Making up vocabulary cards/lists and memorizing them.	7
AIS	9. Using semantic mapping to enlarge vocabulary.	8
RL	2. Using Chinese equivalents in understanding English.	9
CML	7. Remembering words by grouping into categories.	10

AIS = Applying Images and Sounds
CML = Creating Mental Linkages
MS   = Memory Strategies
RL   = Rote Learning
RW = Reviewing Well

rated the ten statements (taken from the trends that emerged from the interview) according to their preferences. The analysis (see Table 1.6) revealed that Strategy 5, an RL strategy 'Reading and writing words many times' was ranked 1st, and that Strategy 10, a Reviewing Well strategy, 'Remembering words by reviewing often', was ranked 2nd. The results appeared consistent with the results from the first two parts of question-naire data as discussed above. Other RL strategies were ranked 5th, 7th and 9th, suggesting that there was not a very clear preference indi-cated here for specific types of strategies. Thus, of the four MS, RL and Reviewing Well were ranked as the first two preferred strategies. With Kendall's coefficient of concordance, Kendall W is 0.1458. A chi-square test suggests that the result is highly significant: chi-square = 131.22; df = 9; p < 0.001. Thus, the results suggest that there is some agreement between learners about their preferred strategies.

The second part of the student interview revealed that RL strate-gies were believed to be used overwhelmingly (89%) in preference to the other MS. When asked if they had ever thought of getting rid of RL, 55% said 'yes' and 45% 'no'; this is an inconclusive result which seems to contradict the previous answer. However, most subjects who answered 'yes' stated that they had to give up the idea of dispensing with RL, because it was very hard to abandon the traditional methods that were so deep-rooted and seen to be beneficial. Those who answered 'no' stated that they failed to try new strategies for several reasons, such as using the EFL environment and the need for accuracy in exams.

Asked what they thought of the relationship between RL and the other MS, 99% of them offered comments such as:

> If there are no rote-learning strategies, there are none of the other memory strategies. (CS 1)

> I only can develop other strategies, such as guessing, on the basis of a large vocabulary obtained by rote learning. (CS2)

Content analysis of the interviews allowed the researchers to divide students into two groups: 'Full RL supporters' and 'Partial RL supporters'. Table 1.7 shows the frequency of beliefs as stated by these two groups.

Turning finally to the teacher questionnaires, it can be said that, generally speaking, the teachers' beliefs about whether RL suits Chinese EFL learners were consistent with the students' statements (see Table 1.8).

Table 1.7   Beliefs about the role of RL by frequency *n = 100*

Full RL	Frequency	Partial RL	Frequency
1. Chinese cultural values	71	10. Too old fashioned	29
2. Easy, simple and effective	89	11. Waste of time/more likely to forget	11
3. Helpful all the time	89	12. Useful for beginners, not advanced learners	11
4. Basis to develop advanced methods	99	13. Not basis to develop other methods	1
5. Always keep it	45	14. Try to drop but have to use	55
6. Only way for accuracy	90	15. No use after exams	10
7. The most effective way	88	16. May not be very effective	1
8. One crucial way of learning	97	17. One not important way of learning	3
9. Benefit of the Chinese language	61	18. Disadvantages of EFL environment	39

Table 1.8   Results of teachers' questionnaire *n = 42*

Questions	Agree		Disagree		Other	
	No.	%	No.	%	No.	%
1. Learners use more RL than other MS	31	74	6	14	5	12
2. RL suits learners best	19	45	8	19	15	36
3. RL works better than other MS	11	26	21	50	10	24
4. Your attitudes to RL	20	48	5	12	17	40

The results of Questions 1, 2 and 4 paralleled those of the students, suggesting that the overall findings could be generalizable.

Question 3 'RL works better than other MS in China. Do you agree?' was the exception: most teachers answered negatively, in marked contradiction with the student questionnaires and interviews. Where the students preferred RL to other MS, the teachers identified other MS as being equally useful and not to be neglected. Examples of reasons given were:

> Besides rote learning, words can be remembered in other ways such as reading novels, learning songs, playing games, using in daily life, so more words can be learned at an advanced level. (CT1)

> It is hard to say if rote learning works better than other memory strategies, for other methods are also very successful. (CT2)

> With China's door wider open to the West, more communicative strategies should be used. (CT3)

1.3.2   RL reflects Chinese CHC values

The student questionnaire showed that they felt that RL 'suits Chinese EFL learners' and that traditional Chinese cultural beliefs were both valued in themselves and identified as having a significant impact on subjects' choice of MS.

Although this chapter does not permit a full account of the results of the factor analysis of the student questionnaires, Table 1.9 is included here to show the results in order to underline the fact that Factor 1 – 'Active CHC-based MS' – topped the list.

Factor 1 reflected Chinese EFL learners' beliefs about the relationship between CHC and strategies for memorizing vocabulary, and indicates that traditional Chinese learning strategies are a combination of repetition, memorization, and practice including reviewing and understanding as

Table 1.9   Results of factor analysis of the use of MS items

Factor	Description	Eigenvalue	% of variance
1	Active CHC-based MS	6.34	22.64
2	Repetition with perseverance	3.20	11.44
3	Repetition with association	2.52	8.99
4	Memorization through practice	2.16	7.72
5	Exam-oriented memory	1.89	6.75
6	Repetition to enhance better use of words	1.47	5.25
	Total		62.79

indicated in literature review. Students in the interviews preferred RL relating to CHC values:

> I am proud of Confucian culture and I have memorized many Confucian sayings and maxims from which I have benefited a lot to guide my way of learning, that is generally, studying, reviewing, practising leading to solving exercise problems. Confucian culture advocates a way of learning through thinking. I am thinking while I am memorizing. I found that each time with the method of thinking and asking myself questions while learning, new understanding will appear. (CS3)

1.3.3   Those who believe in RL perform better in tests

The student attitudes to the relationship between RL and test performance in general were evident in the student interviews. When asked what kinds of strategies could help them to become a better English learner, they equated 'becoming a better English learner' with 'doing well in the exam', offering comments such as:

> Rote learning is helpful to get exact answers for the high marks in the exams. It will affect my results if I give up rote learning. (CS4)

> I mostly use rote-learning strategies in EFL learning, because the exam papers seem to be designed to test fixed, accurate knowledge as presented by the teachers, which require a lot of repetition and memorization. Thus, I do not feel safe enough if I do not keep what I have learnt in class deep in my mind before any tests. (CS5)

There is evidently heavy pressure from the exams; students used RL to meet the exam requirements. They were however aware that RL alone for the exams was fine but that on its own it was not enough to lodge new knowledge in the memory:

> The words learnt through rote learning will be easily forgotten after exams unless it is reviewed very often. (CS6)

The next discussion is about the actual relationship between beliefs and scores in this study's vocabulary test. The test had 100 questions. The traditional Chinese pass mark is 60%. Of the total 100 subjects, 65% passed. See Figure 1.1 for the scores of the test by stage. It is to be expected that the students in higher stages get better scores than the ones in lower stages, because all four stages were given the same test.

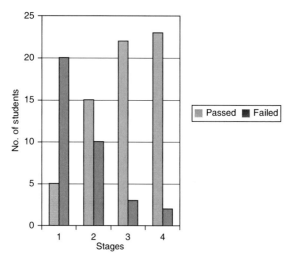

Figure 1.1   Scores of the test by stage

Descriptive statistics showed that the mean score on the test was 62.06% (SD 16.72), which indicates that the test was not difficult for the participants. In order to get a more appropriate proportion, the division was just simply done by the median 64.50 which was rounded off to 65, with 10 marks on either side. In this way, three groups appeared: borderline (between 55% and 75%); high achievers (above 75%); and low achievers (below 55%). When categorized in this way, 44 subjects belonged to the borderline group (between 55% and 75%); 21 to the high achieving group (above 75%); and 35 to the low achieving group (below 55%). The test results suggest no scores between 54 and 60. See Figure 1.2.

The central question was checked with a chi-square test to see whether there was any association between student beliefs about RL and their actual achievement in the English vocabulary test. 'Borderline achievers' were not included in this, so as to make the comparison clearer and avoid the arbitrary. As the contingency table shows (see Table 1.10), there was an association between the Belief Group and Test Result variables: whereas 'Full RL supporters' were divided 50/50 between 'high achievers' and 'low achievers', nearly all the 'Partial RL supporters' got lower scores. A chi-square test suggested that this was a significant association, as shown by the p-value = .003; chi-square = 8.804; df = 1; $p < 0.01$. That is to say, students who were devoted to the value of RL

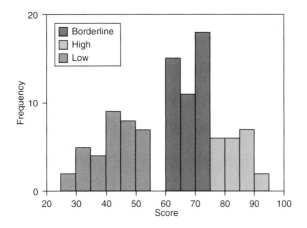

Figure 1.2 All subjects together, divided into three by test scores

Table 1.10 Belief groups and test scores

	High achievers	Low achievers
Full RL supporters	18	16
Partial RL supporters	3	19

got a score that most likely reflected their proficiency. On the other hand, students who were not totally convinced by RL were much more likely to get a low score than a high score.

When the correlation between each of the six factors from the factor analysis and the vocabulary test results was analysed, and the data were plotted onto a scattergraph, it was found that there was little correlation between Factors 2 to 6, but that there was a positive correlation between the Factor 1, beliefs about 'Chinese educational and cultural background: Confucian heritage culture and the use of RL', and test scores. See Figure 1.3, which suggests that the stronger the belief in active CHC-based memory strategies, the higher the test score.

There is of course a strong washback effect. Those who believed in RL were just fitting in with the system and had worked out how to succeed in the test; it does not mean they were better speakers of English. The 'Partial RL supporters' were either very communicative and fluent speakers (none of which the test tests), or they were actually just weak students, in which case their low mark has nothing to do with their RL.

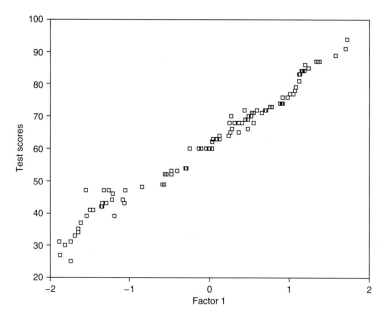

Figure 1.3   Relationship between Factor 1 and test scores

Table 1.11   Summary of results

Hypothesis	Result
1. Chinese EFL students state that they prefer RL strategies to other MS and that they use more RL strategies than other MS	Supported
2. Chinese EFL learners believe that RL works better for memorizing vocabulary than other MS	Mostly supported
3. Those who believe in the effectiveness of RL perform better in vocabulary tests than those who do not	Supported
4. Chinese EFL learners believe that RL is effective in both the initial stages and the higher stages of language learning	Mostly supported
5. Chinese EFL learners believe that RL conveys the basic knowledge to develop other MS	Supported
6. RL is believed to be of Confucian cultural value in China	Mostly supported

1.3.4   Summary

The hypotheses were supported, to a greater or lesser degree. See Table 1.11.

More precisely, the study demonstrated that the students saw RL as involving not just repetition and memorization, but also understanding, practice and reviewing, and they believed that repetition and reviewing were the most effective strategies. This indicates consistency with other studies (Gardner, 1990; Biggs, 1996, 1999; Li, 2001; Kennedy, 2002), and shows that RL involves deeper processes than is supposed by its critics both within and beyond China.

The commitment to RL varied between students and teachers in the study, the students being unlikely to abandon it, and the teachers feeling that other MS were equally useful. The students felt constrained by the exam-oriented system, which rewards accurate memorization. They equated doing well in the exam with being proficient in the language, and most of those who did not totally support RL got a lower score in the test. When CHC learners make passive use of RL and focus on accuracy, this is more likely to be attributable to *keju*, the Imperial Examination System, than with Confucian beliefs.

Times are changing however. Crozier (2002: 6) notes:

> the National University Entrance Examinations still emphasize rote learning far too much, but this is increasingly recognized, as is the level of stress that it places on students. [This aspect of the learning method] may be improved in the future.

As one student in the study astutely pointed out:

> I am sure that we may change our present learning methods if course requirements or exam requirements can be changed towards more creative emphasis. (CS7)

1.4 Conclusion

1.4.1 Implications

The researchers hope that this chapter has explained views from Chinese EFL learners and teachers, in order to establish mutual understanding by challenging the widely held belief that CHC is a negative influence on learning. Because the findings of the study indicate that the CHC learners' use of RL involves far more complex processes than have been supposed to be the case, the researchers suggest a new term 'Active Confucian-Based Memory Strategies' (henceforth ACMS), to distinguish these strategies from passive RL.

They also hope that this chapter will serve as guidance to EFL teachers, test designers, researchers and policy-makers interested in the vocabulary-learning strategies of the Chinese learner. Recognition of the value of ACMS will be of benefit to both CHC and Western learners. The strength of one culture's approach to learning can be combined with the strength of another's, and Chinese learners' positive beliefs about ACMS can be seen as an advantage to their learning.

Although the emphasis on communicative competence is more overt in schools and universities in China, the reform of teaching methodology does not necessarily go hand in hand with a change in teachers' beliefs, especially where these are closely linked to cultural heritage. Williams and Burden (1997: 207) point out:

> Even if a country or an institution adopts a communicative syllabus and course books, what actually goes on in the classroom will reflect a combination of teachers' and learners' beliefs about learning the language and the ultimate purpose of education.

1.4.2   Further research

There is a need for research into active CHC-based MS and other aspects of Chinese EFL teaching and learning, both in China and elsewhere. Research needs to be carried out into the learners' actual use of these strategies to see if it corresponds to what they believe that they do. This requires researchers to go to China and observe learners in the classroom and outside the classroom, when doing homework and learning for tests. It would be beneficial to study Chinese EFL teachers' beliefs about the reform of educational programmes in China, because that will affect everything that they do in the classroom. Examination paper designers could attempt to discover what active MS students are actually using and what strategies they need to develop, and use findings as a framework when designing the paper.

Finally, it would be of benefit to compare integrative and instrumental motivation in Chinese EFL learners. Current requirements of the examination system lead to instrumental rather than integrative motivation. However, changing situations, such as Chinese nationals working in Chinese joint ventures with other countries, within China or beyond China, or settling in foreign countries may lead to higher integrative motivation. This might lead to changes in ACMS choice and usage, and thus affect whether learners find it helpful to use active CHC-based MS or not.

References

Bell, D. (2009) *Confucius*. http://thebrowser.com/books/interviews/bell.
Biggs, J. B. (1996) Enhancing teaching through constructive alignment, *Higher Education*, 32, 329–347.

Biggs, J. (1997) *Demythologising the Teaching of International Students.* http://www.newcastle.edu.au/oldsite/services/iesd/publications/eunexus/articles/teaching-guides/demythologising/demyth-1.htm.

Biggs, J. (1998) Learning from the Confucian heritage: so size doesn't matter?, *International Journal of Educational Research,* 29, 723–738.

Biggs, J. (1999) *Are Chinese Learners Better than Western Learners?* http://www.cityu.edu.hk/celt/rft-usefulpub-chineselearnershtml.

Bond, M. H. (ed.) (1996) *The Handbook of Chinese Psychology.* Oxford and New York: Oxford University Press.

Bond, M. H. & Hwang, K. (1986) The social psychology of Chinese people. In M. H. Bond (ed.) *The Psychology of the Chinese People.* Hong Kong and New York: Oxford University Press, pp. 213–266.

Chang, J. (2001) Chinese speakers. In M. Swan & B. Smith (eds) *Learner English* (2nd edn). Cambridge: Cambridge University Press, pp. 310–324.

Crozier, J. (2002) *A Unique Experiment.* http://www.sacu.org/cifc 12.html.

De Bary, W. T. & Bloom, I. (eds) (1999) *Sources of Chinese Tradition: From Earliest Times to 1600.* New York: Columbia University Press.

Gairns, R. & Redman, S. (1986) *Working with Words: A Guide to Teaching and Learning Vocabulary.* Cambridge: Cambridge University Press.

Gardner, D. K. (1990) *Chu Hsi, Learning to be a Sage: Selections from the Conversations of Master Chu, Arranged Topically.* Berkeley, CA and London: University of California Press.

Greenaway, R. (2002) *What is Reviewing?* http://reviewing.co.uk/-review.htm.

Gu, Y. & Johnson, R. K. (1996) Vocabulary learning strategies and language learning outcomes, *Language Learning,* 46(4), 643–679.

Horwitz, E. K. (1987) Surveying student beliefs about language learning. In A. Wenden & J. Rubin (eds) *Learner Strategies in Language Learning.* New York: Prentice Hall. pp. 119–132.

Horwitz, E. K. (1999) Cultural and situational influences on foreign language learners' beliefs about language learning: a review of BALLI studies, *System,* 27(4), 557–576.

Jiang, X. & Smith, R. (2009) Chinese learners' strategy use in historical perspective: a cross-general interview-based study, *System,* 37(2), 286–299.

Kember, D. (1998) *Learning Experience of Asian Students: A Challenge to Widely-Held Beliefs.* http://www.ouhk.edu.hk/etpwww/AAOU-rep/report.htm.

Kennedy, P. (2002) Learning cultures and learning styles: myth-understandings about adult (Hong Kong) Chinese learners, *International Journal of Lifelong Education,* 21(5), 430–445.

Li, X. (2001) A positive cultural perspective on rote learning in China. Paper presented at EAP PIM Conference focusing on Chinese learners, Sheffield Hallam University, UK. http://www.baleap.org.uk/pimreports/2001/shu/abstracts.htm.

Li, X. (2005) An analysis of Chinese EFL learners' beliefs about the role of rote learning in vocabulary learning strategies, *Asian EFL Journal,* 7(4), 109–110. Abstract of PhD thesis. Full version at http://www.asian-efl-journal.com/xiuping_11-05_thesis.pdf.

Luk, J. C. M. & Lin, A. M. Y. (2007) *Classroom Interactions as Cross-Cultural Encounters.* Mahwah, NJ and London: Lawrence Erlbaum Associates.

Ministry of Education (2007) *College English Curriculum Requirements.* Beijing: Foreign Language Teaching and Research Press.

Oxford, R. (1990) *Language Learning Strategies: What Every Teacher Should Know.* Boston: Heinle.

Parry, K. & Su, X. (eds) (1998) *Culture, Literacy, and Learning English: Voices from the Chinese Classroom.* Portsmouth: Boynton/Cook.

Rao, Z. (1996) Reconciling communicative approaches to the teaching of English with traditional Chinese methods, *Research in the Teaching of English,* 30(4), 458–471.

Schmitt, N. (1997) Vocabulary learning strategies. In N. Schmitt & M. McCarthy (eds) *Vocabulary: Description, Acquisition and Pedagogy.* Cambridge: Cambridge University Press, pp. 199–277.

Thomas, B. J. (1991) *Advanced Vocabulary and Idiom.* Surrey: Nelson.

Watcyn-Jones, P. (1990) *Test your English Idioms.* London: Penguin.

Watkins, D. A. & Biggs, J. B. (eds) (1996) *The Chinese Learner: Cultural, Psychological and Contextual Influences.* Hong Kong: CERC & ACER.

Wenden, A. (1987) How to be a successful language learner: insights and prescriptions from L2 learners. In A. Wenden & J. Rubin (eds) *Learner Strategies in Language Learning.* New York: Prentice Hall, pp. 103–118.

Williams, M. & Burden, R. (1997) *Psychology for Language Teachers: A Social Constructivist Approach.* Cambridge: Cambridge University Press.

2
Cantonese and English Bodies Do Talk: A Cross-Cultural, Metaphor–Metonymy Study on Body-Part Idioms

Danny Chung-hong Leung and Peter Crisp

2.1 Research background

Metaphoric and metonymic forms of language are important because they express underlying metaphoric and metonymic concepts. Metaphoric and metonymic language/concepts are also frequently combined. (For examples of pure metaphor, pure metonymy and combined metaphor/metonymy, see Lakoff & Johnson, 1980.) The results reported in this chapter show that teaching Cantonese L2 learners of English about the conceptual structure underlying the metaphoric/metonymic language of English body-part idioms (the 2Cs method) significantly improves their learning and retention of such idioms. These results also show that teaching them in addition about the similarities and differences between English and Cantonese body-part idioms (the 3Cs method) yet further strikingly improves their learning and retention of these idioms. All human beings have bodies, and this must account for at least much of the striking cross-linguistic similarities in idioms and other forms of metaphoric/metonymic language. The people who own those bodies however belong to differing cultures and this must account for at least much of the cross-linguistic variation also found in this area. The results about to be reported show that an effective L2 pedagogy, at least for idioms, needs to take account of both human, bodily constants and of human, linguistic/cultural variation.

2.1.1 Figurative language

Figurative language has attracted a great deal of attention among applied cognitive linguists in recent years (Deignan *et al.*, 1997; Boers & Demecheleer, 1998; Charteris-Black, 2002; Kövecses, 2002; Deignan, 2005; Boers & Lindstromberg, 2006, to cite a few). The reasons for this are twofold. Firstly, in terms of second language teaching, figurative language is potentially challenging for both second language (L2) learners and teachers due to the fact that figurative meaning typically arises from the role of phrases in discourse rather than from the sum of their grammatical and lexical parts. Take figurative idioms as an example: the meaning of the whole – the underlying figurative meaning – cannot usually be derived as a function of the meanings of the constituent parts, that is, of the literal surface meaning. Faced with this gap between the underlying figurative meaning and the literal surface meaning, L2 learners and teachers find it difficult to approach figurative language systematically and effectively in the L2 classroom. Secondly, in terms of educational applied linguistics there is accumulating evidence showing that many of the fundamental concepts of cognitive linguistics (CL) have major potential for complementing current language pedagogy (e.g. Boers, 2000; Li, 2002; Lazar, 2003; Leung, 2004; Littlemore & Low, 2006). One such fundamental CL concept is that of the role of conceptual metaphor and metonymy in the semantics of natural language and in human cognition generally. CL sees natural language as being an inseparable part of general human cognition (Lakoff & Johnson, 1980; Dirven, 1989). Contrary to the traditional view of metaphor and metonymy as merely rhetorical tools, CL proposes that metaphor and metonymy are central to the semantics of all natural languages and to human thought in general (Lakoff & Johnson, 1980; Lakoff & Turner, 1989; Lakoff, 1993; Lakoff & Johnson, 1999). There are of course many different forms of figurative language; metaphor and metonymy are among the most important and linguistically common of these. In many cases of figurative language, therefore, conceptual metaphor and metonymy are able to provide a systematic explanation of how surface literal meaning is semantically extended to produce underlying figurative meaning. The CL analysis of metaphoric and metonymic language and its underlying conceptual structure has in particular led to a better understanding of the nature of such figurative expressions as idioms and phrasal verbs. This in turn has opened up the possibility of developing a new, more systematic and effective, pedagogical approach to one of the most difficult and challenging issues in second language learning, that of the learning of idioms and phrasal verbs.

2.1.2   Idioms and L2 learning

There are several areas of figurative language in English that are particularly difficult for L2 learners of English to master. Idioms are one of the perennial sources of confusion and frustration in the L2 classroom.

Idioms play a major, pervasive role in the English language, thus constituting a major part of the everyday linguistic repertoire of its L1 speakers. Due to their pervasiveness in L1 English-speaker performance, idioms are crucial for L2 learners to achieve effective communication in English and to obtain native-like fluency. Gibbs (1995) suggests that an L2 learner of English cannot be considered a competent English speaker until he/she is able to master the various idiomatic expressions which are of common use in the language. It follows from this that the level of command of idioms serves as an important indicator of L2 proficiency in general (Yorio, 1989; Weinert, 1995; Howarth, 1998).

Although idioms play an indispensable role for L2 learners of English in achieving native-like proficiency, L2 learners are at a distinct disadvantage in learning and mastering them. There is a general consensus that they constitute one of the most difficult aspects for L2 learners (Kövecses & Szabó, 1996; Cooper, 1998, 1999; Grant & Bauer, 2004; Boers & Lindstromberg, 2006, to cite a few). Kövecses stresses that idioms are 'a notoriously difficult area of foreign language learning and teaching' (2002: 199).

There are several reasons for such difficulty. First, idioms are vast in number. The *Collins COBUILD Idioms Dictionary* suggests that there are over 6000 idioms which are in everyday use in English. Second, idioms belong to a type of conventionalized fixed expressions which are peculiar to a language. Take English idioms as an example: unlike many other linguistic items in the language, they are semantically complex while being syntactically frozen to a greater or lesser degree. One stumbling block of L2 idiom learning is precisely that idioms are very often unpredictable in meaning: they cannot be derived from the literal meanings of their constituent parts. The third reason for difficulty in L2 idiom learning is that idioms are often not taught well in the L2 classroom, because they are semantically complex and linguistically unpredictable. Despite the fact that for idioms the meaning of the whole is not a function of the meanings of the parts, most ESL/EFL textbooks overlook this semantic complexity and present idioms to L2 students using the traditional vocabulary listing method. This method of learning idioms prevents L2 learners from looking for any underlying relationship between the surface linguistic form of an idiom and its figurative meaning. As a result, L2 learners can only learn idioms and their meanings by rote.

2.1.3   A cognitive-linguistic (CL) approach to L2 idiom learning

With regard to the distinct disadvantage facing L2 learners of English in learning idioms, and the inadequacy and ineffectiveness of the traditional vocabulary listing method in presenting idioms in the L2 classroom, a number of applied cognitive linguists (e.g. Kövecses & Szabó, 1996; Boers, 2000; Charteris-Black, 2002, 2003; Boers & Lindstromberg, 2006) have argued for the potential of three CL notions to enhance L2 idiom teaching and learning as a whole. These three CL notions are discussed in the following subsections.

2.1.3.1   Idiom motivation

According to Lakoff (1987) something in language is 'motivated' when it is neither fully predictable nor totally arbitrary; motivation is thus to be distinguished from prediction. It is not the case, Lakoff says, that, given the non-idiomatic meaning of an idiom (e.g. 'emit sparks' for the expression *spark off*), we can entirely predict its idiomatic meaning ('cause to begin'). It follows from this that 'motivation is a much weaker notion than prediction' (Kövecses & Szabó, 1996: 330; Kövecses, 2002: 201). The present study adopts Langlotz's (2006: 45) definition of motivation. This integrates the ideas on motivation of Lakoff and Kövecses. The definition is as follows:

> Motivation refers to a speaker's ability to make sense of an idiomatic expression by reactivating or remotivating its figurativity, i.e. to understand why the idiom has the idiomatic meaning it has with a view to its literal meaning.

As far as L2 idiom learning is concerned, Boers and Lindstromberg (2006) have suggested that explaining the motivation of L2 idioms can assist L2 learners to attain a deeper understanding and a longer lasting retention of them. This is because the process of making these learners aware of idiom motivation involves the activation of semantic networks.

2.1.3.2   Metaphor and metonymy in idioms

The CL concepts of metaphor and metonymy are essential to understanding the motivation for idioms. In *Metaphors We Live By*, Lakoff and Johnson state that 'our ordinary conceptual system, in terms of which we both think and act, is fundamentally metaphorical in nature' (1980: 3). What follows from this is that metaphors are fundamental to the structuring of our thought and language and that we frequently use the concepts and lexis from one semantic area to think and talk about other areas. As suggested by Lakoff (1987), a conceptual metaphor is a cross-domain mapping via which the abstract, target concept/domain is understood in terms of the concrete, source concept/domain. It is used to refer to a connection between semantic areas at the level of thought, such as the metaphorical connection that exists between the concepts of ARGUMENT and WAR (following the Lakoffian typographical convention, concepts are capitalized in order to distinguish them from surface linguistic expressions). Surface linguistic expressions such as *your claims are indefensible, he attacked every weak point of my argument* and *his criticisms are right on target* can be seen as linguistic expressions of the conceptual metaphorical connection between ARGUMENT and WAR. Technically, these surface linguistic expressions are motivated by the underlying conceptual metaphor ARGUMENT IS WAR.

Conceptual metonymy, like conceptual metaphor, plays a fundamental role in the cognitive construction of the semantic extension of concepts with regard to figurative conceptual structures. Kövecses, pursuing the Lakoffian cognitive-linguistic paradigm, defines metonymy as 'a cognitive process in which one conceptual entity, the vehicle, provides mental access to another conceptual entity, the target, within the same domain, or idealized cognitive model (ICM)' (2002: 145). Conceptual metonymy is an underlying conceptual mechanism which can be linguistically realized by metonymic expressions. Surface linguistic expressions such as *I'm reading **Shakespeare*** and *she loves **Picasso*** are motivated by the underlying conceptual metonymy THE PRODUCER FOR THE PRODUCT.

With regard to the motivation of idioms, metaphor, firstly, metonymy, secondly, and the interaction or combination of both metaphor and metonymy, thirdly, can be seen as three different but related cognitive mechanisms linking knowledge domains to underlying figurative meanings. The following examples exemplify these three cognitive mechanisms:

1   He was **overwhelmed** by sadness. (metaphor)
2   We need more **hands** for this task. (metonym)
3   I vividly remember having a **heated** debate with my boss. (interaction of metaphor and metonym)

For the metaphor *overwhelmed* in (1), the domain of NATURAL FORCE is used to understand the domain of EMOTION. The relationship between the concept of sadness and that of being overwhelmed is understood by means of the conceptual metaphor EMOTIONS ARE NATURAL FORCES in which SADNESS is the abstract target domain that is understood in terms of the more concrete source domain of NATURAL FORCES, exemplified by such things as floods. The word *hands* in (2) has the figurative meaning of 'performing an activity'. The basis for the conceptual metonymy THE HANDS STAND FOR THE ACTIVITY is that many prototypical human activities are performed with the hands. As suggested by Kövecses (2002), this metonymy may be a special case of the more general metonymy THE INSTRUMENT USED IN AN ACTIVITY STANDS FOR THE ACTIVITY in which the hand(s) may be viewed as the instrument. The concept of HANDS is not being used here to understand or conceptually structure the concept of ACTIVITY but rather to access or activate it. While metaphor is a matter of structuring, or restructuring, one conceptual domain in terms of another, metonymy is a matter of accessing one concept via another concept where both concepts are part of the same conceptual domain or at least part of the same domain matrix.

The third example is more complex. As explained by Deignan (2005), *heated* in (3) is motivated by the interaction of both metaphor and metonymy. First, it is a part of our everyday, common-sense, belief system that when we are angry or lustful we feel hot and when we are treated distantly or with indifference we feel cold. It is due to this common-sense belief that the conceptual metaphor EMOTION IS TEMPERATURE equates heat with feelings such as anger and lust and coldness with indifference or unfriendliness. The use of *heated* to describe anger involves in the first instance using an 'aspect of something to represent or stand for the thing as a whole' (Gibbs, 1994: 320). Such a 'stand for' relationship within a single conceptual domain, here that of physical/emotional response, is of course a metonymic relationship. Yet the figurative concept EMOTION IS TEMPERATURE is not simply metonymic; it is rather a metonymically motivated metaphor. This is because, although the initial link between the domains of TEMPERATURE and EMOTION is metonymic, rather than simply accessing the concept of EMOTION via that of TEMPERATURE, conceptual structure is actually mapped from TEMPERATURE onto EMOTION. EMOTION is understood in terms of TEMPERATURE. Thus, despite the initial metonymic link between TEMPERATURE and EMOTION, where the first is simply a means of conceptual access to the second within what is construed as a single conceptual domain, EMOTION and TEMPERATURE are ultimately construed as two separate domains with the first being understood in terms of the second. (It has often been noted that it is difficult to find a stable objective basis for differentiating conceptual domains; the increasingly popular, dynamic construal approach to domain delineation assumed here is one possible response to this problem.)

To sum up briefly, the conceptual metaphor EMOTION IS TEMPERATURE, in which emotion is understood in terms of temperature, is metonymically grounded in a common-sense, and at least partially justified, belief about the relation between physical experience and emotional states. In other words, the figurative meaning of *heated* in the example above involves the interaction of both metaphoric and metonymic conceptual elements. The metonymic motivation of metaphor is one of a number of ways in which metaphor and metonymy may be combined or interact (Deignan, 2005).

2.1.3.3 Cross-lingual/cultural comparison for idioms

One of the key theoretical assumptions in CL is that semantics is a matter of conceptualization. In other words, meaning is constructed in the human mind with respect to how language users construe the world anthropocentrically, subjectively and often under the influence of culture-specific preferences (Lakoff, 1987; Langacker, 1987). Given two languages/cultures, any single event or state of affairs may be construed and encoded in one of these languages/cultures in a significantly different way from that in which it is construed and encoded in the other. A cross-lingual/cultural comparison can thus be used to perform a contrastive study on the similarities and differences concerning the treatment of a single type of event or state of affairs in two or more languages/cultures.

Conceptual metaphor and conceptual metonymy will necessarily play a major role in the contrastive analysis of idioms from different languages. The understanding of conceptual metaphor and conceptual metonymy in languages other than English offers both potential for contrastive studies and, pedagogically, raises the possibility of drawing on L1 conceptual knowledge, specifically knowledge of L1 metaphor and metonymy, in the teaching and learning of L2 idioms. As noted by Danesi (1995), a combination of contrastive and cognitive linguistic (i.e. metaphoric and metonymic) approaches should lead to a better understanding of the underlying figurative meanings of idioms because one will be able to see to what extent the metaphors and metonymies in L1 and L2 overlap (i.e. similarities) and/or contrast (i.e. differences). In terms of providing motivation for L2 idiom learning, Boers and Littlemore (2003) and Kövecses (2005) stress that these L1–L2 conceptual similarities and differences should be explicitly and systematically presented to L2 learners. By this means, L2 learners should be able to first reflect on their own L1 concept and then, in the case of finding similarity between L1 and L2, to apply it to learning the L2 idioms directly, and, in the case of finding difference, to disambiguate L1 from L2 concepts before learning the L2 idioms.

2.2 The study

2.2.1 The theoretical rationale

The primary aim of this study was to develop a more systematic and effective L2 idiom pedagogy by drawing on the three above-mentioned CL notions, which are motivation, metaphor and metonymy, and the contrastive analysis of L1–L2 metaphor and metonymy. The study's overall rationale is that a combination of cognitive-linguistic (i.e. metaphor and metonymy) and L1–L2 contrastive approaches to figurative idioms may provide insights into the underlying meaning of these idioms and hence encourage a more systematic and effective L2 pedagogical treatment of these idioms. Lying at the heart of these approaches is the notion of motivation which enables L2 learners to grasp the idioms' semantic analysability and so to make sense of these idioms.

2.2.2 Selection of idioms

The study focused on English idioms involving body-part words. The major reason for this choice is that body-part idioms are 'common' in English, that is, tokens of them are frequently used and their types are vast in number in the language. From the CL point of view, the notion of idiom 'commonness' is explained by the fact that idioms which are based on the most directly experienced source domain can be expected to be the most common and most frequently used in actual discourse. The most directly experienced source domain of all, as argued by Lakoff (1987), Johnson (1987) and Lakoff and Johnson (1999), is the human body itself; idioms involving body parts thus have a direct bodily motivation. Body-part idioms, that is to say, are motivated by means of a connection between source and target based on the direct sensorimotor experience of the world. Nine commonly well-known body parts were chosen for the study, each of which, together with its Cantonese equivalent, is illustrated in Table 2.1.

The English idioms containing the above body-part words were selected as data from the *Collins COBUILD Idioms Dictionary* (2002). To supplement the data, the researcher also consulted three other idiom dictionaries (refer to References for their details). The Cantonese idioms were selected from *Cantonese Colloquial Expressions* (2007). Two more Cantonese idiom dictionaries were consulted to supplement the data

Table 2.1 Nine body parts chosen for the present study

Body parts in English	Body parts in Cantonese [standard Romanized transcription]
head	頭 [tau4]
eye(s)	眼 [ngaan5]
face	面 [min6]
mouth	口 [hau2] / 咀 [zeoi2]
hand(s)	手 [sau2]
foot/feet	腳 [goek3]
heart	心 [sam1]
body	身 [san1]
bone(s)	骨 [gwat1]

(refer to References for their details). As a result, there were 331 and 372 body-part idioms compiled for English and Cantonese respectively, all of which contain at least one word designating at least one of the nine body parts.

2.2.3 Study components and research questions

With an aim to develop a systematic and effective L2 idiom pedagogy, the compiled English and Cantonese idioms served as data for two methodologically independent but theoretically coherent study components which were:

Study One Cross-linguistic/conceptual comparison of English and Cantonese body-part idioms

Study Two Experimental application of the 3Cs method (i.e. conceptual metaphor + conceptual metonymy + cross-linguistic contrastive model) in L2 idiom teaching and learning

The two study components were designed to provide answers to the following three research questions (Questions 1 and 2 for Study One; Question 3 for Study Two):

1 What are the linguistic (i.e. surface linguistic form) and conceptual (i.e. underlying figurative meaning motivated by metaphor and metonymy) similarities and differences in the English and Cantonese body-part idioms?
2 How many types of correspondences can be identified between the English body-part idioms and the Cantonese body-part idioms with regard to their linguistic/conceptual similarities/differences?

3 Does the 3Cs method, which reveals conceptual metaphor and conceptual metonymy as underlying conceptual motivation and draws on a contrastive model between English (L2) and Cantonese (L1) idioms, help Cantonese L2 learners of English learn English figurative idioms better than the traditional, vocabulary listing method?

2.3   Study One: methods and results

Study One distinguished between the surface forms of particular body-part idioms and the underlying cognitive mechanisms (i.e. metaphor and metonymy) motivating the idioms. This results in a typology of idiom comparison which is able to reveal similarities and differences between idioms in English and Cantonese both in surface linguistic form and in underlying conceptual motivation. To provide answers to Research Question 2, the 331 English and 372 Cantonese body-part idioms elicited as data were closely analysed, classified and compared according to their linguistic and conceptual similarities and differences. This contrastive analysis revealed that there are five types of correspondence between the English and Cantonese idiom data. These five correspondences are summarized in Table 2.2 as the cross-linguistic contrastive model.

Regarding Research Question 1, the following discussion will focus on each of the five types of correspondence with reference to the English and Cantonese idioms that were studied.

2.3.1   Type 1

Type	Linguistic form	Figurative meaning	Conceptual metonymy	Conceptual metaphor
1	Equivalent (all terms equivalent)	Equivalent	Equivalent	Equivalent

Table 2.2   Cross-linguistic contrastive model

Type	Linguistic form	Figurative meaning	Conceptual metonymy	Conceptual metaphor
1	Equivalent (all terms equivalent)	Equivalent	Equivalent	Equivalent
2	Similar (only body-part terms equivalent)	Equivalent	Equivalent	Different
3	Equivalent (all terms equivalent)	Different	Equivalent	Different
4	Similar (only body-part terms equivalent)	Different	Equivalent	Different
5	Different (all terms different)	Equivalent	Different	Different

Type 1 was assigned to idioms in English which are linguistically and figuratively (and hence metonymically and metaphorically) equivalent to their Cantonese counterparts. Two examples of idioms involving correspondence of this type are given below (each Cantonese idiom is accompanied with its word-by-word literal English translation and standard Romanized transcription):

English	Cantonese
feet on the ground	腳踏實地
	[goek3 daap6 sat6 dei6]
	foot step firm ground
from the bottom of your heart	打從心底裡
	[daa2 cung4 sam1 dai2 leoi5]
	from heart bottom inside

Both *feet on the ground* and 腳踏實地 mean 'being sensible and practical'. *Feet* and 腳 (foot) are used metonymically to refer to person. As 地 means 'ground' in English, both idioms achieve their figurative meaning via the same conceptual metaphor BEING PRACTICAL AND SENSIBLE IS BEING ON THE GROUND. In the second idiom pair above, the English idiom and its Cantonese counterpart both mean 'to say something really sincerely'. In both English (Kövecses, 2002) and Chinese (Yu, 1995), there is the folk understanding that *heart* is the 'seat of emotion'. In other words, it is this organ which enables human beings to feel. In this way, *heart* in English and 心 in Cantonese are both understood metonymically via HEART FOR ABILITY TO FEEL. Involved in both idioms are the words *bottom* in English and 底 in Cantonese (which also means 'bottom'). Referring to the figurative meaning of the two idioms, it is obvious that both of them are motivated by the same metaphor SOMETHING REAL IS SOMETHING AT THE BOTTOM.

2.3.2 Type 2

Type	Linguistic form	Figurative meaning	Conceptual metonymy	Conceptual metaphor
2	Similar (only body-part terms equivalent)	Equivalent	Equivalent	Different

Type 2 was assigned to idioms in English which are linguistically similar to their Cantonese counterparts. 'Similar' here means that the English and Cantonese idioms have equivalent body-part words whereas other words in the idioms differ. As a result, the two idioms have the same metonymy, as they have equivalent body-part words, but they differ from each other in their underlying metaphorical motivation as the other words in the idioms differ. The two idioms do however have the same figurative meaning. An example of an idiom involving a correspondence of this type is given below:

English	Cantonese
a slap in the face	落面
	[lok6 min2]
	fall face

Both the English and Cantonese idioms share the same figurative meaning, which is 'someone's behaviour upsets you by insulting or rejecting you'. *Face* (面) is commonly used in both languages because they share a common metonymy FACE FOR REPUTATION. It is the face which is often associated with fame and reputation, so its slapping (in English) or its falling (落) (in Cantonese) causes damage to fame and reputation. It is clear by looking at the figurative meaning of the two idioms that they differ from each other in terms of the conceptual metaphors used. In English, the overall figurative meaning is motivated by LOSING YOUR DIGNITY IS HAVING YOUR FACE SLAPPED. In Cantonese, the metaphor is LOSING YOUR DIGNITY IS HAVING YOUR FACE FALL.

2.3.3   Type 3

Type	Linguistic form	Figurative meaning	Conceptual metonymy	Conceptual metaphor
3	Equivalent (all terms equivalent)	Different	Equivalent	Different

As with Type 1, linguistic forms of the English and Cantonese idioms of Type 3 are the same. But unlike Type 1, idioms of this type differ in their figurative meanings and conceptual metaphors, though they have equivalent body-part words and the same conceptual metonymy. An example of idioms of this type is given below:

English	Cantonese
your heart hardens	心都實晒
	[sam1 dou1 sat6 saai3]
	heart is hard all

In English, *your heart hardens* possesses a figurative meaning of 'feeling unfriendly or unsympathetic'. The literal translation of the English idiom gives rise to the Cantonese idiom 心都實晒. They have the same metonymic motivation which is HEART FOR ABILITY TO FEEL. It seems to be a folk understanding shared by many cultures that the heart is the seat of emotion, the place where feelings such as happiness and sadness reside. *Harden* is used in English and the word 實 (hard) has the same meaning as *harden* in the Cantonese idiom. While the two idioms employ equivalent words having the same literal meaning, they also have, interestingly enough, different and in fact opposite meanings. While the English idiom means 'feeling unfriendly or unsympathetic', its Cantonese counterpart means 'feeling sympathetic', which is just the opposite of the meaning of the English idiom. As a result, the two idioms, though motivated by the same metonymy, as they share the same body-part concept, achieve their figurative meanings via two different conceptual metaphors: BEING UNSYMPATHETIC IS BEING HARD in English; BEING SYMPATHETIC IS BEING HARD in Cantonese. Although the two metaphors share the same source domain, the source domain is mapped onto two different and yet opposite target domains in the two languages.

2.3.4   Type 4

Type	Linguistic form	Figurative meaning	Conceptual metonymy	Conceptual metaphor
4	Similar (only body-part terms equivalent)	Different	Equivalent	Different

Linguistic form was labelled 'similar' for idioms in Type 4 because they have equivalent body-part words. Type 4 idioms seem to be in direct contrast to Type 2 idioms because while the latter have equivalent figurative meanings, the former, which are the focus of this section, have different figurative meanings. An example is given below:

English   **Cantonese**
somebody is soft in the head   硬住頭皮
                                     [ngaang6 zyu6 tau4 pei4]
                                     hard head skin

In English, the idiom *somebody is soft in the head* means that 'somebody becomes silly and crazy'. *Head* is always associated with the mind and the brain due to the nature of human anatomy and psychology. It is because of the general function of rational thinking being associated with the mind and the brain that *head* (associated with the mind and the brain) is used metonymically in HEAD FOR THINKING. This is the same as 頭 (head) in the Cantonese idiom. However, other parts of the two idioms differ greatly. In the English idiom, *soft* is used metaphorically in BEING SILLY IS BEING SOFT. In the Cantonese counterpart, 硬 which means 'hard' (the opposite of soft) is used metaphorically in GOING ON WITH SOMETHING IS BEING HARD. As a result, the two idioms achieve very different meanings.

2.3.5   Type 5

Type	Linguistic form	Figurative meaning	Conceptual metonymy	Conceptual metaphor
5	Different (all terms different)	Equivalent	Different	Different

Except for the figurative meaning, all the other parameters were labelled 'different' for idioms belonging to Type 5. It should be noted that what is meant by 'different' here is that the two idioms differ not only with regard to their body-part words but also with regard to their other words. The following idioms are given as an example:

English   **Cantonese**
fall head over heels   神魂顛倒
                       [san4 wan4 din1 dou2]
                       spirit soul mix

As stated before, only the figurative meaning is found to be the same for this type of idiom. In this particular case, the English and Cantonese idioms both mean 'fall in love deeply and suddenly'. In order to conceptualize this meaning, however, English and Cantonese employ very different motivations. In English, *head* is used metonymically in HEAD FOR SENSIBILITY. In Cantonese, the same target concept is used but the metonymic *head* is replaced with *sense* (神) and *soul* (魂) which are believed by Chinese to be the most important elements, the essence of human beings and which govern sensibility. In English, the idiom is motivated by the metaphor FALLING IN LOVE IS SOMERSAULTING. In Chinese, not only does FALLING IN LOVE involve FALLING OVER as in the English idiom, but it also involves

MIXING (顛倒) SENSE WITH THE SOUL, as shown in the metaphor FALLING IN LOVE IS MIXING SENSE WITH THE SOUL. Hence we can see that the underlying motivations for the English idiom and its Cantonese counterpart are totally different, despite the fact that they have the same figurative meaning.

2.4 Study Two: experimental design

The purpose of Study Two was to shed light on the pedagogical soundness of the 3Cs method in enhancing L2 idiom teaching and learning (i.e. providing answers to Research Question 3). A series of experimental tests were developed to investigate L2 English idiom learning in this study. A total of 106 Cantonese advanced L2 learners of English took part in the experimental tests. At the time when the experiment was conducted, they were all second- or third-year undergraduate students majoring either in English or English Language Education. They had received formal L2 English education for at least 13 years starting from Year 1 in primary school. The 106 subjects were divided into three groups: each group received a different method for learning idioms (see Table 2.3).

Subjects in each group went through four stages: (1) Pre-test Paper; (2) Teaching and Learning of Idioms; (3) Post-test Paper; and (4) One-week Delay Test. All the three groups followed the same procedure, except for the part 'Teaching and Learning of Idioms' in which the Control Group received the traditional vocabulary listing method, Experimental Group I received the 2Cs method and Experimental Group II received the 3Cs

Table 2.3 Grouping for experimental study

Group	Nature	Number of subjects	Idiom treatment received
1	Control Group	34	Traditional vocabulary listing method
2	Experimental Group I	38	Cognitive-linguistic method involving CMR and CMY (2Cs method)
3	Experimental Group II	34	Cognitive-linguistic method involving CMR and CMY plus cross-linguistic contrastive (CLC) model (3Cs method)

CMR: conceptual metaphor CMY: conceptual metonymy

method. A total of 24 English idioms were taught at stage 2: the same idioms were also used for the tested items. They were:

eye(s):	*cast an eye on something; can't take your eyes off someone*
face:	*egg on your face; a slap in the face; keep a straight face; a long face*
foot/feet:	*feet on the ground; get your feet wet; bound hand and foot; one foot in the grave*
hand/hands:	*with one hand tied behind your back; turn your hand to something; fall into someone's hand; get your hands on something*
head:	*fall head over heels; somebody is soft in the head*
heart:	*your heart bleeds for someone; your heart hardens; from the bottom of your heart; open your heart*
mouth:	*born with a silver spoon in your mouth; live from hand to mouth; shoot your mouth off; a plum in your mouth*

For the Pre-test, Post-test and One-week Delay Test, each idiom was incorporated into a containing sentence. With each idiom itself the body-part word(s) and some other grammatical words were removed, leaving behind those words which did not provide too much of a hint for subjects, yet still constrained the choice of word in completing the blank in the idiom. After filling in the blank, subjects were also asked to write down the meaning of the idiom on the line provided. Here are two example items:

1 Staying at home to look after a sick parent often means that a person is **bound** _____.
   • Meaning: _____

2 Anne looked so beautiful that no one **could take** _____ _____ **her.**
   • Meaning: _____

Besides the 24 taught idioms, 10 more idioms were added for the Post-test and One-week Delay Test. These 10 idioms were 'untaught idioms' as they did not appear in the Teaching and Learning of Idioms. Subjects in all three groups were asked to complete these 10 idioms in the same way as the 24 taught idioms. The purpose of setting questions with these 10 untaught idioms was to investigate whether subjects from each group were able to make use of what they had learnt in the Teaching and Learning of Idioms and to anticipate the body-part related and figurative meaning of the untaught idioms. Test papers for all the three tests were collected immediately after the experiment. They were marked and scored by the first researcher and then again by two research assistants to ensure validity. All the results were fed into SPSS (ver. 16.0) for statistical analysis using One-way ANOVA and Paired Samples T-test.

A different set of materials for the Teaching and Learning of Idioms was designed for each of the three groups with a view to the experimental rationale applied to the group. Excerpts of the relevant materials are illustrated below:

Control Group: Traditional vocabulary listing method
EYE(S)

| Cast an *eye* on something |

- If you *cast an eye on something*, you examine it carefully and give your opinion about it.

| Can't take your *eyes* off someone |

- If you *can't take your eyes off someone or something*, you find it hard to look at anything else.

Experimental Group I: 2Cs method (CMR + CMY)
  EYE(S)

| Cast an *eye* on something |

- If you *cast an eye on something*, you examine it carefully and give your opinion about it.
  MY: **Eye For Attention**
  MR: **Examining Something Is Throwing Something Else On Something**

| Can't take your *eyes* off someone |

- If you *can't take your eyes off someone or something*, you find it hard to look at anything else.
  MY: **Eyes For Attention**
  MR: **To Stop Looking Is Taking Something Off Something**

Experimental Group II: 3Cs method (CMR + CMY + CLC)

Type	Linguistic form	Figurative meaning	Conceptual metonymy	Conceptual metaphor
1	Equivalent	Equivalent	Equivalent	Equivalent

| *Feet* **on the ground** | 腳踏實地 |

- If someone keeps their *feet on the ground*, they continue to act in a sensible and practical way even when new and exciting things are happening or even when they become successful or powerful.
  MY: **Feet For Person**
  MR: **Being Practical And Sensible Is Being On The Ground**

| **Bound hand and** *foot* | 綁手綁腳 |

- If you say that someone is *bound hand and foot* by something, you mean that they cannot act freely or do what they want because it prevents them.
  MY: **Hand and Foot For Person**
  MR: **Not Acting Freely Is Being Bound**

Type	Linguistic form	Figurative meaning	Conceptual metonymy	Conceptual metaphor
2	Similar	Equivalent	Equivalent	Different

| **Cast an** *eye* **on something** | 一眼關七 |

- If you *cast an eye on something*, you examine it carefully and give your opinion about it.
  MY: **Eye For Attention**
  MR: **Examining Something Is Throwing Something Else On Something**

| **Can't take your** *eyes* **off someone** | 眼金金 |

- If you *can't take your eyes off someone or something*, you find it hard to look at anything else.
  MY: **Eyes For Attention**
  MR: **To Stop Looking Is Taking Something Off Something**

2.4.1 Study Two: SPSS descriptive results

Table 2.4 summarizes the descriptive statistics for the scores of the 24 taught idioms in Pre-test, Post-test and One-week Delay Test for all the three groups. It should be noted that the full score in this part is 120.

The difference between the Pre-test mean scores of CG and EG1 was not statistically significant as the P value is .612. (P > .05). The differences between the Pre-test mean scores of CG and EG1 as well as EG1

Table 2.4 SPSS output for untaught idioms (full score: 120)

	CG	EG1	EG2	P value (sig 2-tailed)
Pre-test (mean)	16.87	18.68		.612
	16.87		20.37	.181
		18.68	20.37	.655
	CG	EG1	EG2	P value (sig 2-tailed)
Post-test (mean)	51.93	74.41		.000
	51.93		93.47	.000
		74.41	93.47	.000
	CG	EG1	EG2	P value (sig 2-tailed)
One-week Delay	36.75	62.54		.000
Test (mean)	36.75		82.38	.000
		62.54	82.38	.000

CG: Control Group EG1: Experimental Group I EG2: Experimental Group II

and EG2 were also not statistically significant as their P values are .181 and .655 respectively (both having P > .05). From these results, it can be concluded that (1) the body-part idioms chosen for the test were generally unknown to the subjects; and (2) subjects in all the three groups possessed a similar knowledge of the body-part idioms tested. In other words, all subjects, before receiving the corresponding teaching and learning treatments for the idioms, started at the same or a similar level of proficiency for the idioms in question.

In the Post-test, EG1 outscored CG and the difference was found to be statistically significant (P = .000). EG2 also outscored CG as EG1 did. Again, the difference was found to be statistically significant (P = .000). This shows that subjects in CG performed the worst among all the three groups in the Post-test. When EG1 and EG2 were in turn compared, EG2 sharply outscored EG1. The difference was found to be statistically significant (P = .000). This shows that subjects in EG2 performed the best among all the three groups. Similar findings were obtained in the One-week Delay Test. EG1 outscored CG. The difference was statistically significant (P = .000). EG2 also outscored CG and the difference was also found to be statistically significant (P = .000). The two findings indicate that subjects in CG performed the worst among all the three groups in the One-week Delay Test. EG2 sharply outscored EG1 and the difference was once again found to have statistical significance (P = .000). This shows that students in EG2 did best among all the three groups in the One-week Delay Test.

Table 2.5 summarizes the SPSS analysis of the mean scores obtained from the 10 untaught idioms in the Post-test and One-week Delay Test for all the three groups. The full score in this part is 50.

Table 2.5   SPSS output for untaught idioms (full score: 50)

	CG	EG1	EG2	P value (sig 2-tailed)
Post-test (mean)	4.41	10.95		.000
	4.41		14.65	.000
		10.95	14.65	.058
	CG	EG1	EG2	P value (sig 2-tailed)
One-week Delay	4.03	9.70		.003
Test (mean)	4.03		14.03	.000
		9.70	14.03	.030

CG: Control Group   EG1: Experimental Group I   EG2: Experimental Group II

In the Post-test, EG1 outscored CG and the difference was found to be statistically significant (P = .000). EG2 also outscored CG as EG1 did. Again, the difference was found to be statistically significant (P = .000). This shows that subjects in CG performed the worst in anticipating the body part and figurative meanings of untaught idioms among all the three groups in the Post-test. When EG1 and EG2 were compared, EG2 (14.65) scored higher than EG1 (10.95). The difference between the mean scores was found to have a P value of .058, which shows that the difference just fails to be significant. However, when comparing the mean scores of the untaught idioms between EG2 and EG1 in the One-week Delay Test, the P value is .030, which means that the difference was statistically significant. The purpose of setting the One-week Delay Test was to examine whether the teaching method exerts any effect for idiom learning on subjects' long-term memory. The statistically significant difference between EG2 and EG1 for the untaught idioms in the One-week Delay Test argues that the effect for idiom learning and its subsequent anticipation on the long-term memory of EG2's subjects was superior to that of EG1's subjects. This finding is more important and should be taken as the more representative finding when compared with the marginal failure to obtain significance in the Post-test. EG1 and EG2 both outscored CG in the One-week Delay Test with statistical significance. Thus the subjects in CG performed the worst in anticipating the untaught idioms among all the three groups in the One-week Delay Test.

For the 24 taught idioms, if it was only memorization that played a positive role in helping subjects complete the Post-test and One-week Delay Test, subjects in all the three groups should have shown a fairly high and similar score without any statistically significant difference. If, however, conceptual metaphor, conceptual metonymy and the cross-linguistic contrastive model play a positive role in motivating the figurative meaning of idioms and arousing subjects' attention to the similar and different idioms in their L1, EG2 should have performed better than EG1 and hence also CG. Our experimental results show that EG2 outperformed the two other groups and hence give strong empirical support for the 3Cs method being the best in enhancing L2 idiom learning.

As for the 10 untaught idioms, if memorization alone played a positive role in helping subjects complete the tests, the scores of the untaught idioms for all three groups should have been low and near random, since memorization has no way of playing a part in helping subjects to anticipate untaught idioms and thus is eliminated as a factor with untaught idioms. If, however, the 3Cs method plays a positive role in motivating the figurative meaning of idioms and allowing subjects to make reference to their L1, EG2 should have performed better than EG1 and hence also CG. It is obvious from our experimental results that the performance of anticipating untaught idioms of EG2 was the best among the three groups. Therefore, there is strong empirical support for the 3Cs method being the best for enhancing L2 learners' ability to anticipate untaught idioms.

2.5   Conclusion

The experimental study has demonstrated that a systematic comparison of idioms based on a cross-linguistic contrastive model (i.e. the 3Cs method) is able to enhance L2 learners' acquisition of L2 idioms. By explicitly informing L2 learners how L2 metaphors and metonymies are similar to and different from those in their L1, not only are L2 learners able to better comprehend and hence remember the lexical components and figurative meanings of L2 idioms, but they are also able to make use of the 'taught' conceptual motivation to help themselves deal with 'untaught' idioms more appropriately and accurately. Two pedagogical insights concerning L2 figurative language arise from this.

Firstly, conceptual mechanisms such as metaphor and metonymy, which play an immense role in motivating figurative language, should be explicitly taught in the L2 classroom. L2 learners should be provided with a list of linguistic expressions which are motivated by a single conceptual metaphor and/or metonymy. L2 teachers should then explain in what ways the linguistic expressions are conceptually linked to the underlying metaphor and/or metonymy. In this way, the underlying conceptual system is made explicit and brought to conscious awareness, thus enabling learners to make sense of the link between the surface lexical components and the underlying figurative meanings.

Secondly, not only should metaphor and metonymy be explicitly introduced to learners, but they should also be compared to those in the learners' L1. Cognitive linguist Ronald Langacker has described language as 'an essential instrument and component of culture, whose reflection in linguistic structure is pervasive and quite significant' (1999: 16). This statement suggests that language is embedded in culture. In this study, although the learners' L1 and L2 cultures are distant from each other, there are, besides variations, overlaps in terms of metaphor and metonymy between the two cultures and a systematic presentation of these facilitates L2 idiom learning. What is implied is that instead of focusing only on the cognitive constraints on metaphor and metonymy, the L2 classroom should also gear itself towards the cultural constraints on them so as to provide L2 learners with cross-cultural conceptualizations associated with the features of the language to be learnt. However, most of the current applications of CL notions in L2 figurative language teaching are constrained by the classroom format in which learners acquire prerequisite cultural knowledge mainly through the media of language and diagrams. They capture only, in Sharifian and Palmer's words, 'glimpses of cultural skeletons' (2007: 5). The richer cultural world indeed takes place outside the cognitive-linguistic classroom. With a view to what has been found in this study as a point of departure, further research should step beyond the classroom format and appeal to cross-cultural conceptualizations to explore pedagogical implications pertaining to L2 figurative language.

References

Boers, F. (2000) Metaphor awareness and vocabulary retention, *Applied Linguistics*, 21, 553–571.

Boers, F. & Demecheleer, M. (1998) A cognitive semantic approach to teaching prepositions, *English Language Teaching Journal*, 53, 197–204.

Boers, F. & Lindstromberg, S. (2006) Cognitive linguistic applications in second and foreign language instruction: rationale, proposals, and evaluation. In G. Kristiansen, M. Achard, R. Dirven & F. J. Ruiz (eds) *Cognitive Linguistics: Current Applications and Future Perspectives*. Berlin and New York: Mouton de Gruyter.

Boers, F. & Littlemore, J. (eds) (2003) Special issue of Cross-cultural differences in conceptual metaphor: applied linguistics perspectives, *Metaphor and Symbol*, 18.

Charteris-Black, J. (2002) Second language figurative proficiency: a comparative study of Malay and English, *Applied Linguistics*, 23, 104–133.

Charteris-Black, J. (2003) Speaking with forked tongue: a comparative study of metaphor and metonymy in English and Malay phraseology, *Metaphor and Symbol*, 18(4), 289–310.

Cooper, T. C. (1998) Teaching idioms, *Foreign Language Annuals*, 31, 255–266.
Cooper, T. C. (1999) Processing of idioms by L2 learners of English, *TESOL Quarterly*, 33, 233–262.
Danesi, M. (1995) Learning and teaching languages: the role of 'conceptual fluency, *International Journal of Applied Linguistics*, 5, 3–20.
Deignan, A. (2005) *Metaphor and Corpus Linguistics*. Amsterdam: John Benjamins.
Deignan, A., Gabrys, D. & Solska, A. (1997) Teaching English metaphors using cross-linguistic awareness-raising activities, *ELT Journal*, 51, 352–360.
Dirven, R. (1989) Cognitive linguistics and pedagogic grammar. In G. Leitner & G. Graustein (eds) *Linguistic Theorizing and Grammar Writing*. Tübingen: Max Niemeyer, pp. 56–75.
Gibbs, R. W. (1994) *The Poetics of Mind: Figurative Thought, Language, and Understanding*. Cambridge: Cambridge University Press.
Gibbs, R. W. (1995) Idiomaticity and human cognition. In M. Everaert, E.-J. van der Linden, A. Schenk, & R. Schreuder (eds) *Idioms: Structural and Psychological Perspectives*. Hillsdale, NJ: Lawrence Erlbaum Associates, pp. 97–116.
Grant, L. E. & Bauer, L. (2004) Criteria for re-defining idioms: are we barking up the wrong tree?, *Applied Linguistics*, 25, 38–61.
Howarth, P. (1998) Phraseology and second language proficiency, *Applied Linguistics*, 19(1), 24–44.
Johnson, M. (1987) *The Body in the Mind: The Bodily Basis of Reason and Imagination*. Chicago: University of Chicago Press.
Kövecses, Z. (2002) *Metaphor: A Practical Introduction*. Oxford: Oxford University Press.
Kövecses, Z. (2005) *Metaphor in Culture: Universality and Variation*. Cambridge: Cambridge University Press.
Kövecses, Z. & Szabó, P. (1996) Idioms: a view from cognitive linguistics, *Applied Linguistics*, 17, 326–355.
Lakoff, G. (1987) *Women, Fire, and Dangerous Things: What Categories Reveal about the Mind*. Chicago: University of Chicago Press.
Lakoff, G. (1993) The contemporary theory of metaphor. In A. Ortony (ed.) *Metaphor and Thought*. Cambridge: Cambridge University Press.
Lakoff, G. & Johnson, M. (1980) *Metaphors We Live By*. Chicago: University of Chicago Press.
Lakoff, G. & Johnson, M. (1999) *Philosophy in the Flesh: The Embodied Mind and its Challenge to Western Thought*. New York: Basic Books.
Lakoff, G. & Turner, M. (1989) *More than Cool Reason: A Field Guide to Poetic Metaphor*. Chicago: University of Chicago Press.
Langacker, R. W. (1987) *Foundations of Cognitive Grammar*, vol. I: *Theoretical Prerequisites*. Stanford, CA: Stanford University Press.
Langacker, R. W. (1999) Assessing the cognitive linguistic enterprise. In T. Janssen & G. Redeker (eds) *Cognitive Linguistics: Foundations, Scope, and Methodology*. Berlin and New York: Mouton de Gruyter, pp. 13–59.
Langlotz, A. (2006) *Idiomatic Creativity: A Cognitive Linguistic Model of Idiom-Representations and Idiom-Variation in English*. Amsterdam and Philadelphia: John Benjamins.
Lazar, G. (2003) *Meaning and Metaphor: Activities to Practise Figurative Language*. Cambridge: Cambridge University Press.

Leung, C. H. (2004) The particle-based learning of English phrasal verbs: a conceptual metaphor and image schema-based approach. MPhil thesis, The Chinese University of Hong Kong.

Li, F. Y. (2002) The acquisition of metaphorical expressions, idioms, and proverbs by Chinese learners of English: a conceptual metaphor and image schema based approach. PhD dissertation, The Chinese University of Hong Kong.

Littlemore, J. & Low, G. (2006) *Figurative Thinking and Foreign Language Learning.* Basingstoke: Palgrave Macmillan.

Sharifian, F. & Palmer, G. B. (2007) *Applied Cultural Linguistics: Implications for Second Language Learning and Intercultural Communication.* Amsterdam and Philadelphia: John Benjamins.

Weinert, R. (1995) The role of formulaic language in second language acquisition: a review, *Applied Linguistics,* 16, 180–205.

Yorio, C. A. (1989) Idiomaticity as an indicator of second language proficiency. In K. Hyltenstam & L. K. Obler (eds) *Bilingualism across the Lifespan: Aspects of Acquisition, Maturity and Loss.* Cambridge: Cambridge University Press.

Yu, N. (1995) Metaphorical expressions of anger and happiness in English and Chinese, *Metaphor and Symbolic Activity,* 10(2), 59–92.

Dictionaries consulted

English idioms

Cambridge International Dictionary of Idioms (1998)
Collins COBUILD Idioms Dictionary (2002)
Longman Idioms Dictionary (1998)
Oxford Idioms Dictionary (1999)

Cantonese idioms

Cantonese Colloquial Expressions (2007)
廣州話口語詞彙
A Dictionary of Cantonese Colloquialisms in English (1990)
英譯廣東口語詞典
A Glossary of Common Cantonese Colloquial Expressions (2002)
常用廣州話口語詞彙

3
More than a Journey: 'Learning' in the Metaphors of Chinese Students and Teachers

Lixian Jin and Martin Cortazzi

In this chapter we aim to get an inside picture of learning from the perspectives of Chinese participants by analysing large numbers of metaphors given by students and teachers in China. Our analysis leads to a complex cultural model of learning but here we focus particularly on one strand of this, which is that 'learning is a journey'. We ask the research question of how Chinese university students represent learning in terms of metaphors and we investigate the major example of how learning is envisaged as a journey, its nature and features, and about the necessary qualities needed to succeed in learning. We show how the picture presented by university teachers in China complements that of students.

3.1 Introduction: investigating Chinese students' ideas about learning

As the Chinese education system turns to more learner-centred approaches, it is vital to analyse how the learners conceive of learning, how they think about the teachers' roles in relation to their own, and what attitudes, values and beliefs they have about learning and teaching. To focus on learning, we need to learn what learners' ideas about learning are. The educational reforms in China since the early and mid-2000s have emphasized more active participation from learners in classrooms and collaboration in learning tasks, together with developing a wider range of learning strategies and students' ability to learn independently and with greater autonomy (Jin & Cortazzi, 2003, 2006; Ministry of Education, 2007), but the success of these initiatives will depend, in part, on students' current conceptions of learning and how new developments relate to their beliefs about learning practices.

Learners' beliefs, classroom contexts, educational policy and practical changes are intertwined: changing contexts will influence what learners believe, yet their beliefs will influence how they learn in these contexts – their beliefs are an important part of this context and may mediate the extent of the enactment of proposed policy changes.

Similarly, for Chinese students who go to study abroad and who are likely to encounter expected ways of learning that are less familiar or new to them, it is crucial for researchers and teachers to have some clear idea of the beliefs and experiences about learning which students from China may hold.

In both these cases, of Chinese learners studying in China or internationally, we do not presume that learners' beliefs and values will be the only determinants of how they will adopt or adapt to different contexts of learning, yet how the students see learning is clearly a significant and influential factor in such educational or socio-cultural adaptation. Further, we should not assume that learners' beliefs will necessarily be a constraining influence on change: this depends on the framework of the beliefs, but in principle some may well facilitate changes which match some attitudes and expectations. Internationally, we should not assume that Chinese students' beliefs will necessarily be conservative, narrow or traditional (it is often supposed that Chinese learners are passive rote-learners but this now seems largely a myth); in principle, learning about Chinese students' learning may well offer useful insights to their teachers and to other international students or students from the 'host' country. This chapter will try to show that this is the case.

However, finding out about students' conceptions of learning is problematic: different research methods favour different kinds of data collection, analysis and interpretation of results which in turn may give different views of learning. This means that we need a variety of complementary research approaches; mixed methods may give a fuller picture, with less risk that researchers are imposing meaning through their choice of approach to find out how learners make meaning in their learning.

It has been suggested that underlying the variety of research approaches in education there are root metaphors underlying investigations into learning (Sfard, 1998; Cortazzi & Jin, 1999; Hodkinson & Macleod, 2010) and that such metaphors – as used by the researchers themselves – construct or skew what learning is, even though data apparently come from learners. Thus large-scale questionnaire surveys often claim to investigate underlying cognitive processes and the root metaphors underlying this are *acquisition* (learners are acquiring propositional knowledge) and developing *skills* (through various processes which can be 'transferred'). In contrast, classroom observations with interviews in a more ethnographic approach of investigating learning activities in a social context may centre on root metaphors of *participation* (learners take part in activities and learning communities) and *construction* (learners actively build up meanings through activity and through 'scaffolded' adult help) or *transformation* (learning includes the learner evolving and perhaps a changing context). Behind these many ways of thinking about learning, it seems there are clusters of metaphors or 'conceptual lenses' (Winch, 1998; Hager & Hodkinson, 2009) which are constrained by contexts and cultures and that reliance on just one metaphor means limiting research and understanding in advance. These indications of a range of metaphors underlying concepts of learning might point to the potential usefulness of investigating learners' metaphors for learning within a particular culture: instead of imposing a research metaphor, the research would be to investigate learners' own metaphors and let the major metaphors emerge from the participants. We might expect the learners' metaphors, like those of researchers within the learning literature, to form clusters.

This is what this chapter does: we report research in which we elicited, collected and analysed large numbers of metaphors of learning from Chinese students – and teachers – in order to look for underlying socio-cultural beliefs which we attempt to put together in clusters into a cultural model which Chinese learners recognize. We believe this model gives knowledge and insight to researchers and teachers, and, more interestingly, encouragement and sustenance to Chinese teachers and students. This approach is intended to be complementary to other approaches rather than exclusive and, like any research approach, it will have advantages and disadvantages, which we will indicate. Some of these strengths and weaknesses may complement or offset some of our previous research into the expectations of students in China about learning and teaching which used the analysis of students' essays, questionnaires, interviews, classroom photography and observations (Cortazzi & Jin 1996a, 1996b, 2001; Jin & Cortazzi, 1998a, 1998b). Thus, while the choice of a research approach is partly determined by the sorts of questions a researcher is asking and the research context, it is also influenced by a researcher's preference for a research orientation and style and what a mixed approach may include (Richards, 2003; Dörnyei, 2007). We propose metaphor analysis as a method which analyses participants' perceptions and which may sit alongside, and combine with, other research approaches.

3.2   Other research on Chinese beliefs about learning

In Hong Kong, Biggs and his colleagues developed the use of questionnaires originally from Australia to ascertain Chinese students' approaches to learning (Biggs, 1987; Biggs & Watkins, 1993; Biggs, 1996; Gow *et al.*, 1996). They distinguished surface and deep approaches and identified a particular Chinese achieving approach which attributed successful outcomes in learning to strong achievement motivation, effort and Chinese cultural values which give great importance to education and diligence in learning. They pointed to a 'paradox of the Chinese learner' in which students were considered as rote-learners (an apparent surface approach in which memorization seems a substitute for understanding) yet scored highly on measures of deep learning (that focuses on underlying meaning, concepts and principles) and had high academic performance (Watkins & Biggs, 1996, 2001). Thus Western ideas about learning may be inappropriate and the contexts of Chinese learners, including the cultural context, needs to be considered (Chan & Rao, 2009). The use of such psychology-based questionnaires, with the underlying metaphor of 'acquisition', is a quantitative approach which allows measurements of large samples and cross-cultural comparisons and can encourage cultural alignment to student predispositions (Biggs, 1999); however, it does not really allow for students' own individual ideas about learning since they respond to question items drawn up by the researchers, although such research is often supplemented with small numbers of interviews.

In a parallel 'acquisition' orientation, questionnaires to investigate learners' language-learning strategies in China (Bedell & Oxford, 1996), while enjoying the cross-cultural strength of a body of quantitative comparisons with other learners' strategies, styles and beliefs about language learning (Wenden & Rubin, 1987; Reid, 1995; Oxford, 1996; Cohen, 1998), also have the disadvantage of applying a top-down inventory of strategies developed in the USA which does not ask for Chinese learners' views in their own words.

An example of a 'participation' or 'construction' approach which elicits free responses from Chinese students is the analysis of word associations (Szalay *et al.*, 1994). Students were asked to quickly write their associations to stimulus words, including 'education', 'study', 'student' and 'knowledge', which were then grouped and compared. Compared with 100 American students, 100 Chinese learners emphasized teacher–student relationships, the moral character of teaching and learning, and the need for student effort and diligence. The Chinese learners gave many metaphors which were absent in the American data: education is *cultivation*, involving a *tree* or *growth*, learning is *cultivating essentials* or *self-cultivation*, knowledge is *a precious treasure* or *wealth*, teachers are *spiritual engineers, industrious gardeners* or *sowers of knowledge* who *cultivate* students. Such metaphors were freely given when participants were thinking about learning and teaching, which suggests that a research method which explicitly elicits metaphors might productively explore Chinese conceptions of learning.

A much more fully worked-out example of a bottom-up, 'participation' approach to investigating Chinese students' beliefs about learning is in the work of Li to develop a cultural model of learning from categorizing and ranking words associated with learning (Li, 2001, 2002a, 2002b, 2009). Such a model is, like a complex collection of schemas, a culturally constructed and shared domain of knowledge which people use to structure and interpret experience and set goals for action and (for our study) would include shared metaphors. Li's approach was to generate a list of freely associated terms from students related to learning; other students sorted them before a further group of students rated their relevance to 'learning'; later, another 100 students sorted the resulting high-rated 225 terms for their similarity, from which, using cluster analysis, a cultural model (like a concept map) was derived and compared with a similarly derived American model. The Chinese model highlights '*heart and mind for wanting to learn*', which had components of pursuing lifelong learning and features of diligence, hardship, steadfastness, concentration, humility and desire. Significant purposes of learning included: learning as an end in itself, the status and benefits of learning, and the learners' contributions to society, while achievements of learning were said to be extensive or deep understanding, developing extraordinary abilities, a moral character and originality or creativity. A later study using a similar categorization approach to explore concepts of 'ideal' learners in written essays (compare the essay approach in Cortazzi & Jin, 1996b) gives detailed aspects of purpose, affect, agency or virtues of learning, and achievement in the 'heart-and-mind' model (Li, 2009). Few of the Chinese aspects of these studies were shared with the American models, which are quite different.

Li's studies do not discuss metaphors (though she quotes some traditional Chinese sayings using metaphors) and they could be complemented and expanded by metaphor analysis. An approach of metaphor analysis would have several advantages over the complex categorization procedures undertaken by students in these psychological word-association studies. Metaphors are commonplace in normal talk and can be elicited from a far wider range of participants; they are currently researched both from the cognitive linguistic point of view of representing people's thinking and from the cultural angle of representing shared social perceptions. Further, metaphors can easily be related to Chinese traditions of learning since they can be identified in both current and classical educational discourse (Jin & Cortazzi, 2010). Also, since metaphors are easily appreciated and interpreted, once analysed they require no specialist knowledge for validation by participants – the students and teachers themselves can recognize and interpret resulting models with reference to classroom and self-study practices, commonplace sayings and official educational documents in which metaphor appear.

3.3   Metaphor analysis as a tool to investigate thinking and cultural beliefs

First, we should consider why people use metaphors. Basic experiences determine how we think about the world and how we talk about it: often this talk includes metaphors which generally present something abstract in terms of a concrete or ordinary aspect of our experience. Metaphors are commonplace in ordinary talk and, in fact, they organize some kinds of talk. In education, metaphors are often systematically used in explanations to help learners understand, visualize, organize and remember concepts. Metaphors work through comparisons, which can be seen through this metaphor: '*Metaphors are bridges to learning*' (this example is from classical Arabic). This compares 'a metaphor' (an abstract idea) to 'a bridge' (a concrete image). Thus metaphors help us to construct alternative visions, which is one reason for studying metaphors from another culture. Metaphors also invite interaction, mentally or socially, since with a metaphor which is new to us we try to work out the point of comparison. In this example we might think, 'By working through the meaning of a metaphor mentally we can travel across a bridge to a new way of understanding on the other side', or we might say, 'Bridges are familiar, they take us from our side of a river to the other side; this is like a metaphor taking us from something familiar to something new, like a new meaning or insight.' In this sense, metaphors are a bridge between language and thought (Cortazzi & Jin, 1999). Metaphors can also often have a dramatic effect in communication through a stylistic highlighting or poetic effect.

Within cognitive linguistics and psychology a widely known approach to metaphor analysis is derived from the work of Lakoff and others (Lakoff & Johnson, 1980; Lakoff, 1987, 1993; Lakoff & Turner, 1989). In this approach metaphors are conceptual: there are systematic 'mappings' or correspondences between sets of language expressions of everyday metaphors and underlying concepts; and the underlying concepts cluster into belief systems. This implies that by collecting and analysing sets of metaphoric expressions in language on a given topic, the concepts of the speakers can be identified which in turn can be used to examine beliefs or, ultimately, underlying ideologies, cognitive models or frames.

An example is 'LEARNING IS A JOURNEY' (Lakoff, 1993; Kövecses, 2005, 2006). This is the overarching 'conceptual metaphor' (conventionally such a conceptual metaphor has small capitals), which is a formal statement of the main idea behind many everyday language expressions (termed 'linguistic metaphors') (see Figure 3.1). In this case, 'learning' is the '*target*' or abstract topic which we are envisaging in terms of a '*source*' (or vehicle) which is the familiar experience of travel from which we pick out features for comparison in order to say something interesting about the target. The linguistic metaphors may not mention 'a journey' but travelling or a journey is implied in many everyday phrases which indicate

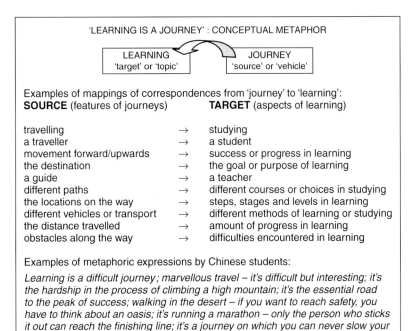

'LEARNING IS A JOURNEY' : CONCEPTUAL METAPHOR

LEARNING	JOURNEY
'target' or 'topic'	'source' or 'vehicle'

Examples of mappings of correspondences from 'journey' to 'learning':

SOURCE (features of journeys)		TARGET (aspects of learning)
travelling	→	studying
a traveller	→	a student
movement forward/upwards	→	success or progress in learning
the destination	→	the goal or purpose of learning
a guide	→	a teacher
different paths	→	different courses or choices in studying
the locations on the way	→	steps, stages and levels in learning
different vehicles or transport	→	different methods of learning or studying
the distance travelled	→	amount of progress in learning
obstacles along the way	→	difficulties encountered in learning

Examples of metaphoric expressions by Chinese students:

Learning is a difficult journey; marvellous travel – it's difficult but interesting; it's the hardship in the process of climbing a high mountain; it's the essential road to the peak of success; walking in the desert – if you want to reach safety, you have to think about an oasis; it's running a marathon – only the person who sticks it out can reach the finishing line; it's a journey on which you can never slow your pace or stop; my teacher is a guide in the way of knowledge for our learning – a pilgrimage which leads to our holy destination; it's a long, long journey – we can't reach the goal if we are not trying to tread a long path.

Figure 3.1 The conceptual metaphor of LEARNING IS A JOURNEY showing mappings and Chinese students' metaphoric expressions

features of journeys which can be 'mapped' to show correspondences with aspects of learning, the 'mapping' is the 'ground' or basis of comparison (Figure 3.1).

A JOURNEY can be thought of as a long-term purposeful activity involving movement in physical space, with direction from a starting point to an end point or destination (Lakoff, 1993; Goatly, 1997). The features of direction and movement in learning are seen in linguistic expressions used when people talk about learning and studying: *advancing, getting ahead, making progress, moving on, going up* or *reaching higher levels.* Underlying ideas are oriented in space and show that 'up' and 'height' are positively valued and imply more learning or achievement, while 'forward' and 'ahead' are also positive evaluations and imply progress or success, often with indications of travel speed, *going forward rapidly, forging ahead, racing along, taking off* or *a high flyer* (in contrast, *staying in one place, going down* or *slipping back* are negative and mean a lack of progress). Common journey metaphors show a path in *following a route, staying on track* or *following guidelines* and a destination in *getting there, reaching my goal* or *attaining a target.* Even clearer examples of the journey metaphor are the expressions about learning which show features of a landscape: *climbing a mountain, reaching a peak, coasting along, going downhill.* Overall, hundreds of similar examples in our data confirm Lakoff's (1993) formulation of a journey metaphor as PURPOSEFUL ACTIVITY, TRAVELLING ALONG A PATH TOWARDS A DESTINATION.

The conceptual metaphors may have further inferences which map ideas beyond the basic correspondences. These are known as 'entailments' (Kövecses, 2005; Berendt, 2008) and they are important for our study of Chinese learners and teachers since they may show cultural aspects which are not obvious to those outside Chinese contexts but may offer insights into Chinese views of learning. What is mapping within a key metaphor in one culture (a normal interpretation or implication) may be an entailment in another (an interpretation that is much less obvious until it is teased out or explained). For example, in the JOURNEY metaphor of Chinese students, learning is often formulated as climbing a mountain with an entailment of reaching or seeing 'beauty': *In learning, I climb to the top of the mountain – the higher you go the more beauty you will see; it is difficult to climb the mountain of learning but when you reach the top you will see the beautiful scenery; learning is painstaking climbing a mountain with the hope of seeing beautiful scenery at the top.* While the entailment of 'struggle' here may be fairly clear from the mapping of 'climbing', the less obvious entailment of 'beauty' can be interpreted by extrapolating from the mapping of 'scenery'. This gives learning an aesthetic dimension which is, according to the entailments in our data, stronger as learning progresses.

Conceptual metaphors are held to be more general or more specific and in the Chinese metaphors for learning studied here the conceptual metaphor for LEARNING IS A JOURNEY subsumes a cluster of specific travel metaphors, which may be thought of as ways of travelling: LEARNING IS CLIMBING, WALKING, RUNNING, SEARCHING, EXPLORING, SAILING AND FLYING. Some of these subsume further specific metaphors, for instance LEARNING IS CLIMBING is associated with particular structures for climbing or crossing: LEARNING IS CLIMBING A LADDER, CLIMBING STAIRS, CROSSING A BRIDGE. This hierarchy of conceptual metaphors which we have found in the Chinese data confirms Goatly's statement (1997: 59) that conceptual metaphors form 'an interacting web'. The hierarchy also follows Yu's investigation (Yu, 1998) into Chinese based on newspaper data which shows that there are cross-matchings between target and source domains in both Chinese and English: the different target domains of LIFE and LOVE both correspond with the source domain of JOURNEY (LIFE IS A JOURNEY; LOVE IS A JOURNEY) and yet the source domain of JOURNEY also cross-matches with the target of HISTORY in Chinese (HISTORY IS A JOURNEY) while LIFE cross-matches with GAME and PLAY (LIFE IS PLAYING A GAME; LIFE IS A PLAY). Yu (1998: 232) speculates that lower levels in such hierarchies will display more diversity and difference across cultures. The hierarchy or web which we find and attempt to model seems theoretically interesting therefore and at the more specific levels, perhaps in entailments, it may have cultural features of Chinese education which are different and present insights to those outside China.

In our research, we follow a more socio-cultural direction in applied linguistics in which the purpose is not so much to investigate cognition but rather to find out about cultural perceptions of central issues in education by analysing participants' metaphors. Here the general research question is:

- How do Chinese students and teachers in universities think about learning?

And the specific focus is:

- What does an analysis of the metaphors given by Chinese students and teachers tell us about their picture of learning as a journey?

In this, we follow a currently accepted approach in applied linguistics – 'the theoretical and empirical study of real world problems in which language plays a central role' (Brumfit, 1995: 27). Within this, metaphor analysis is now recognized as a tool in, among other areas, language and education (Cameron & Low, 1999; Cameron, 2003; Zanotto *et al.*, 2008), which includes investigations of teachers' and learners' metaphors (Cortazzi & Jin, 1999; Ellis & Barkhuizen, 2005; Berendt, 2008).

The real-world problem we investigate is that learners and teachers from different cultures appear to view learning in different ways, according to their educational experience and social expectations deriving from their specific cultural contexts of learning and that in transnational education such differences can lead to difficulties but can positively offer insights if we research them (Cortazzi & Jin, 1996b, 1999; Jin & Cortazzi, 1998a, 1998b, 2006). In the case of China, and specifically in classrooms for learning English, we study conceptions of learning from the view of Chinese learners and teachers in order to present positive insights into learning and make suggestions and recommendations for students and teachers in different contexts such as foreign teachers working in China or teachers elsewhere working with Chinese learners.

3.4 Our method of analysing metaphors

Our approach to researching Chinese metaphors of learning follows the general steps of data collection, grouping and classifying the metaphors under conceptual metaphors, and then recursively examining the classi-fied data to suggest underlying beliefs and values (Cameron & Low, 1999; Ellis & Barkhuizen, 2005). We elicited a database of 3235 metaphors on learning from 1036 undergraduate students in their English classrooms in four key national and provincial universities in China. The students were non-English majors (i.e. their degree is in some other subject but they study English as a required course). We asked them to use meta-phors to complete a sentence frame: '*Learning is...... because.......*' The sentence frame allows myriad responses since it is open-ended – we do not ask specifically for journey metaphors, for instance. These data are supported and checked by analysing a further independent database of 2882 metaphors for '*a teacher*' from 1140 students, and a smaller sample of 471 metaphors for '*learning*' from 258 Chinese university teachers of English (see Table 3.1). The teachers' metaphors and many of those from students were given in English, but we collected 1931 metaphors in Chinese from 496 students. The same major metaphors appear in both languages, though those in Chinese have a slightly larger range and sometimes have more detail.

Table 3.1   Metaphor databases used in this study

	University students in China	University teachers of English in China
Metaphors of 'a teacher'	2882 from 1140 students	541 from 258 teachers
Metaphors of 'learning'	3235 from 1036 students	471 from 258 teachers

This elicitation procedure means that large numbers of metaphors can be collected, largely without the problems of identifying metaphors in a corpus of 'normal' language (Cameron & Low, 1999; Kövecses, 2005; Charteris-Black, 2004), since the vast majority of students understand, given an example, what a metaphor is.

By analysing a large collection of metaphors about *learning* we can see which major metaphors are commonly used as conceptual metaphors. Classification proves difficult because the extreme open-endedness of the task allows, or encourages, a huge range of different responses since students can give any relevant metaphor. To analyse the metaphors we need the participants' meanings for the metaphors (since we want an insider picture of learning and do not want to impose outside ideas on the data) so we analyse both the metaphors *and* the mappings and entailments as given by the participants. This needs great care because the intended meanings of many metaphors cannot be ascertained without reference to what the participants say in the 'because' clause. For example, a number of students say *learning is a needle*. A possible interpretation of this metaphor may be to imagine that a needle is sharp ('learning gives you a sharp mind') or that a needle is used for sewing ('with learning you can embroider the fabric of your life and repair your worn-out clothing or habits'). However, the students in our data give quite different reasons:

• Learning is a needle which pains each bone and each nerve in our bodies, but skilful acupuncture can make you feel warm and comfortable after pain.

This entails that learning brings suffering which can be relieved in the right hands (probably the teacher's) or that learning brings a short-term pain but a long-term gain. These entailments match those about suffering and gain related to other metaphors with different sources and can be classified accordingly.

• Learning is looking for a needle in a bottle of hay.

This implies that learning is a difficult search ('learning is looking for a needle in a haystack') and it can be classified with many 'learning is a search' metaphors.

- Learning is a needle, making steel out of yourself.

Here the student has referred to a traditional Chinese saying which emphasizes that if you make enough effort, you can grind an iron pillar into a needle; you can become a useful tool in society or, here, become steel, a stronger more durable metal than iron. This would be classified with other metaphors about making a strong effort in learning for beneficial results.

In our data-gathering procedure there may be limitations of perceived artificiality and creativity: the elicitation task may seem somewhat artificial and divorced from the classroom (the same can be said of questionnaires or interviews) or it may be interpreted as a creative task, which may mean that students try to give original or unique metaphors which are difficult to compare in a dataset and may not reflect what they think. Some students may give spontaneous individual metaphors which are not particularly connected to their own underlying cognition about learning. Similar limitations may apply to questionnaire and interview data and they are usually held to be overcome with large samples and cross-checking.

We sought to minimize these limitations by analysing a large database of metaphors which includes students' rationales as mappings. In practice, many students give metaphors from Chinese tradition (Jin & Cortazzi, 2008) so there is something of a common basis; the many who give more original metaphors are – as a standard procedure – asked to explain what they mean by completing the *'because'* clause. As the 'needle' examples show, this clause is a crucial element for the research because it is in effect a mapping or partial entailment of the metaphor from the student's perspective. Creative or original metaphors, while they have individual and very different source domains, are likely to draw on common knowledge in mappings and entailments in a cultural context since this is how creative original metaphors usually work – otherwise they risk not being understood (Kövecses, 2005). Thus, for several reasons, we analyse the target domain of 'learning' in terms of source domains but also particularly in terms of mappings and entailments.

Our method is to classify the metaphors with their entailments under conceptual metaphors and then to cross-match different sets of entailments with different linguistic metaphors and overarching conceptual metaphors so that the analysis is not dependent upon any one particular metaphor or on one set of mappings. Here, we focus on the major example of LEARNING IS A JOURNEY but we interpret the broader meaning of this conceptual metaphor in the light of others within the overall system to construct a cultural model. The model is a visual summary of multiple cross-matching of metaphors and entailments and we cross-check the model through comparing the underlying metaphors with common official metaphors in Chinese education and traditional Chinese sayings (Jin & Cortazzi, 2008, 2010) and discussion with Chinese students and teachers.

3.5   Learning is a journey

We now elaborate in some detail the mappings and entailments of the Chinese students' conceptual metaphor LEARNING IS A JOURNEY which has been anticipated in Figure 3.1. Representative quotations from participants are given in italics; the numbers given for each metaphor are relatively high, considering that they are given in an open format which elicits a wide range of different responses.

This journey is essentially a process which is explicitly labelled as 'a journey' by 153 students. The journey is canonically described as 'long', 'hard' and 'difficult': *learning is long and hard travel*; *learning is a long and difficult journey*; *it needs your whole life to complete it*. There are vivid images of difficulty and an ambiguity about the destination, since the journey is 'endless': *learning is a path with many thorns, a way covered with brambles*; *a journey through the desert, we can't get the sweet spring water until we walk through the desert with patience*; *one should not put great emphasis on arriving but keep an eye on the road and appreciate the scenery*; *learning is a journey without destination, it needs your whole life to complete it*. With a specific cultural reference to the military epic journey of a 6000-mile retreat by Mao and the Communists, 'the Long March' (1934–35), 12 students name their journey LEARNING IS A LONG MARCH: *learning is the Long March, step by step we can finish it, it is endlessly walking, we must have patience and a determined decision*. Many other students would agree that this metaphor fits their picture of learning. For many Chinese, the Long March is a story of hardship, risk and danger, a symbol of courage in adversity, struggle and sacrifice, selfless discipline and of how having a strong will can lead to ultimate success.

The journey is characterized as AN EXPLORATION or A SEARCH in 50 metaphors: *learning is a journey of exploration*; *a journey of searching*.

Many entailments of the purpose of learning are ambitious: in learning students explore *time and space; the mysteries of the universe; the mysteries of nature; the vast sea of knowledge* and *the treasures in books.* The search has even wider mappings of both high-minded and practical values. It is a search *for the secret of the world; searching the universe;* and *a spiritual pursuit; an endless pursuit of ideals, perfection and excellence; it is travelling in pursuit of excellence; pursuing the value of life;* and *the process of seeking oneself; searching for your true self; to become a true person* and more practically *looking for jobs; seeking a good job and a bright future.* LEARNING IS A SEARCH blends with 107 metaphors for LEARNING IS WEALTH or LEARNING IS SEEKING TREASURE. For some 24 students this is literally learning to get money: *learning can make a poor person rich; learning is money;* for 28 others it is educational enrichment: *the capital to produce a miracle, the process of enriching ourselves continually; enriching the brain; the process of enriching the soul;* for 46 others it is seeking a valuable object: *seeking a diamond, its brightness lasts forever; looking for a pearl in the deep sea; finding priceless treasure; seeking the palace of mental fortune* or *looking for treasure in the garbage dump.*

The destination of the learning journey is seen as a dream or an ideal by 42 students: *learning is the road to make dreams come true; the wide road to ideals; the endless pursuit of ideals; the process of realizing your dreams; the bridge between a dream and reality; a ladder to climb to the peak of ideals; only by experiencing difficulties can you reach the destination of your heart; learning is the path to your heart, to the ideal palace.* These metaphors blend with the metaphors of 75 students who seem to share a strong belief that the journey leads to future success: *learning is the road to success and to make dreams come true; we are walking on the highway to success, an endless road.* Yet as this last example indicates, the journey of learning is endless because knowledge is seen to be limitless: 74 metaphors characterize learning as *endless, boundless, continual, unceasing,* and the journey continues *without stopping.* Further, in 95 metaphors of using 'ladders' or 'stairs' to climb upwards – metaphors clearly related to LEARNING IS CLIMBING which have been illustrated already with examples of 145 metaphors of mountain climbing in the database – students say: *learning is climbing steps, we must keep on to get to a higher stage, you can't get to the height of your dream unless you keep going up; learning is climbing a long flight of stairs leading to our dreams, only by continual learning can we realize our dreams.*

Thus, paradoxically, learning is limitless and endless, constant and continual efforts must be made, yet achieving success, attaining one's ideals and realizing dreams are within reach, eventually. The necessary effort for learning is a strong theme in LEARNING IS CLIMBING, described as *persistence, perseverance, having determination and a strong will, being diligent, working unremittingly* and *never giving up*. In learning, students say, *we just need to climb unremittingly; only with persistence can you climb to the top; we can never slow our pace and stop; it needs a strong will, only if you keep going can you reach your destination*. The notion of constant effort is reinforced in 64 related journey metaphors of LEARNING IS A RACE: *learning is a marathon, we should keep learning constantly, endlessly; the person who sticks it out can reach the finishing line; only runners who persist to the end can get an eye-catching medal; learning is an endless race, a real learner never gives up; if you want greater success, you must make greater effort*.

This constant effort is visibly deeper and more abiding than simply 'hard work'. The elaboration of 'effort' emerges as a powerful entailment in one category of the journey metaphor, LEARNING IS SAILING. The students give 96 metaphors for 'sailing' as a way of travelling, with a further 68 metaphors for a 'ship' or 'boat' as a means of travel; within these, 58 metaphors stress the need for continual effort with negative consequences of relaxing the determination or pausing in active learning: *learning is sailing against the current, if we don't work hard we will fall behind; learning is sailing against the wind, if you don't strive to go forward, you will go back; learning is taking a boat upstream, not to advance means dropping back; learning is a boat sailing against the tide, if you don't make an effort to go forwards, you'll go backwards*.

3.6   Aesthetic and affective dimensions of learning

In their metaphors, the students make it clear that learning is more than a journey, in the sense that it has more than cognitive functions; it has distinct aesthetic, affective and moral elements that are more than a simple description of a PURPOSEFUL ACTIVITY, TRAVELLING ALONG A PATH TOWARDS A DESTINATION (Lakoff, 1993).

An aesthetic dimension to the learning journey is made specific by 89 students using the term 'beauty'. This dimension characterizes the destination of reaching the top of a mountain (*seeking beautiful scenery at the top; at the top you will see beauty; reaching the final beauty*) and the process of travel (*we enjoy the sightseeing, seeing the most beautiful scenery*), which correlates with progress (*the higher you climb, the more beautiful the view; the higher you go, the more beauty you will see*) (see also earlier examples).

A positive affective dimension to the journey of learning is highlighted by 92 students who explicitly mention 'happiness' (with many others using 'joy' and similar synonyms). Again, this describes the destination (*learning is the obligatory path to happiness; this journey has a happy ending*) and the process (*learning is happy travelling; you become happy during the process of study*). Fifteen students indicate a causative relation in which happiness is the result (*learning is a source of happiness; it brings us happiness; it's the fountainhead of happiness; you become happy during the process of study; after the accomplishment you will feel thrilled*) and 21 others simply equate learning with happiness (*learning is happiness*).

However, this affective dimension involves mixed feelings expressed as oxymorons for 27 students: *the journey is bitter-sweet; the path is full of pain and happiness; the road to success is full of tears and mirth; climbing with both hardship and happiness; happiness and pain mixed together; walking with taking pain and sweetness together, no sweet without sweat; on this road you hear the sadness in your happy laughter.* The bitterness and suffering are sometimes presented as necessary features: *you can't feel happy about learning unless you taste the hardship of it, a bitter experience which includes happiness and pain, sometimes you suffer, sometimes it can be enjoyable.* These two dimensions are further joined and metaphorized as flora and fauna in the landscape of the learning journey: *learning is a road full of thorns but also of fresh fruit; a road full of brambles or of fresh flowers; learning is walking on a road of thorns, we get bloodstained and depressed through loneliness but we can hear the leisurely birds singing.*

The oxymoron of 'bitter-sweet' is a major feature of the entailments of LEARNING IS A DRINK, which includes 23 metaphors for 'tea' and 34 for 'coffee' in which it is clear that 'bitter-sweet' has – at least for many students – a sequence so that those who endure the bitterness get the sweetness later and the sweetness is linked to a positive affect of happiness: *learning is drinking tea, you first taste the bitterness but in the end you can taste sweetness, the comfort and happiness; learning is coffee, there is both sweetness and bitterness in it; it is bitter at first but wonderful forever later, the delicious flavour is hidden in initial bitterness.*

The affective dimension is vigorous in student metaphors which characterize the locations of the destination, or conditions of learning, in LEARNING IS A JOURNEY THROUGH HELL TO HEAVEN. The feature of 'heaven' in 30 metaphors is an extreme of the destination of learning as realizing dreams: *learning is Paradise; the studious student's Garden of Eden; the road leading to heaven; an elevator to heaven and the road to paradise; learning is a church, it's supposed to take you to heaven; learning is a place for fair angels, collecting cotton from heaven while standing without feet on the ground.* However, in 41 metaphors, learning is 'hell': *learning is going to hell; learning is God's punishment for humans, evil, hopeless and painful.*

Similarly, *learning is torture in ice and fire; horror; more suffering than separation and death; a black hole; a bottomless hole; an assassin; a murderer.* For some, however, the 'hell' is temporary, beneficial or part of the route to 'heaven': *learning is a bunch of hell flames, only real gold can bear the fire; learning is a road with thorns, it's too painful for us to walk forward but at the end of the road there's a paradise filled with flowers; learning is death, the process is painful, the result is that you get rid of the pain, it separates flesh from the spirit; learning is the journey from hell to heaven.*

The role of affect is underlined by the frequency with which students and teachers mention '*heart*' and '*mind*'. These are a single term in Chinese, *xin*, which is often translated into English in literature and philosophy as a hyphenated term, '*heart-mind*'. This shows a unity of what Westerners generally think of as separate entities of thinking and feeling so it is natural that for Chinese students and teachers metaphors for learning should have affective dimensions. The moral dimension emerges through the metaphors about teachers, considered below.

3.7   The role of the teacher

We analysed Chinese teachers' metaphors for learning to see whether these metaphors might confirm what students say (since teachers have been successful students and have daily contact with current students) or they may differ in quality and emphasis (since teachers have a professional expertise to focus on teaching and learning). In fact, the teachers' metaphors broadly confirm the details of LEARNING IS A JOURNEY as given by the students, though with fewer mentions of the extremes of 'hell' or 'heaven' and the 'bitter-sweet' emotions.

Among the 471 open-ended learning metaphors from Chinese teachers, the journey metaphor is clearly important: there are 139 metaphors for LEARNING IS A JOURNEY or TRAVELLING and EXPLORING with subsets of LEARNING IS CLIMBING and LEARNING IS SAILING. These portray the learning journey as continuous, endless, hard and difficult with encounters with obstacles and surprises, but it includes a sense of beauty. It is a journey which requires constant effort for the learner and guidance from a teacher and the process and the destination are both important. Example metaphors include: *learning is a long journey, the destination is not the most important thing, but the beautiful scenes on the way; learning is climbing a mountain, the more you climb, the higher you get: the more you learn, the more you achieve, but you must persist; learning is a pilgrimage, the road is long and painstaking but you may arrive at a holy place in the end.* Among the teachers' metaphors for 'teacher', 56 specify their role as a guide or director to lead, show the way, point out the direction and give help: *teachers guide students and take them on a fabulous journey; a teacher points the way and shows you how to get to your destination; a teacher shows you the way to success; they guide us in darkness and give us hope.* Some teachers direct the journey as an accompanying guide, others lead from the perspective of one who has arrived: *with the help of a teacher, we can climb to different scenery from the foot of the hill; a teacher is on a high mountain – everybody around you expects to enjoy the beautiful scenery that you can see.* In these teachers' metaphors, the teacher guides, directs and leads students not only to success, but also to beauty: *teachers guide students to the most beautiful destination; she leads us to a beautiful land-scape; teachers lead the way of touring around the beautiful garden of learning and help everyone to enjoy the beautiful scenery.*

The teacher's role for guidance is strongly confirmed in the student data, where 85 metaphors portray the teacher as a guide, but the map-pings make it clear that the teacher is not just a guide for study matters: *a teacher is our guide for our study and life; a guide of life; a guide leading us in the right path.*

This much wider role for the teacher is reinforced by other meta-phors of A TEACHER IS A FRIEND or A TEACHER IS A PARENT. Among the teach-ers' metaphors, 32 represent mappings which reveal the teacher as 'a friend' or 'a parent'. This is a person who shows concern and under-stands problems, who cares, is close and helps to solve problems. These qualities emerge strongly in the student data, where 78 meta-phors show the teacher as a friend and 48 as a parent. Some attributes are summarized in Table 3.2 and shown in a longer set of mappings by

Table 3.2   The roles of teachers in China as shown in students' metaphors for 'a teacher'

A teacher has roles of:

Directing	*Sharing knowledge*
Guiding	*Leading*
Advising	*Giving friendship*
Caring	*Being close*
Protecting	*Sheltering*
Supporting	*Helping progress*
Nurturing growth	*Understanding students' problems*
Controlling	*Loving*
Mediating	*Purifying students' characters*
Giving enlightenment	*Beautifying life*

Through teachers, students develop *their head, heart, character, life* and *their future.*

one student: *a teacher is my friend, in my heart, who can talk heart to heart with students and become their friend, not only teaching us knowledge but more importantly teaching us how to become a person through the model of their behaviour, caring for us and looking after us, and cultivating our ability to survive in society, teaches us many things without payment, a guide in study but a friend in life.* The picture given here by Chinese students is broadly that of a humane, caring guide – notably it is not the stereotype of an authoritative or authoritarian transmitter of knowledge.

The entailments of many different metaphors from students show teachers' sacrifice. This is typified by A TEACHER IS A CANDLE in 109 metaphors from students and 63 from teachers. This metaphor is traditional in China (and in many places in the Middle East) and it entails that the teacher gives light in a dark place, gives brightness and hope to students in lighting up the way, lighting up the desire for knowledge and showing selfless devotion through sacrifice. Students say: *a teacher is a burning candle, she sacrifices herself to illumine our way; she burns herself out but gives us light; teachers are candles, they burn themselves to enlighten others.* Teachers explain: *teachers are candles, they sacrifice themselves to light the way for students; they brighten others but use themselves drop by drop; they bring light to students but at the same time they are losing their life, even burning themselves down to a small piece of wax.* Interestingly, the student data show many other metaphors for the sacrifices made by Chinese teachers, so the candle metaphor would be subsumed under TEACHING IS SACRIFICE, which outside Chinese contexts may be a surprising metaphor.

The moral dimension is shown in another surprising metaphor of TEACHING IS PURIFYING, given by 53 teachers, and a corresponding metaphor of LEARNING IS CLEANSING, given by 23 students. These complementary metaphors mean that teachers correct students' mistakes and faults, but they go well beyond this, since mappings repeatedly mention 'mind', 'character', 'heart' and 'soul'. This gives 'purifying and cleansing' a moral function, which in turn links with the teacher's sacrifice. Thus, *a teacher is the purifier of our mind; the teacher purifies students' hearts; purifies our spirit; purifies our mind and soul; the teacher gets rid of students' different bad habits, errors, immoral thoughts, purifying our thoughts and souls.* A teacher *cleanses the unclear wastes of our minds* and *learning is the purifier of our mind, the process of cleansing our soul;* a teacher *is the cleaner of the heart and soul; the cleaner of our souls – he helps us to tell the difference between evil and goodness;* teachers *sacrifice themselves to get rid of the dirt in our minds; they sacrifice themselves to erase our mistakes and get rid of our faults.*

3.8 A cultural model of learning as a journey

In the Chinese metaphors for learning studied here, learning has a spatial orientation with clear senses of direction: UP is an increase showing more and better knowledge, raised awareness, progress and happiness, together with increasing control and autonomy; FORWARD shows an advance in learning, progress, success and development. Both of these directions are characteristic of LEARNING IS A JOURNEY, an overarching conceptual metaphor with cultural characteristics which emerge in the detailed entailments of many students and teachers. This is summarized in the model in Figure 3.2.

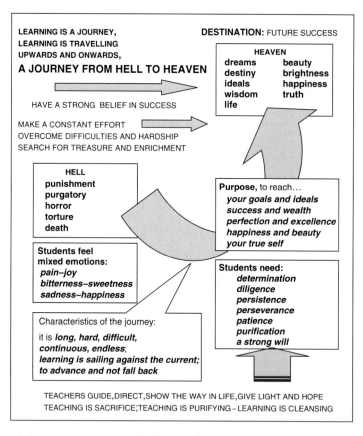

Figure 3.2 LEARNING IS A JOURNEY in the metaphors of Chinese students and teachers with cognitive and practical, aesthetic, affective and moral dimensions

The chief features of this model, which we think are cultural, are that the journey is long, hard, difficult, continuous and endless; many students pass through 'hell' but much larger numbers believe in the ultimate success and 'wealth' of 'heaven'. 'Heaven' summarizes the idealized vision that many students clearly possess: a destination of learning where dreams are realized in happiness and beauty. The driving force in this journey is 'constant effort', a phrase which embraces a range of necessary attributes for successful study: determination, persistence, patience, having a strong will, not giving up. The need for consistency of effort is clear in the common phrases in the metaphors, *learning is sailing against the current, you need to advance and not fall back, if you don't make an effort to go forwards you'll go backwards*. Major characteristics include the aesthetic dimension of envisaged beauty, the affective dimension of experienced mixed feelings, and the moral dimension of exploring, developing and purifying the mind, heart and soul. On this journey, teachers have a clear role of guidance and direction; they also give light, hope and show the way, both in study and in life; they are seen to sacrifice themselves to give light, direction and hope, like 'burning candles'.

The LEARNING IS A JOURNEY metaphor is more than a journey because it has aesthetic, affective and moral elements. However, it is more than a journey in another sense, which means that the conceptual metaphor might well be rephrased as LEARNING IS TRAVELLING. The paradox that learning is endless and continuous yet is aimed at a destination of dreams, desires and perceptions of success can be resolved by recognizing – as some students and teachers do – that the goals are always changing as the learner develops and that the aim is to travel. As Peters (1967: 8) says after a philosophical analysis of the process of 'education', 'To be educated is not to have arrived; it is to travel with a different view.' Some of the Chinese participants in our study emphasize that learning is to admire the scenery on the journey, to enjoy the travelling and be happy with the process, with the implication perhaps that 'heaven' is to travel while 'hell' is neither to arrive nor to enjoy the journey. Thus what shapes the journey is not only the learner's agency of constant effort, determination, persistence, patience and perseverance, but also their interpretation that the learner's attitude shapes the travelling. LEARNING IS TRAVELLING emphasizes the process through the verb; graduating learners are WAYFARERS rather than new arrivals. The model we present is a process of travelling which can be seen as an example of complexity, not a simple linearity, and this complexity has 'operational closure': 'a system that has operational closure is one in which the results of its processes are those processes themselves' (Varela *et al.*, 1991, cited in Larsen-Freeman & Cameron, 2008: 7). There is a sense of this in students' metaphors: *learning is a journey without destination; one should not put great emphasis on arriving but keep an eye on the road and appreciate the landscape*; and in those of teachers: *the more you learn, the less you can see the end of the way; the destination is not the most important thing but the beautiful scenes on the way; during the process of the journey I see all the wonders of thoughts, discover its mysteries and fulfil my life.*

3.9   Conclusions and applications

The journey metaphor of Chinese students and teachers is a very rich picture of learning which can offer linguistic and educational insights to researchers, teachers and students in China and in the wider world beyond China. It has key features of a long-term process of seeking knowledge, growth and cultivation with guidance and direction from teachers, who provide knowledge, cultivation and a moral model. It has interesting and important aesthetic, affective and moral dimensions. The journey metaphor is not, of course, the only model: in our database there are many other important metaphors for learning within the wider network of cultural metaphors in education in China and elsewhere. However, this particular model is, on the whole, not difficult to understand once we have followed key examples and this model gives useful insights about Chinese learners.

The metaphors and model presented here invite comparison with those from other cultures of learning. We need more research to ascertain which elements are common or perhaps universal and which are more localized and particular to Chinese and perhaps East Asian contexts. This is a large project for further research but papers using various methods for data collection and analysis on metaphors for learning in Japanese, Chinese, Malay, Tunisian Arabic, Greek, British and South African English pick out various common and distinctive features (Berendt, 1998, 2008). The journey metaphor has clear resonances with some Western traditions of learning and spiritual progress. This is seen, for example, in hero journeys in myths, the journey through hell and purgatory to paradise in Dante's Italian epic poem, *La Divina Commedia*, and in the now less popular *Pilgrim's Progress* in English of John Bunyan.

The cultural model we present can be usefully discussed by Chinese students – or any other students – to facilitate a meta-awareness of learning and study; individual students might locate their own position, feeling and ideas within the model and could be encouraged to create and share their own metaphors. Some knowledge and insight into students' metaphors for learning, such as LEARNING IS A JOURNEY, should be part of the professional knowledge landscape of teachers. Arguably, too, the metaphors of their teachers should be part of the students' awareness of approaches to learning; after all, in a sense students need to be socialized into their teachers' ways of seeing knowledge, learning and understanding within subject disciplines. In the case of Chinese students, the insights from their metaphors for learning should be useful for their teachers within China and for others who teach Chinese students internationally. Teachers might use some students' metaphors as part of introducing and discussing learning tasks, especially if the tasks are new, different or challenging; metaphors can then help students relate to the task and overcome feelings of unfamiliarity and perhaps gain empowerment.

In our talks with Chinese teachers in China, we have drawn upon metaphors and the cultural model, finding that teachers can readily identify with the metaphors and confirm the general features of the model. We find that the focused discussion of metaphors for learning and teaching can promote reflection and awareness of cultural aspects of professional development with a stronger sense of Chinese educational values imbued in the metaphors.

In our teaching with Chinese students completing master's dissertations in the UK, we have talked through the metaphor of LEARNING IS A JOURNEY as a practical way to envisage the dissertation tasks and formulate plans that may take account of the ups and downs towards success. Such periodic reference with students to features of the journey shows empathy. It is comforting during difficult moments of 'hell' and is encouragement to move through 'bitter-sweet' stages towards the 'heaven' of successful completion and to take steps to further learning and living through professional application of their qualifications.

References

Bedell, D. & Oxford, R. (1996) Cross-cultural comparisons of language learning strategies in the People's Republic of China and other countries. In R. Oxford (ed.) *Language Learning Strategies around the World: Cross-Cultural Perspectives*. Manoa: Second Language Teaching & Curriculum Center, The University of Hawaii, pp. 47–60.

Berendt, E. (ed.) (1998) *Learning: East and West*, Special issue of *Intercultural Communciation Studies*, 7(2).

Berendt, E. A. (ed.) (2008) *Metaphors for Learning*. Amsterdam: John Benjamins.

Biggs, J. B. (1987) *Student Approaches to Learning and Studying.* Melbourne: Australian Council for Educational Research.

Biggs, J. B. (1996) Learning, schooling, and socialization: a Chinese solution to a Western problem. In S. Lau (ed.) *Growing Up the Chinese Way: Chinese Child and Adolescent Development.* Hong Kong: CERC, The University of Hong Kong, pp. 147–167.

Biggs, J. (1999) *Teaching for Quality Learning at University.* Buckingham: Open University Press.

Biggs, J. B. & Watkins, D. (1993) *Learning and Teaching in Hong Kong: What it Is and What it Might Be.* Hong Kong: The University of Hong Kong.

Brumfit, C. (1995) Teacher professionalism and research. In G. Cook & B. Seidlhofer (eds) *Principles and Practice in Applied Linguistics.* Oxford: Oxford University Press, pp. 27–41.

Cameron, L. (2003) *Metaphor in Educational Discourse.* London: Continuum.

Cameron, L. & Low, G. (eds) (1999) *Researching and Applying Metaphor.* Cambridge: Cambridge University Press.

Chan, C. K. K. & Rao, N. (eds) (2009) *Revisiting the Chinese Learner: Changing Contexts, Changing Education.* Hong Kong: CERC, The University of Hong Kong.

Charteris-Black, J. (2004) *Corpus Approaches to Critical Metaphor Analysis.* Basingstoke: Palgrave Macmillan.

Cohen, A. (1998) *Strategies in Learning and Using a Second Language.* London: Longman.

Cortazzi, M. & Jin, L. (1996a) Changes in learning English vocabulary in China. In H. Coleman & L. Cameron (eds) *Change and Language.* Clevedon: Multilingual Matters, pp. 153–165.

Cortazzi, M. & Jin, L. (1996b) Cultures of learning: language classrooms in China. In H. Coleman (ed.) *Society and the Language Classroom.* Cambridge: Cambridge University Press, pp. 169–206.

Cortazzi, M. & Jin, L. (1999) Bridges to learning: metaphors of teaching, learning and language. In L. Cameron & G. Low (eds) *Researching and Applying Metaphor.* Cambridge: Cambridge University Press, pp. 149–176.

Cortazzi, M. & Jin, L. (2001) Large classes in China: 'good' teachers and inter-action. In D. A. Watkins & J. B. Biggs (eds) *Teaching the Chinese Learner: Psychological and Pedagogical Perspectives.* Hong Kong: CERC, The University of Hong Kong, pp. 115–134.

Dörnyei, Z. (2007) *Research Methods in Applied Linguistics.* Oxford: Oxford University Press.

Ellis, R. & Barkhuizen, G. (eds) (2005) *Analysing Learner Language.* Oxford: Oxford University Press.

Goatly, A. (1997) *The Language of Metaphors.* London: Routledge.

Gow, L., Balla, J., Kember, D. & Hau, K. T. (1996) The learning approaches of Chinese people. In M. H. Bond (ed.) *The Handbook of Chinese Psychology.* Hong Kong: Oxford University Press, pp. 109–123.

Hager, P. & Hodkinson, P. (2009) Moving beyond the metaphor of transfer of learning, *British Educational Research Journal,* 35(4), pp. 619–638.

Hodkinson, P. & Macleod, F. (2010) Contrasting concepts of learning and con-trasting research methodologies: affinities and bias, *British Educational Research Journal,* 36(2), pp. 173–189.

Jin, L. & Cortazzi, M. (1998a) The culture the learner brings: a bridge or a barrier? In M. Byram & M. Fleming (eds) *Language Learning in Intercultural Perspective: Approaches through Drama and Ethnography*. Cambridge: Cambridge University Press, pp. 98–118.

Jin, L. & Cortazzi, M. (1998b) Dimensions of dialogue: large classes in China, *International Journal of Educational Research*, 29, 739–761.

Jin, L. & Cortazzi, M. (2003) English language teaching in China: a bridge to the future. In W. H. Ho & R. Y. L. Wong (eds) *English Language Teaching in East Asia Today* (2nd edn). Singapore: Eastern Universities Press.

Jin, L. & Cortazzi, M. (2006) Changing practices in Chinese cultures of learning, *Language, Culture and Curriculum*, 19(1), 5–20.

Jin, L. & Cortazzi, M. (2008) Images of teachers, learning and questioning in Chinese cultures of learning. In E. Berendt (ed.) *Metaphors for Learning: Cross-Cultural Perspectives*. Amsterdam: John Benjamins, pp. 177–204.

Jin, L. & Cortazzi, M. (2010) The changing landscapes of a journey: educational metaphors in China. In J. Ryan (ed.) *Education Reform in China*. London: Routledge.

Kövecses, Z. (2005) *Metaphor in Culture: Universality and Variation*. Cambridge: Cambridge University Press.

Kövecses, Z. (2006) *Language, Mind, and Culture*. Cambridge: Cambridge University Press.

Lakoff, G. (1987) *Women, Fire, and Dangerous Things*. Chicago: University of Chicago Press.

Lakoff, G. (1993) The contemporary theory of metaphor. In A. Ortony (ed.) *Metaphor and Thought* (2nd edn). Cambridge: Cambridge University Press, pp. 202–251.

Lakoff, G. & Johnson, M. (1980) *Metaphors We Live By*. Chicago: University of Chicago Press.

Lakoff, G. & Turner, M. (1989) *More than Cool Reason: A Field Guide to Poetic Metaphor*. Chicago: University of Chicago Press.

Larsen-Freeman, D. & Cameron, L. (2008) *Complex Systems and Applied Linguistics*. Oxford: Oxford University Press.

Li, J. (2001) Chinese conceptualization of learning, *Ethos*, 29(2), 111–137.

Li, J. (2002a) Learning models in different cultures, *New Directions for Child and Adolescent Development*, 96, 45–63.

Li, J. (2002b) A cultural model of learning: Chinese 'heart and mind for wanting to learn', *Journal of Cross-Cultural Psychology*, 33(3), 248–269.

Li, J. (2009) Learning to self-perfect: Chinese beliefs about learning. In C. K. K. Chan & N. Rao (eds) *Revisiting the Chinese Learner: Changing Contexts, Changing Education*. Hong Kong: CERC, the University of Hong Kong, pp. 35–69.

Ministry of Education (2007) *College English Curriculum Requirements*. Beijing: Foreign Language Teaching and Research Press.

Oxford, R. (ed.) (1996) *Language Learning Strategies around the World: Cross-Cultural Perspectives*. Manoa: Second Language Teaching & Curriculum Center, the University of Hawaii.

Peters, R. S. (1967) What is an educational process? In R. S. Peters (ed.) *The Concept of Education*. London: Routledge & Kegan Paul, pp. 1–23.

Reid, J. M. (ed.) (1995) *Learning Styles in the ESL/EFL Classroom*. New York: Heinle & Heinle.

Richards, K. (2003) *Qualitative Inquiry in TESOL*. Basingstoke: Palgrave Macmillan.

Sfard, A. (1998) On two metaphors for learning and the dangers of choosing just one, *Educational Researcher*, 27(2), 4–13.

Szalay, L. B., Strohl, J. B., Fu, L. & Lao, P.-S. (1994) *American and Chinese Perceptions and Belief Systems: A People's Republic of China and Taiwanese Comparison*. New York: Plenum Press.

Watkins, D. A. & Biggs, J. B. (eds) (1996) *The Chinese Learner: Cultural, Psychological and Contextual Influences*. Hong Kong: CERC, The University of Hong Kong.

Watkins, D. A. & Biggs, J. B. (eds) (2001) *Teaching the Chinese Learner: Psychological and Pedagogical Perspectives*. Hong Kong: CERC, The University of Hong Kong.

Wenden, A. & Rubin, J. (1987) *Learner Strategies in Language Learning*. Hemel Hempstead: Prentice Hall.

Winch, P. (1998) *The Philosophy of Human Learning*. London: Routledge.

Yu, N. (1998) *The Contemporary Theory of Metaphor: A Perspective from Chinese*. Amsterdam: John Benjamins.

Zanotto, M. S., Cameron, L. & Cavalcanti, M. C. (eds) (2008) *Confronting Metaphor in Use: An Applied Linguistic Approach*. Amsterdam: John Benjamins.

4
Meeting in the Middle? Intercultural Adaptation in Tertiary Oral English in China

Phiona Stanley

4.1 Introduction

The following vignette shows different perceptions of the same classroom activity:

> A British teacher stands on the podium of a Chinese university oral English classroom. On the chalkboard behind him are the question beginnings: What is your …? Where are you …? What is your favourite …? He asks, 'Can anyone give me an example? Anyone?' He sighs, pauses. 'Anyone?' His 37 students sit in rows; they have to be here for a further 75 minutes this week then they can go. Some have already passed the all-important College English Test (CET4), and all know that it is not compulsory to take an oral English exam in order to graduate. Several read newspapers; others chat quietly in Chinese; most look down or away, embarrassed. These students have been learning English for ten years or more. The sentences are laughably simple, the foreign teacher is an idiot. Back on the podium the teacher scans the room. He steps off the podium and tries a friendlier approach, sitting on one of the tables at the front of the class. He asks again. Still nothing. The class won't talk; the students must be stupid. Welcome to oral English, site of intercultural misunderstandings.

This chapter considers the extent to which Western teachers and their Chinese undergraduate students in non-English disciplines are able to 'meet in the middle' culturally in oral English teaching. It is my contention that the teachers and students in the context make different assumptions about the nature of both language and language learning, and that these unproblematized differences cause intercultural misunderstandings.

Different underlying assumptions are illustrated in the vignette above: in pursuit of student participation, expected by his own culture of learning, the teacher oversimplifies language input and takes a 'friendly' approach by sitting on the table. But to the students, whose culture of learning leads them to expect the teacher to *teach* from the podium, this behaviour may indicate teacher incompetence.

However, the research question discussed in this chapter is not which theory of language or language learning, or which culture of learning, is more 'correct'; much has been written elsewhere on language theory and second language acquisition. Instead, the interplay of the Chinese students' and Western teachers' assumptions is the focus. What happens when these different theories of *language* and *language learning* come into contact? My finding is that students' and teachers' implicit theories of language and language learning serve to build barriers rather than bridges (see Jin & Cortazzi, 1998).

As oral English with a Western teacher is, for many Chinese students, a first encounter with the Western Other, such miscommunications may have an impact beyond the classroom door, as they may serve to create and perpetuate negative Othering more generally. 'Otherization' is discussed by Holliday, Hyde and Kullman (2004: 21–35) and is defined as '[r]educing the foreign Other to less than what they are' (2004: 24). The use of Other and Othering in this chapter refers to this phenomenon. This chapter shows how classroom misunderstandings can serve to create rather than challenge Othering, on both sides.

4.2   Literature review: language teaching in China

This and the next two sections review contextualizing literature and present the theoretical frameworks used in this chapter. These are symbolic interactionism and the contextual and cultural specificity of role-bound behaviours. As described in the review of literature on English language teaching in China, there seem to be fundamental differences between Chinese students' expectations about English language teaching and the norms that the Western teachers bring with them to China. As I will show, these may result in differences in teachers' and students' classroom roles and behaviours, with consequent misunderstandings of each other's intended meanings.

Jin and Cortazzi (2006: 9) define cultures of learning as:

> taken-for-granted frameworks of expectations, attitudes, values and
> beliefs about how to teach or learn successfully and about how to use

talk in interaction ... A culture of learning frames what teachers and students expect to happen in classrooms.

Cultures of learning establish paradigms of what is 'normal' in classrooms, and these differ by context. 'Context' here refers not to essentialist national contexts, such as 'the Chinese context', as if homogeneous, but to the contexts of individual classrooms and institutions, which may differ socio-economically and culturally (Holliday, 2009).

Within this framework, Chinese students have been stereotyped as quiet, passive rote-learners, who are respectful of teachers and teaching materials. Learners are seen as uncritical thinkers and reluctant to express opinions or to question their teachers (Atkinson, 1997; Ballard & Clanchy, 1991; Bodycott & Walker, 2000). This view is echoed by Gu and Maley (2008: 230), who frame their discussion of Chinese university students' 'learning shock' in the UK as attributable in part to the students having:

> travelled from a culture where the educational tradition is textbook-focused to a culture where the educational environment encourages students to independently explore their personal interests in learning.

Additionally and perhaps as both cause and effect of Chinese learners' ostensible passivity, Chinese teachers enjoy high social status, which relies on being seen as knowledgeable and authoritative (Hu, 2002).

Jin and Cortazzi (2006: 14) cite Hinton's (1998) translation of the Confucian dictum: 'to learn and never think – that's delusion. But to think and never learn that is perilous indeed.' Biggs (1996: 55) uses this same dictum to explain Chinese learners' reluctance to express their critiques until they feel they have mastered the material under consideration: 'In the West, we believe in exploring first, then in the development of skill; the Chinese believe in skill development first ... after which there is something to be creative with.' Thus, Chinese learners may not, in fact, be unable or unwilling to think critically, but may see themselves primarily as learners, whose critical analyses should wait until they are in possession of all the facts.

Students' and teachers' cultures of learning affect English language teaching, but these are not the only factors affecting what goes on in classrooms. Classroom teaching of English is subject to myriad influences including examination backwash from predominantly structural exams, teachers' own English language proficiency and preparation, and institutional factors including class sizes and curriculum separation. Examination backwash is an important constraint on language teaching; at tertiary level this means the all-important examination College English Test (CET). This test relies heavily on discrete-item testing of vocabulary and, as a result, teachers complain they are under pressure to cover the syllabus, which is expressed quantitatively as a large number of lexical areas to be learned. The *College English Curriculum*, on which the CET exams are based, includes a 156-page list of all the words and phrases a graduating student is expected to 'know', although the document is vague about what s/he might be expected to 'know' about them in terms of language in *use* (Ministry of Education, 2007: 60–228). As a result, teachers may complain they have no time for 'activities' in which students might *use* English (e.g. Ng & Tang, 1999). Even where teaching materials are designed to be used for communicative language teaching (CLT), teachers may not use them as such (Hu, 2002; Hui, 1997; Jin *et al.*, 2005), perhaps thinking communicative materials are only for 'strengthening the students' oral expression and not for improving their grammar' (Li & Song, 2007: 63).

Additionally, large class sizes constrain teachers' classroom practices, as may teachers' own English language and teaching abilities (Groves, 2002; Ng & Tang, 1999). Many Chinese teachers of English have limited communicative competence in English themselves, and many have had little pedagogical training, instead perhaps having been schooled in a declarative knowledge *about* English language (Anderson, 1993; Groves, 2002; Hu, 2005a, 2005b; Nunan, 2003; Yu, 2001; Zheng & Davidson, 2008: 11). Another issue is the separation of university-level English language teaching into different courses in listening comprehension, writing and 'intensive reading'; the latter comprises micro-analysis of lexis presented through texts. At the research site these three courses comprise English language study for the first two years of tertiary education. Although each course is ostensibly macro-skills based, language-dense assessment backwash from CET examinations reduces time that can be spent on actual skills development and as a result all these courses may, in practice, become vehicles for discrete-item grammar and lexis transmission (Gu & Liu, 2005; Ji, 2005; Jin, 2008; Jin *et al.*, 2005). The development of students' macro *skills* (i.e. holistic, process-oriented, meaning-focused language *use*) is therefore marginalized. This means that the development of students' speaking macro skill, as conceived by Folse (2006), appears to be regarded as separate from and subsequent to the 'learning' of English by learning its discrete parts.

These influences combine to produce an educational environment in which:

> learning involves mastering a body of knowledge ... Both teachers and learners are concerned with the end product of learning – that is, they expect that the learner will, at an appropriate time, be able to reproduce the knowledge ... [D]eductive presentation tends to be favoured over inductive, and the teaching and use of learning strategies such as prediction and contextualization are in general neglected. A further result is that, in language teaching, the use of the mother tongue tends to be stressed. (Brick, 2004: 149–150)

This is a *product approach* to learning, in which learning objects are transmitted by teachers and acquired by learners. This can also be framed as the dichotomy of 'teaching the book' (product) versus 'educating the person' (process); Wette and Barkhuizen (2009) found that tertiary English teachers struggled to reconcile these potentially conflicting objectives. This is because examination backwash creates a demand for *product* more than *process* learning, and Huang (2006) encountered resistance to skills-development teaching. This characterization of English teaching corresponds with the teacher's practice in the case study presented by Xinmin and Adamson (2003) and with other accounts of English language teaching practices in China (e.g. Boyle, 2000; Degen & Absalom, 1998; Jin & Cortazzi, 2003; Wang, 2001; Xu, 2002). Into this context come Western teachers trained in communicative language teaching (CLT).

4.2.1   Literature review: communicative language teaching in China

CLT is defined by Hiep (2007) as comprising three tenets. Firstly, language proficiency is understood as communicative competence (Canale & Swain, 1980; Hymes, 1971). Secondly, second languages are thought to be acquired by learners *using* the language meaningfully as opposed to, for example, learning *about* language or manipulating language form. Thirdly, CLT takes a 'communicative approach' to classroom teaching, including, for example, pair work and group work activities in which students negotiate meaning and produce language output. Within CLT there exists a continuum from 'weak' to 'strong' versions, the main difference being the extent to which focus on language form is included to enable communication (Wesche & Skehan, 2002). While 'strong' CLT has been largely discredited as unable to produce language accuracy,

Lightbown and Spada (1999: 141–149) cite research supporting a weak CLT approach.

However, much of the research into second language acquisition, including that cited by Lightbown and Spada (1999), has been undertaken in Western learning environments, and the finding that an approach worked in one context may not prove that it would work equally well elsewhere. Many writers have argued this point (e.g. Holliday, 1994; Kramsch & O'Sullivan, 1996; Pennycook, 1989; Tudor, 2001), and Bax (2003: 279) condemns what he terms the 'CLT attitude', held by some teachers, that those contexts that do not employ CLT are 'somehow backward' and that CLT is the single correct way to learn a language.

Much has been written on the contextual appropriateness, or otherwise, of CLT in China. Some writers, for example Liao (2004), enthusiastically advocate off-the-shelf CLT, although Liao's (2004) paper both lacks convincing evidence and makes problematic assumptions about CLT and Chinese contexts (Hu, 2005c). In contrast, Yu (2001) rejects CLT for China on the grounds of situational constraints including examination backwash and the issue of under-qualified, sometimes near-monolingual, Chinese teachers who 'basically teach English in Chinese' (2001: 197). Similarly, Zhang (2004) reported a commonly held teacher belief that:

> it is not feasible to adopt CLT because China has its special characteristics, including lack of real English environment, teachers' inability to teach communicatively, and grammar-focused examination pressures. (Zhang, 2004: 102)

Other writers have found a third way in the CLT-in-China debate, and Bjorning-Gyde and Doogan (2004) proposed a fusion model of teaching for China, in which the strengths of Western and Chinese methodologies can be blended, drawing upon the similar goals identified by Senior and Xu (2002). Perhaps, then, an answer lies in blending CLT with traditional Chinese approaches.

However, Hu (2002) argues that CLT and Chinese cultures of learning are at irreconcilable odds, embodying, as they do, very different underlying ideologies and philosophies, and espousing contradictory roles of teachers and learners. Hu argues that the processes, strategies and goals of CLT are simply too different, and that:

> a methodology is only effective to the extent that teachers and students are willing to accept and implement it with good faith, and

whether it is accepted or not is largely determined by the set of values and beliefs that these teachers and students have been socialized into. (Hu, 2002: 102)

One key difference between CLT and Chinese traditional teaching methods is CLT's *process* approach compared to a *product* approach to learning. Writing about CLT in Confucian cultures, Greenholtz (2003: 123) notes that:

Students from non-Socratic, teacher-centred, canonical learning environments may not recognize that they are being taught anything ... If students come from an education tradition that does not emphasize the process of generating knowledge (but rather, the product), they may not recognize what is happening in a Socratic classroom as legitimate pedagogy.

CLT may therefore lack face validity. This is problematic when there is a one-to-one association with communicative-style, skills-focused oral English teaching and Western teachers, as there is in the university studied in this context. This may result in misunderstandings, the causes of which are theorized next.

4.3 Theoretical framework: symbolic interactionism and role expectations

When we communicate, we encode meaning into signs (words, images, etc.) so as to represent those meanings. Signs unite two concepts: the signifier (the sign) and the signified (the intended meaning). Such signs are arbitrary; the same sign may have different meanings in different contexts (Barthes, 1967). This has important consequences for symbolic interactionism, the theoretical framework used in this study. Blumer (1969) proposed three premises of symbolic interactionism in a classic statement. Firstly, people act towards things on the basis of the meanings that those things have *for them*. Secondly, the meanings of things are derived from social interaction. Thirdly, those meanings are negotiated and modified through individuals' interpretive processes as they deal with the things they encounter. Symbolic interaction, then, investigates the interpretation of meaning through social interaction. Central is the idea that people respond to others' outward perform-ances (i.e. behaviours and other signs) according to what those signs mean *to them*, and not necessarily the *intended* meanings. Herein lies one source of intercultural miscommunication. One outward signifier that might be (mis)interpreted is behaviour within roles. Roles themselves are constantly negotiated and constructed and, like signs, they are context-specific.

Role-bound behaviours depend on socially inculcated systems of meanings. These are culture-specific, and Ong (1999: 14) describes the 'inescapabilities and particularities' that transnational people bring with them to a new place. Western teachers in China are often typical examples, having possibly worked in several other countries prior to going to China. Previously acculturated by different influences and places, each teacher arrives in China with his or her own prior *habitus* that is then shaped by their experiences in China. This may mean engaging in cultural 'Othering' so as to protect their own culturally informed *habitus* by providing the self with 'a relatively constant universe of situations tending to reinforce its dispositions' (Bourdieu, 1990: 61). *Habitus* is defined as 'an open system of dispositions that is constantly subjected to experiences, and therefore constantly affected by them in a way that either reinforces or modifies its structures' (Bourdieu & Wacquant, 1992: 133). This means our unconscious ways of being and ways of doing that inform our actions and our interpretations of events; our *habitus* includes our predispositions, patterns of thoughts, beliefs and preferences that are based on past experiences and which are constructed by events and social practices. Bourdieu (1990) posits that individuals acquire their own internal *habitus* that cannot be consciously accessed and that although people are constructions of their socio-contextual milieus, this process creates coherent individual 'selves' that are carried from one social context to another.

Within this, individuals enact performances that may or may not fulfil expectations borne of their role, with the latter judged as deficient against role norms (Butler, 2005). This means that, for example, the role and accepted norms of behaviour of a teacher (which are socially constructed) may differ across contexts; the role of a teacher in a Chinese university may not be the same as the expected 'teacher' role that Western teachers bring with them to China. Western teachers whose behaviour does not 'fit' the role as it is constructed by Chinese students may be judged as deficient. Similarly, students whose behaviours do not fit teachers' expectations of students' roles may cause teachers to evaluate the students as poor. This is because of each side's different expectations and their use of different implicit criteria to judge the other.

4.4   Contexts and research method

The context of this study is People's Square University in Shanghai (PSU; a pseudonym). PSU is a publicly funded university administered by Shanghai Municipality. It is considered a 'second tier university' as it is not administered directly by the national Ministry of Education, although PSU ranks in the top hundred of 1700 tertiary institutions nationally on the list compiled by the Chinese Academy of Management Science (2009). The teacher and student participants in this study were recruited through my research at PSU as a participant among the teachers' professional and social milieu. The teachers are native English speakers from the UK, the USA and Canada, and all are university graduates in disciplines other than education. Most are experienced English language teachers and they have a mean average of two years' teaching experience, with most having taught previously in Western and other Asian contexts including language schools in the UK, Thailand and Taiwan. Most of the teachers hold a short-course English language teaching qualification such as the Cambridge CELTA. The students are Chinese undergraduates in their early twenties; most were in their third year of university study in disciplines other than English. This is different from the situation at some Chinese universities, where English language teaching is restricted to the first two years of undergraduate study; at PSU the students take oral English in the third year. By the time they reach oral English many have already passed the CET4 examination.

This study took a qualitative case study approach that aims to illuminate the field rather than represent a wider population from a sample (Stake, 2005). As a result, I have resisted the use of a quantitative logic, in which many recurrences of the same point in the data might be assumed to be indicative of the significance of the point. It may be that the findings are atypical, and instead of attempting to represent all of College English students or Western teachers I present this context as a case study of what *may* be a wider issue. Further research is suggested to ascertain the extent of this phenomenon in other contexts. This has meant I have resisted summarizing my findings numerically (along the lines of, for instance, 27 out of 40 participants agreed) as my participants may be unrepresentative. Instead, I have allowed for participants' own voices to recount their experiences of *this* context.

This study draws upon data collected over two years (2007–09) and three visits to Shanghai, totalling four months. The data and discussion in this chapter are taken from a larger study on the cognition and identities of Western English language teachers in Shanghai.

The study made use of 200+ hours of recorded data gathered in semi-structured conversations, both individual interviews and focus groups. This information was triangulated against other data sources including classroom observations, ethnographic participant research and document analyses. Grounded theory informed the data collection, coding and analysis (Charmaz, 2006). All quotes in this chapter are taken from audio-recorded interviews and focus groups conducted between 2007 and 2009. Throughout this chapter, the Western teachers are referred to as WT and the Chinese students are CS; they are numbered for ease of reference (WT2, CS4, etc.).

A note on terminology is necessary. In China, the term 'Western' usually denotes Whiteness but includes a notion of 'cultural' Westernness (Zheng, 2006: 170). So, for example, WT6 is from London and his parents are Chinese. He is considered 'Western' in that he has a London accent, speaks little Chinese, associates mainly with White people, and behaves in ways constructed in China as stereotypically 'Western', for example he portrays outward self-confidence. 'Western' is a different construct from 'native English speaker', and some White, non-native English speakers are employed at PSU as foreign teachers. Another term used here is 'foreign', a translation of the Chinese terms *waiguoren* and *laowai*. These Chinese terms lack the negative connotations of 'foreigner', and all are terms the participants have appropriated to describe themselves.

4.5   Findings: implicit theories of language

Implicit theories of language learning often emerge not only from classroom practice, but also from curriculum documents that underlie that practice. An implicit theory of language learning in Chinese education might, arguably, be seen from curriculum documents in which the Chinese language is counted quantifiably. Pupils in different years of schooling are expected to have mastered different quantities of Chinese characters, and it is an oft-quoted statistic in China that it takes proficiency in about 2000 characters to read Chinese newspapers. Language, including English, appears to be seen as a series of discrete items that can be measured and counted in curriculum documents, test preparation word lists and in assessment. Implicit in this is a view of language in which 'knowing' a language means knowing its discrete parts, that is, a view of language as words and structures rather than as discourse in contexts. Current curriculum documents for College English present an updated view of language learning to include active use of English, application to real contexts and critical thinking (Jin & Cortazzi, 2006), but understandably some institutions are slower than others to move towards newer expected practices. Thus the implicit theory evolves slowly. This is a different theory of language from that implicitly underpinning communicative language teaching (Richards & Rodgers, 2001), and this section examines teachers' and students' conceptualizations of language.

My own observational data from PSU and other contexts suggest that Chinese students may have a good explicit knowledge *about* grammar and may be able to translate the propositional meanings of many lexical items, but that there is often a lack of awareness of connotation, context appropriateness and collocation. Additionally, learners may have little communicative competence in using discrete language items they have memorized. As a result, students may struggle to speak and understand English because of insufficient listening and speaking *skills* development. Two PSU students give their views:

> The Chinese English teacher, he will stress on the grammar, the words, and not the accent, the speaking, so we learn English just to prepare our test, not practising our oral exercising. So this is why we are eager to meet a foreign teacher because we want to learn some native accent. (CS1)

> If you just learn from [a] book, or class you cannot understand the native speaker. English is changing quickly, for example the slang, you couldn't understand the slang, and it is different from what you learn from book[s], so I think it is very important to study oral English. You need to learn from native speaker. (CS2)

To these students, the problem seems to be a lack of language items, whether a 'native accent' or 'slang' words. While the barrier to comprehension *may* be accent or slang, a more persuasive explanation here might be the lack of listening *skills* development. Metaphorically, these students seem to assume that the jigsaw is missing vital pieces, rather than that they lack skill in putting together jigsaw puzzles.

The implicit assumption of language as quantifiable also allows for a correct/incorrect binary distinction to inform teaching. As a result, another student complains:

> English people don't care too much about the words, don't care the tense. Because you have to take written tests including the grammars and the words so you have to master the language from a second language teacher … Native speakers, yes, they make mistakes. (CS3)

This student appears to be assuming a Chomskyan model of underlying linguistic competence and observable language performance, attributing the latter to native speakers' use of language and the former to the language competence students may need to acquire in order to be successful at CET-type exams. In this model, language is a set of discrete, prescriptive variables that may be correct or incorrect; contextual differences are seemingly discounted in explaining language variance, including whether language is written or oral. As the above quote (CS3) demonstrates, Chinese students and teachers may value a right/wrong, quantifiable approach to language.

The implicit view of language quantifiability for learners contrasts with the view of language assumed by most of the teachers in this study, whose English teaching training was undertaken in contexts in which communicative language teaching (CLT) is the norm. Discussing error correction, one Western teacher exposes her assumed model of language as a system for communicating:

> If the students are telling me about their weekend or something and they'll say something and I'll be like 'sorry? I didn't understand that' ... I mean if it's only a small thing ... I won't pick up on it. But, yeah, I focus on where it's causing a breakdown of communication. (WT2)

So the Western teachers and the Chinese students in this study assume different underlying theories of language; to the students, language is a set of discrete variables that can be learned atomistically whereas to the teachers language is a holistic, meaning-making system. These implicit theories of language inform their language *teaching*, to which I turn next.

4.5.1   Findings: implicit theories of language learning

A quantifiable view of language appears to be enacted in classrooms as an expectation that students will learn more lexical and grammatical items as they progress through the years of English language teaching in school and university, with testing at each stage comprising testing of the items learned rather than testing of language *proficiency* across macro skills. This culminates, in the third year at PSU, in oral English as a capstone course designed to 'activate' language already learned 'in theory'.

Cameron (1999) describes metaphor as linguistic evidence that allows researchers access to mental representations, and I asked my PSU students for metaphors of how they understand the language-learning process. Two metaphors are particularly vivid in understanding students' conceptualizations of the process. The first is that language is first 'downloaded' through years of learning English 'in Chinese'; it is then 'installed' through the oral English course, which 'runs' the program and 'activates' English for the students. The second metaphor is that of Frankenstein: English is gradually and lifelessly built before being 'sparked to life' through oral English. These metaphors have in common the idea that English needs to be first learned, *then* used, rather than learned *through use*. This idea is shown in Figure 4.1. This may be explainable as a fear of error fossilization:

> You have to know some grammars ... because [if] you doesn't know any grammars and your English just poor, and you speak wrong English, [then, as a result] you speak like that again. And you form wrong ways, the wrong habit, not good habit, and after you have formed this habit you have, maybe you have to do a lot of things to rid of this habit ... First you have to learn from the book, then you use. (CS4)

This student's repeated use of 'habit' to describe language acquisition is evocative of Skinner's behaviourism, in which language acquisition was believed to be the acquisition of language *habits*; this is the theory of learning behind language-teaching methodologies such as the audio-lingual method (Richards & Rodgers, 2001).

This implicit theory of learning language may explain the concern of one of my Chinese colleagues at PSU who observed me teach, that

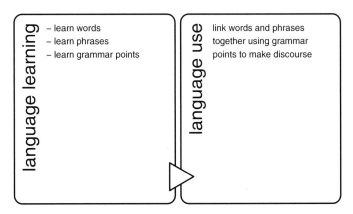

Figure 4.1   Conceptual model of the understanding of how languages are learned implicit in students' metaphors

students in my class were making mistakes in an oral fluency exercise. She perceived that this was problematic and unintended, and explained that she regards students' errors as evidence that learning has not succeeded, and that bad habits will ensue. A PSU foreign teacher participant described a similar discord with a Chinese colleague, in which the Chinese teacher made use of some of the communicative activities he had suggested, but used them as controlled practice following a thorough explanation of the language items, so as to 'prevent the students from making mistakes'. The Western teacher described this situation as:

> She seemed to think the activities ... were some kind of break from learning ... not that an activity can actually be the learning ... For her, the activity is the dispensable bit if she's running out of time. For me, it's the explaining bit that's dispensable. (WT3)

These very different views of classroom practice appear to indicate very different models of language acquisition as well as different cultures of learning. Although one of the Western teachers noted that 'content subjects' are often taught via lectures in Western education, she describes languages at her university in the USA as taught in small tutorials focused on meaningful student output, and were:

> More holistic, so you did get up some level of fluency ... [At PSU], students give back only the same output they've received, so they don't need to manipulate the language. (WT4)

Consequently, having a tangible, transmittable 'little sack of English', as WT3 put it, appears to be valued. One of the students summarizes her assumed model of language learning:

> The teacher is teaching to the students, the students are receiving information from the teacher. (CS3)

The sequential learning of tangible facts contrasts with skills development inherent to communicative language teaching, which assumes that languages are learned through use and that errors are evidence of learning (Richards & Rodgers, 2001). But *using* English so as to learn it may appear nebulous to students and may lack face validity; the students may expect learning to be explicit and measurable. But explicit, measurable learning contrasts with the aim of oral *skills* development in which the objective

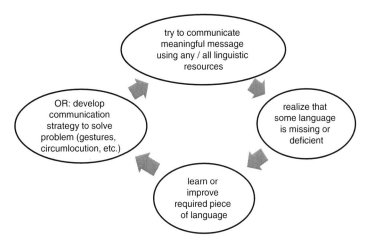

Figure 4.2   Conceptual model of the understanding of how languages are learned implicit in communicative language teaching

is not the acquisition of new language items but instead improvement in the *use* of students' existing store of language; this model is shown in Figure 4.2, in which the top circle is understood to represent the bulk of (oral) English teaching through the use of communication activities. However, students whose culture of learning assumes knowledge acquisition may struggle to see the purpose of skills development. The issue is students' and teachers' different theories of language and language learning *in contact*. This is the topic of the next section.

4.6   Discussion: crossing cultures of learning

Oral English is ostensibly a capstone course to 'activate' students' existing English, but it may feel redundant to the students as it lacks the face validity of learning new language items. Two teachers describe the problem of trying to get students to practise existing language items that they perceive they already 'know':

> [Foreign teachers] turn the students off because [the students] they think they know it, they feel like they've already ticked that box, they've closed that page in the book ... they haven't necessarily internalized it but they've seen it, so they perceive they've learned it. (WT7)

[The students] look at the book and see 'maybe you could plus verb', and they think 'I know those words, that's not new, I already know that' ... [and] they'll dismiss it and go 'boring', [and put their] head down on the desk. And then you go ask them, like, 'what would you say: you just killed a friend and you don't know what to do with the body?' And they'll be like 'uhhh, I say go to police' ... So they're not using it at all. (WT8)

One origin of students' resistance may therefore be a perception that, in practising ostensibly 'known' language items through communicative activities, the teachers appear to be pitching the level of the material too low, as students may perceive they have already covered the language in question.

But students' resistance, that the teacher above describes as students' putting their heads down on the desk and 'tuning out', may cause the teachers to reduce the level of challenge further so as to elicit a response, as their *own* cultures of learning would lead them to expect this. One of the Western teachers explains this process:

It's so hard to get them to talk. You know when you sort of say 'what did anyone think? Can anyone tell me what this means?' and, you know, you'll have people sitting there looking away ... It could be that maybe I'm speaking too quickly or maybe they don't understand the question. So I try to make it easier and I ask again. (WT1)

This problem seems to be caused by the inert knowledge problem, where students have a large passive knowledge that oral English is supposed to 'activate'. Teachers may erroneously interpret students' silence as incomprehension, and, as their own cultures of learning expect students' participation in class, may pitch their lessons too low. This problem then self-perpetuates, as shown in Table 4.1.

Students' perceptions of the intangibility of oral English, and of the low-level objectives of their foreign teachers, may result in students negatively evaluating their foreign teachers' professional competence. As discussed above, symbolic interactionism theorizes that people respond to things on the basis of the meanings those things hold *for them*. As a result, PSU students may, quite naturally, judge foreign teachers from within their own symbolic paradigm, in which the foreign teachers do not appear to be serious or competent given their constructed notion of a 'teacher' role. From this, it may be that the

Table 4.1 Conceptual model of a source of misunderstanding in oral English

	Perceived purpose of oral English	In oral English classes	As a result
Teachers	Teachers think the purpose of oral English is to develop skills through the use of communication activities.	Teachers behave in ways borne of communicative language teaching; they adopt a friendly approach and expect students to participate.	Teachers oversimplify the content.
Students	Students think oral English is a waste of time, as it does not appear to add content to their store of language items.	Students do not respond in the ways Western teachers expect; some refuse to participate in communication activities.	Students' view is confirmed that oral English is a waste of time. Some also think their foreign teacher is an idiot.
Teachers		Teachers think students' unresponsiveness is because they do not understand, and think they are pitching the level of the material too high.	Some teachers think Chinese students are stupid and/or immature.

students judge foreign teachers negatively *as a category*. Three PSU students explain:

> [Foreign teachers] sit on the tables, and you never see a Chinese teacher sit on the tables, never. So maybe the Western teachers give us the impression they are fun and we have highly expectation of them, be the foreign friends. A different expectation for the foreign teachers. (CS4)

> We see the TV dramas, we see Western teachers always willing [to] communicate with students … But I don't understand. In the Western education is talk, talk, talk, and so how someone will learning? (CS2)

> The foreign teachers, they don't bring books to class and the students think the teacher don't bring books and seems doesn't have a lot of plans, they just pick a topic and write on the board and say

'this class we just talk a topic'. This is not a way Chinese teacher do a class, so this is not a good teacher ... We think the foreign teacher is an idiot. (CS1)

It may be that teachers' intended meanings are being (mis)understood through (mis)interpretations of their outward signifiers and what these mean *to the students*. Some student interpretations of teachers' outward behaviours are shown in Table 4.2.

These misunderstandings of teachers' intended meanings may lead students to the conclusion that foreign teachers are incompetent, and therefore expecting little of them. One Western teacher reports:

My engineering students have the opportunity to go to America at the end of their junior year ... They didn't tell me at first, I found out a little over halfway through. And I asked, 'Why didn't you tell me earlier? This class would have been completely different if I'd have known. I would have structured it to make it more useful for you going abroad.' And they're 'oh, well, you know, it's just our English class' ... It just hadn't occurred to them ... they have all of their real classes and then they just get to come to our class and goof around and have fun. (WT4)

Students' constructions of foreign teachers may sometimes go beyond low educational expectations, with some students also ridiculing their foreign teachers. WT2 describes an incident that took place in May 2008, following a university-wide minute's silence for the victims of the Sichuan earthquake. All the students and teachers had taken part in a minute's silence in the morning, and the class WT2 describes took place in the afternoon of the same day.

[The students] think of Western people as clowns. And I think that's dangerous, like, for example, what the students did in [a non-participant teacher's] class, with the minute's silence. There [were three Western teachers team teaching] and [the students] wanted them to stand up the front, the three of them, face the class, and do a minute's silence, heads bowed, just the three of them, to, like, show their respect to China because of the earthquake ... I think we need to be careful that they're not just viewing us as these kind of toys that they can do what they want with ... I think they need to realize that that's not how all Western people are. And like, OK, we're outgoing and we're open about things, but we're not just,

Table 4.2 Some Western teachers' classroom behaviours and intentions compared with possible Chinese student misinterpretations borne of symbolic interactionism

Shared outward signifier	Teachers' intended meaning	Students' potential interpretation
The teachers sit on the tables, chew gum in class, laugh with the students, tell funny stories about their travel and other experiences, etc.	Language learning is about communication; I am trying to be friendly and approachable. I am trying to get students to respond.	Our teacher is nice but is not a 'proper' teacher; our teacher seems more like a friend than a teacher.
Students are expected to talk, in groups, without the teacher necessarily being part of the discussion.	The aim is to increase students' total output opportunities, output being a route to speaking-skills development.	All I am doing is talking to my friends. I am not learning anything; the teacher cannot teach properly.
Learning outcomes may appear to be intangible; there is no clear list of quantifiable language items to be learned.	Oral English aims at skills development rather than language input; teachers aim to improve students' oral fluency not add to their stock of language	We're not learning anything; this is too basic; the foreign teacher can only teach low-level language points; we *know* this!
Teachers do not correct much.	The aim is fluency rather than accuracy.	The teacher does not know how (or cannot be bothered) to correct our mistakes.
The textbook is used as a resource and is not covered in great depth.	*A textbook cannot provide* speaking-skills development, so textbook topics are used selectively to achieve the aims of oral English skills development.	The teacher does not 'know' grammar; the course (or the teacher) is not serious because we don't need to 'learn' the whole textbook.
There are no 'correct' answers to discussion questions.	The aim is to have students use English in discussions, as a route to speaking-skills development.	Either: the answers cannot be very important (so this is pointless), or: the teacher doesn't know the answers.
Teachers expect student responses because this is part of their culture of learning.	They resort to 'fun' games to get students' responses.	Western teachers are fun (but not very good teachers); all they do is pointless games.

yeah. I think a lot of my students do portray Western people as idiots. (WT2)

It appears that students' constructions of Western oral English teachers may affect how students perceive and portray Westerners more generally. If so, this would have important and negative implications for students' intercultural competence as it might be that by learning to disrespect foreign oral English *teachers*, Chinese students may transfer this judgement more widely to other 'foreigners'.

At the same time the *teachers* in this situation may reduce the perceived status of their Chinese students as a result of their experiences of teaching oral English. Some of the PSU foreign teachers construct and refer to their students as 'kids'. In addition, some teachers used very childish games/activities in class. One example was an activity that one of the foreign teachers recounted at a teachers' meeting; he had asked his students to bring crayons to class so as to do a 'colouring' dictation (i.e. colouring a picture according to his instructions). Another activity, also suggested at a teachers' meeting, was to have the students act out a dating agency role-play and have them explain to the teacher, playing the role of their 'father', why the partner they had chosen was appropriate.

The foreign teachers' use of the word 'kids' to refer to their students may be attributable to teachers' own struggles with their professional role and their perception that the students do not take them entirely seriously as teachers. Because of this, the teachers may seek to protect their *habitus* and professional standing. A different explanation is offered by symbolic interactionism and is the possibility that the foreign teachers interpret learning culture-induced behaviours as immaturity:

> They speak a lot of Chinese [in class] and I think it's only to be expected, 'cause they're at that sort of age, aren't they, where they don't want to seem like they're speaking English all the time and be showing off to their friends. (WT1)

This teacher, it appears, may be taking students' outward signifying behaviours and interpreting their meanings for what these would mean in her own paradigm; other participants did the same with different examples of students' behaviours. This is similar to the process described above, in which the students misinterpret the Western teachers' behaviours for what they would mean in their own paradigm.

4.7 Conclusion and a suggestion

It appears, then, that rather than crossing cultures, the contact situation at PSU is actually erecting barriers to intercultural communication, as both students and teachers leave the situation with negative constructions of the foreign Other created or confirmed rather than challenged by first-hand experience. If so, this is clearly a negative force in a globalizing world, as there may be implications for other contexts in which Westerners collaborate with Chinese people.

How can this problem be solved? One possibility is that oral English classes at PSU might take as their subject matter for discussion exactly the intercultural misunderstandings described in this chapter, transforming the somewhat intangible oral English course into a more tangible cultural studies course; the teaching of culture is also given as one of the stated objectives of the *College English* curriculum. This would allow for awareness raising of both sides' intended meanings behind outward behaviours, and for an intercultural 'third space' (Bhabha, 1990) to be found and negotiated. This could focus on classroom behaviours, and/or could focus on intercultural miscommunications borne of symbolic interactionism more generally. Cultural-awareness raising could be combined with oral English skills development in such as way as to increase the face validity of the process objectives of the latter by seeming to comprise the product of the former; this is a sleight of hand in which oral fluency development could be disguised as content-based culture teaching.

As an example, I used an activity in my teaching at PSU, in which the theories of language and language learning described above were explored through group-based discussions. This activity also aimed to develop students' oral fluency in English. Students began by working alone, making notes on one set of questions each. These included the following guided discussions that focused on the nature of language and on the nature of language learning as partially based on skill development:

Can you swim? Can you drive? Can you play a musical instrument? If you can do any of these, think about how you learned to do it. Is learning English similar to learning one of these things? Why or why not? How are they similar? How are they different?

Think about how you learned to speak and understand your first language when you were a child, before you went to primary school.

If you know any young children, think about how their language develops. Which comes first in a child's language development: meanings, or good grammar and complex vocabulary? Do children make grammar mistakes? Can they communicate meanings? Is learning English (as an adult) similar to learning your first language (as a child)? Why or why not?

Students worked in small groups, with each student presenting their thoughts on one set of questions before the group discussed the topics. Students were engaged by these discussions and were also able to make salient comments at whole-class feedback. This activity allows for exploration of the nature and purpose of oral English language practice activities that may seem intangible and for clarification to be provided as necessary as to the meanings behind the Western teachers' classroom behaviours.

Intercultural exploration with a focus on students' *own* norms as much as those of their Western teachers is therefore my suggestion for the content of foreign teachers' classes. This needs careful handling, and might be best co-taught bilingually by local and foreign teachers. 'Culture teaching' would likely require substantial teacher development, which could be achieved in two ways. Firstly, academic managers could draw upon resources from intercultural development; as an example, some of the texts and activities in Holliday, Hyde and Kullman's (2004) book *Intercultural Communication: An Advanced Resource Book* would be an excellent starting place for teachers' guided intercultural explorations. Secondly, culture-focused materials could be developed, perhaps based on Holliday *et al.*'s (2004) work, for use in other contexts where oral English teaching's seeming intangibility marginalizes it, as appears to be the case at PSU. Further research into this type of hybrid programme is necessary, but it is offered here as a suggestion for moving forward.

What is certainly clear is that the current situation described here is flawed, and that it may serve to hinder rather than help Chinese students to use English to communicate interculturally, as their contact with foreign Others in this situation appears to create and confirm Othering rather then help them build understandings. As I have described in this essay, students' and teachers' distinct cultures of learning, based on different assumptions about language and language learning, are misinterpreted through each side viewing the other's meanings through its own semiotic paradigm. This results in Western teachers infantilizing their Chinese students and the students judging their teachers as deficient.

References

Anderson, J. (1993) Is a communicative approach practical for teaching English in China? Pros and cons, *System*, 4, 471–480.

Atkinson, D. (1997) A critical approach to critical thinking in TESOL, *TESOL Quarterly*, 31(1), 9–37.

Ballard, B. & Clanchy, J. (1991) *Teaching Students from Overseas: A Brief Guide for Lecturers and Supervisors*. Melbourne: Longman Cheshire.

Barthes, R. (1967) *Elements of Semiology*. London: Cape Publications.

Bax, S. (2003) The end of CLT: a context approach to language teaching, *ELT Journal*, 57(3), 278–287.

Bhabha, H. K. (1990) The third space: interview with Homi Bhabha. In J. Rutherford (ed.) *Identity, Community, Culture, Difference*. London: Lawrence and Wishart, pp. 207–221.

Biggs, J. B. (1996) Western misperceptions of the Confucian-heritage learning culture. In D. A. Watkins & J. B. Biggs (eds) *The Chinese Learner: Cultural, Psychological and Contextual Influences*. Hong Kong: Comparative Education Research Centre, University of Hong Kong, pp. 45–67.

Bjorning-Gyde, M. & Doogan, F. (2004) TEFL practice and reform in China: learning, adapting, succeeding, creating. Paper presented at the 2nd International Conference of IATEFL China, Tonghua, China, 24–28 May.

Blumer, H. (1969) *Symbolic Interactionism: Perspective and Method*. Berkeley, CA: University of California.

Bodycott, P. & Walker, A. (2000) Teaching abroad: lessons learned about intercultural understanding for teachers in higher education, *Teaching in Higher Education*, 5(1), 79–94.

Bourdieu, P. (1990) *The Logic of Practice*. Palo Alto, CA: Stanford University Press.

Bourdieu, P. & Wacquant, L. T. D. (1992) *An Invitation to Reflexive Sociology*. Chicago: University of Chicago Press.

Boyle, J. (2000) Education for teachers of English in China, *Journal of Education for Teaching*, 26(2), 147–155.

Brick, J. (2004) *China: A Handbook in Intercultural Communication*. Sydney: NCELTR.

Butler, J. (2005) *Giving an Account of Oneself*. New York: Fordham University Press.

Cameron, L. (1999) Operationalising 'metaphor' for applied linguistics research. In L. Cameron & G. Low (eds) *Researching and Applying Metaphor*. Cambridge: Cambridge University Press, pp. 3–28.

Canale, M. & Swain, M. (1980) Theoretical bases of communicative approaches to second language teaching and testing, *Applied Linguistics*, 1(1), 1–47.

Charmaz, K. (2006) *Constructing Grounded Theory*. London: Sage.

Chinese Academy of Management Science (2009) Chinese university ranking. http://edu.sina.com.cn/gaokao/09utop/index.html.

Degen, T. & Absalom, D. (1998) Teaching across cultures: considerations for Western EFL teachers in China, *Hong Kong Journal of Applied Linguistics*, 3(2), 117–132.

Folse, K. S. (2006) *The Art of Teaching Speaking*. Mahwah, NJ: Lawrence Erlbaum Associates.

Greenholtz, J. (2003) Socratic teachers and Confucian learners: examining the benefits and pitfalls of a year abroad, *Language and Intercultural Communication*, 3(2), 122–130.

Groves, I. (2002) Ma, why can't my English teacher speak English? *The Amity Foundation Newsletter*. http://www.amitynewsletter.org/index.php? issueNo=60.

Gu, Q. & Maley, A. (2008) Changing places: a study of Chinese students in the UK, *Language and Intercultural Communication*, 8(4), 224–242.

Gu, W. & Liu, J. (2005) Test analysis of college students' communicative competence in English. *Asian EFL Journal*, 7. http://www.asian-efl-journal.com/ June_05_gw&lj.php.

Hiep, P. H. (2007) Communicative language teaching: unity within diversity, *ELT Journal*, 61(3), 193–201.

Hinton, D. (trans.) (1998) *The Analects*. Washington, DC: Counterpoint.

Holliday, A. (1994) *Appropriate Methodology and Social Context*. Cambridge: Cambridge University Press.

Holliday, A. (2009) The role of culture in English language teaching: key challenges, *Language and Intercultural Communication*, 9(3), 144–155.

Holliday, A., Hyde, M. & Kullman, J. (2004) *Intercultural Communication: An Advanced Resource Book*. London: Routledge.

Hu, G. (2002) Potential cultural resistance to pedagogical imports: the case of communicative language teaching in China, *Language, Culture and Curriculum*, 15(2), 93–105.

Hu, G. (2005a) Contextual influences on instructional practices: a Chinese case for an ecological approach to ELT, *TESOL Quarterly*, 39(4), 635–660.

Hu, G. (2005b) Professional development of secondary EFL teachers: lessons from China. *Teachers College Record*. http://www.tcrecord.org/content.asp? contentid=11816.

Hu, G. (2005c) Readers respond: 'CLT is best for China': an untenable absolutist claim, *ELT Journal*, 59(1), 65–68.

Huang, J. (2006) Learner resistance in metacognition training? An exploration of mismatches between learner and teacher groups, *Language Teaching Research*, 10(1), 95–117.

Hui, L. (1997) New bottles, old wine: communicative language teaching in China, *Forum*, 35. http://exchanges.state.gov/forum/vols/vol35/no4/ p38.htm.

Hymes, D. H. (1971) On communicative competence. In J. B. Pride & J. Holmes (eds) *Sociolinguistics*. London: Penguin Books.

Ji, L. (2005) Pronunciation: stepping stones to improvement, *English Teaching Professional*, 39, 18–22.

Jin, G. (2008) Application of communicative approach in college English teaching, *Asian Social Science*, 4(4), 81–85.

Jin, L. & Cortazzi, M. (1998) The culture the learner brings: a bridge or a barrier? In M. Byram & M. Fleming (eds) *Language Learning in Intercultural Perspective: Approaches through Drama and Ethnography*. Cambridge: Cambridge University Press, pp. 98–118.

Jin, L. & Cortazzi, M. (2003) English language teaching in China: a bridge to the future. In H. W. Kam & R. Y. K. Wong (eds) *English Language Teaching in East Asia Today*. Singapore: Times Academic Press, pp. 131–145.

Jin, L. & Cortazzi, M. (2006) Changing practices in Chinese cultures of learning, *Language, Culture and Curriculum*, 19(1), 5–20.

Jin, L., Singh, M. & Li, L. (2005) Communicative language teaching in China: misconceptions, applications and perceptions. Paper presented at the Australian Association for Research in Education Conference, Parramatta, NSW, 27 November–1 December.

Kramsch, C. & O'Sullivan, P. (1996) Appropriate pedagogy, *ELT Journal*, 50(3), 199–212.

Li, Z. & Song, M. (2007) The relationship between traditional English grammar teaching and communicative language teaching, *US–China Education Review*, 4(1), 62–65.

Liao, X. (2004) The need for communicative language teaching in China, *ELT Journal*, 58(3), 270–273.

Lightbown, P. M. & Spada, N. (1999) *How Languages are Learned*. Oxford: Oxford University Press.

Ministry of Education (2007) *College English Curriculum Requirements*. Beijing: Foreign Language Teaching and Research Press.

Ng, C. & Tang, E. (1999) Teachers' needs in the process of EFL reform in China: a report from Shanghai. http://sunzi1.lib.hku.hk/hkjo/view/10/1000116.pdf.

Nunan, D. (2003) The impact of English as a global language on educational policies and practices in the Asia-Pacific region, *TESOL Quarterly*, 37(4), 589–613.

Ong, A. (1999) *Flexible Citizenship: The Cultural Logics of Transnationality*. Durham, NC and London: Duke University Press.

Pennycook, A. (1989) The concept of method, interested knowledge, and the politics of language teaching, *TESOL Quarterly*, 23(4), 589–618.

Richards, J. C. & Rodgers, T. S. (2001) *Approaches and Methods in Language Teaching* (2nd edn). Cambridge: Cambridge University Press.

Senior, R. & Xu, Z. (2002) East meets West: language teachers from different contexts discover similar goals, *English Australia Journal*, 19(1), 65–74.

Stake, R. E. (2005) Qualitative case studies. In N. K. Denzin & Y. S. Lincoln (eds) *The SAGE Handbook of Qualitative Research*. Thousand Oaks, CA: Sage, pp. 443–466.

Tudor, I. (2001) *The Dynamics of the Language Classroom*. Cambridge: Cambridge University Press.

Wang, M. J. (2001) The cultural characteristics of Chinese students: a study of basic attitudes and approaches to their English studies, *RELC Journal*, 32(1), 16–33.

Wesche, M. B. & Skehan, P. (2002) Communicative, task-based and content-based language instruction. In R. B. Kaplan (ed.) *The Oxford Handbook of Applied Linguistics*. New York: Oxford University Press, pp. 207–228.

Wette, R. & Barkhuizen, G. (2009) Teaching the book and educating the person: challenges for university English language teachers in China, *Asia Pacific Journal of Education*, 29(2), 195–212.

Xinmin, Z. & Adamson, B. (2003) The pedagogy of a secondary school teacher of English in the People's Republic of China: challenging the stereotypes, *RELC Journal*, 34(3), 323–337.

Xu, Z. C. (2002) From TEFL to TEIL: changes in perceptions and practices: teaching English as an international language (EIL) in Chinese universities in

P.R. China. In A. Kirkpatrick (ed.) *Englishes in Asia: Communication, Identity, Power and Education*. Melbourne: Language Australia, pp. 225–244.

Yu, L. (2001) Communicative language teaching in China: progress and resistance, *TESOL Quarterly*, 35(1), 194–198.

Zhang, L. (2004) CLT in China: frustrations, misconceptions and clarifications, *Hwa Kang Journal of TEFL*, 10, 101–114.

Zheng, T. (2006) Cool masculinity: male sex clients' sex consumption and business alliance in urban China's sex industry, *Journal of Contemporary China*, 15(46), 161–182.

Zheng, X. & Davidson, C. (2008) *Changing Pedagogy: Analyzing ELT Teachers in China*. London: Continuum.

5
Reticence and Anxiety in Oral English Lessons: A Case Study in China

Meihua Liu and Jane Jackson

5.1   Introduction

In recent decades, research has revealed that reticence and anxiety can have a debilitating impact on second language (L2) learning (Horwitz *et al.*, 1986; MacIntyre & Gardner, 1991a; Tsui, 1996; Jackson, 2002a; Liu, 2006a; Liu & Jackson, 2008). It is widely agreed that reticent students often speak less and exhibit more negative forms of arousal (e.g. anxiety, tension, unpleasant effect), with speech that tends to be brief and less comprehensible. Likewise, high-anxious people are more reluctant to speak in L2 classroom activities and this often hinders their learning. Reticence and anxiety are complex constructs that stem from a range of linguistic, educational and cultural elements as well as personality attributes. This chapter reviews key research in this area before focusing on an investigation of factors that influenced the behaviour of students in oral English lessons at a university in Mainland China.

5.2   Review of the literature

Reticence and anxiety are closely interrelated, as Phillips explains: 'Reticence often masks strong emotions. It is often accompanied by anxiety that can impede both performance and receptivity to instruction' (1997: 142). Moreover, level of language proficiency, self-efficacy, personality, motivation, willingness to speak the target language and other factors may interact with each other to determine whether a learner is passive or active/confident or nervous in the classroom (Ely, 1986; Jackson, 2002b). The impact of these variables on learning in L2 classrooms underscores the need for further research in this area. This is especially important in Mainland China where many EFL learners have been observed to be quiet and/or to speak English with a trembling voice, make numerous unnecessary stops, or have shaking hands or legs during English lessons (Cortazzi & Jin, 1996; Zou, 2004; Liu, 2006a, 2006b). As there is growing pressure on Chinese students to master oral English, it is vital for educators both in China and internationally to be familiar with research on reticence and anxiety.

5.2.1   Reticence

Reticence research that centres on native speakers in social interactions has a long history (Burgoon, 1976; McCroskey, 1977; Keaten & Kelly, 2000). Findings indicate that many people are apprehensive when communicating in their native language and are reluctant to voice their opinions in conversations. When people speak in an L2, they may become even more apprehensive, tense and unwilling to participate in conversations (Horwitz *et al.*, 1986; MacIntyre & Gardner, 1989). As one might expect, many learners are quiet in classrooms for learning L2 or in content courses in which they learn through L2, rarely responding to teachers' questions or actively taking part in discussions (Dwyer & Heller-Murphy, 1996; Chen, 2003; Jackson, 2003; Zou, 2004; Liu, 2006a).

By way of interviews and journals, researchers have found that student reticence may arise due to a plethora of reasons: fear of making mistakes, low target language proficiency, incomprehensible input, habit, lack of confidence, limited experience with oral communication, personality attributes, little investment in language learning and so on (Tsui, 1996; Liu & Littlewood, 1997; Jackson, 2002a, 2002b; Liu, 2006b). Studies in Asian contexts (Cortazzi & Jin, 1996; Dwyer & Heller-Murphy, 1996; Tsui, 1996; Jackson, 2002a) report that Asian EFL learners are often reticent and passive in classroom situations. It is speculated that a principal reason for this is cultural beliefs which are prevalent in these countries. Sato (1990) and Cortazzi and Jin (1996), for example, maintain that many Asian students are reluctant to express their ideas in class due to the prevailing social hierarchy as well as concerns about preserving 'face'; they may fear making a mistake and suffering embarrassment in front of peers and teachers or they might be concerned for the teacher who would lose face if unable to answer their questions (Cortazzi & Jin, 1996).

Although students may express a willingness to participate in classroom activities, this does not guarantee they will actually do so. Jackson's (2002a, 2003) three-year ethnographic study of business majors in Hong Kong showed that while aware of the benefits of case discussions, the students often remained reticent in classroom discussions conducted in their L2. This was due to a wide range of cultural, psychological and linguistic factors: lack of vocabulary, anxiety about making mistakes and 'losing face', the fear of speaking in public, personality attributes, lack of familiarity with the subject matter, lack of confidence in their ideas or 'points', unwillingness to challenge professors and limited oral English proficiency. Clearly, student reticence in L2 classrooms is a complicated phenomenon.

5.2.2 Foreign language anxiety

Similar to reticence, anxiety is a significant psychological variable in general education. Research indicates that it plays an important or even deciding role in determining academic achievement levels (Tobias, 1979; MacIntyre & Gardner, 1994). The situation is the same in L2 teaching and learning (Gardner, 1985; Horwitz, 1995).

As a form of situation-specific anxiety (Horwitz *et al.*, 1986; MacIntyre & Gardner, 1989), foreign language anxiety is a complex, multidimensional phenomenon (Young, 1991), which refers to 'the feeling of tension and apprehension specifically associated with second language contexts, including speaking, listening, and learning' (MacIntyre & Gardner, 1994: 284). Students in L2 classes may engage in negative self-talk, ruminating over a poor performance; this, in turn, affects their ability to process information in the L2 (MacIntyre & Gardner, 1991b). Some students with very high levels of anxiety may even have a mental block (Tobias, 1979) and find it too challenging to learn an L2.

Quantitative research often examines the effect of anxiety on L2 learning and/or the relationship between anxiety and other variables such as confidence, personality, motivation, unwillingness to communicate, learning style and learning strategies, gender and cultural differences (MacIntyre & Gardner, 1991a; Oxford, 1999; Pappamihiel, 2001; Liu & Jackson, 2008). It is widely agreed that foreign language anxiety is common in L2 learners; it is closely related to public speaking and mainly has a debilitating role in L2 learning. Low-anxious learners often perform better in the target language than their high-anxious peers.

Using such methods as interviews, diaries and observations, qualitative researchers have explored the nature, characteristics, sources and consequences of L2 anxiety (Cohen & Norst, 1989; Price, 1991; Hilleson, 1996; Mak & White, 1997). They have discovered that high-anxious students may use emotive language to describe their experiences and feelings in L2 classes (e.g. 'horrible', 'frightening' and 'awful'). Many 'resent' or even 'hate' the way they feel in these situations. Various factors have been found to contribute to their malaise: the pursuit of perfectionism, fear of public speaking, negative classroom experiences, lack of confidence, fear of being criticized and ridiculed, lack of preparation, unfamiliar teaching styles, incomprehensible input and a competitive environment.

Anxiety exists in almost every aspect of L2 learning and is most often associated with trying to comprehend oral discourse and speak the target language (Young, 1991; Phillips, 1997; Jackson, 2002a). Similar to reticence, it may be a by-product of a range of linguistic, cultural, educational and personality factors. As it can serve as a debilitating force in L2 learning, it merits scrutiny by L2 educators and researchers.

5.3   A case study of L2 learners in Mainland China

The review of the literature suggests that both reticence and anxiety in L2 classrooms are complex constructs that may adversely affect student learning. In Asian contexts, where English language learning has become increasingly important, there is a pressing need to better understand these phenomena. As previous research has shown that Asian learners are often reticent and anxious in oral L2 lessons, it is vital that we identify effective ways to empower students to optimize learning in classroom situations. Though reticence and anxiety have been found to be closely related to each other (Hilleson, 1996; Tsui, 1996; Jackson, 2002a), few researchers have systematically examined both constructs in the same situation (Liu & Jackson, 2008). Drawing on several modes of qualitative data (e.g. observation, interviews, diaries and videotapes), the following case study of L2 learners in Mainland China aims to fill this void.

5.3.1   Research questions

At a key comprehensive university in Beijing, the present research explored student reticence and anxiety in oral English lessons, focusing on the perspective of the students. For this purpose, the following research questions were formulated:

1 What is the general profile of student reticence and anxiety in oral English lessons?
2 What is the impact of reticence and anxiety on the students' learning of oral English?

3 What causes the students to be reticent and anxious in oral English lessons?

4 What strategies do they employ to cope with reticence and anxiety in oral English lessons?

5.3.2 Research methods

Participants

Three intact classes of the *English Listening & Speaking* course at a top university in China were randomly selected for this study. A total of 93 freshmen (78 males and 15 females) with an average age of 18.5 participated. All of them were non-English majors from various disciplines such as Computer Science, Architecture and Business Management. As one of the few highly prestigious universities in China, this university recruits top students from each province of the country, who (especially those who do not plan to major in English) are often considered at the highest level of English of the same student population.

Instruments

For this study, data were collected via observations (videotaped lessons), reflective journals and interviews, as detailed below.

Reflective journal: this was used to gather data about personal and affective dimensions of English language learning. The 93 students were asked to write reflective journal entries on a weekly basis for six consecutive weeks. Prompts were provided in both English and Chinese to stimulate reflection on such topics as their level of participation and anxiety during the English language lessons and their reasons for their behaviour in class activities (e.g. reticence and feelings). Students were also encouraged to write about their overall English language learning experiences in English. If they had any difficulty in expressing ideas in English, they could turn to Chinese. To motivate the students to write, each week their entries were photocopied, reviewed and returned with feedback.

Semi-structured interview: this was used to obtain a more comprehensive insider view of reticence and anxiety in English language classrooms. Seven students from each class were randomly invited to participate in a semi-structured interview. While English was used occasionally, most interviews took place in Mandarin as it was easier for the students to express themselves in this language. The questions covered such aspects as educational experience, attitudes towards active students, behaviour in university English lessons, feelings of anxiety when speaking English in class, reasons for being reticent and anxious, and coping strategies.

Classroom observation: this method was adopted during the semester. Oral activities were observed and videotaped on three separate occasions in each of the three classes.

Procedure

The study was conducted during 14 weeks of the first term of the academic year, as soon as the formal classroom teaching and learning started. The students started journal writing in the second week of the course and kept on writing for six weeks consecutively, with one entry per week. In the last two months, one of the researchers observed and videotaped each of the three classes three times, with each taping lasting 90 minutes. This provided an overall picture of what was happening in the classroom and insight into the students' degree of participation in various activities (e.g. pair work, group work, student–teacher inter-action and presentations). To reduce the potential influence of anxiety due to the presence of the equipment/observer, only the last two videotapings were analysed. The semi-structured interviews took place when the final-term exam was over. Twenty students were interviewed/audiotaped, with each session lasting about 50 minutes. The aim was to talk with seven students in each class who represented a range of reticence and anxiety; however, one student was unable to attend the interview.

Data analysis

The interviews were transcribed by the first researcher and checked by the second. Together with the journals and observations, the trans-criptions were then triangulated and subjected to a thematic content analysis (Neuendorf, 2002; Grbich, 2007). The primary purpose was to ascertain the source, frequency and context of reticence and anxiety in the oral English lessons and to determine whether this negatively affected their learning.

5.4   Outcomes and results

5.4.1   Self-reported reticence and anxiety in class

The reflective journals revealed that the participants wished to learn and speak English well for a variety of reasons. The following statements were typical: 'English is important and useful'; 'I want to communicate with foreigners'; 'Speaking English well makes me more self-confident'; 'It's fun and interesting to speak another language'; and 'It's a necessary ability for a university graduate to speak a second language'. Sixty-two respondents (66.7%) expressed a willingness to communicate with others in English in the classroom in order to 'improve their spoken English' and/or enhance their 'communication with others'. Similar to Jackson's (2002a) study, however, their desire did not translate into practice. As observed by the researchers and acknowledged by the students, few actively participated in class activities. They did not volunteer to respond to their teacher's questions and did not ask questions even though they were often encouraged to do so.

Interestingly, 66 (70.97%) of them reported that they were most active during pair work; only 7 (7.5%) were most active when responding to the teacher; and only 4 (4.3%) during group work. The video-recorded observations verified their self-assessment. Most of the learners in each class played a more active role in pair work; around a third responded to the teacher when the questions were easy to answer but few volunteered if the questions were difficult or challenging; most either gazed down at their books or looked as though they were deep in thought. Even if singled out by the teacher for a question, they tended to offer very brief responses and some were barely audible. While a few appeared to be disinterested in the questions, nearly two-thirds of the class appeared to listen attentively even though they remained silent.

Significantly, the students wished that the class was more interactive and held positive views about active peers. In particular, they admired those who responded to the teachers, referring to them as courageous and confident. The participants also believed that these active individuals spoke better English and set a good example for other students. These role models appeared to stimulate their peers to at least contemplate becoming more active in class.

The content analysis of the journal entries revealed that of the 93 students, 56 (60.2%) felt anxious or nervous to varying degrees when speaking English in class. Fifteen (16.1%) were 'a little nervous' and 9 (9.7%) were 'sometimes nervous'; only 13 (14.0%) declared that they were not nervous. Their level of preparedness to speak had an impact on their anxiety level, with 20 (21.5%) stating that their nervousness lessened when they were prepared; 14 (15.1%) declared that they were not nervous when ready to speak. Even with preparation, however, 46 (49.5%) remained fearful. Although it might not eliminate the anxiety altogether, preparation did help some to feel better about speaking in class.

The students' level of apprehension varied depending on the activity, in part because of the different audience they faced in each situation. During pair work, the students needed to speak with only one peer;

thus, most of them felt at ease in this situation, especially when both partners knew each other and possessed a similar level of proficiency in English. Group work often involved three or four students, which made some nervous because the audience was bigger and they might not have yet become acquainted with everyone in the group. Most grew more comfortable speaking English in a small group as soon as they became familiar with their group members. The following statement from one of the participants was typical:

> I feel nervous when speaking English in class because I'm afraid of making mistakes. But I'm not nervous during pair work and group work because we are at a similar English proficiency level. (CS1, journal and interview)

Being singled out to answer questions and make presentations (usually without a prepared script) was the most anxiety-provoking activity. In the fifth reflective journal entry, the students again discussed their anxiety in different classroom activities. Of the 93 students, 83 (89.2%) were still the most anxious when responding to questions from their teacher, 81 (87.1%) were the least anxious when doing pair work activities. At this stage, 75 (80.6%) were less anxious in group work situations.

The students provided further insight into the source of their anxiety. Many attributed it to a lack of confidence in their English language proficiency and fear of making mistakes. The following comment was typical:

> I was most anxious when asked to stand up and speak only English because I thought that it was a shame to show my poor English to my classmates. (CS2, journal)

Some students felt the most anxious when speaking English to the whole class because 'all the classmates were looking at me' (CS3, journal). When the students were ill-prepared or failed to understand the teacher, they became particularly anxious when asked to speak English because they were unsure what to say.

The students' revelations about their behaviour were generally confirmed by the video-recordings of the oral English lessons. As in previous studies (Hilleson, 1996; Tsui, 1996; Jackson, 2002a; Liu, 2006b), many students appeared to be anxious when speaking English in class and their level of discomfort appeared to vary depending on

Table 5.1 Students' change in anxiety reflected in journals *n* = 93

Week	Anxious %	A little anxious %	Sometimes anxious %	Not anxious %
2	39/41.9	23/24.7	11/11.8	20/21.5
3	27/29	27/29	6/6.5	33/35.5
4	22/23.7	31/33.3	9/9.7	30/32.3
5	21/22.6	23/24.7	12/12.9	37/39.8
6	20/21.5	30/32.3	2/2.2	41/44.1
7	17/18.3	25/26.9	6/6.5	45/48.4

the activity. In sum, the students felt the least anxious during pair work and group work, but the most anxious when asked to speak in front of the whole class, especially when unprepared. As they became more familiar with the classroom environment and used to speaking English, some of their nervousness subsided, as evidenced in Table 5.1.

Similar to Bailey (1983) who was learning French, the students in the present study tended to be anxious in the second lesson, with only around 20% not feeling nervous when speaking English to others in class. As they had more access to spoken English and became more familiar with the new environment, more and more students, however, did not feel nervous when speaking the language in class. For example, from the fifth week on, around or even more than 40% of the students reported not feeling nervous in class. Moreover, even among those who still felt nervous when speaking English in class, many reported feeling better than they used to in the previous lesson(s). As a student said, 'but I turned more comfortable and not felt as nervous as I did last time' (CS19, journal), and many students became less anxious when they came to be 'more confident' (CS20, journal) and/or 'get used to the situation and those activities' (CS21, journal).

5.5 Impact of reticence and anxiety on students' performance in oral English

All of the students held the view that active students spoke better English and were likely to continue to make good progress. Only two were not sure whether reticence negatively affected their performance in spoken English. Those who tended to be reticent and anxious in class acknowledged that their behaviour limited their practice of speaking English. Because they spoke so little in class they were unable to pinpoint their specific weaknesses in oral English, as one of the students explained:

> If a person doesn't speak English, he won't be able to know his real oral proficiency ... As a result, his performance must be affected. At least, his spoken English can't be improved. (CS4, journal)

Reticence also had a negative impact on the willingness of all students to take an active role in class, similar to the findings of Zou's (2004) study. Not wishing to be put into an out-group by behaving differently from their peers, some students became reluctant to speak up even though they were capable of doing so and wished to participate. This phenomenon is best explained by the following excerpt:

> If most students in class kept quiet, those who wanted to be active would feel that they were special in class. To be the same as others, they would also be quiet so the negative circumstances were certain to affect everyone's oral English. (CS5, journal)

Only three students thought that anxiety could be positive. For example, CS6 stated in his interview that 'it will encourage you to perform much better'. By contrast, nearly all (more than 90%) of the students believed that anxiety negatively affected their performance in spoken English. The following comments were common:

> Because of nervousness and anxiety, I can't speak as well as I should and this makes me insecure. For example, I usually make mistakes in tense because of nervousness. (CS7, journal)

As well as being nervous in particular classroom situations, anxiety negatively affected their performance in the long term, as the following student explained: 'If you feel nervous, you can't go on. If you can't go on, you don't want to speak any more. Gradually you are not willing to speak English. Thus, you can't improve your English' (CS8, interview).

The respondents claimed that anxiety in oral English lessons made them afraid of, or even hate, speaking English; some were unable to even say anything about a very easy topic; they were unable to think clearly, became less and less interested in English, and stammered during a speech. Their anxiety caused them to make many mistakes and forget words and expressions and this made them even more nervous and afraid to speak. Due to their elevated level of stress, many students chose not to speak the language, which made it harder for them to improve their spoken English. A negative cycle was set in motion.

Most participants were convinced that confident students would gradually become better English speakers while anxious students would become less willing to speak the language and therefore speak poorer English:

> Confident students often speak more and their English certainly gets better and better. If you are nervous and for example your mouth is shaking when speaking English, you can't speak it well. (CS9, journal and interview)

5.6 Source of reticence and anxiety in oral English lessons

Though often encouraged by their teachers to speak English, most of the participants remained reticent and felt (very) anxious when using English in class. In their journals and interviews, the most widely cited explanations for reticence were: low English language proficiency (47.3%), Chinese cultural beliefs (44.1%), personality (mainly introversion and shyness) (39.8%), the Chinese educational system (31.2%) and anxiety (25.8%). As one of the female students explained, her level of English held her back from participating in class:

> I think what keeps me reticent is my poor English proficiency ... I lose many chances to show myself to the class. All is owing to my poor English proficiency. (CS10, journal)

Chinese cultural beliefs also played a major role in student reticence in L2 classroom situations, a similar finding to earlier studies (Sato, 1990; Cortazzi & Jin, 1996; Jackson, 2003). In the students' opinion, Chinese culture values modesty rather than standing out and expressing one's views and this affected their behaviour in class. As traditional Chinese culture also emphasizes respect for elders, in Chinese classrooms teachers are often considered figures of authority, who should be respected and obeyed but not challenged (Bond, 1996; Phillips, 1997; Chen, 2003). Consequently, most of the students did not like to be regarded as 'show-offs' and thus kept quiet in class, as the following student explained:

> If you are too active, you will be thought of as one who likes to show off. People will not like you. (CS11, journal)

Another student also cited Confucian ideology as the source of students' unwillingness to volunteer to speak in class:

> Chinese culture teaches us not to be the first nor last, so that the majority prefer to wait for someone to speak first rather than make themselves the first one to try. (CS12, journal)

Personality also affected student reticence in English language lessons. Some kept quiet because they were too shy or introverted to speak; some just did not like to speak to others. Some preferred thinking to speaking though they could speak English quite well:

> In the classroom, though I didn't answer any question, I think I could answer very well if the teacher asked me to. (CS13, journal)

Reticence was also partly attributed to the Chinese educational system, as a participant explained in the following journal entry:

> Silence ... is a historic question in Chinese universities. When we were in primary school, the teacher told us to be quiet in the classroom, to listen to the teacher and to speak only if the teacher asked you to do so. The people who made noise were punished by the teacher ... Though everything changed at the University, time is needed to change our mindset. (CS14, journal)

Over time, the students formed the habit of waiting to be singled out, like those in Jackson's (2002a, 2003) studies. The testing system also impacted on their behaviour. Due to the format of the examinations, Chinese students had to 'pay great attention to reading and writing, not to listening and speaking' (CS15, journal).

Similar to Jackson's (2002a) study of Hong Kong students, the participants considered anxiety a main reason for student reticence. Many students acknowledged that they kept quiet in class because 'they are too nervous to speak out' (CS6, journal). This finding further supports Keaten and Kelly's (2000) belief that reticent individuals experience communication anxiety.

In addition to these most commonly cited reasons, a range of other factors played a role in student reticence in English language lessons, including the difficulty of the task, fear of making mistakes and being laughed at, and lack of familiarity with partners and the environment. Interestingly, one student held the belief that keeping quiet could make him more attentive in class and thus enable him to acquire more knowledge. He downplayed the benefits of practising the oral language. The content analysis of the journals and interview transcripts also revealed that the three main factors that the students believed were the causes of student anxiety in English language lessons were: lack of practice (71%), insufficient vocabulary (51.6%) and low English language proficiency (34.4%). The majority did not practise speaking English when in middle school as their focus was on written examinations. When they started to speak English in class at the university, it is not surprising that they became nervous. Further, the university did not offer many chances for them to access spoken English outside class, as a student explained:

> I think the bigger problem is practice ... As I didn't practice speaking English in the past few years, my pronunciation is poor so I'm afraid to stand up and give others my opinion. (CS11, journal)

This view was held by more than 70% of the participants, who emphasized that, as a foreign language, English was seldom used or needed in their daily life.

The students were also anxious because they felt they had a lack of vocabulary when speaking English in class. The following excerpt best explains the situation:

> Because students don't know how to express themselves, they can't identify the names of objects. They don't know enough adjectives and adverbs to express their opinions. (CS16, journal)

For nearly one-third of the students, anxiety was also related to their low level of proficiency in English. The next three sources were personality (introversion and shyness) (43.3%), fear of making mistakes (30%) and lack of preparation (20%). Other factors included incomprehensible input, lack of confidence, fear of being laughed at, fear of being the focus of attention and so on.

In addition to the factors found in previous studies (Bailey, 1983; Price, 1991; Hilleson, 1996; Tsui, 1996; Jackson, 2002a), other reasons for anxiety were cited by the students in the present study including having a poor memory and family communication patterns that inhibited their desire to speak. Some participants also commented that fear of speaking 'Chinese English' and the desire to speak English fluently made them anxious in oral lessons. This suggests that the students lacked confidence in their English and set unrealistic expectations for themselves. The following excerpt illustrates this phenomenon:

> Everybody at the university wants to do everything perfectly. No one wants to make a mistake in the English class. (CS17, journal)

The fear of making mistakes and the desire to speak perfect English inhibited their performance, a situation observed by Price (1991) in other L2 contexts. Several students also reported that speaking in class was anxiety-provoking whether in Chinese or English. This fear of speaking in public or in front of the whole class has been noted by other researchers (Horwitz *et al.*, 1986; MacIntyre & Gardner, 1989).

5.7   Strategies to cope with reticence and anxiety in oral English lessons

Through interviews and journal entries, most students confided that they seldom employed any specific strategies to cope with reticence and anxiety in their oral English lessons. Only a few encouraged themselves to speak up by saying 'I must do this' or 'I must speak more.' Several also reminded themselves of the potential benefits of practice: 'English is important for my further education and future jobs' (CS18, journal and interview). Before giving a presentation in class, a few told themselves, 'don't be nervous, don't be nervous', but this approach proved ineffective. While dismayed by their reticence, the majority were unsure how to overcome it, similar to the findings of Keaten and Kelly (2000).

The students were encouraged to offer suggestions for English teachers and L2 students to cope with reticence and anxiety. Most believed that students would become more active and less anxious when speaking English if teachers would prepare more interesting topics (e.g. current affairs), create a relaxing classroom environment, encourage students to speak more and provide more opportunity to practise speaking the language in class. In their view, teachers should give students more thinking time, praise them more and create more chances for English conversations so that students can become more self-assured. Many of their ideas echoed the recommendations offered by Tsui (1996).

In addition, many participants suggested that teachers should treat their students as friends and build up their self-confidence through comments such as, 'making mistakes is unavoidable'. They also thought that teachers should motivate students to learn spoken English by repeatedly emphasizing its importance and creating more time in class for pair work and asking questions. Taking steps to enhance the vocabulary of students would also be welcome. Some students challenged teachers to find creative ways to open the mouths of their students.

To become more active and confident in speaking English in class, all of the participants stressed that students should not be afraid of failure or making mistakes. They should be well prepared for class, practise more and support each other. Their ideas were in line with the suggestions of researchers (Tsui, 1996; Jackson 2002a, 2002b).

5.8 Implications and applications

Despite expressing (strong) willingness to speak English with their peers in class, most of the students remained silent and nervous during classroom activities. This was especially the case when asked to address the whole class. Their behaviour was due to a complex mix of linguistic, cultural, educational, psychological and personality factors. While aware that reticence and anxiety negatively affected their performance in oral English lessons, most felt helpless about overcoming these barriers to their participation. Even so, when prompted, they proposed a number of useful strategies for teachers and L2 learners to enhance oral English skills, which are discussed here along with the suggestions of the researchers.

In English language classrooms, teachers can take a number of steps to help reduce student reticence and anxiety. At the beginning of a term, student profiles can be created to develop a better understanding of the class members. Data can be gathered about their educational and family background, English proficiency, previous language-learning experiences, attitude towards English and oral English lessons, and learning objectives/expectations. Early on, teachers should familiarize students with the English-learning environment and encourage them to take advantage of opportunities to practise the language outside class.

It is essential for students to understand the aims and teaching format that will be used in oral English lessons. As found in the present research and previous studies (MacIntyre & Gardner, 1994; Oxford, 1999; Zou, 2004), when students are not familiar with the classroom environment they are more reluctant to speak and feel anxious when unsure what is expected of them, especially if they have little previous experience with oral language lessons. Thus, as suggested by Donley (1998) and Zou (2004), teachers should clearly explain the rationale behind activities and encourage open discussion about the most effective ways to learn to speak an L2 well.

To create a situation that is conducive to learning, teachers should design a variety of activities to help students get to know one another and become familiar with the English-learning facilities on campus. This should happen early in the course. Students will become less anxious and more willing to speak the target language in oral English lessons if the classroom-learning environment is friendly, supportive and encouraging, as suggested by the participants in the present research and previous studies (Horwitz *et al.*, 1986; Price, 1991; Jackson, 2002b; Yan, 2003).

For Chinese learners who have little contact with English in their daily life, abundant practice is essential. They need to practise speaking English both in and outside the classroom with different people in a range of situations. This can help them build up their confidence and comfort level when using the language. To facilitate this, English teachers may create tasks that require the students to practise speaking their L2 outside class. Throughout a course, teachers have a responsibility to encourage students to become active and autonomous learners to take full advantage of linguistic affordances in their surroundings. For this to be effective, the students must become familiar with L2 learning facilities and opportunities in their environment. This additional practice has the potential to enhance their self-perception of their competence in the language and thereby reduce their anxiety level when trying to express themselves in their L2 (Baker & MacIntyre, 2000).

It is important for students to reflect on and discuss issues related to the use of their L2. Students could respond to journal prompts on this topic and then discuss their concerns in small groups, with group representatives sharing their findings in a full-class discussion. In subsequent discussions, the students could discuss strategies that could be used to cope with reticence and anxiety in oral English lessons. According to Donley (1998), students feel more comfortable and become (more) active in their language class once they realize that other students and their teacher empathize with their fears. This approach was also shown to be effective in Kondo and Yang's (2004) study.

There are also steps that learners can take to enhance their own learning. Early in a course, they should take the initiative to become familiar with their classmates and English-learning facilities that are available on campus and in the wider community. To enhance their participation in oral English lessons, they need to accept that mistakes and errors are a natural part of language learning (Donley, 1998). Further, it is essential for them to identify realistic targets for learning rather than set themselves up to fail (Gregersen & Horwitz, 2002). With achievable term goals, students may gradually become more confident and active in language-learning activities in class. Instead of remaining silent, learners need to actively seek chances to increase the amount of oral English practice and take advantage of opportunities both in and outside class. Lastly, it is beneficial for learners to be well prepared for language lessons. With adequate preparation, their anxiety level should diminish; they may feel more at ease when speaking English and thus become more willing to use the language in a range of situations (Kondo & Yang, 2004). Reticence and anxiety can be overcome.

Finally, it is important to note that if this phenomenon is prevalent among students who have a relatively high level of proficiency in English, as in the present study, one might expect even greater levels of anxiety and reticence at less prestigious universities in China and other non-English-speaking countries. At institutions where students generally have (much) less access and exposure to the language, they may be even less willing to participate in oral English lessons, although this may not always be the case. It is conceivable, for example, that students may be less sensitive to the potential loss of face when speaking English since they are not expected to be highly competent in the language. As competition in these universities is less fierce, they may actually experience lower levels of anxiety and reticence. Investigations in a variety of settings with students who have differing levels of proficiency are urgently needed to better understand this complex phenomenon and offer context-appropriate advice.

References

Bailey, K. M. (1983) Competitiveness and anxiety in adult second language learning: looking at and through the diary studies. In H. W. Seliger & M. H. Long (eds) *Classroom Oriented Research in Second Language Acquisition*. Rowley, MA: Newbury House Publishers, pp. 67–103.

Baker, S. C. & MacIntyre, P. D. (2000) The role of gender and immersion in communication and second language orientations, *Language Learning*, 50, 311–341.

Bond, M. H. (1996) *The Handbook of Chinese Psychology*. Oxford: Oxford University Press.

Burgoon, J. K. (1976) The Unwillingness-to-communicate scale: development and validation, *Communication Monographs*, 43, 60–69.

Chen, T. (2003) Reticence in class and on-line: two ESL students' experiences with communicative language teaching, *System*, 31, 259–281.

Cohen, Y. & Norst, M. J. (1989) Fear, dependence, and loss of self-esteem: affective barriers in second language learning among adults, *RELC Journal: A Journal of Language Teaching and Research in Southeast Asia*, 20, 61–77.

Cortazzi, M. & Jin, L. (1996) Cultures of learning: language classrooms in China. In H. Coleman (ed.) *Society and the Language Classroom*. Cambridge: Cambridge University Press, pp. 169–206.

Donley, P. (1998) Ten ways to cope with foreign language anxiety. In A. Mollica (ed.) *Teaching and Learning Language: Selected Reading from Mosaic.* Welland, ON: Soleil Publishing, pp. 109–110.

Dwyer, E. & Heller-Murphy, A. (1996) Japanese learners in speaking classes, *Edinburgh Working Papers in Applied Linguistics*, 7, 46–55.

Ely, C. M. (1986) An analysis of discomfort, risk-taking, sociability, and motivation in the L2 classroom, *Language Learning*, 36, 1–25.

Gardner, R. C. (1985) *Social Psychology and Second Language Learning: The Role of Attitudes and Motivation.* London: Edward Arnold.

Grbich, C. (2007) *Qualitative Data Analysis.* London: Sage.

Gregersen, T. & Horwitz, E. K. (2002) Language learning and perfectionism: anxious and non-anxious language learners' reactions to their own oral performance, *The Modern Language Journal*, 86, 562–570.

Hilleson, M. (1996) 'I want to talk with them, but I don't want them to hear': an introspective study of second language anxiety in an English-medium school. In K. M. Bailey & D. Nunan (eds) *Voices from the Language Classroom.* Cambridge: Cambridge University Press, pp. 248–282.

Horwitz, E. K. (1995) Student affective reactions and the teaching and learning of foreign languages. *Journal of Educational Research*, 23, 569–652.

Horwitz, E. K., Horwitz, M. & Cope, J. (1986) Foreign language classroom anxiety, *The Modern Language Journal*, 1, 125–132.

Jackson, J. (2002a) Reticence in second language case discussions: anxiety and aspirations, *System*, 30, 65–84.

Jackson, J. (2002b) Diversity and the case leader: linguistic, cultural, psychological and contextual insights, *Journal on Excellence in College Teaching. Special Focus: Issues in Case Method Teaching*, 13(2 & 3), 87–101.

Jackson, J. (2003) Case-based learning and reticence in a bilingual context: perceptions of business students in Hong Kong, *System*, 31, 457–469.

Keaten, J. A. & Kelly, L. (2000) Reticence: an affirmation and revision, *Communication Education*, 49, 165–177.

Kondo, D. S. & Yang, Y. L. (2004) Strategies for coping with language anxiety: the case of students of English in Japan, *ELT Journal*, 58, 258–265.

Liu, M. (2006a) Anxiety in Chinese EFL students at different proficiency levels, *System*, 34, 301–316.

Liu, M. (2006b) Reticence in oral English classrooms: causes and consequences, *Asian Journal of English Language Teaching*, 16, 45–66.

Liu, M. & Jackson, J. (2008) An exploration of Chinese EFL learners' unwillingness to communicate and foreign language anxiety, *The Modern Language Journal*, 92, 71–86.

Liu, N. & Littlewood, W. (1997) Why do many students appear reluctant to participate in classroom learning discourse?, *System*, 25, 371–384.

MacIntyre, P. D. & Gardner, R. C. (1989) Anxiety and second-language learning: toward a theoretical clarification, *Language Learning*, 39, 251–275.

MacIntyre, P. D. & Gardner, R. C. (1991a) Investigating language class anxiety using the focused essay technique, *The Modern Language Journal*, 75, 296–304.

MacIntyre, P. D. & Gardner, R. C. (1991b) Methods and results in the study of anxiety and language learning: a review of the literature, *Language Learning*, 41, 85–117.

MacIntyre, P. D. & Gardner, R. C. (1994) The subtle effects of language anxiety on cognitive processing in the second language, *Language Learning*, 44, 283–305.

Mak, B. S. & White, C. (1997) Communication apprehension of Chinese ESL students, *Hong Kong Journal of Applied Linguistics*, 2, 81–95.

McCroskey, J. C. (1977) Oral communication apprehension: a summary of recent theory and research, *Human Communication Research*, 4, 78–96.

Neuendorf, K. A. (2002) *The Content Analysis: Guidebook*. Thousands Oaks, CA: Sage.

Oxford, R. L. (1999) 'Style wars' as a source of anxiety in language classrooms. In D. J. Young (ed.) *Affect in Foreign Language and Second Language Learning: A Practical Guide to Creating a Low-Anxiety Classroom Atmosphere*. Boston: McGraw-Hill, pp. 216–237.

Pappamihiel, N. E. (2001) Moving from the ESL classroom into the mainstream: an investigation of English language anxiety in Mexican girls, *Bilingual Research Journal*, 25, 31–38.

Phillips, G. M. (1997) Reticence: a perspective on social withdrawal. In J. A. Daly, J. C. McCroskey, J. Ayres, T. Hopf & D. M. Ayres (eds) *Avoiding Communication: Shyness, Reticence, and Communication Apprehension* (2nd edn). Creswill, NJ: Hampton Press, pp. 129–150.

Price, M. L. (1991) The subjective experience of foreign language anxiety: interviews with highly anxious students. In E. K. Horwitz & D. J. Young (eds) *Language Anxiety: From Theory and Research to Classroom Implications*. Englewood Cliffs, NJ: Prentice Hall, pp. 101–108.

Sato, C. J. (1990) Ethnic styles in classroom discourse. In R. C. Scarcella, E. S. Anderson & S. D. Krashen (eds) *Developing Communicative Competence in a Second Language*. Boston: Heinle, pp. 107–119.

Tobias, S. (1979) Anxiety research in educational psychology, *Journal of Educational Psychology*, 71, 573–582.

Tsui, A. B. M. (1996) Reticence and anxiety in second language learning. In K. M. Bailey & D. Nunan (eds) *Voices from the Language Classroom*. Cambridge: Cambridge University Press, pp. 145–167.

Yan, Y. (2003) Language anxiety and the teaching of spoken English, *Journal of Liaoning Technical University*, 5, 73–74.

Young, D. J. (1991) The relationship between anxiety and foreign language oral proficiency ratings. In E. K. Horwitz & D. J. Young (eds) *Language Anxiety: From Theory and Research to Classroom Implications*. Englewood Cliffs, NJ: Prentice Hall, pp. 57–63.

Zou, M. (2004) EFL learners' perceptions of in-class relationships and their voluntary responses. In Y. Gao (ed.) *The Social Psychology of English Learning by Chinese College Students*. Beijing: Foreign Language Teaching and Research Press, pp. 149–167.

6
Intercultural Competence and EFL Teaching in China

Yi Zhou, Shijing Xu and Jonathan Bayley

6.1 Introduction

This chapter is built on the research data of a study with 20 Chinese university teachers of English as a Foreign Language (EFL) regarding their intercultural competence teaching. This work also draws on our own lived experience as former EFL teachers in China and as learners and researchers in Canada (Xu, 2000; Xu & Stevens, 2005; Xu, 2006; Zhou, 2007; Xu & Connelly, 2009). In addition to linguistic competence, it is also necessary for Chinese English teachers and learners to develop intercultural competence, the ability of intercultural understanding and mediation, in order to achieve effective and smooth intercultural and international communication (Corbett, 2003).

Many EFL educators have come to realize that foreign language teaching is expected to promote and facilitate students' acquisition of intercultural competence which allows them to view different cultures from a perspective of informed understanding and prepares them for intercultural encounters (e.g. Byram, 1997; Xu, 2000; Corbett, 2003; Sercu *et al.*, 2005; Xu & Stevens, 2005; Wu, 2006; Y. Wu, 2007; Z. Wu, 2007; Xu & Connelly, 2009). Teaching intercultural competence requires attention to, respect for and an understanding of the dynamic system of values, beliefs and ideologies in both the target and one's home cultures and their influence on the process of individual and social behaviours and interactions (Byram, 1997; Corbett, 2003).

Through a survey questionnaire and follow-up interviews, this research investigated the teacher knowledge among Chinese EFL teachers with a focus on their intercultural competence teaching. Findings from this study will inform teacher educators and researchers in both Chinese and Western institutions and other educational agencies where professional training is offered to Chinese EFL teachers, in order to better accommodate Chinese teachers' needs and help them to promote intercultural competence teaching when planning and conducting their programmes. Knowing Chinese teachers' cultural teaching practices will also inform Western English teachers and curriculum designers about their Chinese students' cultural learning experience in China in order to help overseas Chinese students to achieve successful intercultural communication and adaptation.

6.2   Context and background to the research

6.2.1   Our stories

This study was originated from Yi Zhou's personal and professional cross-cultural experience of moving from China to Canada. Yi was a Chinese university teacher of English from 2001 to 2004, during which time she was not aware of the importance of cultural competence. She expected no difficulties in her communication with Canadians upon her arrival in Canada in 2004. However, Yi soon found that well-developed language skills alone did not guarantee effective and successful intercultural understanding and communication.

For instance, Yi and a white English-speaking Canadian friend, Jack, had difficulty in communicating over a discussion of the death of a family member. Yi said that when her grandfather was diagnosed with cancer the diagnosis was withheld from him. Jack, on the other hand, said that when his father was diagnosed with cancer he was fully informed by the doctor and the family. The different ways in which this fundamental life problem was handled generated a discussion between Yi and Jack and reveals underlying values that influence practices. In this situation it seemed that expressing truth and showing care for others were conflicting cultural values in relation to death, which itself can be a topic which is treated quite differently in talk between different cultures and even within Chinese and Canadian cultures. The cultural value expressed in Yi's story is not necessarily unique to the Chinese. It is, however, important in Chinese culture in which people believe that one's physical wellbeing depends heavily on one's emotional and spiritual wellbeing. Jack, on the other hand, interpreted the situation from the point of view of a human rights-based society in which an individual has the right to know the truth.

Ultimately Yi realized that her thinking and language expression were embedded in her cultural values. Experiences such as this led her to undertake the study of the cultural dimension of EFL education that had been largely missing in her teaching and learning experience.

In China, a large body of literature has discussed intercultural communication and (inter)cultural competence from a theoretical and pedagogical perspective (Chen, 2000; Lin, 2006; Zhang, 2006; Pan, 2007; Xiao, 2007; Yang & Zhuang, 2007; Wang, 2008); however, few researchers have conducted empirical studies regarding (inter)cultural competence teaching and learning. There have been many studies on intercultural learning experiences of Chinese students in British, North American and New Zealand universities (e.g. Holmes, 2005; Wang & Falconer, 2005; Spencer-Oatey & Xiong, 2006; Gu & Maley, 2008). These studies mainly aimed to explore Chinese students' intercultural experiences and their social and academic challenges in adapting to a new country and educational system, in order to improve the intercultural learning experiences of Chinese students in Western institutions. They also provided useful information for the universities to offer appropriate support and programmes to assist Chinese students in terms of academic and intercultural adaptation. In her research in Canada, Yi Zhou (2007) identified issues related to language-learning experiences and motivation in an intercultural context involving Chinese learners. Shijing Xu (2000) examined issues of English teaching for non-English major students from the perspectives of Chinese visiting scholars in Toronto. She identified the importance of intercultural competence in international communications as well as in EFL teacher education (Xu & Stevens, 2005; Xu & Connelly, 2009). Her work with Chinese newcomer families in Toronto reveals different ways of knowing and being among people of different cultural traditions (Xu, 2006).

Our work in this study returns to the EFL context in China where overseas Chinese learners come from.

6.2.2   Research context

With the increasing interconnectivity among people from different linguistic and cultural backgrounds in the context of globalization, many researchers have called for communicative competence (a primary goal of language education for more than two decades) to be broadened to include the notion of intercultural competence (Damen, 1987; Byram, 1997; Wen, 2004; Sercu *et al.*, 2005; Fantini, 2006). Intercultural competence requires not only the development of socio-cultural competence (as a part of communicative competence), which refers to the knowledge and familiarity with the socio-cultural context in which native speakers use the target language (van Ek, 1986; Byram, 1997), but also emphasizes an equally important ability of intercultural understanding and mediation (Corbett, 2003). According to Byram (1997), intercultural competence allows individuals to act as a mediator between their home culture and target cultures. It represents the psychological readiness and willingness to seek out opportunities to interact with people from the target community, explore the target culture and make necessary changes to prepare for intercultural encounters.

Compared to previous decades, Chinese people engage in more face-to-face interactions with people from different cultural backgrounds and English serves as the dominant medium for such interactions. In recent years, Chinese EFL educators have considered more seriously the role culture plays in foreign language learning to address the need to integrate cultural dimensions into English classrooms (Wen, 2004; Lin, 2006; Zhang, 2006; Pan, 2007; Xiao, 2007; Yang & Zhuang, 2007; Wang & Liu, 2008). EFL teaching objectives, as outlined in China's national *College English Curriculum Requirements* (for non-English major programmes in all universities and colleges), include an enhancement of students' cultural competence to help China's development and international communication (Ministry of Education, 2007). Intercultural competence teaching has started to gain attention from Chinese university EFL teachers and researchers as an initiative (Liang, 2008; Wang & Liu, 2008).

The drive for us to conduct this study is to gain an insight into teachers' existing perceptions and practices of cultural teaching and hence to understand how to prepare teachers for this initiative in their professional development.

6.3   Research focus

6.3.1   Research questions

Empirical data were collected and analysed to answer the following research questions:

1   What are Chinese university EFL teachers' perceptions of cultural teaching?
2   What are Chinese university EFL teachers' cultural teaching practices?
3   To what extent can their perceptions and teaching practices be characterized as intercultural competence teaching?

This study aimed to inform teacher educators and researchers in both Chinese and Western institutions and other educational agencies where professional training is offered to Chinese EFL teachers, in order to better accommodate Chinese teachers' needs and help them to promote intercultural competence teaching in their programmes. Knowing Chinese teachers' cultural teaching practices will also inform Western teachers and curriculum designers about their Chinese students' cultural learning experience in China in order to help overseas Chinese students to achieve successful intercultural communication and adaptation. This study was conducted in China, but we hope it will help teacher educators and researchers in other contexts.

6.3.2   Research design

For this study, we employed a design of mixed methods shaped in a narrative inquiry framework. Narrative inquiry is a very recent addition to the social science research literature first introduced in 1990 (Connelly & Clandinin, 1990). Since then the field has expanded rapidly and is found in virtually all social science and humanity disciplines (Riessman & Speedy, 2007) as reflected in a recent *Handbook of Narrative Inquiry* (Clandinin, 2007). Because of this rapid development there are many forms of narrative inquiry (Polkinghorne, 1995; Mishler, 1999; Pinnegar & Daynes, 2007). The research described herein follows narrative inquiry shaped by Connelly and Clandinin (Clandinin & Connelly, 2000; Connelly & Xu, 2008). In this view, narrative inquiry is a way of thinking about experience. It has phenomenological qualities in that what is studied is life experience; and it is methodological in that narrative inquiry is a way of studying experience. It is both method and phenomena, and, at bottom, is a way of thinking. Philosophically, the work draws heavily on Dewey (1932, 1938). One of the principal lines of educational research using this framework is on teacher knowledge in which a distinction is made between *knowledge for teachers* and *teacher knowledge* (Connelly & Clandinin, 1995; Xu & Connelly, 2008). *Teacher knowledge* refers to the things that a teacher knows by way of their experience (Elbaz, 1983). Briefly put, a teacher's experience represents a historical personal and cultural expression rather than an indication of liquid or inadequate knowledge for the situation (Xu & Connelly, 2008).

In recent years, narrative inquiry has been increasingly employed in cross-cultural teacher education and development research (e.g. Xu & Stevens, 2005; Yang, 2007; Barkhuizen & Wette, 2008; Xu & Connelly, 2009). A narrative approach allows us to 'hear teachers' voices and begin to understand their culture from the inside' (Cortazzi, 1993: 1); and learn from their lived experience in order to examine the 'representations and explanations of experience' (1993: 2) and the way they make meanings out of it. In this study, we begin with one of the researchers' lived stories of intercultural experience and later share more stories of participating teachers' intercultural experience. A teacher's opinion or behaviour might be judged as good or bad, competent or incompetent, from a *knowledge-for-teachers* point of view, but from a narrative *teacher-knowledge* point of view, the teacher's opinion or behaviour would be seen as an expression of his or her experience with its past, present and future, and a judgement of adequacy would not be made (Xu & Connelly, 2008).

Quantitative data were first collected through a survey questionnaire. The questionnaire consists of three sections: the first obtained partici-pants' demographic information, including overseas experiences; the second explored participants' perceptions of cultural teaching and their self-reported cultural teaching practices, guided by Sercu *et al.*'s (2005) survey instrument with Likert-scale questions; the third measured participants' intercultural competence using a modified version of Fantini's (2006) Assessment of Intercultural Competence (AIC).

Qualitative data were used to gain a more in-depth understanding of Chinese EFL teachers' cultural teaching experience; these were generated from follow-up email responses and phone interviews. We attempted to develop a narrative understanding of Chinese EFL teachers' experience using narrative inquiry as a method for con-structing meaning out of people's lived experience and personal growth (Connelly & Clandinin, 1990).

Cortazzi and Jin (2006) proposed a framework of socio-cultural issues in narrative data collection and interpretation in cross-cultural research. They argued that context is necessary in order for the audience to understand cross-cultural narrative. In this study, two of the research-ers have cross-cultural learning and teaching experience and both participated in narrative data collection and analysis process, which allows them to identify and provide 'sufficient contextual and back-ground information' of the narrative (Cortazzi & Jin, 2006: 42) in order for a Western audience to understand the socio-cultural issues involved in Chinese EFL education.

6.3.3   Participants

The survey involved 20 EFL teachers from different universities in China, who were attending a summer programme in Beijing in 2009 to prepare them for doctoral programmes in universities outside China. Based on the preliminary data analysis of the survey, we developed six follow-up questions in Chinese and sent them to the participants by email. We also asked in the email if they would like to participate in our follow-up interviews. It is not very common for Chinese EFL teachers, especially senior teachers, to conduct or participate in empirical research studies. We assumed that some teachers might not be comfortable with interviews. Therefore, we gave them the option to respond to our questions by email and to make it clear whether they would mind us following up with them in a phone interview. Seven teachers emailed us their responses to our interview questions and three of them indicated that they would like us to follow up with them over a phone interview. Though the number of participants is small, they are well qualified: all hold a master's degree and have an average of ten years' teaching experience.

We conducted a three-way phone interview in Chinese with three email respondents individually, with Yi in Hamilton, Shijing in Windsor and each participant in a different university in China. The three interviewees also had visited an English-speaking country as a visiting scholar for 3 to 12 months. Yi and Shijing are also participants in the study and interviewed each other with the same set of interview protocol. During the phone interviews, we drew on our own lived experiences in China and Canada as we discussed with the participants issues of our shared interest.

6.4   Results

6.4.1   Quantitative data

The Statistical Package for Social Sciences (SPSS) was used to analyse survey data.

6.4.1.1   Demographic information

Among the 20 participating teachers, 13 are female and 7 are male (see Table 6.1). The majority (84.2%) of them are between 31–40 years old. They all hold a master's degree. On average, they have been teaching EFL for nearly ten years and teach 11–13 hours per week. Teachers reported that the average number of students in their class is 41–50. Thirty-five per cent of the teachers have been to another country and the average time of stay is five months. Eight of them teach English major courses, six teach College English courses (a two-year undergraduate English course compulsory for all non-English major students at Chinese universities and colleges) and six teach both.

6.4.1.2   Teachers' perceptions of cultural teaching

Teachers' perceptions of cultural teaching were assessed in terms of their beliefs about the objectives of EFL teaching and their understanding of

Table 6.1 Demographic information *n = 20*

Gender	13 female
	7 male
Age	31–40 years old (majority)
Degree	Master's degree
Teaching experience	10 years +
Teaching load	11–13 hours per week
No. of students	41–50 per class
Overseas experience	35% of participants
Length of time	5 months, average
Courses taught	
College English	6 participants
English major	8 participants
Both	6 participants

specific aspects and issues about cultural teaching. Six objectives for EFL teaching were listed which reflect the teaching objectives required by China's national *College English Curriculum Requirements* (for non-English major programmes in all universities and colleges) (Ministry of Education, 2007). Participants were asked to indicate the degree to which they believed the objectives were important on a four-point Likert scale from *Not important* to *Very important*. The six objectives can be categorized into three groups: linguistic objectives, cultural objectives and other objectives (see Table 6.2). The objectives are ranked according to the mean which is based on participants' responses. Collectively, linguistic objectives rank higher than other objectives. However, teachers consider 'Foster students' interest in English learning and their self-learning ability' to be the most important objective for EFL teaching. In terms of cultural objectives, teachers rank 'Promote students' interest in and understanding of English cultures' as important as the two linguistic objectives.

Among the demographic factors, only teachers' years of teaching experience is found correlated with the mean score of the six objectives of EFL education ($r = .462, p < .5$). Teachers with more years of teaching experience tend to give higher scores on the importance of the objectives.

Participating teachers were asked to indicate their attitudes towards six statements about cultural teaching on a seven-point Likert scale from *Strongly disagree* to *Strongly agree* (see Table 6.3). They are positive towards the integration of English language and cultures of English-speaking countries. They somewhat disagree that poor language skill is the major cause of misunderstandings in intercultural communication

Table 6.2 Teachers' beliefs about the objectives of EFL education *n* = 20

Item	Range			
	Not important 1	Somewhat important 2	Important 3	Very important 4
			Mean	Rank
Linguistic objectives				
1 Help students to acquire listening and speaking skills in English for effective oral communication			3.37	2
2 Help students to acquire reading and writing skills			3.37	2
Cultural objectives				
3 Promote students' interest in and understanding of English cultures			3.37	2
4 Help students to develop ability to communicate with people from other cultural backgrounds			3.21	5
Other objectives				
5 Foster students' interest in English learning and their self-learning ability			3.58	1
6 Help students to pass College English Test (CET) 4			2.39	6

(*M* = 3.84). Teachers also indicate that both English and Chinese cultures should be included in EFL teaching (*M* = 5.89). Teachers are positive towards the statement 'English teachers should generally present a positive image of English culture and society' (*M* = 4.68). Teachers indicate their support for cultural teaching as reflected in their responses to items five and six.

6.4.1.3 *Teachers' cultural teaching practices*

Teachers' cultural teaching practices were explored through the content of their teaching (the frequency that English and Chinese cultural topics are addressed in class) as well as cultural teaching pedagogies (the frequency that teaching activities and practices are employed). Teachers were required to indicate the frequency on a four-point Likert scale from *Never* to *Always*.

Seventeen topics related to English culture were listed; they include the arts, customs, political system, different social groups, conventions of communication, etc. The frequency of teachers addressing these topics is low with an overall mean score between *Seldom* to *Sometimes* (*M* = 2.68),

Table 6.3 Teachers' attitudes towards cultural teaching *n* = 20

Item	Range							Mean
	Strongly disagree 1	Disagree 2	Somewhat disagree 3	Neutral 4	Somewhat agree 5	Agree 6	Strongly agree 7	
1. Based on your experience, English language and cultures can be taught in an integrated way								5.84
2. Poor language skill is the major cause of misunderstandings in communication between Chinese and people from other countries								3.84
3. English teaching should touch upon both English and Chinese culture in order to help students to mediate between the two in communications								5.89
4. English teachers should generally present a positive image of English culture and society								4.68
5. I would like to teach about English cultures in my class								5.84
6. Besides English cultures, English teachers should also touch upon cultures of other countries								5.31

which suggests that cultural teaching might not be a regular focus of their teaching (assuming that the topics are reasonably representative). Seven topics related to Chinese culture were listed, such as customs, different ethnic groups, people's values and beliefs, etc. The frequency of teachers addressing these topics is similarly low.

Teachers indicated how frequently they apply eight cultural teaching activities and practices in their teaching (see Table 6.4). The overall average score for these activities is relatively low ($M = 2.93$). This again suggests that cultural teaching might not be an integral component of the teaching in the participating teachers' classes. The items are ranked according to the mean which is based on participants' responses.

The frequency of applying cultural teaching activities and touching upon topics related to English culture are positively correlated with each other ($r = .490$, $p < .5$). How frequently teachers address cultural contents is consistent with how often they employ cultural teaching activities. The frequency of applying cultural teaching activities is also positively correlated with their attitude towards the EFL teaching

Table 6.4   Teachers' cultural teaching activities and practices $n = 20$

Item	Range			
	Never 1	Seldom 2	Sometimes 3	Always 4
			Mean	Rank
1. I ask students to present a particular cultural topic			2.67	7
2. I introduce to students what they should know about a topic			3.17	2
3. I divide students into pairs or small groups to discuss a topic			3.39	1
4. I ask students to participate in role-play situations in which people from English-speaking countries communicate			2.83	5
5. In written assignments, I ask students to discuss a particular cultural perspective or event			2.53	8
6. I use technology to illustrate a cultural topic (e.g. videos, CD-ROMs, PowerPoint and the Internet, etc.)			3.06	3
7. I engage students in a debate regarding a controversial cultural issue			2.78	6
8. I ask students to compare Chinese and English culture regarding a particular topic			3.00	4
Overall average			*2.93*	

objective to 'Help students to develop ability to communicate with people from other cultural backgrounds' ($r = .466, p < .5$). Teachers who believe this objective is more important as compared to their peers tend to employ more cultural teaching activities.

6.4.1.4 *Teachers' intercultural competence*

Fantini's (2006) Assessment of Intercultural Competence (AIC) measures intercultural competence quantitatively and it has achieved both validity and reliability (Fantini, 2006). AIC was modified to fit this study. In total, the modified AIC contains 20 six-point Likert-scale items. Participants were asked to indicate their ability or opinion towards each item from *Not at all* to *Very high*.

Teachers' average AIC score, namely their intercultural competence, is 4.35, which is just beyond *Average* on the six-point Likert scale. Demographic factors are not found to have an influence on their AIC score. Teachers' intercultural competence positively correlates with how frequently they apply cultural teaching activities ($r = .626, p < .5$) and address topics related to English culture ($r = .478, p < .5$). Teachers with a higher level of intercultural competence tend to conduct cultural teaching practices more frequently.

6.4.2 Qualitative data

Based on the quantitative data analysis, we generated six key questions to ask our participants to use specific examples or stories to respond more in detail to the questions we had asked in the questionnaire. The designations of CT with numbers are pseudonyms used to identify our email respondents. Built on the email correspondence, we conducted a phone interview, in which we had a conversational and in-depth discussion with CT2, CT6 and CT7 individually over the key questions derived from the quantitative and email responses. The main themes that emerge from the qualitative data are as follows: teachers' perceptions of culture, communication and cultural teaching, teachers' cultural teaching practices, the integration of cultural teaching and teachers' professional development. The quantitative data on cultural knowledge and teaching, particularly as found in Tables 6.2, 6.3 and 6.4, are enriched and given in-depth meaning by the specific examples given or stories shared during the conversations. As in much narrative inquiry, stories generate stories and there is a rich development of thought as participants speak with one another, hear and resonate in each other's stories, and relate to their own (Connelly & Clandinin, 1988; Conle, 1996). One of the purposes of the interviews, and the follow-up stories, is to find out why people give certain numerical ratings found in the survey and the tabulated data. The combination of the quantitative and qualitative data hence results in heightened validity.

6.4.2.1   *Perceptions of culture and communication*

The interview methodology was structured in such a way that discussion revolved around specific topics that emerged in the quantitative data. For instance, in her email response to our request for specific examples to reveal how she rated the importance of cultural teaching in EFL, CT3 used a story of her friend who was invited to a potluck party and was told to 'bring your plate'. Her friend brought an empty plate to the party only to find that other guests all brought their dishes of food. She learned to understand that in English culture, 'bring your plate' to a potluck party means 'bring your dish of prepared food'.

CT2 shared a story, in his email response, about his first contact with Western culture. When he was a visiting scholar in a North American city, he found a cellphone and informed the owner to pick it up. Before he returned the cellphone to its owner, he asked the person what she knew about the cellphone in terms of its colour and brand name to make sure that she was indeed the owner. The woman was very upset. CT2 was puzzled why the woman was angry rather than grateful when he returned her lost cellphone. He reflected that in Chinese culture responsibilities are valued; in a Western culture, trust is more important in this context.

Shijing, following CT2's story in his email response, began the phone interview with him by sharing her initial contact with Mary, her first Canadian landlady. Shijing always offered to share her homemade meal when Mary arrived home. At first, Mary was very pleased to take the offer, but became annoyed after one week. After a two-hour conversation, Shijing and Mary understood the cultural differences that existed between them: in Chinese culture, it is rude not to offer your food to others around you before you eat and it is a customary courtesy understood among Chinese people that the offer can be declined. In Canadian culture, people mostly value self-independence, which makes them uncomfortable in face of too much care from others.

The narrative approach adopted in this research allowed us, then, to engage in such conversations with the participating teachers to listen to their voices. It is crucial for the purpose of this inquiry to understand the teachers' perceptions and their understandings without intervention and criticism by us as researchers. In this way they are able to participate in and think through this inquiry to understand the role of language and culture in the building of cross-cultural understanding.

In the conversational interviews with our participants, the process of sharing our own cross-cultural experiences raised the topic that people's values, thoughts and behaviours are culturally embedded. In our discussion, cultural differences were perceived not as being right or wrong, but as being different. Participants found that people are not always aware of their beliefs, mindsets and behaviours which have been shaped by their individual cultural experience. All cultures share certain values such as hospitality and independence although they may be enacted in different ways. It is through such intercultural experience that teachers came to realize that cultural teaching would bring such awareness and get learners to think about and reflect on their own customs and values.

CT7 and CT6 each talked about their respective teaching situations. Their students have little opportunity in intercultural communication. In their opinions, the major obstacle and cause of misunderstanding in intercultural communication for Chinese students are a lack of language proficiency. For instance, CT7 said:

> To a large extent, especially in China, if they [students] communicate [with foreigners], they are afraid of not being able to understand and speak it. It seems that they do not worry about the cultural perspective involved. (CT7 Interview data)

CT2, however, held a different view:

> They [researchers and policy-makers] have a biased understanding of communication; communication does not have to be oral only ... Writing a letter can be communication; email is communication. (CT2)

Yi added:

> It also includes reading. Actually, when you read an English article, even though you are not interacting with people, this is also a kind of communication. (CT2 Interview data)

6.4.2.2 *Perceptions of cultural teaching*

In the research process, participating teachers indicated their view about cultural teaching objectives and the cultural image they usually present to students.

CT4, CT7 and CT2 stated that, in their opinions, the purpose of cultural teaching is to foster students' knowledge about and understanding of the target culture, nurture their minds for critical and open-minded thinking, enhance divergent perspectives of thinking and facilitate communication. They emphasize to their students the importance of learning the target culture and the impact it has on the development of their understanding of both the target language and the culture. For instance, CT7 said, 'I always tell this to my students' (Interview data CT7).

In another interview, Shijing used a *window* metaphor to describe how cultural teaching can encourage the exchange of information: Chinese people can learn about the outside world through the window of culture and introduce China and Chinese culture to the outside.

We asked CT7 and CT6 what Western cultural image they presented to their students in their teaching. They said that they mostly present a positive image of Western cultures and society. Students spend most of their time understanding and learning Western cultures, values and views, which in CT6's words, 'it seems that we spend most of the time learning from the West'. According to their observations, students are not able to critically think and evaluate Western cultures and lack critical thinking in cultural learning. Some tend to admire and even worship Western cultures without reflection; for instance, students often follow Western pop culture and celebrate Western holidays even though they may not know their origins. This is partly because reflection on Chinese cultures is rarely developed in English classes so students lack a critical framework of cultural concepts for comparison and are not used to making cultural behaviours and values explicit for discussion and reflection.

In our interview with CT2, we talked about the sense of inferiority Chinese people tend to have in intercultural and international communications with Western people on various social levels and discussed the cause of such phenomena from a historical perspective. Regarding how foreign language education could help change the situation, CT2 stated:

> As a teacher, I think it is our responsibility and obligation to guide students towards this direction. I mean, you cannot say because you teach a foreign language and you should exaggerate the good side of foreign countries and ask students to accept those good stuff. It is also our necessary responsibility to warn students against the negative side of foreign countries. (CT2 Interview data)

In his teaching, CT2 believes that he discussed both positive and negative sides of foreign cultures and presented foreign social and cultural contexts to students in an objective manner. His teaching was based on a comprehensive analysis of what the media presented in both China and abroad.

6.4.2.3 Cultural teaching practices

In the research process, participants described how and what cultural teaching is carried out in their English classes. In this section we present the contents and pedagogies of their cultural teaching.

CT6 and CT7 said in their interviews that decisions on what culture to teach depend on their expertise, personal preference, the connection with the textbook and perceived students' interests in cultural learning. The content of their teaching is, as CT7 described, 'not very systematic', and they each are able to cover some 'shallow knowledge' about English cultures, for instance customs, holidays, TV programmes, and different religious beliefs and traditions. It is partly due to the fact that English textbooks published in China traditionally included very few materials or activities designed to explicitly raise learners' intercultural understanding. Only a few textbooks since around 2005 have begun to do this and even fewer do this systematically.

Though most participating teachers indicated that consideration of Chinese culture should be included in EFL teaching, CT6 and CT7 pointed out that limited course hours restrict them from including the teaching of Chinese culture in their English classes. The shortage of time implies an add-on view of cultural teaching rather than an aspect of communication that has to be integrated into language teaching as a way of using existing time differently.

In their teaching, Chinese culture is dealt with only when they need to compare some cultural issues or perspectives between Chinese and Western cultures. They spoke of 'they' vs 'we' referring to Chinese and foreign cultures. People within a culture are perceived as a homogeneous group. CT6 stated the following:

> Yes, there is no comparison [between Chinese and Western cultures]. Only when a teacher recognizes that there is a need for students to think about the [cultural] difference or make comparison between East and West, he [or she] may add in. Otherwise, Chinese culture should not be included. (CT6 Interview data)

This we–they binary division in Chinese EFL teaching practice reveals the views held in the East and West dichotomy in which the West, or China, is perceived as culturally homogeneous, rather than more realistic, multidimensional and multicultural societies with greatly diverse populations and different ways of living. In the discussion section, we will discuss the importance of challenging such East and West dichotomy in EFL classrooms to bring forward critical thinking and cultural awareness among Chinese EFL learners.

Reflecting on her lived experience abroad, Yi stated that how people from foreign cultures see Chinese culture and people should also be included in EFL teaching. Yi sees Chinese EFL education as being still East to West, unidirectional in cultural teaching.

In our discussion about teaching non-English cultures in EFL classes in China, CT2 described how he engaged his students, discussing the difference between Chinese and Japanese businessmen in their negotiation styles. CT6 believes, however, that it is too large a topic for EFL teachers to teach non-English cultures. She said that her teaching does not involve much about the cultures of non-English-speaking countries and the textbook does not include much information on this aspect, either.

This raises questions for EFL teacher educators when it comes to the issues of the role of EFL teachers and the role of English in this more and more globalized world. Teachers assume that their role is to teach cultural content rather than to raise widely applicable cultural issues through selected examples; and that English is learned in relation to targeted English-speaking countries, rather than the current view that English is used globally, often between 'non-native' speakers. The broader current view would imply the inclusion of cultural situations involving 'non-English' cultures.

From our conversations with the interviewed teachers, we know that they often 'introduce' students to and 'tell' them about cultural knowledge as well as their own understanding of cultural issues. With the constraints that many EFL teachers do not have direct lived experience in English-speaking countries, culture is often perceived as knowledge rather than behaviours or values and ways of interpreting experience in their English teaching. Cultural teaching therefore appears to be transmission of knowledge, rather than giving students direct or vicarious experience. Cultural teaching tends to stay at a superficial and introductory level, even after several years' learning of English or in more advanced language levels.

With EFL teachers who have visited English-speaking countries, students are engaged in activities which involve discussions of cultural topics. For instance, in CT7's class, her students are asked to do individual presentations. Some students pick culture-related topics, such as introducing an American movie. She once involved her students in a discussion about whether to forgive the killer in a campus shooting incident in a North American city that she visited. In the discussion, most students were unable to make sense of why some local people actually went to the killer's funeral. With her cross-cultural lived experience, she was able to engage her students in discussion like this to help develop a range of language and thinking skills simultaneously with intercultural awareness and understanding.

In CT2's class, cultural issues are discussed more frequently. For instance, he once asked his students to propose a new civilization by projecting in a thousand years' time. With open-ended questions, he engaged his students in discussing the issues of what social groups would still exist in the new civilization in one thousand years and did not provide any conclusion. CT2 explained:

> From the cultural perspective, it is all right as long as they [students] think, analyse, and judge. I cannot make a conclusion about an issue ... I hope to engage my students in critical thinking. (CT2 Interview data)

6.4.2.4 *Integration of cultural teaching*

The participating teachers talked about, in email responses and interviews, the proportion of cultural teaching in their English classes and the factors that constrain them from integrating more cultural teaching practice.

Teachers indicated that cultural teaching is important in EFL teaching and that more teaching time should be allocated to it. In their opinions, the amount of cultural teaching that should be involved in an EFL class depends on the development of students' English proficiency. Language levels are perceived as somehow correlated with cultural learning, and English proficiency is a prerequisite for cultural learning. This again implies the same perception discussed earlier, that is, that many EFL teachers see language and culture as separate rather than embedded. Such a perception, along with the practical constraints in EFL contexts, has prevented many Chinese EFL learners from reaching the English level needed in real-life communication as English language teaching has been focused on the linguistic competence of language only.

Limited class time and the test-oriented system are the main constraints for integrating cultural content in language teaching. CT5, CT1 and CT2 indicated in their email responses that although cultural teaching should reach 30 to 40% of EFL teaching, it often does not. CT1 said he gave no more than five minutes to cultural teaching in each class. The constraints for cultural teaching indicated by the teachers are as follows:

First, students have a heavy work load on language learning and their drive to pass language exams overrides their motivation to cultural learning and hence teachers are forced to spend most of the time on language teaching. Second, teachers have to follow the EFL syllabus which focuses mainly on the linguistic dimension of language teaching. Third, teachers feel that they lack the knowledge for cultural teaching. They believe that EFL teachers need to have a true, in-depth and comprehensive understanding of the target culture in order to conduct effective cultural teaching. Most EFL teachers do not have overseas living or working experience and their primary source of cultural knowledge is gained from reading books.

Such constraints have set up a vicious circle in which raising culture awareness is viewed as an add-on that requires extra time, rather than an integral element of language which will necessarily be engaged in whatever time is available, and teachers presume that their classes cannot really engage in cultural learning at higher levels because they lack experience and knowledge. This raises critical issues for EFL teacher educators as to how to prepare and help EFL teachers to go beyond these obstacles to integrate culture in English teaching.

6.4.2.5 Teacher development

Three of the interviewed respondents happen to have overseas experience in an English-speaking country. We shared our own cross-cultural and intercultural experiences and talked about how our perceptions and practices of EFL teaching, cultural teaching in particular, have changed. CT7 and CT2 said that prior to their overseas experience they felt a lack of confidence about their cultural knowledge and understanding. They indicated that they became more confident with cultural teaching after experiencing the target culture in person. For instance, CT2 said:

> I have more understanding towards cultural teaching than before. I did not have a deep experience regarding this before going abroad. I had a general knowledge about what the foreigners would be like. But now, I would explain more [to students] and spend a bit more class time [on cultural teaching] when a text has culture-related topics. (CT2 Interview data)

Yi described how she perceived Western people as being more or less the same when she was in China and what individual differences she noticed after she came to Canada. Yi attributed this to the stereotypical way of teaching Western cultures in our EFL classes. Shijing pointed out the same problem in the West; for instance, their perceptions and understandings of China are very stereotyped. Hence, it is important to keep in mind the overgeneralization of different cultures in Western terms and categories that tend to reinforce the stereotyped and biased view of other parts of the world. Yi found that direct communication and interaction among people of different cultures in Canada helped her to develop an understanding of the concept of culture from a simplistic view to one with multi-layered perspectives.

Apart from what teachers can learn from their overseas experience, professional development is also seen in their day-to-day lived experience of teaching and learning. For instance, CT2 explained how he made an effort to gain an in-depth understanding of culture and cultural teaching. For CT2, deep thinking and reflection are the key in the development of his cultural competence and teaching:

> I have the habit of deep thinking. When a social phenomenon, or something related to Western cultures, comes out, I would reflect on the reason why it would be like this ... So when I teach students, my ideas do not come from nowhere but have their historical evidence. (CT2 Interview data)

6.5 Discussion

Our study used both quantitative and qualitative data to explore to what extent Chinese EFL teachers' perceptions and practices of cultural teaching reflect an intercultural perspective. As researchers, we also participated in the study as one of our research strategies. With both outside perspectives as researchers and inside perspectives as participants we will discuss the insights we have gained from this study about cultural teaching in China.

6.5.1 Teachers' perceptions

In our interviews, the notion of cultural difference is approached from an intercultural perspective. Ethnorelativism is reflected in some participants' perceptions of cultural difference but other comments show an 'us–them' ethnocentrism. 'Fundamental to ethnorelativism is the assumption that cultures can only be understood relative to one another and that particular behaviour can only be understood within a cultural context' (Bennett, 1993: 46). Some of the participants perceive intercultural communication as direct interaction (including oral and written form) with foreigners, while others believe that for many Chinese students, who may never get a chance to have communication with people from other cultures, intercultural communication implies indirect vicarious interactions with other cultures through multimedia such as books, magazines, newspapers, movies, TV programmes and the Internet, etc. (Byram, 1997). EFL teachers' understanding of a broad notion of intercultural communication, integrated into concepts of language development, would help enrich their understanding of the nature, significance and objectives of cultural teaching.

The participants emphasize fostering students' ability of understanding and interpreting the target cultures and also recognize the 'interactive' perspective of cultural understanding and interpreting between one's home and target cultures. What are also recognized are students' needs to have an understanding of the target people's culturally determined values and behaviours, which has been generally regarded as an essential objective for intercultural language teaching (Byram, 1997; Knutson, 2006). What participants fail to perceive is that cultural teaching also needs to inform students that the notion of culturally determined values and behaviours also applies to their home cultural identity. Students need to be aware of their culturally constructed self, that is, to develop their social and cultural self-awareness (Byram, 1997; Knutson, 2006). An important objective of intercultural competence teaching is to see both target and home cultures from an informed understanding (Byram, 1997), thus developing an intercultural understanding and awareness (Byram, 1997; Fantini, 2006).

6.5.2 Cultural teaching practice

This section discusses the contents and pedagogies of participants' cultural teaching and issues that emerged in their teaching practice.

We learn from both the quantitative and the qualitative data that participants recognize the importance of cultural teaching and make attempts to help develop students' ability of intercultural understanding. However, cultural teaching has not been a regular focus of EFL teaching, and most of the time teachers focus on the traditional way of cultural teaching – transmitting to their students some superficial and introductory cultural knowledge, often as an add-on element. This is understandable given the fact that most Chinese EFL teachers lack training in cultural study and do not have overseas experience. It is difficult for them to have an in-depth and comprehensive understanding of the target cultures. In such cases, introducing some simple and superficial cultural knowledge seems to be an easy solution. This is not just a problem for Chinese EFL teaching, since many English textbooks for French learners mainly include such 'vital but superficial' contents (Fries, n.d.: 4). Language teachers only scratch the surface level of cultural teaching, which multicultural educators deride as the Four Fs: food, fashion, festivals and folklore (Banks, 2002). Culture is a dynamic system that changes over time and it is meaningful for students to acquire the skills and strategies to learn a culture or adapt to these changes rather than merely learning static factual knowledge (Damen, 1987; Knutson, 2006). Byram (1997) proposes that intercultural competence encompasses skills to learn new knowledge of a culture.

Monoculturalism holds the notion that cultural teaching is to promote language learners' ability to understand and use the target language in appropriate ways perceived by native-language speakers (Phillipson, 1992; Kumaravadivelu, 2003). In this study, participants' cultural teaching practice tends to be monocultural: teachers mainly focus on developing students' understanding of English cultures, which is closely associated with their perceived cultural teaching objectives. Consequently, Chinese English learners' voices and their native cultural identity are marginalized (Kumaravadivelu, 2003) and Chinese university EFL learners have been found to have a limited knowledge and understanding of their native culture (Shi & Wang, 2001; Han, 2002). Shijing Xu pointed out in the interview that Chinese EFL learners need to regain their lost Chinese identity in face of the impact of Westernization, and EFL teaching should help to achieve this goal. Teachers could assist students to perceive themselves as culturally determined and individually framed and understand their home culture from 'an "external" perspective' (Larzén-Östermark, 2008: 527), which will help foster students' intercultural understanding and interpreting of both the home and the target cultures.

In this study, both quantitative and qualitative data indicate that teachers mostly touch upon the positive side of Western countries and present to students a positive image of their cultures. Some cultural issues are oversimplified, which may consequently lead to stereotypes and reinforce students' blind admiration and even worship of Western cultures. Shijing Xu and CT2 recognize the need for EFL teachers to touch upon both positive and negative sides of Western cultures. Shijing discusses the ideological impact of colonialism and neocolonialism and points out that Chinese people as a whole tend to perceive Western cultures as superior and advanced; and hence Chinese EFL educators need to help change biased perceptions and help Chinese learners to recover and reconstruct their own identity through intercultural competence teaching.

What may also contribute to students' stereotypes is the 'we' vs 'they' binary division. It is suggested that teachers remind students not to oversimplify culturally determined beliefs and behaviours and to be aware of the existence of variations among members of a culture (Fries, n.d.). Special attention could be given to the differences between social, racial and regional groups as subcultures within both the home and the target cultures. Teachers could lead students to consider their impression and expectation about cultural beliefs, behaviours and issues in their home and the target cultures, and prepare them to suspend and modify their stereotypes or disbeliefs if the reality does not meet their expectations (Byram, 1997; Fries, n.d.). This implication also applies to teacher education in multicultural settings (Xu *et al.*, 2007; Xu, 2010; Xu & Connelly, 2010).

6.5.3   Teacher knowledge

The participating teachers in this study believe that cultural teaching is equally important and should be given more attention, though they are not often able to do this in practice. Teachers believe that language and its culture can be taught in an integrated way, though it is apparent that few do this. However, in reality, cultural teaching sometimes has to give way to linguistic teaching in order to satisfy curriculum requirements, and students' need to pass exams, both of which exclusively focus on the linguistic dimension. However, contrary to the norm, CT2 manages to obtain a dynamic balance between linguistic and cultural teaching. His decision about what to focus on in a particular unit, linguistic or cultural dimensions, depends on how much cultural content is involved in the unit. He switches between the two dimensions from unit to unit to maintain a balance.

Though CT2 faces the same constraints as other EFL teachers, he manages to overcome some of them and successfully incorporates a larger amount of cultural teaching in his class. He is able to do so because he implicitly adopts inquiry-based learning and reflective practice in his teaching. He demonstrates an in-depth understanding of cultural phenomena and perspectives and a critical awareness of cultural teaching while employing cultural teaching techniques. We learn from CT2 that what matters is a teacher's mindset and approach in developing integration of cultural teaching.

CT2's case illustrates the point that Xu and Connelly have made to Chinese language teacher educators: 'begin with the teacher knowledge' and 'Chinese teachers are not blank slates' (2009: 225). That is, teacher educators need to respect and build on teacher knowledge cultivated in teachers' teaching practice, not treating them as blank slates as if they know little of cultural teaching.

'New knowledge and skills in a teacher education and development programme are not bricks in a knowledge edifice; they are enrichment for a flowing river of life. Everything taught enters this flow and is changed as it joins in what teachers know and do' (Xu & Connelly, 2009: 225). This flowing river captures the notion of teacher knowledge, which refers to 'a narrative construct which references the totality of a person's personal practical knowledge gained from formal and informal educational experience' (2009: 221).

Narrative inquiry allows participating teachers to reflect on their lived teaching and learning experience and develop a new construct of what it means to be an EFL teacher in a Chinese cultural and social context and an understanding and knowledge of what cultural teaching practice they want to conduct. Teachers' ways of knowing, that is, their narrative understanding of personal and professional experiences, help to shape and develop their language teaching. We did not enter the inquiry process with an attitude of having something to teach the teachers. Our purpose is to reveal how they know and understand their perception in their own terms. It is only with data of this sort that we may be able to rethink teacher education and curriculum programmes in such a way as to meet teachers' needs and the needs of the modern cross-cultural world.

Our inquiry into Chinese EFL teachers' lived experience of language teaching in China and their intercultural learning outside China helps us learn about their teacher knowledge regarding intercultural competence teaching – how EFL teachers developed their perceptions and practices of cultural teaching over time through their teaching practice as well as their personal intercultural experience and professional development.

6.6   Implications and applications

This research provides an insight into Chinese university EFL teachers' perceptions and practices of intercultural competence teaching: these are quite limited in some respects and are developing in others. While it focuses on the Chinese EFL context, the insight gained is also applicable to other second or foreign language contexts and multilingual and multicultural contexts.

As Xu and Connelly (2009: 225) point out: 'Because teacher knowledge is tacit and embodies all that a teacher has experienced, teacher knowledge and teacher identity are closely connected.' Teacher education and professional development programmes could help promote intercultural competence teaching by helping teachers to reflect on their teaching practice, recognize the nature, objectives and significance of intercultural competence teaching, and identify practical teaching methods. As illustrated in CT2's successful intercultural competence teaching, we suggest that teachers be encouraged and guided to achieve this professional development through reflective, experiential and inquiry-based practices in their teaching practices.

CT2's story suggests that teachers develop their pedagogical skills through their personal professional knowledge generated in their teaching practice. Teacher knowledge needs to be brought forward when new knowledge, in terms of intercultural competence teaching and related pedagogy, is introduced in teachers' professional development programmes in order to assist teachers to transform and realize this new knowledge in teaching practice. It is recommended that teacher educators develop teacher education programmes that provide opportunities for experienced teachers like CT2 to share his teacher knowledge with novice teachers, which CT2, as he indicated in his interview, has always wanted to do but does not have appropriate avenues.

It is difficult for language teachers, Chinese EFL teachers included, to 'acquire familiarity with, let alone expertise in, the wide range of regions and cultural topics typically included in textbook material' (Knutson, 2006: 596), as in many cases, they 'may not have first-hand experience with one or more of the target cultures, or, if they do, it may not be recent or in depth' (2006: 596). It is neither necessary nor feasible for teachers to study all aspects of target cultures. Teachers should select and teach their teaching materials according to the personal and professional needs of their learners to meet the social needs in the society. It is also important to help teachers to build their confidence and recognize their culturally embedded teacher identity for cultural teaching if we 'first begin at home in China' (Xu & Connelly, 2009: 225). That is, 'Chinese teacher knowledge reflects their personal narrative histories and the cultural narrative history of China. These ways of *knowing* and *being* reach back to ancient Chinese traditions of thought and need to be the starting point for any kind of teacher education and development' (2009: 225).

Hence when it comes to intercultural competence teaching, it is essential to help EFL teachers understand and mediate both their home cultural traditions and the target cultures and develop a deep understanding and awareness of their own culturally determined and individually constructed values, beliefs and knowledge. EFL teachers are both teachers and learners of intercultural competence in their teaching. This ongoing professional development resonates in Confucian tradition: 'Teaching and learning grow together.' With the advancement of technology in the forms of the Internet and mass media, EFL teachers have increasing accessibility to different cultures in the world. As a result, it is more of a matter of how to maximize teacher knowledge as well as the use of such accessibility to cultivate teachers' intercultural competence in teacher education and professional development programmes in order to promote intercultural competence teaching in their teaching practices.

References

Banks, J. (2002) *Cultural Diversity and Education: Foundations, Curriculum, and Teaching* (4th edn). New York: John Wiley & Sons.

Barkhuizen, G. & Wette, R. (2008) Narrative frames for investigating the experiences of language teachers, *System*, 36(3), 372–387.

Bennett, M. J. (1993) Towards ethnorelativism: a developmental model of intercultural sensitivity. In R. M. Paige (ed.) *Education for the Intercultural Experience*. Yarmouth, ME: Intercultural Press, pp. 21–71.

Byram, M. (1997) *Teaching and Assessing Intercultural Competence*. Clevedon: Multilingual Matters.

Chen, W. Y. (2000) Intercultural communication and college English teaching, *Journal of Xi'an Foreign Language University*, 8(1), 86–89.

Clandinin, D. J. (ed.) (2007) *Handbook of Narrative Inquiry: Mapping a Methodology*. Thousand Oaks, CA: Sage.

Clandinin, D. J. & Connelly, F. M. (2000) *Narrative Inquiry: Experience and Story in Qualitative Research*. San Francisco, CA: Jossey-Bass Publishers.

Conle, C. (1996) Resonance in preservice teacher inquiry, *American Educational Research Journal*, 33(2), 297–325.

Connelly, F. M. & Clandinin, D. J. (1988) *Teachers as Curriculum Planners: Narratives of Experience*. New York: Teachers College Press.

Connelly, F. M. & Clandinin, D. J. (1990) Stories of experience and narrative inquiry, *Educational Researcher*, 19(5), 2–14.

Connelly, F. M. & Clandinin, D. J. (1995) Narrative and education, *Teachers and Teaching: Theory and Practice*, 1(1), 73–85.

Connelly, F. M. & Xu, S. J. (2008) Narrative inquiry: concept and method. In X. M. Chen (ed.) *Research Methodologies in Social Sciences*. Chongqing, China: Chongqing University Press (in Chinese).

Corbett, J. (2003) *An Intercultural Approach to English Language Teaching*. Clevedon: Multilingual Matters.

Cortazzi, M. (1993) *Narrative Analysis*. Falmer Social Research and Educational Studies Series: 12. London: Falmer Press.

Cortazzi, M. & Jin, L. (2006) Asking questions, sharing stories and identity construction: sociocultural issues in narrative research. In S. Trahar (ed.) *Narrative Research on Learning: Comparative and International Perspectives.* Oxford: Symposium Books, pp. 27–46.

Damen, L. (1987) *Culture Learning: The Fifth Dimension in the Language Classroom.* Reading, MA: Addison-Wesley.

Dewey, J. (1932) *The School and Society.* Chicago: University of Chicago Press.

Dewey, J. (1938) *Experience and Education.* New York: Collier Books.

Elbaz, F. (1983) *Teacher Thinking: A Study of Practical Knowledge.* London: Croom Helm.

Fantini, A. E. (2006) Exploring and assessing intercultural competence. http://www.sit.edu/publications/docs/feil_research_report.pdf.

Fries, S. (n.d.) *Cultural, Multicultural, Cross-Cultural, Intercultural: A Moderator's Proposal,* TESOL France. http://www.tesol-france.org/articles/fries.pdf.

Gu, Q. & Maley, A. (2008) Changing places: a study of Chinese students in the UK, *Language and Intercultural Communication,* 8(4), 224–245.

Han, H. (2002) Cross-cultural concept of foreign language teaching in the globalized context, *Foreign Language Research,* 25(1), 105–111.

Holmes, P. (2005) Ethnic Chinese students' communication with cultural others in a New Zealand university, *Communication Education,* 54(4), 289–311.

Knutson, E. M. (2006) Cross-cultural awareness for second/foreign language learners, *The Canadian Modern Language Review,* 62(4), 591–610.

Kumaravadivelu, B. (2003) Critical language pedagogy: a postmethod perspective on English language teaching, *World English,* 22(4), 539–550.

Larzén-Östermark, E. (2008) The intercultural dimension in EFL-teaching: a study of conceptions among Finland–Swedish comprehensive school teachers, *Scandinavian Journal of Educational Research,* 52(5), 527–547.

Liang, H. J. (2008) Viewing foreign language classroom teaching innovation from cultural teaching evaluation, *Journal of Changchu Normal University,* 27(1), 124–126.

Lin, J. J. (2006) Research on intercultural teaching strategies, *Foreign Languages and their Teaching,* 28(4), 31–58.

Ministry of Education (2007) *College English Curriculum Requirements.* Beijing: Ministry of Education of the People's Republic of China.

Mishler, E. G. (1999) *Storylines: Craftartists' Narratives of Identity.* London: Harvard University Press.

Pan, D. T. (2007) Cultural awareness in foreign language teaching, *Foreign Language Research,* 30(6), 141–143.

Phillipson, R. (1992) *Linguistic Imperialism.* Oxford: Oxford University Press.

Pinnegar, S. & Daynes, J. G. (2007) Locating narrative inquiry historically: thematics in the turn to narrative. In D. J. Clandinin (ed.) *Handbook of Narrative Inquiry: Mapping a Methodology,* vol. 1. Thousand Oaks, CA: Sage, pp. 3–34.

Polkinghorne, D. E. (1995) Narrative configuration in qualitative analysis. In J. A. Hatch & R. Wisniewski (eds) *Life History and Narrative.* Washington, DC: The Falmer Press, pp. 5–24.

Riessman, C. K. & Speedy, J. (2007) Narrative inquiry in the psychotherapy professions: a critical review. In D. J. Clandinin (ed.) *Handbook of Narrative Inquiry: Mapping a Methodology,* vol. 17. Thousand Oaks, CA: Sage, pp. 426–456.

Sercu, L., Bandura, E., Castro, P., Davcheva, L., Laskaridou, C., Lundgren, U., Carmen, M., Garcla, M. & Ryan, P. (2005) *Foreign Language Teachers and Intercultural Communication: An International Investigation*. Clevedon: Multilingual Matters.

Shi, G. Q. & Wang, Y. X. (2001) The new syllabus and cultural elements in English teaching, *Foreign Languages and their Teaching*, 23(7), 33–35.

Spencer-Oatey, H. & Xiong, Z. (2006) Chinese students' psychological and sociocultural adjustments to Britain: an empirical study, *Language, Culture and Curriculum*, 19(1), 37–53.

Van Ek, J. A. (1986) *Objectives for Foreign Language Learning*, vol. 1: *Scope*. Strasbourg: Council of Europe.

Wang, B. & Liu, A. Z. (2008) On implementing culture teaching in college English classroom based on the model of intercultural communicative competence, *Journal of Higher Education Management*, 30(2), 83–86.

Wang, J. K. (2008) English teaching in cultural context, *Foreign Language Research*, 31(3), 134–136.

Wang, Y. & Falconer, R. (2005) Experiences of Asian-Chinese students in the United States: a case study, *Research in the Schools*, 12(1), 20–31.

Wen, Q. (2004) Globalization and intercultural competence. In K. Tam and T. Weiss (eds) *English and Globalization: Perspectives from Hong Kong and Mainland China*. Hong Kong: The Chinese University of Hong Kong, pp. 169–180.

Wu, Y. (2007) University EFL teacher development: goal and route. Keynote speech at the Second National Conference on Foreign Language Teacher Education and Development. Beijing, China, September.

Wu, Z. (2006) Understanding practitioner research as a form of life: an Eastern interpretation of exploratory practice, *Language Teaching Research*, 10(3), 331–350.

Wu, Z. (2007) Cultural interpretation of Chinese pedagogic discourse. Keynote speech at the Second National Conference on Foreign Language Teacher Education and Development. Beijing, China, September.

Xiao, S. Y. (2007) Cultural teaching in twenty years: reflection and thinking, *Academic Forum*, 30(4), 197–201.

Xu, S. J. (2000) Perspectives of Chinese visiting scholars on English teaching and learning for non-English majors in China. Master's research paper, York University, Toronto.

Xu, S. J. (2006) In search of home on landscapes in transition: narratives of newcomer families' cross-cultural schooling experience. Doctoral dissertation, University of Toronto, Toronto.

Xu, S. J. (2010) Cultural and linguistic differences. In Craig Kridel (ed.) *SAGE Encyclopedia of Curriculum Studies*. Thousand Oaks, CA: Sage, pp. 162–164.

Xu, S. J. & Connelly, F. M. (2008) Narrative inquiry and teacher development, *Peking University Education Review*, 6(1), 51–69 (in Chinese).

Xu, S. J. & Connelly, F. M. (2009) Narrative inquiry for teacher education and development: focus on English as a foreign language in China, *Teaching and Teacher Education*, 25(2), 219–227.

Xu, S. J. & Connelly, F. M. (2010) On the need for curious and creative minds in multicultural and cross-cultural educational settings: narrative possibilities. In Cheryl Craig & Louise F. Deretchin (eds) *Teacher Education Yearbook XVIII: Cultivating Curious and Creative Minds: The Role of Teachers and Teacher Educators*. Lanham, MD: Rowman & Littlefield Education, pp. 252–266.

Xu, S. J., Connelly, F. M., He, M. F. & Phillion, J. (2007) Immigrant students' experience of schooling: a narrative inquiry theoretical framework, *Journal of Curriculum Studies*, 39(4), 399–422.

Xu, S. J. & Stevens, E. D. (2005) Living in stories through images and metaphors: recognizing unity in diversity, *McGill Journal of Education*, 40(2), 303–319.

Yang, S. H. (2007) Narrative of a cross-cultural language teaching experience: conflicts between theory and practice, *Teaching and Teacher Education*, 24(6), 1564–1572.

Yang, Y. & Zhuang, E. P. (2007) Constructing a framework of intercultural communication competence in foreign language teaching, *Foreign Language World*, 28(4), 13–21.

Zhang, L. X. (2006) Teaching English in China: language, literature, culture, and social implications, *Foreign Language Teaching and Research*, 50(5), 248–253.

Zhou, Y. (2007) Attitudes and motivation towards learning a second language in an Internet-based informal context: perceptions of university ESL students. Master's thesis, University of Windsor, Canada.

Part II
Intercultural Adaptation: Chinese Learners in International Contexts

7
Cultures of Learning and Student Participation: Chinese Learners in a Multicultural English Class in Australia

Heather Parris-Kidd and Jenny Barnett

7.1 Introduction

Chinese students coming to Australia for university studies usually undertake preliminary general and academic English classes in a private college of some kind. Such classes are multicultural, although they may have a larger proportion of one cultural group than others. For example, at the turn of the century Koreans were heavily predominant, whereas by 2009 this was rather less so and there were more Chinese and Indian students. This chapter is a case study of three Chinese students in one such multicultural pre-university English class. It focuses on their patterns of classroom participation, the factors they identified as significant in their participation and our analysis of these factors in terms of cultures of learning (Jin, 1992).

The data on which this account is based were generated as part of a larger study (Parris, 2007), which found that differences in cultures of learning were highly relevant to how students participated in such classes. Our interest in returning to the data is twofold: to focus specifically on Chinese learners and to explore more deeply the notion of cultures of learning as a factor in students' classroom participation.

7.2 Framing the study

Cortazzi and Jin (1996) developed a definition for cultures of learning which has been used subsequently in their work as well as by others investigating into this area (Kato, 2001; Kennedy, 2002):

> By the term 'culture of learning' we mean that much behaviour in language classrooms is set within taken-for-granted frameworks of

expectations, attitudes, values and beliefs about what constitutes good learning, about how to teach or learn, whether and how to ask questions, what textbooks are for, and how language teaching relates to broader issues of the nature and purpose of education. (Cortazzi & Jin, 1996: 169)

This definition acknowledges the culture that learners and teachers bring with them to the English language classroom and the ways in which it might shape how teachers and students perceive language learning and how they evaluate each other's roles and classroom performance. This is not to overlook individual differences, nor the 'danger of over-generalization' (Kennedy, 2002: 442) through talking about cultural groups as one entity, not taking into sufficient account age, gender, geographical location or other factors that influence learning. Rather it is to adopt the position that 'socio-cultural insight and an understanding of students' previous learning experiences can undoubtedly help L2 teachers to develop more culturally sensitive pedagogies' (Kennedy, 2002: 442). This is because cultures of learning directly shape our ideas about teaching and learning, forming the basis of our ideas and beliefs of ideal classroom behaviour and participation (Cortazzi & Jin, 1996; Jin & Cortazzi, 1998; Aldridge *et al.*, 1999; Kato, 2001).

Cultures of learning are of course shaped by the broader cultures within which they sit, whether, for example, these are predominantly collectivist, as Chinese culture is generally considered to be, or predominantly individualist, as in Australian culture (Triandis, 1995; Hofstede & Hofstede, 2005). The constructs of individualism and collectivism are, of course, broad social trends and should not be confused with being determinants of individual behaviour, though they may influence the particular behaviour of some people in relevant contexts (Smith & Bond, 1993). While Chinese society may be characterized as predominantly collectivist, there are some individualist trends too (Ho & Chiu, 1994). Whether the society is, broadly, collectivist or individualist, there is a shared culture of norms, perceptions and ideals in regard to education which are likely to frame the contexts of behaviour. Chinese collectivism is specific to role relationships (Ho & Chiu, 1994) and so may be expected to influence student–teacher roles.

In more individualist societies, teaching methods are generally intended to inspire and encourage students to form their own meaning from the information and experiences they come across rather than reproducing the knowledge of others (Biggs *et al.*, 1997; Ngwainmbi, 2000). Originality and creativity are encouraged and there is a lot of attention paid to learning contexts, learner-centred pedagogies and task-based problem solving, with a strong focus on classroom interaction and student participation. In Aldridge, Fraser and Huang (1999), one Australian teacher commented that 'developing the students' ability as learners is more important than the acquisition of content knowledge' (1999: 57).

By contrast, more collectivist cultures in Asia place considerable emphasis on the transfer of knowledge and the authority of those holding it. Ng (2000) affirms that students in collectivist societies are trained from an early age to respect their teachers as masters of all essential knowledge and that in order to pass exams they must demonstrate their understanding by repeating back what the master has told them. Jin and Cortazzi (1998, 2006) affirm that in more collectivist cultures of learning the teacher and other sources of information, such as textbooks, are intended to give or transmit knowledge to the student.

How knowledge is tested and how success is measured is also a factor of the culture of learning. As in many other Asian societies, education in China is strongly results-driven (Tsui, 1996; Jin & Cortazzi, 1998) and consequently cultural attitudes towards effort and achievement in Asian cultures differ from those in Western cultures. In Asia, poor attainment is attributed to lack of effort, not a shortage of ability, whereas in the West poor attainment is often attributed to a lack of ability rather than a lack of effort (Deveney, 2005).

Effort includes classroom participation, but the nature of valued participation is shaped by the nature of the learning culture. Biggs (1996) and Jin and Cortazzi (2006) explain that Chinese learners' apparent reluctance to participate in Western classrooms is due to the Confucian value given to mastering the material first. So what Western teachers may see as reluctance to participate is in the students' eyes the fulfilment of their role as learners who must acquire the necessary skills first before putting them into practice. Jin and Cortazzi (2006) also point out that Chinese students look at their academic life in a collective way and, in their care for positive relationships and communication with others, 'they are tolerant and avoid situations which may cause anybody (both themselves and others) to lose face' (2006: 112).

In the study by Parris (2007), students from several Asian collectivist societies discussed the nature of classroom participation expected from them in a multicultural Australian classroom, as well as the factors shaping their own participation patterns. The data, from two classes, indicated factors having a clear link with the concept of distance and synergy between cultures of learning (Jin, 1992; Jin & Cortazzi, 1998), where difference between cultures of learning can be described in terms of social, academic and psychological distance. Social distance factors related to interpersonal relations between groups and individuals. Academic distance factors are related to the instructional environment, including the classroom and its English language learning goals. Psychological distance factors are related to students' attitudes and responses to their experiences, including anxiety and concern over loss of face. In this chapter, we illustrate the application of these concepts and develop a framework of 'cultures-of-learning factors' relevant to understanding students' classroom participation and the choices available to learners, teachers and institutions in helping bridge the distances encountered.

7.3   Research base

This is a phenomenological study in that it questions the way people experience the world in their everyday existence, and attempts 'to uncover and describe the structures, the internal meaning structures, of lived experience' (von Manen, 1990: 10). The focus is the lived experience of classroom participation by three out of six Chinese students who were enrolled in a multicultural General English class in Adelaide, South Australia. The class was at an upper intermediate level, and was conducted full time (five hours per day) over a ten-week term, with a mid-term entry and exit option. Of the three Chinese students we are focusing on, two were present from weeks 1 to 5 and one from weeks 6 to 10.

The data were generated through non-participant classroom observations and semi-structured individual interviews with the three Chinese students and their Australian teacher. Observations took place during weeks one, two, four, five, six, seven, nine and ten which allowed the observer to build a relationship with the class as a whole and for students to act naturally despite her presence. The interviews were conducted at the start and finish of the students' period of study in that class. The first interview was to obtain information regarding the students' previous learning experiences and their intentions and expectations regarding their time in Australia, plus their initial impressions. The second interview was constructed on the basis of the data from the first interview and the observations of participation patterns shown by the student in relation to the class and the teacher. The questions were about their experiences of learning English in their home countries and in Australia, focusing on similarities and differences.

In analysing the data from the three Chinese students, we first took a thematic approach to the interview data, focusing on what the students said about (a) their participation patterns, and (b) factors relating to these participation patterns. We then trawled through the field notes to identify evidence of the identified participation patterns and factors, from any of the Chinese students. The next level of analysis was to see whether these patterns and factors could be related to the dimensions of distance between cultures of learning, and if so in what ways. This then allowed us to identify a set of 'cultures-of-learning factors' in classroom participation, and led us to consider these Chinese students' classroom participation at the intersection of cultures of learning in terms of choices made by the learner, the teacher and the institution. We see this as a useful tool for teachers and students endeavouring to understand and negotiate interculturality in their classrooms.

7.3.1   Introducing the class

The observed class initially consisted of 14 students of various nationalities predominantly from South East Asia, with just one European student, from Italy, in the group. Five weeks into the ten-week course, the class composition changed with some students leaving the class and new students arriving; however, the demographic stayed the same. This changing of the make-up of classes is quite common in language schools around the world. In some schools there is continual enrolment on a weekly basis but in this school the students entered and left every five weeks, which meant that the classes were made up of a mix of both new and established students.

For the first five weeks in this class there were four Chinese students. In week 5, three of these Chinese students left and three more arrived. All of the Chinese students observed in this study were from large cities in China, and all had already completed at least one degree in China. They had either funded themselves or been funded by their families to undertake further higher education in Australia.

The learning aim for most students in this upper intermediate General English class was to pass a test of some description, either IELTS or the University entrance test, in order to go onto further study in Australia. Some were dismayed to find their English language proficiency was not what they had thought it to be. For example, one Chinese student (CS1), in his early twenties, had achieved the necessary results in his International English Language Testing Service (IELTS) test while in

China, but was forced to question the validity of those results once he arrived in Australia:

> My IELTS test is listening 6.5, reading 6, speaking 6 and writing 4. But when I got here I can't understand a lot of things and even though I try my speak is not very good, it's normal but not a 6. I think in here really my speaking point would be 4 and listen point maybe 4.5 or 5, which is not good ... I think I get lots of trouble because my speaking, so I was feel very uncomfortable because IELTS test was 6, but nothing. I feel very bad. (CS1)

From these words, we can see that it unsettled CS1 considerably to find such a gap between his test scores and his capabilities in practice, and one wonders if he does not feel somewhat betrayed by the system. Certainly it seems appropriate that the class he has been allocated to should have a focus on speaking and on Australian settings.

The teacher of this class (AT) is an experienced English as Additional Language (EAL) professional in his fifties. He has been working in the school for over ten years and has much experience in teaching this level. He has been in Australia for over 20 years, but was born in Europe and English is not his first language. He tells the students this and explains that he understands what they are going through as he too had to learn English, albeit a long time ago. His emphasis is on teaching communication skills and introducing the students to natural aspects of Australian life. Throughout the observations there are many examples of how he tries to introduce the students to aspects of Australian culture and creates situations where they can interact with local people, who ordinarily they may not have had the chance to meet.

The teacher has a dialogic teaching approach encouraging democratic participation in classroom activities, which emphasize speaking and communication skills. He uses games and humour to provoke talk; discussions to encourage the students to think critically and develop and express their own opinions; and deliberate strategies to encourage students to take responsibility for their own learning. He openly admits that he sometimes tries things that do not work, but because of his experience he has the confidence to do this and mostly gets very good results from trying different things. He is also ready to give his reasons for asking students to do things they may not be comfortable with, such as asking questions of strangers:

> The reason I am doing this is that here you are in Australia; you are going to meet many new people and have many new experiences,

and it's normal here that when you meet new people you ask them questions to find out about them. So here we are practising where it is safe and you can say/ask anything. (AT)

He challenges the students to move beyond the comfort zone of their familiar cultural practices and to engage in a culture of learning that is reflective of Australian values and practices.

7.4   Research findings and discussion

7.4.1   Academic distance between cultures of learning

This case study has examined the Chinese students' views about distance in the academic dimensions of their old and new cultures of learning – specifically the Chinese culture of English language learning and the culture of English language learning they were experiencing in Australia. Features of the academic dimension relevant to classroom participation include features of broad educational practice, such as assessment and homework, and also specific curriculum priorities in English language teaching.

CS1 had previously studied English at high school and university in China. He explains that Chinese students are very focused on test achievement, and the curriculum is built around what will best prepare them for that:

> In China grammar is very important, all the time. Like all people want practical for the IELTS test. So it's very important. And writing, writing, reading, no speaking but some listening. (CS1)

The importance of testing and test practice in the Chinese culture of learning is well documented (Ng & Liu, 1999; Jin & Cortazzi, 2003; Zhang, 2004). However, this is in contrast to the Australian system where the focus is on learning, and where preparing students for university education emphasizes developing the skills and abilities to work independently, think critically and find alternative solutions. Achieving a good test score may not address the actuality of coping with academic life in Australia, which is a matter of concern in an Australian setting.

The emphasis CS1 identifies on reading and writing in the Chinese classroom is endorsed by another case study student in his early twenties, referred to here as CS2:

> Chinese English teacher tell student a lot of grammar rule, so his write and read ability is very strong ... Chinese teacher educated

in China so his teaching skill is Chinese skill, it's different. A lot of China teachers never come to the English world, so he never know how to speak and how to explain the idea in English way. (CS2)

CS1's description of classrooms in China indicates a text-based and teacher-centred academic environment:

> Chinese class we have lots of texts and the teacher writes lots of words and explain them. Then when we go home we have a lot of homework ... and in China there is not so much talking in class. And in China teacher is very strict. (CS1)

Other sources also tell us that classes in China are traditionally text-based (Jin & Cortazzi, 1998; Ng, 2000) with the teacher as the expert in making sense of texts and adopting an authoritarian stance in the classroom. This is in contrast to the learner-centred democratic style of teaching in CS1's Australian classroom, where the teacher seldom uses a textbook, does not use a transmission approach and requires a lot of talk by the students themselves.

This emphasis on speaking created a certain tension for most students, particularly in the early days of their enrolment. In CS2's first class, where he was one of six new students in a class with several established and continuing students, he was paired with another new student and the two of them spoke very little. They observed the other couples chatting and even commented on it and yet at this point seemed to lack the skills or confidence to do the same. However, over the course of just a few short weeks CS2's behaviour changed from that of a very passive and dependent student to one who was willing to take risks and think and act independently. In the lesson observed after he had been in the school just four weeks, he was asking questions without being prompted and participating animatedly in discussions. When asked about participating in class and asking questions he said that

> some first time I felt different because in China don't do this ... but after time will be know each other well and talk each other well and understand so we will make some feel better. And asking and speaking is now OK. (CS2)

Students thus adjusted to the requirement to talk. However, they were also called upon to make some more challenging adjustments.

The third case study student, a nurse in her early thirties whom we will call CS3 and who studied English throughout her school years in China, highlights one such challenge:

> [I]n China the education system is different. Teacher always tell you what to do and give a lot of homework assignment, but here you yourself have to push not the teacher. (CS3)

In making this assessment, CS3 shows her awareness of the teacher dependence characteristic of her primary culture of learning and the independence valued in the new culture of learning. However, she is not entirely happy with the expectations:

> I think it's good for people to create their own ideas, yeah, but sometimes for international students we really need some kind of teacher instructions from teachers as we really don't know.

CS3's awareness of dependence and her interest in students creating their own ideas suggests that she is open to adjusting to the new culture of learning. However, she maintains her preference for teacher guidance and is clearly not ready to fully adjust. As Auerbach points out, 'ESL learners have their own ideas about what counts as language learning, and having a democratic classroom may not be one of them' (2000: 152).

As part of his strategy to develop learner independence and responsibility for learning, the teacher in this class rarely sets required homework, but tells the students that 'it would be good for' their English if they were to write a diary and make an effort to engage socially in English language conversations. On the one hand he makes it clear that this is the homework he wants them to do, even though he will not be assessing it; on the other hand he tells the students it is up to them whether they do it or not, encouraging them to take an active role in their learning.

CS2 is excited by this approach:

> It is very important you know how to work, how to study in Australia, [the teacher] not only tells you the words, but more – this is the most important thing – no homework not mean you have nothing to do after class, because the study here is the whole thing, not only in class. He teach about the way, the manner how to communicate, so we can communicate with other student after class and this is study all. (CS2)

This shows considerable depth of understanding into the role of the independent learner in an Australian classroom.

CS3, on the other hand, expresses some difficulty in taking an active role in her learning without any formal requirement from the teacher:

> In this class it's different, there's no homework or rather there is homework but if you don't want to do it that's fine ... It's good to finish the homework, but because I have no pressure ... sometimes I'm busy or because I'm doing a part-time job, sometimes I'm really tired ... I don't do. (CS3)

It appears her difficulty is not entirely related to culture-of-learning factors, but also has to do with the personal factors she mentions. This is relevant, because in other aspects, as becomes apparent in the next section, CS3 is one of the students who adapted well to the new culture of learning.

7.4.2   Social distance between cultures of learning

In regard to classroom participation, features of the social dimension in a culture of learning include (a) broad societal characteristics and (b) expectations of students' participation and use of spoken English within the framework of valued curriculum content and pedagogy. Social distance between cultures of learning can be identified through the tensions students experience in regard to complying with teacher expectations of participation in the new setting. Some of these tensions are illustrated here, all of them suggesting choices that the students felt they had to make in regard to participation.

CS1 explained that in the beginning he found it

> quite frightening as Australian teacher like to make us laugh and if in China, in Chinese classroom, if you laugh it is wrong. In first week, I just arrive here and couldn't laugh you know, I think it's wrong but although there were others laughing and although I understood the joke but I don't laugh only underneath. (CS1)

This difference in socio-cultural behaviour patterns was evidently quite alarming to CS1. He has been taken right out of his comfort zone by something that is seen as normal practice in this Australian classroom, where the teacher regularly uses humour as part of his pedagogy. However, although initially CS1 is awkward with the situation he quickly adjusts since by 'the second week I felt more relaxed, comfortable' (CS1).

When asked why, he answered: 'It's because everyone else was ok.' The established students in the class modelled not only the adoption of a new behaviour pattern, but the letting go of a traditional pattern (Parris, 2007).

Another widely mentioned traditional pattern among students from some parts of Asia is a reluctance to ask questions in class when they have not understood what to do (Liu & Littlewood, 1997; Greenholtz, 2003). CS2 demonstrates this in a lesson shortly after he joined the class at the five-week entry point.

At the start of the class the teacher explains to all the students that as a way of introducing themselves they must say their name and give an adjective and do an action that describes them, both the adjective and the action beginning with the same letter as their name. He asks 'Do you understand?' All the students nod, including CS2. The student the teacher chooses to go first is an established Korean student who has been in the school for several months. He is very relaxed in his manner, follows the instructions correctly and generates a lot of laughter. CS2 seems very uncomfortable especially with people doing actions; and he does not join in with the laughter. When it is his turn to say his name, adjective and action, he says his name, which begins with F, and then an adjective that begins with K and a noun that begins with R, indicating that he has not understood the instruction to use the first letter of his name. The other students say 'No' out loud and he looks confused by this. Several of the established students try to explain to him what he should do, but he continues to look confused. The teacher explains again and tells him which letter his words should begin with, after which he does as he should, but is reluctant to do any actions.

Although CS2 himself does not comment on why he didn't want to admit lack of understanding, such behaviour is explained by another Chinese student in a different class, who says that in China the whole culture of asking questions is very different and as such is something that many Chinese students struggle to come to terms with in Australia. When asked why he didn't ask the teacher questions when the teacher invited the class to do so, he replies:

> I think it's not ok ... Because I think in the class is all of students' time, if I ask teacher I think I waste another student's time, so I want to ask after the class. (CS4)

When it was suggested to him that perhaps if he didn't understand then maybe the other students also didn't understand and so by asking a question it could be clarified for everyone, he replied: 'Yes, but they understand, just me I don't understand' (CS4). This response suggests a related reason not to ask questions, which is for fear of making mistakes and thus losing face or looking stupid in front of your classmates.

Loss of face is also a factor that can impact on the level of comfort students feel in complying with the teacher's expectations for talk. Jin and Cortazzi point out that Chinese students are 'tolerant and avoid situations where they may cause anybody (both themselves and others) to lose face' (2006: 112).

In one lesson the topic up for discussion was 'elections', chosen to coincide with the upcoming local elections. The teacher put the students into groups of mixed nationalities and asked them to tell their groups about elections in their own countries and compare how they were similar or different to other countries. While the groups were speaking together CS3 left her group and went to talk directly to the teacher. After the groups had stopped talking, the teacher then said '(CS3) has been talking to me and telling me something very interesting. Will you please share it with the others?' She was very reluctant to do so and says 'No, I don't want to' (CS3 Observation). However, the teacher persists and even after her saying to him 'Why don't you say or you ask?' he says 'No, it was your point.' She then turns to a Taiwanese student and says 'I'm really sorry but he is forcing me to ask. I saw on TV that they fight in parliament in your country, is it true? Sorry.' The Taiwanese student answers 'Yes it's true' and she does not seem to mind. In this incident CS3 is clearly reluctant to speak out since it is for her culturally inappropriate to risk embarrassing someone else in such a way, and yet it is also culturally inappropriate to refuse to do what the teacher insists upon. It is this latter imperative that wins out, but she nevertheless prefaces and concludes her question with apology, thereby attempting to address any potential loss of face for the other student.

This example from the observation data points to the complexity of decisions students must make about their classroom participation in the hybrid social space between two disparate cultures of learning. Under pressure from the teacher, students must somehow respond to the challenge of being asked to do something they consider inappropriate, and each one of them will respond in their own way, demonstrating their own take on the psychological dimension of cultural synergy. In this study, such challenges arose not only from the teacher's emphasis on talk and on learner responsibility, but from the types of guest introduced into the classroom and from the types of topic selected for discussion.

Introducing guests to the classroom allowed students to meet with members of the Australian community whom they might otherwise not have connected with. CS3's view of this was very positive:

> I think is very useful for me as he introduced some different person. If I didn't meet the teacher I think I have never get a chance to met that person. For example we met a gay Australian and you can question anything what we want. So I can find a difference of culture between my country and here. So is very useful method. (CS3)

However for CS2, a newer student, the experience of the teacher introducing the class to an openly gay friend of his, named Ray for present purposes, was not one he was comfortable to talk about in a subsequent lesson.

The teacher is trying to get the students who had met Ray to explain to those who had been absent who he was. CS2 looks a little confused, so the teacher says, 'Do you remember Ray?' And CS2 says, 'Yes,' to which the teacher responds: 'So tell us about his life, his emotional life, why he was here.' CS2 looks very uncomfortable and doesn't say anything for a while, so the teacher says, 'He was here to explain about how he came out.' CS2 laughs nervously and says, 'I don't know the meaning.' He looks very embarrassed, is going red and looking at the floor squirming. He really doesn't want to say anything. Although we cannot tell from observation if this is because he doesn't understand or because he feels uncomfortable talking about homosexuality, when asked later how he felt talking about controversial topics he merely said:

> Chinese English teacher [do not] tell student how to spoke, how to explain, how to express idea so Chinese student have a poor ability to communication with other people.

This teacher loved to get the students to talk about somewhat controversial topics, without giving any particular direction. As CS3 said in regard to set presentations, 'the teacher doesn't give his opinion, he just give our topic' (CS3). Some of these topics would definitely be seen as taboo in the classroom in their own countries, but most of the students did what was asked of them even though some were a little more reluctant than others. Referring to her early days in the class, CS3 said, 'I can't imagine talk about sex in class, but we did in class so I feel a little bit astonished.' Then as time progressed she came to believe that 'I'm old to understand about that so [now] I think is no difficult.' CS3 also came to express quite strong opinions in class and was not afraid to disagree with others. When asked about this she said:

> I don't mind because I'm not in China. I'm in an international situation. You will have all sorts of international people here; they have their own opinion, they have their own educational background, so that's their opinion. And because they come here it means they don't mind too. (CS3)

However, as we saw earlier, not minding giving her own opinions in the international classroom situation did not mean that she would readily risk another student minding, as when answering a question reflecting an implicit negative opinion on the behaviour of parliamentarians.

These intercultural negotiations that students made in order to participate in their new culture of learning evidently came about as a result of two factors: first, the social and academic distance between their own and their teacher's cultures of learning, and, second, the requirement to bridge the gaps between the two, which involved addressing psychological distance. As the students make clear, they each experienced psychological distance in terms of the positive or negative values they attributed to particular behaviours, based on their cultural heritage; their fear of unknown cultural expectations; the degree of culture shock they experienced; and how they managed that shock. Bridging the gaps of academic and social distance between classroom cultures thus involved choice and agency, and a call to negotiate.

7.5   Conclusion: negotiating a new culture of learning

This study has illustrated the features of social and academic distance encountered by three Chinese students in an Australian classroom, as compared with what they were accustomed to. At the same time, it has shown how the students negotiated their new culture of learning by making conscious or unconscious choices reflecting their personal psychological distance in relation to those academic and social features. Sometimes they chose resistance, even refusal to comply; sometimes they succumbed to confusion or embarrassment; and other times they chose to adapt, gradually shifting their own psychological distance closer to the expectations of the new classroom.

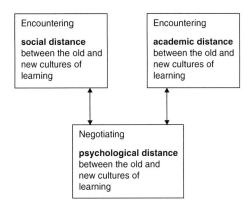

Figure 7.1   Negotiating a new culture of learning

The students' own agency in making such choices indicates that in a cultures-of-learning model it is the psychological dimension which shapes the responses of each individual student to their experience of academic and social distance. This relationship is captured in Figure 7.1.

To help students negotiate a new culture of learning, it may be helpful for teachers to themselves identify features of academic and social distance that newcomers might experience in their classrooms, and then to either explicitly or implicitly assist students to likewise consciously identify them.

As a support for this process, we have summarized in Table 7.1 the features of academic and social distance indicated by the three students in this study, acknowledging that other features may occur in other settings, with other participants and in other times. Each item comprises a characteristic typical of the Chinese culture of learning and a contrasting characteristic typical of the culture of learning in this particular multicultural Australian classroom (separated, and simultaneously connected, by the symbol ↔). While a feature list developed in another setting might highlight different features, they may similarly be in contrast with one another.

The use of ↔ to separate the points of distance across the cultures of learning highlights the fact that the distance may be bridged from both directions. This is done through choices made consciously or unconsciously by the learner, by the teacher and by the institution. In this study, choices made by the learner included letting go of inhibitions about speaking out, laughing and giving opinions; taking

Table 7.1   Features of academic and social distance in a multicultural General English class

Academic distance	Social distance
* teacher centred ↔ learner centred * dependent learner ↔ independent learner * authoritative teaching style ↔ democratic teaching style * test focused ↔ learning focused * passive learner ↔ active learner * reproduction of ideas ↔ creation of ideas	* collective society ↔ individualist society * face as highly important ↔ face as marginally important * classroom laughter unacceptable ↔ classroom laughter acceptable
Classroom language use:	**Classroom language use:**
* text-based activities ↔ talk-based activities * accuracy ↔ fluency * little student talk ↔ lots of student talk	* pretending to understand ↔ asking for clarification * withholding opinions ↔ giving opinions * keeping to safe topics ↔ venturing into controversial topics

responsibility for homework and asking for clarification and help. Choices made by the teacher included deliberately eliciting talk in culturally challenging situations and on culturally avoided topics; giving reasons for teaching strategies; and facilitating participation through 'setting the tone – creating an atmosphere where students feel respected and comfortable' (Auerbach, 2000: 152). Choices made by the institution included not setting required textbooks; giving teachers a degree of autonomy over curriculum; and having a mid-term entry and exit point after five weeks.

It is clear that choices made by the institution to some degree shaped choices made by the teacher which in turn shaped the opportunity for choice among the learners. However, we believe there is also a flow in the opposite direction, even though it may be weaker, and that the teacher in the middle has a mediating role between the institution and the learner. This is illustrated in Figure 7.2.

As this chapter has indicated, changes in patterns of participation occur over time, and also as a result of new students observing other 'established' students participating comfortably and with confidence. We believe that such changes can be facilitated through application of a 'cultures-of-learning model' in curriculum and pedagogy, highlighting distance in the academic and social dimensions of the relevant cultures

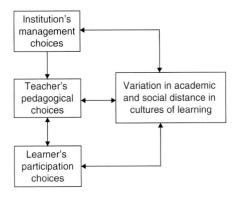

Figure 7.2 Negotiating academic and social distance across cultures of learning

of learning. For example, teachers and students could together investigate features of distance, building up their own summary of features as in Table 7.1, and then explicitly addressing the psychological aspects of bridging the gaps between different features. This in turn would facilitate learner choice and agency in classroom participation, as well as teacher responsiveness to student choices. Finally, institutions could incorporate use of a cultures-of-learning framework in curriculum and pedagogy, and provide professional development for teachers, helping them to apply the framework and explore ways of improving intercultural interaction in their classrooms.

References

Aldridge, J. M., Fraser, B. J. & Huang, T.-C. I. (1999) Investigating classroom environments in Taiwan and Australia with multiple research methods, *Journal of Educational Research*, 93(1), 48–62.
Auerbach, E. (2000) Creating participatory learning communities: paradoxes and possibilities. In J. K. Hall & W. Eggington (eds) *Sociopolitics of English Language Teaching*. Clevedon: Multilingual Matters, pp. 143–164.
Biggs, J. B. (1996) Western misperceptions of the Confucian-heritage learning culture. In D. A. Watkins & J. B. Biggs (eds) *The Chinese Learner: Cultural, Psychological and Contextual Influences*. Hong Kong: Comparative Education Research Centre, University of Hong Kong, pp. 45–67.
Biggs, J. B., Murray-Harvey, R. & Silins, H. C. (eds) (1997) Teaching across and within cultures: the issue of international students. In *Learning and Teaching in Higher Education: Advancing International Perspectives (Special Edition)*. Adelaide: Flinders Press, Proceedings of the Higher Education Research and Development Society of Australasia (HERDSA) Conference, Adelaide, South Australia, July, pp. 1–22.

Cortazzi, M. & Jin, L. (1996) Cultures of learning: language classrooms in China. In H. Coleman (ed.) *Society and the Language Classroom*. Cambridge: Cambridge University Press, pp. 169–203.

Deveney, B. (2005) An investigation into aspects of Thai culture and its impact on Thai students in an international school in Thailand, *Journal of Research in International Education*, 4(2), 153–171.

Greenholtz, J. (2003) Socratic teachers and Confucian learners: examining the benefits and pitfalls of a year abroad, *Language and Intercultural Communication*, 3(2), 122–130.

Ho, D. Y.-F. & Chiu, C.-Y. (1994) Component ideas of individualism, collectivism, and social organization: an application in the study of Chinese culture. In U. Kim, H. C. Triandis, C. Kagitcibasi, S.-C. Choi & G. Yoon (eds) *Individualism and Collectivism: Theory, Method, and Application*. Thousand Oaks, CA: Sage, pp. 137–156.

Hofstede, G. & Hofstede, G. J. (2005) *Cultures and Organisations: Software of the Mind* (2nd edn). New York: McGraw-Hill.

Jin, L. (1992) Academic cultural expectations and second language use: Chinese postgraduate students in the UK – a cultural synergy model. PhD thesis, University of Leicester.

Jin, L. & Cortazzi, M. (1998) The culture the learner brings: a bridge or a barrier? In M. Byram & M. Fleming (eds) *Language Learning in Intercultural Perspective*. Cambridge: Cambridge University Press, pp. 98–118.

Jin, L. & Cortazzi, M. (2003) English language teaching in China: a bridge to the future. In H. W. Kam & R. Y. K. Wong (eds) *English Language Teaching in East Asia Today*. Singapore: Times Academic Press, pp. 131–145.

Jin, L. & Cortazzi, M. (2006) Changing practices in Chinese cultures of learning, *Language, Culture and Curriculum*, 19(1), 5–20.

Kato, K. (2001) Exploring 'cultures of learning': a case study of Japanese and Australian classrooms, *Journal of Intercultural Studies*, 22(1), 51–67.

Kennedy, P. (2002) Learning cultures and learning styles: myth-understandings about adult (Hong Kong) Chinese learners, *International Journal of Lifelong Education*, 21(5), 430–445.

Liu, N.-F. & Littlewood, W. (1997) Why do many students appear reluctant to participate in classroom learning discourse?, *System*, 25(3), 371–384.

Ng, C. and Liu, C. (1999) Teaching English to Chinese immigrants in Hong Kong secondary schools, *Language, Culture and Curriculum*, 12(3), 229–238.

Ng, G. A. (2000) From Confucian Master Teacher to Freirian mutual learner: challenges in pedagogical practice and religious education, *Religious Education*, 95(3), 308–319.

Ngwainmbi, E. K. (2000) Communication in the Chinese classroom, *Education*, 125(1), 62–76.

Parris, H. (2007) Cultures of learning and student participation: a study in two multicultural classrooms for English as an Additional Language. Masters by Research thesis, University of South Australia.

Smith, P. B. & Bond, M. H. (1993) *Social Psychology across Cultures*. London: Prentice Hall Europe.

Triandis, H. C. (1995) *Individualism and Collectivism*. Boulder, CO: Westview Press.

Tsui, A. B. M. (1996) Reticence and anxiety in second language learning. In K. M. Bailey & D. Nunan (eds) *Voices from the Language Classroom*. Cambridge: Cambridge University Press, pp. 145–167.

von Manen, M. (1990) *Researching Lived Experience: Human Science for an Action Sensitive Pedagogy*. Albany, NY: State University of New York Press.

Zhang, L. (2004) CLT in China: frustrations, misconceptions and clarifications, *Hwa Kang Journal of TEFL*, 10, 101–114.

8
Getting the Big Picture: A Longitudinal Study of Adaptation and Identity in a New Zealand University

Gillian Skyrme and Cynthia White

8.1 Introduction to the project

In the early years of this decade, certain sections of New Zealand universities were taken by surprise by the unprecedented demand for places from a new cohort of students of which they had very limited experience, and whose previous educational experience had been within a markedly different academic culture: Chinese international students. The presence of international students was not a novelty. New Zealand had a history of providing university education for international students as part of its close relationship with Pacific Island nations, and through participation in the Colombo Plan, a British Commonwealth initiative to promote influence on developing Asian countries (which for historical reasons did not include the People's Republic of China). By the end of the last century, however, self-interested altruism had been replaced by a business model of recruiting full-fee-paying students, and the primary sources of such students were changing. National statistics provide something of the story: in 1998, 89 university students came from China to New Zealand; by 2002, that number had jumped to 11,700, more than half the full-fee students at public tertiary institutions (Tarling, 2004: 223). What these statistics do not show, however, is their concentration in particular subjects, such as undergraduate business studies. In late 2003, for example, a newspaper article (Matthews, 2003) reported that more than 70% of students were international in some first-year business courses in one university. The vast majority of these were Chinese.

Understandably, this situation was the subject of an enormous amount of discussion and scrutiny from teachers, students, international and domestic, and the wider community. Greater understanding was called for: a doctoral research project which closely examined the meanings of the experience for the Chinese students themselves. Gillian, the doctoral candidate, and Cynthia, the supervisor, both had long-standing experience with Chinese students and had taught in China. We decided the focus should be on students studying business and information sciences, where the concentration was highest. Thus began a rewarding study to investigate from a socio-cultural perspective the expectations with which the students arrived, the issues that led to change and the nature of the changes they underwent. While the findings were wide ranging, in this chapter we trace the affective dimensions of evolving student identity, and the methodological choices made at key points to best capture the emerging meaning of their experience.

8.2   Developing the methodology

Decisions about how best to inquire into the research problem required consideration of a number of complexities and some creativity. The choice of a qualitative paradigm was easily made. Entry into an institution of higher education, especially in a foreign country, implies a restructuring of behaviour, viewpoints, understandings and identities. Such restructuring is not confined to behaviour in classrooms or in respect to classmates and teachers but extends to decisions about where and with whom to live, part-time work, leisure activities, personal relationships, time management – decisions which potentially impact on every aspect of one's life and sense of who one is. The effects of these students' decision to undertake study abroad were potentially infinitely diverse responses to complex variables, such as personality, prior experience and choices made about their study. The qualitative paradigm, which 'looks for patterns of interrelationship between many categories rather than a sharply delineated relationship between a limited set of them' (McCracken, 1988: 16) offered the best hope of capturing that. Semistructured interviews were chosen as the basic framework for collecting data, combined throughout with a range of other tools which gave visual support to the process of eliciting verbal accounts, both designed by the researcher and selected by the interviewees. The role of three of these visual methods – feeling graphs, big pictures of the individuals' journeys and self-selected photos – will be discussed in this chapter at the points at which they were brought into play in the study.

   Another aspect to be considered was the temporal element. Metaphors of journey are endemic in discourses of learning (Jin & Cortazzi, 2008, forthcoming), and we needed to present a sense of trajectory in students' accounts of their learning journeys. This takes account of the cyclical nature of life in an educational institution, as well as phases of acculturation to new settings (e.g. Ward *et al.*, 2001; Burnett & Gardener, 2006), and enabled us to locate moments of that journey that were particularly significant in promoting new learning for participants. The full project used two approaches to elongating the temporal reach of the study: the retrospective, interviewing students nearing the end of their undergraduate degrees, and the longitudinal, following a group of newly enrolled students through their first semester and then throughout their degrees. It is the longitudinal phase that will provide the focus of this chapter.

Ortega and Iberri-Shea (2005) and Dörnyei (2007) argue strongly for the value of longitudinal studies in applied linguistics research. While the areas of interest here were not confined to language learning, as they encompass a wider purview informed by the communities of practice perspective (Lave & Wenger, 1991), the importance of tracing learning across time applies. Measurement effects have been highlighted as a potential drawback of longitudinal studies (Cohen *et al.*, 2007; Dornyei, 2007), but this needs to be balanced against the value of the developing trust between researcher and participant which a longitudinal study facilitates. In their study, Tian and Lowe (2009: 664) describe a 'gradually gained closeness between researcher and participants [which] helped to produce the depth in the data that the study sought', and which 'handed power over to the participants, so that they could speak of their perceptions and present personal stories with an assurance that their voices would be met with respect, empathy and objectivity'. The development of this relationship and the enhanced involvement of participants in the research process facilitated by measures described below proved to be enriching aspects of this study.

Planning for the project took place during 2003. The first data collection began at the end of that year, and the central longitudinal project started in February 2004, the beginning of the New Zealand academic year. From the outset Cynthia's advice was that time in the field would suggest new directions, so we purposefully left the later stages of the design open. A timeline for the process can be seen in Figure 8.1.

8.3   Applying the methodology

This study concerned the experiences of a group of novice students entering a complex community of practice, or rather, a constellation of communities of practice (Wenger, 1998: 126). We were very aware from our own observations and discussion with colleagues that the large

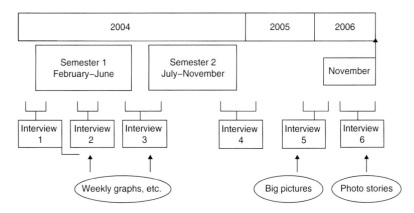

Figure 8.1   Timeline of data collection

first-year classes which would provide their initial experiences presented huge challenges to many of these students. It was important to us to limit the extra complexity that the research design itself might add. McCracken (1988: 12) points out that the extended one-to-one research interview bears little resemblance to more familiar interactions. In this case, it would be conducted in the second language of the participants by an interviewer initially unknown to them who was a representative of the community with which they were in an as yet unresolved process of coming to terms. On the planes of age, culture, profession and institutional relationship, the interviewer could be seen to be at considerably greater ease in the setting than they were. It was important to adopt an appropriate tone to mitigate this potential power imbalance and ensure that they felt some degree of control over the situation and in their choices of self-expression, and also that they found the process engaging: 'Unless respondents feel the interviewing process offers them some personal involvement and satisfaction, the possibility of repeated, in-depth interviews is unlikely' (Cotterill, 1992: 595).

In resolving how to mitigate these factors, Gillian, recognizing her own novice status in relation to the research process, drew on the kinds of teacherly understandings which Senior (2006) recognizes as part of the repertoire of the experienced teacher. She had formulated strong beliefs about how talk might be supported and encouraged through years of teaching students in New Zealand language centres where a communicative approach held sway. Among these, and pertinent here, was a belief in the usefulness of varying the dynamic over an extended session to ensure renewal of focus, and in the value of paper-based resources as a means of doing this. Such resources provide an infinite variety of ways of inviting the respondent to take a new angle on the matter in hand, but also allow a mental retreat from the intensity of gaze that the one-to-one interview imposes.

It was also recognized that the language around research itself can be daunting. An intervention to reduce the 'technologized discourses' which Holliday (2002: 152) suggests can stand between us and our informants, arose early on in the process of gaining consent from participants. The information sheet required to establish the ethical boundaries of the research process for the students remained a dense text in an unfamiliar genre, even when the language of the original model had been adjusted. To ensure that this would not be a barrier, a clear abbreviated cover sheet in both English and Chinese, as well as a Chinese version of the full text, served both to address their need for accessible information and to present the researcher as someone concerned about such issues.

8.3.1   Getting started

For both researcher and participants, the first steps took place during the flurry of orientation week, 2004, when copious amounts of information about matters pastoral, financial, educational and even climatic (a major flooding event affecting the nearby river happened to be taking place), were delivered in a large hall to a multilingual audience. This information was scaffolded (or not) by varying amounts of visual support and adjusted language. The request for participation in our project was a small voice in that deluge, but Gillian's efforts to make it fully communicative, even putting herself in a linguistically vulnerable position by introducing herself in Mandarin, were rewarded by a round of applause. This was followed up with first-week visits to small tutorial-sized classes for English for Academic Purposes where a more interactive process was possible. This contrast replicated in many ways the students' learning programmes, in which some courses were primarily delivered in monologic lectures which were poorly attuned to L2 difficulties, while in others havens of access were to be found in weekly tutorial classes.

As a result, 12 students were recruited into the longitudinal study, making an initial commitment to one semester's involvement, and the first interviews were held. Demographic details can be seen in Table 8.1.

From the beginning, we attached fundamental importance to getting close to the students' voices and meanings. On Cynthia's advice, the data analysis was based on repeated listening to the recorded interviews and

Table 8.1 Participants in the longitudinal study

Code	Sex	Age	IELTS	Highest study in China	Time in NZ at enrolment	Degree	Length of time in the study
CS1	M	23	5.5	3-year DB	1 year	BBS	1 semester
CS2	M	23	6	3-year Dip Computing	8 months	BIS	3 years*
CS3	F	24	6.5	High school	18 months	BBS	1 year
CS4	M	20	6	High school	1 year	BBS	1 semester
CS5	F	22	6	Incomplete Dip Teaching	1 year	BBS	1 semester
CS6	F	25	5.5	College DB	1 year	BBS	1 semester
CS7	F	22	5.5	College DB	1 year	BBS	2 years*
CS8	M	24	5.5	College DB	1 year	BBS	2 years*
CS9	M	24	6	College DB	2½ years	BBS	3 years*
CS10	M	25	5.5	College DB	1 year	BBS	3 years*
CS11	F	24	5.5	College DB	18 months	BBS	1 semester
CS12	M	25	5.5	College DB	1 year	BBS	1 semester

DB=Diploma of Business; BBS=Bachelor of Business Studies; BIS=Bachelor of Information Sciences
*The full length of their undergraduate study at the university

close attention to the transcripts, which Gillian made herself. This almost poetic attention allowed for an intimate awareness of nuance, and an almost memorized recall of the content. Throughout the study this proved invaluable, enabling Gillian to recognize points of commonality across interviews and to shape understanding of themes derived from a large pool of data.

The focus of the first interview was the expectations that students arrived with. This was achieved by asking them to move from the known, their experience of tertiary study in China, to the unknown, speculation on whether the New Zealand experience would be similar. However, it was clear their expectations drew more on their recent study in New Zealand English language centres than on their previous education in China. These students had not on the whole been highly successful or enthusiastic in China; most had not attended universities, and several of them felt short-changed by 'college-level' education which had left them undereducated:

When I working and then I meet some foreigner, especially Japanese, and always they talk about some economy or something, but I study computing, I don't know any. (CS8 I1. I1 indicates this is from Interview 1. See Figure 8.1)

In the highly interactive learning process of the language centre environments, 'scaffolded' on neo-Vygotskyan principles (Lantolf, 2000; Kozulin *et al.*, 2003), they had found a new enthusiasm for study which they expected to carry them through their degree study:

> In China I forced to study, but here I want to study, so my opinion has changed. (CS2 I1)

Added to this was a sense of efficacy arising out of their recent hard-won success in the IELTS examination that had gained them their places in the university. The majority had had at least one experience of failure which was shocking at first since it transgressed their assumptions that learning English in an English-speaking country would be easy. However, this failure allowed their eventual achievement of the goal to be construed as indicative of their ability to persevere and overcome adversity by their own efforts:

> So this year when I come to [the university] I feel I can taste little bit sweet of the successful, because I achieve a goal and I never give up, and keep trying, keep trying, keep trying. (CS9 I1)

These experiences built a rather consistent picture of apprehensive readiness, an expectation of challenges and hard work, in particular in developing independent learning skills, but a tentative optimism and excitement about their new identity in the university. This was imagined as an active, interactive student, intrinsically motivated by an encouraging study atmosphere, in a non-hierarchical accessible relationship with teachers, and with emergent, though perhaps barriered, relations with New Zealand peers. English would be demanding, but the student would be able to put the level already attained to use to draw understanding, from reading initially. Ease in listening to lectures, writing and speaking in university settings would take longer to acquire. Learning would take place step by step through channels opened to new entrants by university teachers and the university system.

This identity was interim, and it was clear that these Chinese students already had a vision of a future self, the endpoint of the process, as graduates of a 'Western' university. This graduate would be able to speak English, not perhaps as fluently as expected on departure, but nevertheless with sufficient command to engage in easy relations with foreigners, supported by intercultural communication skills. He or she would be prized in the employment market in China, and, if returning home, would bring back skills that allowed responsibilities to family, society and country to be fulfilled. He or she would also be a fully realized, independent, educated individual who had retained learning from the degree study and could use it to understand the world.

8.3.2   Completing the first semester experience

The next two rounds of interviews were held around the middle and the end of the semester, and focused on adjustments to these expectations and development of new understandings and skills brought about by the reality of the university experience. The interviews revealed that for none of the students had access to learning, either of content or of process, been as open as they had imagined. Their programme included compulsory first-level courses held in large, packed lecture halls, in some cases without accompanying tutorial classes. It was a long way from the accessible interaction they had dreamed of:

> I just in the university I just be a number, just be my ID number and they cannot remember all the ID number. (CS4 I2)

All of this was exacerbated by the extreme time demands made by internal assessment which left no room for experimentation:

> That assignment they will get the marks in the final exam, that is a little pressures for us, if they didn't they just to say that the exercise, just practice I will do it and to correct it and I will say, 'Oh, is that problem? Oh, I will understand,' but now, no, they will get the mark, so I will thinking about that is a little difficult for me. (CS7 I2)

CS10's initial assumption that 'the university life is quite free and quite relaxable' had proved misleading: 'It's quite, quite tough' (CS10 I2).

In these two sets of interviews, a series of paper-based visual instruments were used to trace the emotional journey that ran through their accounts of new demands and attempts to negotiate them. These included a graph introduced in the second interview and adapted in the third which asked students to mark their emotional state in each week (see Figure 8.2). As they filled it in, they spoke, creating a close tracking of their affective trajectories and the events which shaped them; for example:

> And the other thing is during the three and four week I'm, how to say? Time management trouble, everything what I thinking about before. But I think the most important thing I'm worry about the

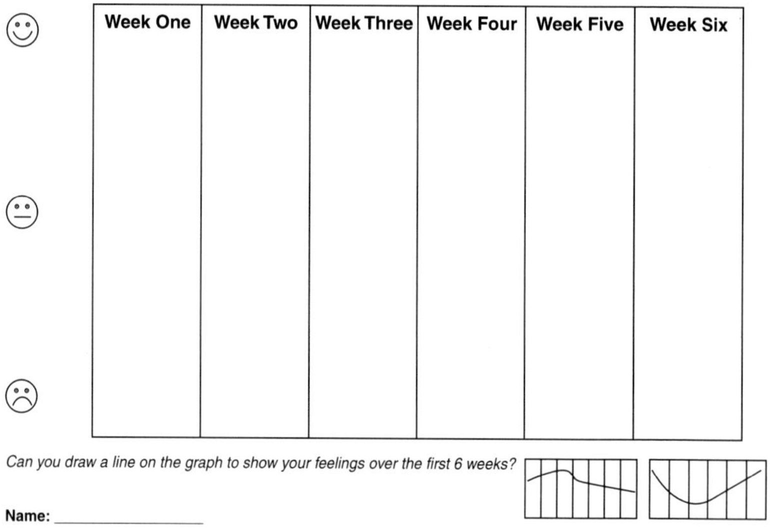

☺	Week One	Week Two	Week Three	Week Four	Week Five	Week Six
😐						
☹						

Can you draw a line on the graph to show your feelings over the first 6 weeks?

Name: _____

Figure 8.2   Feelings graph, longitudinal study

assignment result because they count for quite important in my total result. (CS10 I2)

Inevitably the first semester was a destabilized period as students sought to make sense of their environment. Confusion and false steps occurred, and could be debilitating if the sense of overarching progress was lost, so signs of successful adjustment to new demands, such as greater time-management skills, or working out how to read textbooks more effectively, were heartening, helping them inhabit more convincingly the identity of a New Zealand university student.

There were also indications that the students' attitudes centred more fully on the new academic culture. They moved from resentment of some of its features (such as the lack of daily present sources of personal academic guidance) which had in many cases swept away their initial enthusiasm, to an acceptance and apparent adoption of its values. For example, in response to a question about whether they were learning useful new skills, a number of them highlighted deeper insight into self-study and an appreciation of it:

I just find maybe I'm more flexible than what I used to be. Not just follow the lecture. Actually it's to teach you the ability to find the information you need to what you want. (CS5 I2)

Yeah, useful, because I'm already 24 and 24 I learn how to study on my own. Yeah, I waste lots of time. (CS11 I2)

By the end of the semester, there was a firm assertion from most students in the longitudinal study that they were learning better than they had in China:

> I think I learn much better [than] in China ... Because now I know what I should do. Yes, in China ... actually I'm study and, how to say, no goals for me, I just study and even I got bad result and good result, no matter. When after my college I went on work and I think, 'Oh, I don't know nothing.' (CS8 I3)

There remained difficulties and confusions, though. Inhabiting this complex community with a sense of competence would take more than four months. The language barrier still filtered content from them and assessment pressures were extreme. One had found the exams

> just like gambling. Because we don't know what lecturers or teachers think and some teacher didn't told us how to give us the guide or way. (CS1 I3)

The students were on a continuum, at one end of which were those who seemed to have retained their sense of agency, not yet arrived at expertise, but still seeing ways towards it, feeling they had learned valuable lessons and adopted specific measures that would help them navigate. They could be seen to be in a situation of 'legitimate peripheral practice' (Lave & Wenger, 1991). The other end was a much more sombre spot where there was a real anxiety about their ability to succeed and no clear plan to change current approaches in spite of their apparent inadequacy. CS4, for example, described a well-structured plan in interviews 2 and 3 for improving his learning, involving preview and review reading and high attendance, but admitted that he did not have time to implement it. CS9 had brief moments when he experienced a sense of competence (as when he realized that he actually had more confidence participating in discussion than some of his native-speaker classmates), but the semester was characterized by confusion about what he should do and puzzlement that hours spent studying in ways which had served him well in the past were not being rewarded by the good marks that he craved. He was driven forward only by his belief in the value of persistence (Skyrme, 2007).

There were, too, points in between these extremes, and students who fluctuated between positive and negative feelings. CS11, for example, struggled with her course work and was too timid to seek help, leading to great anxiety. She was nevertheless excited to observe other students at the end of the lectures engaging in the interaction with teachers that she aspired to: 'I love it!' she said (CS 11 I2 & I3).

8.4   Extending the study

The original invitation to participate in the longitudinal study had been for the duration of the first semester. The richness of the data emerging and the sense that the adaptive process remained incomplete, as illustrated by the patterns above, suggested that an expansion over the length of the degree would be rewarding: the original 12 participants were invited to continue their involvement by taking part in an interview at the end of their first year, and thereafter annually until completion of their degrees. Six took part in the next interview of whom five continued till the end of their study.

8.4.1   Getting the big picture

The iterative nature of the longitudinal study calls for close and continual data analysis, the 'constant comparison' familiar in grounded theory (Glaser, 1998; Strauss & Corbin, 1998). Comparisons are not just between subjects; there is also a need for recurring deep analysis of each subject's accumulating data so as to be ready at each successive interview with a sense of the elements of the evolving narrative that warrant further probing. Successive interviews also facilitate a process of member checking, 'taking data and interpretations back to participants in the study so that they can confirm the credibility of the information and narrative account', which Creswell and Miller (2000: 127) establish as one of the procedures for establishing validity in qualitative research. It was important to find an effective way to achieve this.

As she prepared for the second-year interviews, Gillian revisited the transcripts, subjecting them to line-by-line scrutiny (Glaser, 1998; Strauss & Corbin, 1998), heightening recognition of subtle positioning, nuances and echoing phrases which clarified a growing awareness of patterned individual difference within their responses and experiences. These patterns were building up in her mind into visual representations of each student's journey through the first year of study. She had been looking for a way to mark this interview out from the previous four, both to keep up participant interest, and to open them to new ways of investigating their personal experience. This needed to include a process for member checking which could, as well, invite students to elaborate on previous comments in the light of new perspectives. After discussion with Cynthia, she decided to develop the mental pictures into actual graphic representations on large charts for these purposes. Each of these 'big pictures', as she came to call them, enjoying the aptness of both literal and idiomatic meanings, had a central representation of adjustment pattern, learning style and chronological narrative, with important influences, aspirations and representations of identity depicted in relation to those in some detail. CS8's big picture can be seen in Figure 8.3. Inevitably they highlighted the individuality of each journey, while also reflecting commonalities such as the greater sense of membership that the second semester had brought.

The fifth interview, which for two of the students, because of cross-crediting from their Chinese qualifications, was also the interview which marked the completion of their undergraduate studies, began with an account from them of significant events in the second year. The big pictures were then introduced. The visual aspect allowed for an efficient consideration of a great deal of material without painstaking verbal reconstruction, reduced the dependence on spoken English as our only means of reflection and provided an engaging new way to think about their experience. The participants were all interested in the graphic representations, which gave them a greater understanding of the research process, and some were obviously flattered that their accounts had been subject to such close attention ('Oh, for me! Only for me! Oh, the privilege!' CS9, I5).

The pictures prompted rich discussion in directions often led by the student, providing more detail about earlier events and indications that stances had been elaborated or altered, or new skills had opened up further possibilities. For example, with hindsight, distance and subsequent success to cushion the pain, CS2 was able to provide a more detailed account of his first few weeks which he had previously referred to as a 'disaster' (I4). In China, he recalled:

we had to do assessment frequently. And the teachers they tell us, 'OK, you got to hand in these tomorrow and you got to hand in that next week,' so they all notice you and they sort of control. Not a good word but, you know, you know what to do, but when I was at [the New Zealand university] in the first week, second week, maybe first month, I didn't know what to do [laughs], apart from going to the lecture

200

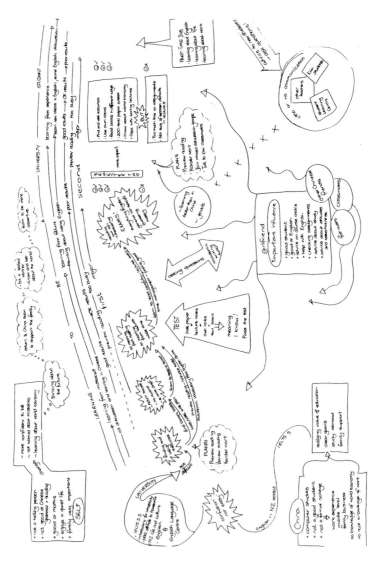

Figure 8.3 CS8's big picture

I didn't know what to do, when should I hand in assignments and when should I start? You know, I didn't know when to start. (CS2 I5)

He also reflected on a practice depicted on the chart which had proved highly valuable to him in the previous year in enabling him to overcome these difficulties, that of consulting his lecturers during their office hours, and discussed how, with greater understanding and ease with the university, he had moved on from that:

I changed myself a little bit from, especially in this semester I don't go to see my Professor very often 'cause I want to sort of test myself to see what can I do by myself rather than getting some help from my teachers. And also I would say if I want to really carry on with my study I got to have that ability to do it by myself, self-study and things. (CS2 I5)

CS8 looked back with hindsight on a key skill, reading books for assignments, to unpack what had blocked him in his first year and described his growing expertise:

But at that time I'm just know how to find the book. I find a number of books but I can not really get the message from books ... Now? It's more confident to find the *exactly* useful book and then I will just looking for the major part, so it's more quickly, more effective ... Yes, and then I will compare this book and the other book, the ideas, and textbook so I will choose just one useful. In the first year I will put all the related topic together, so sometimes confused. (CS8 I5)

CS9 added a nuance to the suggestion that he had found the tutor in one of his first-year courses helpful:

Oh, no they're *helpful*, but its not very – I don't know, it's kind of cold, or kind of superficial ... Yes. Because I'm too emotional, I'm too sensitive, so I try to get the information from their hearts rather than their face. That's my feeling. (CS9 I5)

For CS10 (see Figure 8.4), it even proved to be a source of self-recognition. When Gillian asked him about his future plans he laughed:

After I check your [indicating the big picture], yeah, I am quite changeable. (CS10 I5)

202

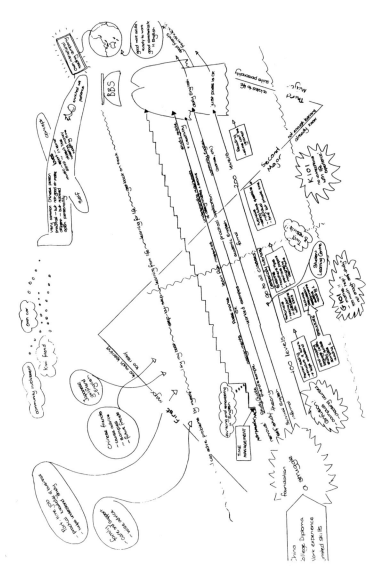

Figure 8.4 CS10's big picture

8.4.2   Photographic accounts

Following the success of the visual representations in the fifth interview, Cynthia suggested inviting the three students still completing their degrees to provide the centrepiece for the next one themselves. Some weeks beforehand, Gillian asked them whether they would be prepared to bring along photographs of 'times, events, people, places that have been important for you in your time at the university' (email communication). All three readily agreed and this proved highly successful as a way of framing the final interviews, since it provided the students with the opportunity to control how they summed up their experience, an opportunity they clearly relished. Their manners of doing so were very different and very reflective of the differences referred to above. For example, CS2, whose journey Gillian came to characterize as one of strategic preparation and adventurous experimentation, produced a series of pictures presenting himself in a range of situations outside the university itself and drew analogies from them with his personal development in areas as diverse as his 'religious and identity exploration' (I6) and the learning about himself and others that he derived from seasonal work in agriculture, culminating in this account of a time in a remote national park (Skyrme, 2008):

> I did walk into a bush. And I was quite scared at the beginning because I was only by myself. Was OK weather, but was a bit dark in the bush so bit scared. I was walking by myself for like nearly an hour and suddenly I met one person, oh finally, I felt a little bit safer. I really want to relate this to my life, feel like in my life I'm walking in a bush as well, I don't really see the destination, the only thing I can do is just explore all things. I'm still in the bush I would think even though I could see a little light somewhere. Still. (CS2 I6)

CS10 also liked to extend himself, but in a more cautious manner, based on carefully staged 'step-by-step' learning, with a focus very much on promoting his two important goals of succeeding at the university and preparing himself for employment after graduation. His photos were all firmly centred on the university experience and provided a catalyst for accounts of his growing sense of membership. For example, one of them was of the library shelves that were most pertinent to his area of study:

> Normally when I get in, I say, even I close my eyes I know how to go. This area I should go, so before, compared with I just first year's

student, really confusing, probably how to get the book right, how to get the subject right, right now I don't need to, just go directly, and I even don't need to use computer search for the book I need, I just go to this column and then have a look and then pick up some book useful for me. (CS10 I6)

The third of these students, CS9, reported above craving a warm personal relationship with his teachers, struggled in many of the core courses for his business degree, but flourished where teachers were tolerant of the multiple visits he made to check their intentions for assignments. He felt it was 'totally waste of time' to try to 'guess' what was required, as he felt his peers did, instead of consulting the lecturer, since the point was to find out

how the assignments will achieve *his* opinion and what's about *his* idea to analyse this assignment, what's *he* think about assignments. (CS9 I6)

Significantly, he found himself unable to make his own selection of photographs and produced several albums so that Gillian could tell him what kind she wanted.

This final device for summing up the experience, therefore, proved highly revealing as process as well as through content.

8.5   Reaching the end

To sum up the students' journeys in terms of the affective dimensions of evolving identity, this study revealed a progressive movement from a position on enrolment of peripheral, indeed sometimes marginal, participation in the practices of the university, to a far more centralized membership, predicated on the acquisition of growing language skills, but also, importantly, the recognition of wider social practices, such as consultation with teachers, and the participants' own exercise of agency in negotiating a fit between the student they wanted to be and the university's demands of them, as can be seen in CS9's frequent consultations with lecturers over assignments.

There were important measures of success. By far the majority of these participants, and all those who stayed with the longitudinal study, completed their degrees; two of them continued to postgraduate study. They conceptualized a significant part of the journey as being about process rather than product, in particular the development of independent study and life skills. This was perceived as a highly valued aspect of what they had learned, a source of pride, and the essential added value of the New Zealand degree. CS8 had found the demands of English difficult through the whole process, but when Gillian asked him whether, given the chance, a university education in China would have been preferable, he responded:

> I think this style is better for learning. Yeah. You do it by yourself, you look at the resource and everything. (CS8 I5)

Another educational goal mentioned had been to retain and apply learning beyond the confines of their exams, to be educated human beings in their ongoing experience of the world, and CS8, among others, was pleased to have achieved this:

> I'm watching the news and newspaper and I will put the what I'm learn relate to that. Now think about more and talk to friends. (CS8 I5)

His new understanding had implications beyond himself. He envisaged a future self explaining the ways of foreigners to Chinese people:

> I'm already experienced about the foreign culture, so I will understand what they are doing in Chinese, so I am not surprised ... On the other hand I want many foreigner to China to see what China is. It's better than stay in their own country and just the newspaper or other people say ... Understand each other the world will be better. (CS8 I5)

This was an insight he would have liked to share with his mono-cultural domestic classmates.

The ultimate test of being-and-doing (Gee, 2004) a university student in New Zealand was feeling oneself to be, and to be recognized as, equal to 'Kiwi' students. By the end of his first semester, CS2 claimed equality within the classroom, but felt to the end that they were treated as 'foreigners' (I5) outside its confines. CS8 was reluctant to equate himself with local counterparts:

> It's hard to equal to the Kiwi students because they already stay here, they haven't got the other culture. (CS8 I5)

Interestingly, in terms of membership of the university community, having access to two cultures was clearly not seen as an advantage.

All of them had appreciated opportunities for personal growth and reassessment of values which were, no doubt, partly age-related, but which this experience had facilitated and broadened. These reached beyond study experiences, as CS2 indicates:

> Especially I like the exploration part, like after I came to New Zealand actually I faced more challenges and more issues, more questions about myself, yeah, even like say self-identity, things like that, feel like things I never thought about before, 'cause back home that's the way I was and the way of my life, but here, coming to New Zealand is like open another window for me, even a door for me, I could really explore different things, different views. It's towering because I have to face different things, but I really enjoy the overseas experience. (CS2 I6)

A fuller model of this journey can be found in Figure 8.5.

8.6 Reflecting on the research process

This account has also been about the research process itself, and we will conclude with some reflection on that. From the point of view of the primary aim of a researcher to elicit rich and reliable data, we believe that the processes and tools that were developed revealed a fine-grained picture of the lived experience of these students. The longitudinal study included 50 interviews, most of them around 45 minutes long, and produced a wealth of data on many aspects of their learning (Skyrme, 2004, 2005, 2007, 2008).

A longitudinal study of this length was new for both of us, and both the design and our understanding of its potential evolved over the period. For example, the importance of spending adequate time in the field (Ortega & Iberri-Shea, 2005) is clearly demonstrated by the case of CS9. At the end of the first semester he was struggling, stressed and unable to turn his undoubted diligence to good effect in this academic culture. Following his progress to the end of his first year (see Figure 8.6), and then to the end of his degree study, however, allowed us to witness the emergence of a different picture. Although puzzlement continued to plague him in courses in unfamiliar disciplines, within his major discipline, where teachers tolerated, or even welcomed, his frequent visits, he felt secure, even ebullient, in his

207

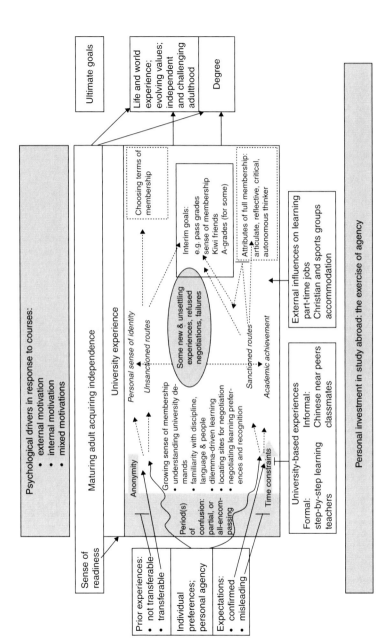

Figure 8.5 Chinese international students: the New Zealand university experience

208

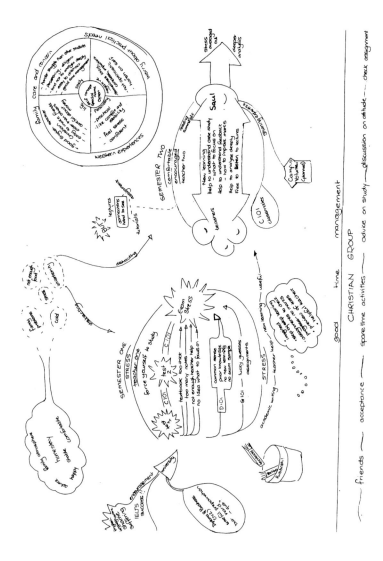

Figure 8.6 CS9's big picture

role as student. More widely, he prided himself on his acquired self-knowledge, his ability to conduct his life and personal relationships satisfactorily, and his English, which was enabling him to get jobs such as telemarketing, generally seen as beyond the ambit of second language speakers. He had made his university life 'fruitful' (CS9 I6) by taking up a volunteering opportunity to assist new students and agreed with Gillian that he had become '*full* student, yeah, full member of the uni' (I6).

Another aspiration of the research was to ensure that benefit did not just flow in the direction of the researcher. Gillian gave small gifts at each interview, but, to our satisfaction, the greatest appreciation arose out of the artefacts that flowed from the process itself. This can be illustrated by responses to the final summary sent out to the students remaining for the last round of interviews. CS2 immediately contacted her to thank her for it effusively, saying:

I spent about 40mins just reading through it without a stop. You know, not many articles from academic perspective I could enjoy reading through but this is definitely one of them. (CS2, email communication)

He thanked her for sharing 'our special journey' with other educators and policy-makers. CS9 needed a second copy since his mother wanted the one he had received, and CS10 immediately invited Gillian to his graduation ceremony and dinner, during the course of which he told her that she was one of only two New Zealanders to whom he had ever talked about his feelings and problems during the four years of his stay.

It seemed that the processes, and in particular the innovations, which allowed close cooperative scrutiny of significant aspects of the experience by using graphic elements supported by talk, and an invitation to the students to contribute their own photographs to this, had been instrumental in achieving our intentions. A growing interest in the use of visual elements is evident in other studies with L2 learners (e.g. Kalaja *et al.*, 2008; Nikula & Pitkanen-Huhta, 2008; Gu *et al.*, 2010). However, we have found no published accounts of their use incorporating both researcher and participant contributions in the manner represented here, and we would recommend them for other researchers. Holliday (2002: 161) suggests that the term 'participant' may often be a misnomer as the life which the subjects of research 'participate' in may be largely removed from brief encounters with researchers and the interpretation which those researchers put on them. However, the responses quoted above suggest to us that these informants had truly felt they were participating in a collaborative process of understanding the significant issues and changes that study abroad had brought for them.

References

Burnett, C. & Gardener, J. (2006) The one less traveled by ...: the experience of Chinese students in a UK university. In M. Bryam & A. Feng (eds) *Living and Studying Abroad: Research and Practice*. Clevedon: Multilingual Matters, pp. 64–90.
Cohen, L., Manion, L. & Morrison, K. (2007) *Research Methods in Education* (6th edn). London: Routledge.
Cotterill, P. (1992) Interviewing women: issues of friendship, vulnerability and power, *Women's Studies International Forum*, 15(5/6), 593–606.
Creswell, J. W. & Miller, D. L. (2000) Determining validity in qualitative inquiry, *Theory into Practice*, 39(3), 124–130.
Dörnyei, Z. (2007) *Research Methods in Applied Linguistics: Quantitative, Qualitative, and Mixed Methodologies*. Oxford: Oxford University Press.
Gee, J. P. (2004) Learning language as a matter of learning social languages within discourses. In M. R. Hawkins (ed.) *Language Learning and Teacher Education: A Sociocultural Approach*. Buffalo, NY: Multilingual Matters, pp. 11–31.
Glaser, B. G. (1998) *Doing Grounded Theory: Issues and Discussions*. Mill Valley, CA: Sociology Press.
Gu, Q., Schweisfurth, M. & Day, C. (2010) Learning and growing in a 'foreign' context: intercultural experiences of international students, *Compare*, 40(1), 7–23.
Holliday, A. (2002) *Doing and Writing Qualitative Research*. London: Sage.
Jin, L. & Cortazzi, M. (2008) Images of teachers, learning and questioning in Chinese cultures of learning, In E. Berendt (ed.) *Metaphors of Learning: Cross-Cultural Perspectives*. Amsterdam: John Benjamins, pp. 177–202.
Jin, L. & Cortazzi, M. (forthcoming) The changing landscapes of a journey: educational metaphors in China. In Janette Ryan (ed.) *Understanding China's Education Reform*. London: Routledge.
Kalaja, P., Alanen, R. & Dufva, H. (2008) Self-portraits of EFL learners: Finnish students draw and tell. In P. Kalaja, V. Menezes & A. M. F. Barcelos (eds) *Narratives of Learning and Teaching EFL*. New York: Palgrave Macmillan, pp. 186–198.
Kozulin, A., Gindis, B., Ageyev, V. S. & Miller, S. M. (eds) *Vygotsky's Educational Theory in Cultural Context*. Cambridge: Cambridge University Press.
Lantolf, J. P. (ed.) (2000) *Sociocultural Theory and Second Language Learning*. Oxford: Oxford University Press.
Lave, J. & Wenger, E. (1991) *Situated Learning: Legitimate Peripheral Participation*. New York: Cambridge University Press.
Matthews, L. (2003) International students crowding out lectures, *Manawatu Evening Standard*, 18 August, 1.
McCracken, G. (1988) *The Long Interview*. Newbury Park, CA: Sage.

Nikula, T. & Pitkanen-Huhta, A. (2008) Using photographs to access stories of learning English. In P. Kalaja, V. Menezes & A. M. F. Barcelos (eds) *Narratives of Learning and Teaching EFL*. New York: Palgrave Macmillan, pp. 171–185.

Ortega, L. & Iberri-Shea, G. (2005) Longitudinal research in second language acquisition: recent trends and future directions, *Annual Review of Applied Linguistics*, 25, 26–45.

Senior, R. M. (2006) *The Experience of Language Teaching*. Cambridge: Cambridge University Press.

Skyrme, G. (2004) Stepping over the threshold: Chinese international students in transition from language centre to university, *New Zealand Studies in Applied Linguistics*, 10(2), 93–102.

Skyrme, G. (2005) The reflective learner: Chinese international students' use of strategies to enhance university study, *Research Paper Series*. http://www.crie.org.nz/research_paper/G.Skyrme%20WP%2016.pdf.

Skyrme, G. (2007) Entering the university: the differentiated experience of two Chinese international students in a New Zealand university, *Studies in Higher Education*, 32(3), 357–372.

Skyrme, G. (2008) I am who I am: new senses of self in a New Zealand university. Paper presented at the CLESOL Conference 2008, Auckland, New Zealand.

Strauss, A. L. & Corbin, J. (1998) *Basics of Qualitative Research: Techniques and Procedures for Developing Grounded Theory*. Thousand Oaks, CA: Sage.

Tarling, N. (2004) *International Students in New Zealand: The Making of Policy since 1950*. Auckland, NZ: New Zealand Asia Institute, University of Auckland.

Tian, M. & Lowe, J. (2009) Existentialist internationalisation and the Chinese student experience in English universities, *Compare: A Journal of Comparative and International Education*, 39(5), 659–676.

Ward, C. A., Bochner, S. & Furnham, A. (2001) *The Psychology of Culture Shock* (2nd edn). New York: Routledge.

Wenger, E. (1998) *Communities of Practice: Learning, Meaning and Identity*. Cambridge: Cambridge University Press.

9
An Emotional Journey of Change: The Case of Chinese Students in UK Higher Education

Qing Gu

9.1 Introduction

This chapter outlines some key challenges that Chinese students face while studying in UK higher education and the nature of their learning and personal growth in intercultural contexts. The empirical work is based upon a series of research projects that the author has led over the past five years (2004–09), including a two-year Economic and Social Research Council (ESRC) research project on the experiences of international undergraduate students at British universities (Gu *et al.*, 2010) and a British Academy-funded two-year research project which investigated how, why and to what extent overseas educational experiences may (or may not) contribute to the personal, professional and career development of Chinese students who return to work in China (Gu *et al.*, 2009).

The research uncovers the fragmentation of Chinese students' intercultural experiences. It reveals the role of agency in their ability to make sense of their learning experiences during their study abroad and to make use of these in their working lives when they returned to their home country. The findings contribute to understanding the impact and transferability of the study abroad experiences on individuals' change and development over time.

9.2 The internationalization of higher education: the policy contexts

Despite the apparent recency of the current growth, proliferation and diversification in global higher education, internationalization is not a new phenomenon for universities. Historical accounts of scholar exchanges and intercultural education can be traced back to 272–222 BC (Ward *et al.*, 2001). However, the concepts, forms, focus and movement of the internationalization agenda have changed profoundly in identifiable phases in modern times: from aid in the 1970s, cooperation and exchange in the 1980s to trade by the end of the twentieth century (de Wit, 2008). Now, at the end of the first decade of the twenty-first century, the competition for international students, particularly in the form of the provision of cross-border education in the developed world, has increased significantly (de Wit, 2008; OECD, 2008; UNESCO, 2009). Cross-border tertiary education refers to 'the movement of people, programmes, providers, curricula, projects, research and services in tertiary (or higher) education across national jurisdictional borders' (OECD, 2007: 11). As new forms of cross-border education emerge and grow, so too the complexity of the internationalization of higher education has increased. The latest phase of the internationalization of higher education is thus qualitatively distinct.

Not surprisingly, internationalization is perceived by some as the most revolutionary development in higher education in the twenty-first century (Seddoh, 2001). The sheer rapidity of change in the 1990s has seen institutions of higher education become active players in the global marketplace. In the UK, both Government and universities have been engaged in a push to improve the international competitiveness of the higher education offering (*Guardian*, 2006; also Blair, 1999; UKCOSA, 2004; UKCISA, 2007; Universities UK, 2006). The then Prime Minister Tony Blair in 1999 called upon universities to 'open a window on the world' (Blair, 1999). One of the key objectives of the second Prime Minister's Initiative (PMI2), launched in 2006, was to consolidate the success of the PMI1 through understanding the expectations of international students and improving the quality of all aspects of their experience while studying and living in the UK (British Council, 2007).

The Government's initiatives to secure UK's success in the global education competition have come to fruition. The United Kingdom remained the second favourite study destination for international students between 1999 and 2007, sharing approximately 12.6% of the world's mobile students (UNESCO, 2009). It has, also, been the second largest overseas destination for Chinese students, behind the United States first and ahead of Australia third (*People's Daily Online*, 14 December 2009).

The upsurge of Chinese students studying abroad can be traced back to China's reformist and former leader Deng Xiaoping's speech in June 1978: 'We are going to send thousands or tens of thousands of students to receive overseas education' (Xinhua News Agency). Three decades after Deng's speech, the number of Chinese students studying abroad has indisputably met his expectations. According to statistics from the Chinese Academy of Social Sciences, 1.07 million Chinese students studied overseas in China's reform and opening-up period between 1978 and 2006. In 2007, an additional 421,000 Chinese students contributed to the statistics of international student mobility (UNESCO, 2009). Following the internationalization of China's economy and the trend of globalization, central and local Chinese education authorities have placed greater emphasis on international education exchanges, 'including permitting large numbers of young Chinese to study abroad on their own or at government expense' (British Council, 2008). This has, no doubt, further contributed to China's important presence on the world stage of global higher education competition.

In the case of the UK in particular, given the launch of the British Government's long-term worldwide educational campaign in 1999 and the subsequent introduction of a series of national policies to boost the recruitment of international students, soaring interest among students in China has led to a major influx of Chinese students into British universities. Figure 9.1 illustrates the number of UK Universities and Colleges Admissions Service (UCAS) applications from China and accepted Chinese

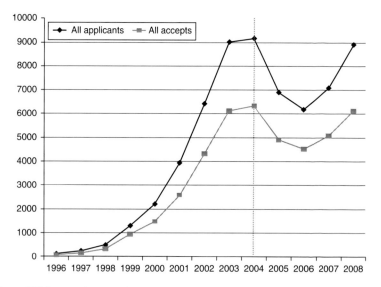

Source: UCAS press releases, various years
Figure 9.1   Numbers of applications from China and accepted Chinese applicants by qualification (degree, foundation degree and HND), between 1996 and 2007

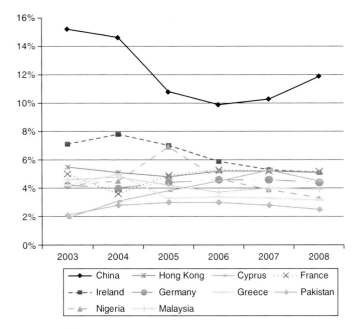

Source: UCAS press releases, various years
Figure 9.2   Percentages of accepted applicants by country, between 2003 and 2008

applicants between 1996 and 2008. These applicants all applied to full-time, undergraduate higher education courses offered by universities and colleges in membership of the UCAS scheme. After a drastic rise from 104 in 1996 to a peak of around 9141 in 2004, the number of Chinese applications for UK degree courses showed a decline in 2005 and 2006, which was then reversed by a rapid recovery in 2007 and 2008. In 2008, close to 9000 Chinese students submitted their applications to undergraduate courses at British universities and over 6000 departed for overseas study in the UK. As Figure 9.2 shows, Chinese students have been the largest single international student group in the UK since 2003.

9.3   Reconceptualizing the intercultural experiences of student sojourners: the research contexts

The psychological and educational literature on international students and Chinese students in particular is substantial (e.g. Bond, 1986; Cortazzi & Jin, 1997; Bochner *et al.*, 2001; Ward *et al.*, 2001;

Grimshaw, 2007; Kingston & Forland, 2008; Gan, 2009; Dimmock & Leong, 2010; Rizvi, 2010). Each expanding body of research, however, has its distinct focus.

Empirical research in psychology tends to be primarily concerned with stress levels and coping strategies and the quality of the support mechanism that is available to promote (or inhibit) student sojourners' intercultural adaptation, intra- and interpersonal interactions and psychological wellbeing. Such a focus is reflected in their conceptualization of students' study-abroad experiences which are defined as 'a significant transitional event that brings with it a considerable amount of accompanying stress, involving both confrontation and adaptation to unfamiliar physical and psychological experiences and changes' (Cushner & Karim, 2004: 292). With regard to specific patterns of intercultural adaptation, Ward and Kennedy (1993: 222) suggest two major types of reactions to intercultural stress: psychological adjustment (i.e. psychological wellbeing or satisfaction that is interwoven with stress and coping process) and socio-cultural adaptation (i.e. relating to social skills and predicted on cultural learning) (see also Searle & Ward, 1990; Ward & Kennedy, 1993; Mori, 2000; Li & Gasser, 2005; Leung *et al.*, 2006).

While the above studies are valuable as a means of identifying key issues in intercultural education, most are predominantly quantitative and 'objectivistic in nature' (Gudykunst, 2005: 25) and attempt to predict patterns of intercultural interactions and factors that determine the observed patterns. Such methodological concerns of psychological research often fail to take into account the role of human agency in the management by international students of their overseas learning experiences. Moreover, psychological researchers are relatively less concerned with the cultural backgrounds of the individuals involved in intercultural interactions (Ward *et al.*, 2001), making it almost impossible for them to explain the complexity of international student identity negotiations and sense making in the cultural, social and educational environments in which they are engaged. Not surprisingly, psychological research, at best, can only provide a rather limited account of how, why and to what extent the frustrations, tensions and challenges embedded in intercultural experiences are managed (or not managed) by international students over time.

The educational literature, on the other hand, tends to be based upon small-scale, qualitative studies (e.g. Gu & Brooks, 2008; Kingston & Forland, 2008; Montgomery & McDowell, 2009) and has been increasingly criticized for having focused far too much upon the deterministic role of culture in international students' experiences (Jones, 2005;

Gu & Schweisfurth, 2006; Grimshaw, 2007; Schweisfurth & Gu, 2009; Signorini *et al.*, 2009). The level of difference in cultural norms, values and behaviour patterns between the host country and the international students' country of origin tends to be perceived as *the* factor that has contributed to the struggles and challenges that many students experience while studying abroad. There are at least four critical limitations in such conceptualization.

First and foremost, the international student population is not a homogeneous group. However, despite their diverse cultural, social and linguistic backgrounds, international students are too often uncritically regarded as 'an undifferentiated block' (Jones, 2005: 341). 'The' Chinese (or Asian) learner (e.g. Watkins & Biggs, 1996, 2001) is probably one of the most frequently researched student groups in the educational literature – a phrase which paints too simplistic a picture of their often fragmented, differentiated and complex individual and collective study-abroad experiences. Given the heterogeneity of the student group, it can be argued that the tendency to use cultural models alone to identify and remedy the challenges that Chinese students experience should be treated with caution.

Second, the deterministic notion of culture tends to work on a deficit model and problematize international students in that they perform less well academically and require more institutional support (Morrison *et al.*, 2005). In the case of Chinese students, despite the empirical evidence which suggests that Chinese students are also cognitively able learners (e.g. Biggs, 1996), Chineseness has been defined in terms of deviation from Western norms (Chang, 2000), implying that they are significantly different from Western learners and thus less adequate in a Western learning environment (Jones, 2005). In their research which compared academic achievement levels of UK-domiciled undergraduate students with non-UK domiciled undergraduate students, Morrison *et al.* (2005) found that the performance of Chinese students did not differ significantly from that of UK students. This observation was 'a surprise' because it did not support the expectation that 'students domiciled in China – who are generally considered to face significant problems in adapting to linguistic, cultural and educational differences in the UK – would do worse than UK-domiciled students' (Morrison *et al.*, 2005: 335).

Third, the deterministic notion of culture also fails to take into account the role of individual agency and resilience in managing setbacks and challenges in adverse circumstances. These qualities are individualized and may vary greatly even within a mono-cultural group. Gu and Schweisfurth (2006) carried out a mixed-method comparative pilot study on Chinese learners' experiences in the UK and in British Council's language-teacher education projects in China and found that in addition to culture, factors such as the identities and motivations of the learners and the power relationships between them and their teachers were also significant issues in the strategic adaptations made by Chinese students. Moreover, an excessive emphasis upon the impact of cultural models tends to overlook the 'maturing process' (Murphy-Lejeune, 2003: 113) that many international students experience while studying abroad. They are found to go through two types of transition while studying abroad: (1) maturation and human development and (2) intercultural adaptation (Gu *et al.*, 2010). These transitional experiences interactively influence the nature and process of their change and development in a different educational environment and a different culture and society over time.

Finally, culture is itself a fluid and dynamic construct. It is even more so when the world has entered the third phase of globalization in which knowledge, information, skills, values, cultures and systems have been able to interact on the 'flat-world platform' more easily and more seamlessly than ever before (Friedman, 2005). The sheer rapidity of change and its accumulated effects have altered the character of work and many features of contemporary living in a fundamental way (Held *et al.*, 1999; Coolahan, 2002; Little & Green, 2009). A fixed and static view to compare cultural models in such an increasingly globalized world may, therefore, be of limited and dubious value. Culture evolves and 'the' Chinese learner transforms within the changing cultures.

In sum, important though it may be, culture is not the only determinant of teaching and learning practices, preferences and experiences. All too easily teachers and learners may fall into the trap of cultural stereotyping. However, it is clear that other factors are at least as influential: the backgrounds and aspirations of learners, their specific motivation for learning, the settings in which the interactions take place, and the nature of the relationship between teachers and learners. In particular, the cultural blinkers may screen out the importance of the individual personality of learners. Moreover, a rigid view of cultural essentialism will, unfortunately, fail to capture a profound change process of maturation that many Chinese students learn to manage over time.

In the following section, the chapter will explore the nature of several samples of Chinese students' experiences at British universities, drawing upon a synthesis of findings of four studies (Gu & Brooks, 2008; Gu & Maley, 2008; Gu *et al.*, 2009, 2010), investigating different aspects of Chinese students' study and living experiences in UK higher education.

The first study was set up in 2004 and the last ended in October 2009. A distinctive strength of the studies is the holistic and developmental perspective that the author and her colleagues adopt to probe into a learning process that is itself holistic and developmental in nature.

9.4 Change as transition and development: managing challenges at British universities

All four studies on which this chapter is based combined quantitative and qualitative methodologies. The first stage was a questionnaire survey which provided a baseline description of the sample students' purposes for their overseas studies, expectations and initial impressions and a range of personal, social and academic challenges that they had experienced by the time of the survey. A series of individual interviews and group meetings to explore their experiences were then carried out, with special attention to critical incidents, changes over time and respondents' explanations for how their experiences were unfolding.

In the study funded by ESRC (Gu *et al.*, 2010), the qualitative data gathering also used narrative interviews with assistance of an instrument adapted from the VITAE study (Day *et al.*, 2006). This instrument required students to recall peaks and troughs during their stay in the UK and to identify 'turning points' (Strauss, 1959), that is, key moments and experiences that had had a significantly positive or negative impact on their perceptions of their effective management of their study, lives and communication with others. They related how these were managed (or not managed) over time (the lines were known as 'Managing the ups and downs of living and studying (MUDLS)', see Figure 9.3 for an example).

The integration and synthesis of the findings of both qualitative and quantitative instruments enabled the identification of the extent to which intercultural, personal and professional experiences in the UK and China over time influenced the experiences of the informants involved.

By bringing together patterns and themes identified in the three studies, it becomes clear that despite various intercultural challenges and struggles, most students have managed to survive the demands of the learning and living environment, and to adapt and develop. Key observations of their journey of study abroad include:

- Chinese students come to the UK for language and cultural experiences, but, primarily, for academic accreditation.
- Academic achievement and personal independence are the most important achievements for most students.

220

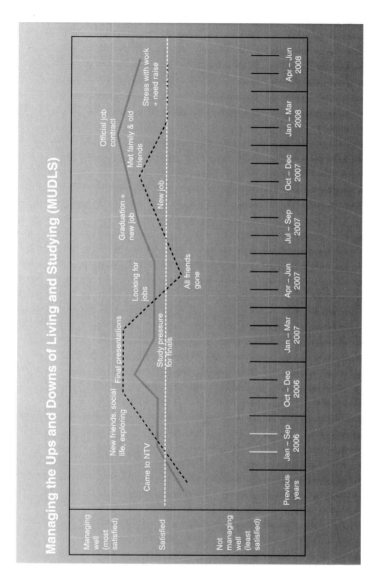

Figure 9.3 Managing the ups and downs of living and studying (MUDLS)

- While some students may have fitted in better socially than others, most have managed to achieve in their academic studies.
- The most profound change lies in their success (or otherwise) in managing the influences which challenge existing identities.
- There is an important relationship between students' sense of belonging, identity and self-efficacy (the belief that they can achieve and succeed).
- They have experienced three major aspects of change: (1) interculturality: cross/intercultural experiences; (2) maturity: human growth and development; and (3) intellectual development.

9.4.1 Change as transition: managing academic challenges

Students' learning processes are holistic and developmental in nature. Evidence suggests that the challenges of adapting to a different academic culture can be more acute and overwhelming than settling into a different cultural and social environment on students' arrival. A widely acknowledged initial learning shock was experienced by the Chinese students who were involved in the studies.

9.4.1.1 *Learning shock*

Learning shock refers to some unpleasant feelings and difficult experiences that learners encounter when they are exposed to a new learning environment. Such unpleasant feelings can be intensified and may impose a deeper psychological and emotional strain on learners when they study abroad. The psychological, cognitive and affective struggles that learners experience primarily result from their unfamiliarity with different teaching and learning traditions and a lack of confidence in using the English language for communication in the new learning environment. For example:

> When I first started studying here, I was not used to either the study or the life here. I did not know where to start. In class, I did not understand the purposes of the teaching, and sometimes I did not quite understanding the teacher. (CS1)

Lewthwaite (1986) argues that the experience of crossing cultural borders is a learning process in which there are many obstacles to overcome. The experiences of the following postgraduate student indicate that differences in cultural, social and historical roots between the societies from which students are drawn and in which they are currently based are most likely to lead to an uphill struggle for them to participate fully and confidently in class activities, particularly in the initial phase of their studies. In addition, their stress to cope with an unfamiliar linguistic learning environment would have further contributed to the intensity of their initial struggles. In this sense, learning shock cannot be separated from cultural shock; it is an important aspect of cultural shock:

> When I first started my MA, I felt very strongly that I was not used to the teaching and learning environment at all ... The teaching style was very different from that in China. Chinese students were taught like stuffed ducks in China, whilst here students are encouraged to take part in group discussions ... I also found that language could be a barrier, particularly in listening. I could not quite understand students from countries like Malaysia. A particular teacher had a very strong local accent, which I could hardly understand. (CS2)

Chinese students' learning shock and academic stresses were also noted by their tutors:

> Yes, they have serious difficulty adjusting to expectations of the British education system ... We are trying to encourage an autonomous approach to study ... Understanding that difference [in teaching] is extremely challenging to learners when they come on the course, because they are expecting to be told what to learn, what to read, the answers to produce, and they are ready to work hard doing that ... Some students welcome that. Some students are worried, intimidated, confused by that shift of responsibility ... Yes, the language can be a problem. But I think cultural issues are far more important. (BT1)

9.4.1.2 Beyond frustration

While cultural differences may play a crucial part in Chinese students' initial struggle and frustration when adjusting to a 'foreign' academic environment, conclusions from all four studies indicate that the large majority of Chinese students (like most other international students) have experienced positive adaptation and development in their academic studies over time. This can be seen in their improved linguistic competence, increased self-confidence and involvement in class activities and a strong sense of independence in learning. Thus, by the end of their studies, it is unlikely that culture will continue to function as 'a source of conflict', as Hofstede (2009) maintains on his website, or a source of stress and struggle. Rather, different fabrics of the host culture of learning and teaching will have been absorbed, integrated and personalized by individual students to take on different forms which enable them to perform in their studies and fuel them with strength, confidence and power.

The development of students' independent learning abilities and greater responsibility for their own study is evidenced in the following quote:

> I have become more independent in my life here. As for study, I enjoy my studying because I like my subject very much ... I have a lot of spare time at university. But I am mostly doing my own stuff in my spare time, something about my subject Art Design. Due to the nature of my subject, I often make connections of what I encounter in my spare time with my subject. (CS3)

Some British lecturers have also noticed their Chinese students' conscious and reflexive change towards more independent learning. For example:

> I had an interesting example of a Chinese student who started a degree with us and she had problems. Very often the Chinese students have problems finding themselves extending from one to two years. But she went from a student who in her first year suffered all sorts of problems to a student who in a second year took a piece of research which she found, challenged it, researched it and actually came up with some original research data disputing quite an important article which she based her research on. (BT2)

Students' change, adaptation, improvement and rebirth experience in their studies can also be seen in their enlightened understanding of the notion of plagiarism over time. Learning to write using unfamiliar academic discourse patterns requires, at the deepest level, the students' cultural appropriation of a possibly different conceptual understanding of the way of writing and of the meaning of using the literature to develop their written argumentation (Gu & Brooks, 2008). This learning process spans a developmental continuum involving the learners overcoming emotional tensions which arise from changes in their cognition, senses of identity and socio-cultural values. Ample evidence from the experiences of the case study students shows that the intercultural learning experience is also a transitional and rebirth experience. Thus, change in students' perception of plagiarism is indeed part of their wider adaptation to the academic conventions of their host countries. For example, Cui, the female student in English Literature, commented:

> But now [on a master's course] the situation is very different. I have been reading materials in my subject as the course goes along. So I have, consciously and subconsciously, gained some understanding in the field. Sometimes when I come across something interesting in a book, I put it down in my notebook. So when I am writing up my essay, I can use my old notes which are very useful. I also look for more references according to the specific subject of my essay. So the process of preparing for my essays is very different from before. (CS4)

It is clear that what she has acquired over time is not only an improved understanding of her subject. She has also acquired a deeper understanding of ways of writing in the host, dominant academic community. However, the most profound change in her goes beyond her improved understanding and ability to write in a way that is deemed as 'normal' in the dominant academic community. She managed to engage confidently with the academic conventions as an active and competent learner. What shines through is her successful development and adaptation.

9.4.2   Change as transition: managing social and cultural challenges

Furnham and Bochner (1986) argue that 'foreign students face several difficulties, some exclusive to them (as opposed to native students)' (cited in Furnham, 2004: 17). In addition to the need of adjusting academically to the local teaching and learning environment, students who study abroad also encounter challenges of acculturation and socialization simultaneously. On the one hand, the differences in values, attitudes and beliefs between home and host cultures, coupled with the sense of loss of the familiar (including food), put considerable pressure on their acculturation (Lewthwaite, 1986). On the other hand, they are also engaged in a process of socialization – an ongoing dialectic process in which individuals define and redefine themselves and their relationships with others in the 'outside' society (Jenkins, 2004). Jenkins argues that '"Society" is a conversation between people; the mind is the internalization of that conversation; the self lies within and between the two' (2004: 42).

Establishing a 'conversation' with people who share different, unfamiliar and sometimes contrasting traditions, societal values and social expectations can be emotionally draining and physically exhausting.

9.4.2.1 *'Enjoying loneliness'*

'Enjoy' and 'loneliness' do not normally collocate well together. However, when they were put together by a postgraduate student to summarize his social life in the UK, the term conveyed a powerful and profound psychological frustration that this student had coped with in his student life. This frustration was additional to the learning-shock-related stress and tensions that he might have also suffered.

Leading a boring and lonely social life and feeling a lack of sense of belonging contribute to their sense of alienation in the host society. For example:

> I was just wondering why I didn't feel lonely at all when I first came here. Because I didn't know what was going to happen. So every day was a new day ... But this time I came back [after Easter break] I knew what was going to happen to me. I knew I was going to have a presentation and lots of study ... and every day is normal. To be honest I don't like my personal life here. I enjoy my study life but my personal life is kind of boring ... Everyone [friends in England] has got their [own] stuff to do ... I just feel that I don't belong here. It's not my place. I'm the guest and the guest is always less powerful; and also they are the host or something like that. (CS5)

This student's story is not, unfortunately, unique. Her experience reflects certain aspects of cultural shock, typically featured with 'a sense of loss and feelings of deprivation in regard to friends, status, profession and possessions', 'being rejected by, or rejecting, members of the new culture', and 'feelings of impotence due to not being able to cope with the new environment' (Oberg, 1960, cited in Furnham, 2004: 17).

9.4.2.2 *Friendship patterns*

CS5's journey of her student life in England was accompanied by her constant intention to retain friendships and seek a sense of belonging within her class, her accommodation and the local society. She retained friendships with the Japanese and French students whom she met on her pre-sessional English course. In order to keep the friendships, she went to the campus student club with her Japanese friend regularly, despite the fact that she did not like clubbing: 'I sometimes feel lonely when everyone is dancing.' Towards the end of her first academic year, she began to feel strongly that she wanted to have a close Chinese friend – someone who would have a deep understanding of her cultural values.

More than three decades ago, Bochner (1977) had already expressed a contrasting view to those who were against the co-national friendship network in a 'foreign' context:

> Thus mono-cultural (conational) bonds are of vital importance to foreign students, and should therefore not be administratively interfered with, regulated against, obstructed, or sneered at. On the contrary, such bonds should be encouraged, and if possible, shaped to become more open to bi- [foreign student-host national] or multicultural [bonds between non-compatriot foreign students] influences. (Bochner, 1977: 292)

The following quote provides further evidence supporting the important role of co-national friendship patterns in students' social and cultural adjustment in the host society:

> I realized my weaknesses when I had to independently deal with everything in life, things like communicating with people and solving problems. When I was in China, I had my parents, relatives and good friends with me ... When I came here, I strongly felt that this country was a strange place to me. So naturally I had made some Chinese friends. I was a little worried that staying with my Chinese friends all the time might not help me to improve my English quickly. But then I found it rather difficult to communicate with English people. (CS6)

9.4.3   Identity change: maturity and interculturality

Analysis of data from all four studies suggests that it is important to adopt a holistic and developmental lens to view and interpret Chinese students' experiences while they are studying in UK higher education. This is because change at the deepest level is related to their perceptions of self, that is, identity change. Given the distinctive intercultural environment in which they live and study, the process of their identity change has been interwoven with the growth in their maturity (i.e. human development) and interculturality.

The experience of travelling across cultural and social boundaries presents individuals with opportunities to broaden and develop their intercultural awareness and intra-/interpersonal competence. In this process, 'identity is constructed in transactions at and across the boundary' (Jenkins, 2004: 22). Jenkins asserts that during these transactions, 'a balance is struck between (internal) group identification and (external) categorisation by others' (2004: 22). To achieve such balance, the social actor is constantly engaged in a process of identity negotiations: in terms of how they perceive themselves and how they would like to be perceived by others each time when they cross the boundary. 'I've got two sets of values: one is for here and one is for China,' because 'I don't want to be treated as a foreigner in either context' (CS5).

Our research on the impact of UK educational experiences on Chinese returnees' careers and personal lives (Gu *et al.*, 2009) revealed that returnees' overseas learning experiences are both transitional and trans-formational and necessitate identity change to a greater or lesser extent. In the research Chinese returnees negotiated and reconstructed their personal and professional identities at the interface between cultural and social values, norms and behaviours while studying abroad. Having returned to China, their study-abroad experiences were found to continue to influence the change in their personal and professional self over time. This is despite that certain 'primary identities' (Jenkins, 2004) and values which were established earlier in life in China are more resilient and robust to change than others.

> I used to have a very stubborn attitude. But gradually, I felt that I'd become more flexible and open-minded. I've learned to accept the diversity of the world which is created by different people with different behaviours and values. (CS7)

Thus, study-abroad experience is also a personal journey. For some, this journey is filled with happiness, joy and fulfilment of personal, academic and social achievements, despite the ups and downs. For others, however, it is a lonely journey that is filled with bitter experiences, struggles, frustrations and failures. Coleman argues that as a result of the 'huge range' of internal and external factors, many of which are not associated with culture, the outcomes of study abroad vary considerably from one individual to another:

> In each individual case, biographical, affective, cognitive and circum-stantial variables come into play, with students' previous language learning and aptitude impacted upon by their motivation, attitudes, anxiety, learning style and strategies, as well as by unpredictable elements such as location, type of accommodation, and degree of contact with native speakers. (Coleman 2004: 583)

Nonetheless, it is encouraging to see that for the large majority of the students involved in our studies, the study-abroad experience has provided them with an excellent opportunity for personal growth, which Anderson (1994) describes as a 'reborn' experience (see also Montuori & Fahim, 2004). They enjoyed the achievement of personal independence, broadened life experiences and interests and improved interpersonal and communication skills. For example:

> I think the biggest change is my ability to independently manage my life. I have to think everything for myself. It is a feeling that there is nobody around to help me with all this. My life in the UK has improved my ability to communicate with people. I came here on my own. I realized that I had to get used to a completely different environment and meet different people. Sometimes when I come across problems, I need to learn to ask for help from those new friends. I feel that my interpersonal abilities have greatly increased. And, I have had some part-time working experience. (CS8)

For CS9, in addition to change in his authorial self, he also demonstrated a personal identity change, refining and modifying his 'ideological' (values that he acquired from his social and cultural background) and 'logical' identities (the 'natural' way he used to organize and express his thoughts in Chinese writing) (Shen, 1989: 459):

> I think the biggest change for me is that my way of thinking has changed profoundly. I begin to feel that my personal views are equally importantly. I seem to have developed a stronger personality ... I wouldn't take someone's views for granted any more. (CS9)

9.5   Conclusion

This chapter has examined the border-crossing experiences of Chinese students in the UK. Analyses of Chinese students' experiences were set out in the wider context of the internationalization of higher education. A synthesis of key findings from the literature and empirical studies led by the author has identified distinctive patterns of struggles, changes and achievements that different groups of Chinese students have experienced over time. Through these, the chapter sends messages to academics, administrators and policy-makers, reminding them that the experience of international students' intercultural adaptation 'takes on the shape of a personal expansion' (Murphy-Lejeune, 2003: 113). The driving force and essential qualities learners require to achieve such 'personal expansion' transcend the boundaries of cultural models.

It is the interaction of these learners with their particular living and studying environments that facilitates change. This suggests not only that constructs shaped by culture can be changed, but that the nature and characteristics of each individual's motivations and experiences are major factors. This is in contrast to deterministic notions of culture and learner. It suggests that culture – as one factor in the emotional journey of change – is not only clearly linked to other factors, such as those discussed above, but that it is itself a flexible and dynamically changing factor. Culture is implicated in Chinese students' study experiences as culture shock and adjustments and continues as an influence on students after their return. For some, it may influence their professional work and subsequent contributions to Chinese society: for those who are teachers, this may include work with future Chinese students who will study abroad in future cycles of study and social and cultural learning.

In *Lost in Translation*, Eva Hoffman concluded that her Polish insights could not be regained in their purity because 'there is something I know in English too' (1989: 273). The Polish and English languages and cultures had been blended into her sense of self in creation of the 'new woman'. Such a fragmented but empowered image is also mirrored by the Chinese students discussed in this chapter:

> No, there's no returning to the point of origin, no regaining of childhood unity. Experience creates style, and style, in turn, creates a new woman. Polish is no longer the one, true language against which others live their secondary life. Polish insights cannot be regained in their purity; there's something I know in English too. The wholeness of childhood truths is intermingled with the divisiveness of adult doubt. When I speak Polish now, it is infiltrated, permeated, and inflected by the English in my head. Each language modified the other, crossbreeds with it, fertilizes it ... Like everybody, I am the sum of my languages – the languages of my family and childhood, and education and friendship, and love, and the larger, changing world – though perhaps I tend to be more aware than most of the fractures between them, and of the building blocks. The fissures sometimes cause me pain, but in a way, they're how I know that I'm alive. (Hoffman 1989: 273)

References

Anderson, L. E. (1994) A new look at an old construct: cross-cultural adaptation, *International Journal of Intercultural Relationships*, 18(3), 293–328.

230   *Qing Gu*

Biggs, J. (1996) Western misperceptions of the Confucian-heritage learning culture. In D. Watkins & J. Biggs (eds) *The Chinese Learner: Cultural, Psychological and Contextual Influences*. Hong Kong: CERC and ACER.

Blair, T. (1999) *Attracting More International Students*, 18 June. http://www.number10. gov.uk/output/Page3369.asp.

Bochner, S. (1977) Friendship patterns of overseas students: a functional model, *International Journal of Psychology*, 12(4), 277–294.

Bochner, S., Hutnik, N. & Furnham, A. (2001) The friendship patterns of overseas and host students in an Oxford student residence, *Journal of Social Psychology*, 125(6), 689–694.

Bond, M. (ed.) (1986) *The Psychology of the Chinese People*. Hong Kong: The Chinese University Press.

British Council (2007) *The Prime Minister's Initiative for International Education*. http://www.britishcouncil.org/eumd-pmi.htm.

British Council (2008) *China Market Information*. http://www.britishcouncil.org/ eumd-information-background-china.htm.

Chang, W. C. (2000) In search of the Chinese in all the wrong places!, *Journal of Psychology in Chinese Societies*, 1(1), 125–142.

Coleman, J. A. (2004) Study abroad. In M. Byram (ed.) *Routledge Encyclopaedia of Language Teaching and Learning*. London: Routledge, pp. 582–584.

Coolahan, J. (2002) *Teacher Education and the Teaching Career in an Era of Lifelong Learning*. OECD Education Working Papers, no. 2. Paris: OECD. http://www. oecd.org/edu/workingpapers.

Cortazzi, M. & Jin, L. (1997) Communication for learning across cultures. In D. McNamara & R. Harris (eds) *Overseas Students in Higher Education: Issues in Teaching and Learning*. London and New York: Routledge, pp. 76–90.

Cushner, K. & Karim, A. (2004) Study abroad at the university level. In D. Landis, J. Bennett & M. Bennet (eds) *Handbook of Intercultural Training* (3rd edn). Thousand Oaks, CA: Sage, pp. 289–308.

Day, C. W., Stobart, G., Sammons, P., Kington, A., Gu, Q., Smees, R. & Mujtaba, T. (2006) *Variations in Teachers' Work, Lives and Effectiveness*. Final report for the VITAE Project. London: DfES.

de Wit, H. (2008) *Changing Trends in the Internationalisation of Higher Education*. http://www.cshe.unimelb.edu.au/research/seminarpapers/deWitPres061008.pdf.

Dimmock, C. & Ong Soon Leong, J. (2010) Studying overseas: Mainland Chinese students in Singapore, *Compare*, 40(1), 25–42.

Friedman, T. L. (2005) *The World is Flat*. London: Penguin Books.

Furnham, A. (2004) Foreign students education and culture shock, *The Psychologist* 17(1), 16–19.

Furnham, A. & Bochner, S. (1986) *Culture Shock*. London: Methuen.

Gan, A. (2009) Chinese students' adjustment to the International Baccalaureate Diploma Programme: experiences of an Australian high school, *Journal of Research in International Education*, 8(3), 283–304.

Grimshaw, T. (2007) Problematizing the construct of 'the Chinese learner': insights from ethnographic research, *Educational Studies*, 33(3), 299–311.

Gu, Q. & Brooks, J. (2008) Beyond the accusation of plagiarism, *System*, 36(3), 337–352.

Gu, Q. & Maley, A. (2008) Changing places: a study of Chinese students in the UK, *Language and Intercultural Communication*, 8(4), 224–245.

Gu, Q. & Schweisfurth, M. (2006) Who adapts? Beyond cultural models of 'the' Chinese learner, *Language, Culture and Curriculum*, 19(1), 74–89.

Gu, Q., Schweisfurth, M., Day, C. & Li, F. (2009) *The Impact of UK Educational Experiences on Chinese Returnees' Lives and Careers: Final Report*. London: British Academy Small Research Grant.

Gu, Q., Schweisfurth, M. & Day, C. (2010) Learning and growing in a 'foreign' context: intercultural experiences of international students, *Compare*, 40(1), 7–23.

Guardian (2006) Who will be welcomed to Britain, 8 March. http://politics.guardian. co.uk/homeaffairs/story/0,,1725982,00.html#article_continue.

Gudykunst, W. (ed.) (2005) *Theorizing about Intercultural Communication*. Thousand Oaks, CA: Sage.

Held, D., McGrew, A., Goldblatt, D. & Parraton, J. (1999) *Global Transformation: Politics, Economics and Culture*. Palo Alto: Stanford University Press.

Hoffman, E. (1989) *Lost in Translation*. London: William Heinemann.

Hofstede, G. (2009) *Geert Hofstede Cultural Dimensions*. http://www.geert-hofstede. com.

Jenkins, R. (2004) *Social Identity* (2nd edn). Abingdon: Routledge.

Jones, A. (2005) Culture and context: critical thinking and student learning in introductory macroeconomics, *Studies in Higher Education*, 30(3), 339–354.

Kingston, E. & Forland, H. (2008) Bridging the gap in expectations between international students and academic staff, *Journal of Studies in International Education*, 12(2), 204–221.

Leung, C., Pe-Puab, R. & Karnilowicz, W. (2006) Psychological adaptation and autonomy among adolescents in Australia: a comparison of Anglo-Celtic and three Asian groups, *International Journal of Intercultural Relations*, 30(1), 99–118.

Lewthwaite, M. (1986) A study on international students' perspectives on cross-cultural adaptation, *International Journal for the Advancement of Counselling*, 19, 167–185.

Li, A. & Gasser, M. (2005) Predicting Asian international students' sociocultural adjustment: a test of two mediation models, *International Journal of Intercultural Relations*, 29, 561–576.

Little, A. & Green, A. (2009) Successful globalisation, education and sustainable development, *International Journal of Educational Development*, 29, 166–174.

Montgomery, C. & McDowell, L. (2009) Social networks and the international student experience, *Journal of Studies in International Education*, 13(4), 455–466.

Montuori, A. & Fahim, U. (2004) Cross-cultural encounter as an opportunity for personal growth, *Journal of Humanistic Psychology*, 44(2), 243–265.

Mori, S. (2000) Addressing the mental health concerns of international students, *Journal of Counselling and Development*, 78(2), 137–144.

Morrison, J., Merrick, B., Higgs, S. & Le Métais, J. (2005) Researching the performance of international students in the UK, *Studies in Higher Education*, 30(3), 327–337.

Murphy-Lejeune, E. (2003) An experience of interculturality: student travellers abroad. In G. Alred, M. Byram & M. Fleming (eds) *Intercultural Experience and Education*. Clevedon: Multilingual Matters, pp. 101–113.

Oberg, K. (1960) Culture shock: adjustment to new cultural environment, *Practical Anthropology*, 7, 177–182.

OECD (2007) *Cross-Border Tertiary Education: A Way Towards Capacity Development*. Paris: OECD.

OECD (2008) *Policy Brief: Cross-Border Higher Education and Development*. Paris: OECD.

Rizvi, R. (2010) International students and doctoral studies in transnational spaces. In P. Thompson & M. Walker (eds) *The Routledge Doctoral Companion (Students)*. London: Routledge.

Schweisfurth, M. & Gu, Q. (2009) Exploring the experiences of international students in UK higher education: possibilities and limits of interculturality in university life, Special issue of *Intercultural Education*, 20(5), 463–473.

Searle, W. & Ward, C. (1990) The prediction of psychological and socio-cultural adjustment during cross-cultural transition, *International Journal of Intercultural Relations*, 14, 449–464.

Seddoh, F. K. (2001) Internationalisation of higher education: what for, how and at what cost?, *International Association of Universities Newsletter*, 7(3), 1–3.

Shen, F. (1989) The classroom and the wider culture: identity as a key to learning English composition, *College Composition and Communication*, 40(4), 459–466.

Signorini, P., Wiesemes, R. & Murphy, R. (2009) Developing alternative frameworks for exploring intercultural learning: a critique of Hofstede's cultural difference model, *Teaching in Higher Education*, 14(3), 253–264.

Strauss, A. (1959) *Mirrors and Masks: The Search for Identity*. San Francisco: Sociology Press.

UKCISA (2007) *Benchmarking the Provision of Services for International Students in Higher Education Institutions*. London: The Council for International Education.

UKCOSA (2004) *International Students in UK Universities and Colleges: Broadening Our Horizons – Report of the UKCOSA Survey*. London: The Council for International Education.

UNESCO (2009) *Global Education Digest 2009*. Paris: UNESCO.

Universities UK (2006) *Universities UK Response to Immigration Point System Proposal*, 7 March. http://www.universitiesuk.ac.uk/mediareleases/show.asp?MR=451.

Ward, C., Bochner, S. & Furnham, A. (2001) *The Psychology of Culture Shock* (2nd edn). Hove: Routledge.

Ward, C. & Kennedy, A. (1993) Where's the 'culture' in cross-cultural transition?: Comparative studies of sojourner adjustment, *Journal of Cross-Cultural Psychology*, 24(2), 221–249.

Watkins, D. & Biggs, J. (eds) (1996) *The Chinese Learner: Cultural, Psychological and Contextual Influences*. Hong Kong: CERC and ACER.

Watkins, D. & Biggs, J. (eds) (2001) *Teaching the Chinese Learner: Psychological and Pedagogical Perspectives*. Hong Kong: CERC.

10
Intercultural Adaptation of Chinese Postgraduate Students and their UK Tutors

Yuefang Zhou, Keith Topping and Divya Jindal-Snape

10.1 Theoretical contexts

Student sojourners are probably the best-researched group of cross-cultural travellers, as they tend to be located together and are more easily accessed as subjects of research (Zhou, 2006). More recent research has also started to investigate the dynamics of intercultural classrooms, for example considering factors influencing intercultural interaction, including individualism-collectivism (e.g. McCargar, 1993; Liberman, 1994) and teacher–student expectations (Cortazzi & Jin, 1997). Over the past 20 years, an increasing number of researchers have started longitudinal studies to find predictors of intercultural and educational adaptation (e.g. Ying & Liese, 1990, 1991; Kennedy, 1999) and to monitor adaptation over time (e.g. Lu, 1990; Ying & Liese, 1991; Ward & Kennedy, 1996, 1999).

Two main strands of longitudinal investigation of student sojourners can be identified, namely predictive studies and monitoring studies. Predictive studies have found that pre-departure language competence is a strong predictor of all three aspects of adaptation: psychological, socio-cultural and educational (e.g. Yeh & Inose, 2003; Andrade, 2006). For specifically educational (academic) post-arrival performance, motivation and pre-departure expectations are among the other important predictor variables (e.g. Kennedy, 1999). Regarding changing patterns of adaptation, the general trend is that both psychological and socio-cultural adaptation problems appear to be greatest in the early stages of transition and decrease over time (Ward & Kennedy, 1996). However, there is little in the literature suggesting consistent patterns in students' educational adaptation, and longitudinal studies to investigate the process of educational adaptation of student sojourners seem urgent.

233

Further, in the area of international students' adaptation, although literature has focused on psychological, socio-cultural and educational adaptation, studies in these three areas have mostly been pursued separately. We suggest that a good strategy for understanding the adaptation experiences of international students is to explore their pre-departure expectations and subsequent experiences in these three areas simultaneously over a period of time.

In this chapter, we will focus on the adaptation of one group of international students, that is, Chinese students coming to the UK for postgraduate studies. In 2007–08 over 45,000 Chinese students were studying in the UK for a higher education award (UKCISA, n.d.), and a majority were postgraduate students. Many came in large groups under Sino-UK collaborative programmes and might have benefited from specific pre-departure adaptation programmes, so their adaptation experience might be different from those who came to the UK individually. Similarly students coming from UK partner universities in China might have had different experiences from those who are travelling individually. We refer students' coming to the UK individually or in groups as the manner of coming. In view of the large groups of Chinese students studying abroad, it seems also important to investigate the different adaptation experiences of students coming to study in the UK in a different manner.

Although studies investigating the pattern of educational adaptation of international students are sparse, there are some studies that suggest that problems relating to intercultural classrooms are mainly due to mismatched cross-cultural educational expectations (e.g. Jin & Cortazzi, 1998; Jin & Hill, 2001; Jin & Cortazzi, 2006). As an example, independence of mind and critical evaluation are highly encouraged in UK education, but acceptance of authority is common in Chinese educational traditions. These mismatched expectations are likely to result in dissatisfying and unpleasant classroom encounters (Ward *et al.*, 2001). Some recent research has pursued the problem of resolving mismatched expectations within a *cultural synergy* approach. It remains necessary, however, to explore whether and how promoting shared perceptions to student problems may actually help smooth the adaptation process. The *cultural synergy* model (Cortazzi & Jin, 1997; Jin & Cortazzi, 1998; Cortazzi & Jin, 2002) suggests that mutual effort is required from both (UK) teachers and (Chinese) students to understand each other's culture and learn from each other, rather than simply expecting Chinese students to assimilate UK ways. In its concern with the acquisition of social and behavioural skills that differ among cultures (Ward *et al.*, 2001), this view of two-way learning reflects the core theme of recent developments in the theory of culture learning.

This adaptation goes beyond mutual efforts to understand one another's cultures, to include necessary mutual behavioural adaptations that follow from the cross-cultural understandings. It may be viewed as an extension of the *cultural synergy* process. Since the idea of *cultural synergy* was advanced, much has changed in terms of increased intercultural awareness and readiness for accommodation from both teachers and students. It is, therefore, important to investigate whether and to what extent both parties have adjusted, and continue to adjust, their teaching and learning strategies in pursuit of more satisfactory academic outcomes (Cadman, 2000). Thus, it is essential to investigate the process that UK staff go through in terms of adapting learning and teaching according to the needs of the international students (Chalmers & Volet, 1997; Zhou, 2006; Zhou & Todman, 2008; Zhou, Topping & Jindal-Snape, 2009).

With these issues in mind, a longitudinal study was undertaken with Chinese postgraduate students and UK staff. The main research objectives were:

- To explore the nature of Chinese postgraduate students' psychological, socio-cultural and educational aspects of adaptation.
- To explore how adaptation across these three areas differs.
- To explore whether the adaptation of Chinese students to UK styles of teaching and learning differs between those coming in groups and those coming individually.
- To explore the effect on adaptation of students' and teachers' shared perceptions of students' problems.
- To explore whether this adaptation is a two-way reciprocal process in which both students and teachers adapt to one another.

10.2 Methods

10.2.1 Participants

The participants included 257 Chinese postgraduate students from two Scottish universities (University A and B in this chapter), who completed one or more stages of a three-stage longitudinal questionnaire over a period of two years. They included students from two Chinese universities (Wanli and Nanchang), the majority of whom came in groups under China–UK educational cooperation programmes to study in the UK.

The remainder came from a wide range of Chinese universities and travelled individually to study in a wide range of disciplines at the two UK universities. Participants were recruited for this study either in China before departure for the UK (Stage I), soon after arrival in the UK (Stage II) or after being in the UK for about six months (Stage III). Forty-five of the students who came to the UK in groups under China–UK cooperation programmes completed all three stages of the questionnaire. Of the latter group, 28 were further interviewed and 26 of those interviewed participated in focus group discussions. Other participants completed one or two stages according to their convenience and availability. The questionnaire responses of 18 students who completed the Stage III questionnaire were matched with the responses of staff to an equivalent questionnaire administered during a semi-structured interview. The staff responses were in reference to individual students for whom the staff member had educational responsibilities, such as teaching or supervision.

A total of 26 staff members from the two Scottish universities participated in a semi-structured interview with a questionnaire component. In addition to the 18 matched staff who responded with respect to individual students known to them, another 8 staff responded with respect to Chinese postgraduate students in general.

10.2.2   Measures

10.2.2.1   *Student questionnaires*

Questionnaires were constructed for each of the three stages. They included items in both English and Chinese. The Stage I questionnaire included a question (Item 2) about difficulties anticipated when coming to the UK to study. The list of difficulties, such as language problems, financial problems, difficulties in understanding lectures and finding friends, was based on an examination of the literature. The Stage I questionnaire also included nine statements about aspects of differences between teaching and learning traditions and practices in China and the UK, such as 'Classroom discussion and debate are less encouraged in China than in UK universities.' For the nine items (3–11) concerning differences between China/UK teaching and learning, responses were requested on a six-point Likert scale ranging from 1 (*totally disagree*) to 6 (*totally agree*). Stage II and Stage III questionnaires were identical to the Stage I questionnaire except for necessary changes in tense to investigate the change over time.

10.2.2.2   *Student interviews*

A semi-structured interview schedule was developed to probe more deeply into students' positive and negative pre-departure expectations and post-arrival experiences in relation to general life, social life and study life.

10.2.2.3 Student focus group discussions

Four focus group discussions involving students who had been interviewed were conducted to get a more in-depth understanding of the participants' perspectives on the interview issues. Three of the discussion points in the discussion guideline were relevant to the issues addressed here. The first point began with a general discussion of culture shock, and invited examples from students' stay in the UK. The second was about their learning experiences in the UK and examples of educational adaptation stories. The third probed more deeply into similarities and differences in educational adaptation stories and coping strategies.

10.2.2.4 Staff interviews

Staff interviews were designed to gain an insight into staff perspectives on students' and their own adaptation. The interview schedule was semi-structured and included both quantitative and qualitative components. The quantitative component matched the Likert-type items on the student questionnaire, with staff being asked to indicate the extent of their agreement/disagreement with nine statements. The qualitative component included two open-ended questions, which explored students' motivations and difficulties when studying in the UK, and elaborations on staff responses to the quantitative items.

10.2.3 Procedures

The three-stage administration of the questionnaire took place over a period of two years as new students arrived or as contact was made with students who had been in the UK for some months. Forty-five students completed questionnaires at all three stages. The remainder completed questionnaires at Stages II and/or III only. The 45 students who completed a questionnaire at all three stages agreed to participate in a follow-up interview. Student interviews between two Chinese native speakers (Yuefang Zhou and a student) were conducted in Chinese without audio recording in order to encourage openness and elicit natural and in-depth conversations. Each interview lasted approximately an hour. Conversations were recorded in note form in Chinese during the interview and these note-form sentences were expanded into the original sentences as accurately as possible directly after the interview. The expanded sentences were then translated into English for data analysis. Four focus group discussions were facilitated by Yuefang Zhou using the discussion points in the guideline and each session lasted about 45 minutes. They were conducted in Chinese and audio-recorded with notes taken during the discussions. With the help of notes, the Chinese recordings were transcribed and carefully translated into English for data analysis. Staff interviews were audio-recorded and notes of key points were taken during the interviews. Recordings were transcribed with help of the written notes immediately after each interview. Themes from student interviews were first generated using content analysis. Student focus group discussions and staff interviews were analysed using a similar approach: clustering topics and summarizing characteristics of topic clusters. The findings were finally related back to the previous findings derived from student interviews.

10.3   Results and discussion

10.3.1   The nature of Chinese postgraduate students' psychological, socio-cultural and educational aspects of adaptation

The student questionnaire data on expected and experienced difficulties (Item 2) at the three stages were analysed separately for two groups of participants: students in groups completed all three stages of the questionnaire (Group G, $n = 45$) and students came individually and completed the questionnaire at one or more stages (Group I, Stage I: $n = 46$; Stage II: $n = 18$; Stage III: $n = 46$). For each of the three stages and for each of the nine difficulties listed in Item 2, the number of participants in the two groups who ticked that difficulty as applying to them was compared. In each case, the difference between groups in frequency of a perceived difficulty was evaluated using the chi-square test (for details, see Zhou & Todman, 2009). There were two main findings. First, shortly after their arrival (Stage II), Group G was significantly more concerned about regional accents than Group I. Second, with regard to academic concerns (reading and understanding lectures), Group G was more concerned at Stage I, and Group I was more concerned at Stage II. As the size and composition of Group G did not change from stage to stage, it was possible to carry out a McNemar test of differences between any two stages. With regard to both of these potential difficulties concerning academic reading and understanding lectures, students in Group G were more worried about them before leaving China (Stage I) than soon after arrival in the UK (Stage II). All the major findings discussed here are statistically significant with the p value between $p < .001$ and $p < .01$ (see Table 10.1). Figure 10.1 shows the changes in frequency of perceived difficulties for Group G over three stages.

Table 10.1 Positive and negative aspects of perceptions pre- and post-arrival in relation to general life, social life and study life

Domain	Alternatives	Result of Wilcoxon test
Pre-departure vs post-arrival perceptions		
General life	Positive perceptions	$T = 102, N = 20, p > .05$
	Negative perceptions	(post>pre) $T = 35.5, N = 26, p < .001$
Social life	Positive perceptions	(pre>post) $T = 3, N = 8, p < .05$
	Negative perceptions	(post>pre) $T = 11, N = 20, p < .001$
Study life	Positive perceptions	(post>pre) $T = 30, N = 19, p < .01$
	Negative perceptions	(post>pre) $T = 6, N = 25, p < .001$
Positive vs negative perceptions		
General life	Pre-departure	$T = 52, N = 18, p > .05$
	Post-arrival	(neg>pos) $T = 23, N = 21, p < .001$
Social life	Pre-departure	$T = 17.5, N = 11, p > .05$
	Post-arrival	(neg>pos) $T = 0, N = 18, p < .001$
Study life	Pre-departure	(pos>neg) $T = 27, N = 17, p < .01$
	Post-arrival	(neg>pos) $T = 78.5, N = 24, p < .05$

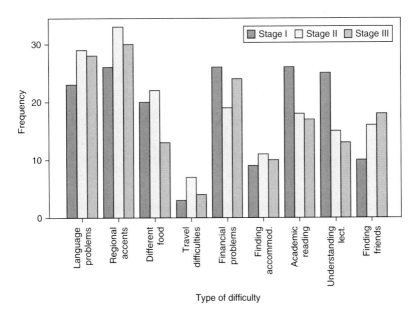

Figure 10.1 Frequency of perceived difficulties for Group G over three stages

Regarding the overall patterns of change in Figure 10.1, it is important to note that the frequency of difficulties relating to general life, social life and study life each changed over time, and that the pattern of changes differed among the three aspects of students' adaptation. At Stage I, academic problems loomed large but reduced to such an extent at Stages II and III that they were overtaken by some of the general life issues (e.g. different food and financial problems) and even by social problems (e.g. finding friends) at Stage III. This pattern of changes across the three domains reflects the more general relatedness of changes in affect (A), behaviour (B) and cognition (C) expressed in the ABC model in the social psychological literature (Zhou *et al.*, 2008), and makes it unlikely that educational adaptation can be considered in isolation from general life and social aspects of students' adaptation.

Data from the student interviews were recorded in the form of the number of references made to positive and negative aspects of pre-departure expectations and post-arrival experiences in relation to general life, social life and study life. Table 10.1 summarizes the findings for the differences in pre/post perceptions and positive/negative perceptions.

As can be seen in Table 10.1, in all domains (general, social and study life) there tended to be more negative post-arrival experiences than pre-departure negative expectations ($p < 0.001$). Positive perceptions were more mixed and less statistically convincing. Positive perceptions regarding general life did not change significantly, whereas positive perceptions decreased after arrival with respect to social life ($p < 0.05$) and increased after arrival with respect to study life ($p < 0.01$). With regard to differences in the number of positive and negative perceptions, after arrival in the UK there were significantly more negative than positive perceptions in all domains (general life, $p < 0.001$; social life, $p < 0.001$; study life, $p < 0.05$). Before departure from China, however, there was only one significant difference, that being a greater number of positive than negative perceptions in the study domain ($p < 0.01$).

It emerged from the student interview data that the frequency of negative experiences was greater than students had expected with regard to all three domains (general life, social life and study life). However, it was only for study life that the frequency of positive experiences was also greater than they had anticipated. This balance between positive experiences (enjoyments) and negative experiences (challenges) in the area of study life may have contributed to the reduction over time in the importance of academic problems. There were always positive academic experiences to alleviate the impact of negative academic experiences.

10.3.2   The adaptation differences between those coming in groups and those coming individually

Reliability of a single scale comprising all nine items (3 to 11) was computed (Cronbach's α = 0.74) for the group of 45 students who completed all three questionnaires (for detailed report on factor analysis, see Zhou, 2006). A repeated measures ANOVA, followed by post hoc *t*-tests, was used to evaluate longitudinal effects using the data from the 45 students. The ANOVA revealed a significant difference among the three stages, $F(2,88)$ = 3.85, $p < 0.05$. Follow-up *t*-tests suggested that only the difference between Stage I (in China: M = 4.70, SD = 0.53) and Stage II (soon after arrival: M = 4.46, SD = 0.49) was significant: $t(44)$ = 2.50, $p < 0.05$. This suggests that shortly after arrival in the UK, the Group G students perceived the differences between Chinese and UK teaching and learning traditions and practices to be fewer than expected before departure, which may have been related to the systematic pre-departure preparation for groups.

It emerged from the student focus group discussions that whether students came in groups or came individually had different impacts on both students' adaptation and UK staff responses in dealing with such students. Table 10.2 summarizes the pros and cons of the manner of coming on students' adaptation.

The results suggested that students in the more protected environment that existed when they came in groups were more likely to adapt quickly and enjoyably to the new learning environment. A typical comment from a Chinese student (CS) who came in a group was:

> They [UK teachers] certainly are working very hard to help us now we are here a big group of students. I don't think the tutors in some

Table 10.2   Focus group pros and cons of students coming in groups or individually

	Coming in groups	Coming individually
Pros	• Help each other within groups • UK teachers take special care • Initial adaptation likely to be smoother	• Learn English more quickly • Learn about a different culture
Cons	• Prone to speak Chinese and practise less in English • Fewer chances to learn about a different culture	• Initial adaptation likely to be more difficult

Source: Zhou & Todman, 2008; reproduced by permission of Taylor & Francis Ltd.

other department, where there are one or two international students, would be so willing and so ready to adjust their teaching strategies to meet our needs. (CS1)

Another student in the group followed on the topic about the benefits of helping each other among Chinese students:

> I think only our Chinese students understand our problems best, not the UK teachers. We've got someone to talk to and to share problems with somebody who has similar experience. We [2nd group of Chinese students who came to a UK university from the UK partner university in China] really benefited a lot from the first group students. They [1st group] reminded us of some most tricky things in life and in study (once we arrived in the UK). (CS2)

However, discussants also suggested that coming as groups of Chinese students and helping each other to deal with study problems was not necessarily seen as having a positive impact on students. It was in fact sometimes seen more as an implicit negative impact, via the effect on the UK teachers, in that they may have remained unaware of their students' problems. One negative view about coming in groups was expressed as follows:

> I can see these UK teachers would feel the life a bit easier if we come together. You know, we helped each other, and we don't have to ask them for help for every single question. We can solve a lot of problems all by ourselves by helping and supporting each other within groups. I suppose, if we come individually, we would bother these tutors far more frequently than now. But on the other hand, the UK teachers might not see the real problems we have had. They might have lost opportunities to understand us, because helping us solve problems in our studies could understand us deeper. (CS3)

Nonetheless, in terms of the overall impact of the manner of coming on UK staff, it was confirmed that UK teachers did make some adjustments to accommodate these students, especially when they comprised a big group of Chinese students on the course. There were two reasons for UK staff adjustments in their teaching and support strategies that emerged in the discussions. First, they were responding to the university's mission to provide better services to 'customers', as Chinese students now form a large proportion of international students in UK universities in general. Second, they were attempting to meet the challenge of improving teaching quality and learning outcomes, for example by selection of experienced teaching staff.

The fact that students coming in groups experienced fewer differences in teaching and learning in general than they had anticipated, may have contributed to the fact that they also experienced fewer academic difficulties after arrival than they had anticipated. Another possibility is that the differences may have been softened by a willingness of their tutors to meet them halfway in the adaptation process. The most intriguing result concerning perceived difficulties was the reversal of the difference between Group G and Group I from Stage I to Stage II with respect to study difficulties (academic reading and understanding lectures). A 'group' hypothesis focusing on the supportive aspects of being in a group of Chinese peers seems plausible (Lin, 2006). Students in Group G might be less motivated to study in the UK and they therefore expected academic difficulties. However, they benefited from group support after arrival. Students in Group I, on the other hand, may have been more academically motivated (having sought out a course for themselves), which might have resulted in their being more academically confident before departure. After arrival, however, they may have found the unfamiliar academic demands hard to deal with initially, due to their relative isolation and lack of preparation. This is a clear example of an interaction between manner of coming and the stage at which problems present, suggesting that different solutions are likely to be required. For students in groups, pre-departure familiarization with the substantive content of their intended courses may be helpful, together with a post-arrival emphasis on making effective use of their tutors instead of relying on help from their peers. For students coming individually, however, the greatest benefit may be attained from pre-departure and post-arrival familiarization with teaching/learning differences.

10.3.3   The effect on adaptation of students' and teachers' shared perceptions of students' problems

As we can see from Table 10.3, regarding student and staff responses to the questionnaire, the difference between the means of the matched pairs of students and staff, that is, staff talking about their own individual students, was not significant. The difference between the means of staff focusing on an individual student and those focusing on Chinese students in general was not significant either. In addition, the correlation between the views of the 18 matched students and staff was low and non-significant.

Table 10.3 Results of staff and student responses to the nine quantitative items of the student questionnaire/staff interview

Differences and correlations	Results
Difference between the matched pairs of students and staff talking about their own individual students	$t\ (df = 17) = 1.70, p > .05$ Staff: $M = 4.38\ (SD = 0.87)$ Students: $M = 4.79\ (SD = 0.63)$
Difference between staff talking about individual students and staff talking about Chinese students in general	$t\ (df = 24) = 1.64, p > .05$ Individual student: $M = 4.38$ $(SD = 0.87)$ Students in general: $M = 4.99$ $(SD = 0.69)$
Correlation between the 18 matched students and the staff talking about the 18 individual students	$r\ (N = 18) = 0.11, p > .05$

The absence of a significant difference between means of staff focusing on a matched student and those focusing on Chinese students in general is consistent with the finding from the qualitative data that staff were often unaware of the problems of their individual students. It appeared that, when Chinese students came in groups, they tended to rely on helping one another to deal with their study problems, which may have had a negative impact on the UK teachers, in that they were more likely to remain unaware of their students' problems. There was very little agreement between the staff views and the matched student views on the nature of the expected differences between China and the UK. This suggested that discrepancies remained between teacher and student views about student adaptations (for details, see Zhou & Todman, 2008). In view of the lack of staff awareness of their students' problems and the low level of shared perception between students and staff, we may have to accept that much remains to be done in terms of *cultural synergy* before there is substantial scope for resolving students' problems based on common understandings.

10.3.4 Two-way reciprocal process of students' and teachers' adaptation

The staff interviews suggested that most of the UK staff adjusted their teaching strategies in response to Chinese students both at an individual level and at the departmental and university levels. As one staff interviewee (BT) said:

> As they come in groups, I did pay special attention to my teaching. I use less jargon and I slow down my English. I think about how to

get them actively involved in classroom activities. You know, sometimes it is hopeless; they all speak Chinese in their groups. (BT1)

It also emerged from the staff interviews that departments and universities have also adopted procedures to solve problems arising from working with large groups of Chinese students:

> We recently did a survey about what they [Chinese students] like and what they don't like about our course, and we have student representatives to collect their study problems. It is hard to work with such a large number of Chinese students and we want to solve their problems. (BT2)

A different view also emerged from staff data, to the effect that UK universities should be careful about how much adjustment should be made for Chinese students. For example, a lecturer in Applied Computing strongly advocated that some core issues in UK teaching and learning should not be flexible for anyone:

> I agree that UK tutors and supervisors should be aware of the culture difference when teaching Chinese students and in some sense we need to adjust our teaching strategies to achieve better academic outcomes. However, UK tutors and supervisors should always stick to the rules and regulations about some core issues in teaching and learning, such as in dealing with the issue of plagiarism. (BT3)

The finding from students' focus group discussions that the UK universities lacked serious consideration of the suitability of some courses for Chinese students was confirmed from staff interviews. As one of the lecturers in English for Professional Development said:

> Chinese students on the course have some problems that are related to the course design. They are required to relate what they have learned to their working context. It is very hard for them as they don't have any working experiences. I think on the whole the University has picked up the wrong modules for them. (BT4)

A new theme that emerged in the staff interviews was the issue of whether UK-based master's degrees or tailor-made programmes would be more appropriate for collaborative programmes involving Chinese students. It was admitted that both Chinese students and

UK staff were struggling to deal with the mismatch of educational expectations. A lecturer in Information Technology described the issue in the following terms:

> The master's degree ... requires independent thinking, problem-solving and analytical skills. The current module does not build in enough time to train them [Chinese students]. There is also a vacuum of context here. The organizations and businesses we talked about are Western companies and British organizations, which they don't have a lot of knowledge about. They have a lot of knowledge about the organizations in China, which we don't know about. From the UK university point of view, we need to decide what the final product is that we are going to sell to Chinese students. Is it a UK-based master's degree or a special programme tailored to Chinese students? Based on the answer to that, we could either design specific programmes that enable Chinese students to do the tailored master's course or we could choose specific students, or type of students. (BT5)

Findings from student focus group discussions and staff interviews were consistent with the situation discussed in the literature by Ward *et al.* (2001), that, as international students became a major source of revenue for a lot of Western universities and institutions, staff members had to respond to the university's mission to provide good customer services. The evidence from the data was also consistent with two-way conse-quences implied in discussions of *cultural synergy* (Jin & Cortazzi, 1998; Cortazzi & Jin, 2002). Findings from staff interviews suggested that they also gained new professional insights into intercultural teaching and learning when working with international students. In this sense, it can be seen as a reciprocal adaptation process, in that both parties had gains and enjoyment.

Regarding the issue of who makes the greater adaptation, findings from student group discussions suggested that students realized that the wholesale adoption of Western values and approaches (assimila-tion) was not the preferred solution for them; and UK staff members suggested that some core aspects (e.g. attitudes towards plagiarism) of the UK system were non-negotiable. Our results suggest that HE insti-tutions in the UK need to find ways to adapt to international student requirements that do not challenge their core academic beliefs. Marcy (2004) suggests that ideas involving quite profound institutional transformation will be required to meet the needs of an increasingly diverse student body.

Our data suggested that there might be potential problems with some China–UK educational cooperation programmes. For example, some UK contexts used in teaching were unfamiliar and inapplicable to the Chinese students. There was further discussion around the desirability of adopting standard UK-based master's degree courses, contrasted with the development of tailor-made programmes for international students. Evaluative research is urgently needed in this area and attempts are indeed beginning to be made to examine the appropriateness and effectiveness of knowledge transfer and knowledge sharing within educational cooperation programmes (e.g. Peelo & Luxon, 2007; Richard, 2007).

10.4   Limitations and future research

The student sample in the study primarily comprised two groups of Chinese students from two areas of China coming to two Scottish universities. Therefore, in view of the sample characteristics, the findings relating to students' educational adaptation experiences need to be interpreted with caution. In addition, differences between coming in groups and coming individually must be treated with circumspection because the manner of coming may be confounded with other variables such as specific universities in China and different disciplines being studied in the UK.

In response to these limitations of the sample, future research should aim to achieve a more even balance between students coming individually and students coming in groups so that the two groups of students' adaptation experiences can be better compared. On a broader scale, joint research needs to be undertaken across universities to evaluate their cooperation programmes and to explore suitable modules and courses for large groups of Chinese students coming to study in the UK. Research is needed to clarify what kinds of preparation, at which stages, are most effective. Finally, there is also a need to learn more about the conditions that encourage *cultural synergy* and effective reciprocal adaptation.

10.5   Conclusion

Different patterns of adaptation in different domains of student life have suggested that the focus of preparation and support will need to shift among general, social and study issues during the course of student adaptation. In addition, staff working with international students, or home students who are planning to study abroad, should be aware that there might be different preparation and support needs for students travelling individually or in groups. An implication of the low level of shared perceptions about student adaptation is that it may be necessary to put in place additional individual support procedures to ensure that staff become aware of individual student problems. With regard to reciprocal adaptation that staff also gain professional insights into intercultural teaching and learning, it would be useful to disseminate this finding widely for good practice. In the context of educational cooperation programmes, further research should address the issue of increasing internationalization of higher education.

Acknowledgement

We wish to express our gratitude to John Todman for his valuable input into this research project and we also thank all the research participants.

References

Andrade, M. S. (2006) International students in English-speaking universities, *Journal of Research in International Education*, 5(2), 131–154.

Cadman, K. (2000) 'Voices in the air': evaluations of the learning experiences of international postgraduates and their supervisors, *Teaching in Higher Education*, 5, 475–491.

Chalmers, D. & Volet, S. (1997) Common misconceptions about students from South-East Asia studying in Australia, *Higher Education Research & Development*, 16(1), 87–99.

Cortazzi, M. & Jin, L. (1997) Communication for learning across cultures. In D. McNamara & R. Harris (eds) *Overseas Students in Higher Education*. London: Routledge, pp. 76–90.

Cortazzi, M. & Jin, L. (2002) Cultures of learning: the social construction of educational identities. In D. C. S. Li (ed.) *Discourses in Search of Members: In Honour of Ron Scollon*. New York: University Press of America, pp. 49–77.

Jin, L. & Cortazzi, M. (1998) Expectations and questions in intercultural classrooms, *Intercultural Communication Studies*, 7(2), 37–62.

Jin, L. & Cortazzi, M. (2006) Changing practices in Chinese cultures of learning, *Language, Culture and Curriculum*, 19(1), 5–20.

Jin, L. & Hill, H. (2001) Students' expectations of learning key skills and knowledge, *International Journal of Language and Communication Disorders*, 36 (Supplement), 333–338.

Kennedy, A. (1999) Singaporean sojourners: meeting the demands of cross-cultural transition. Doctoral thesis, National University of Singapore.

Liberman, K. (1994) Asian student perspectives on American university instruction, *International Journal of Intercultural Relations*, 18, 173–192.

Lin, C. (2006) Culture shock and social support: an investigation of a Chinese student organization on a US campus, *Journal of Intercultural Communication Research*, 35(2), 117–137.

Lu, L. (1990) Adaptation to British universities: homesickness and mental health of Chinese students, *Counselling Psychology Quarterly*, 3, 225–232.

Marcy, M. B. (2004) When diversity and dollars collide: challenges for higher education, *Innovative Higher Education*, 28, 205–218.

McCargar, D. F. (1993) Teacher and student role expectations: cross-cultural differences and implications, *The Modern Language Journal*, 77, 192–207.

Peelo, M. & Luxon, T. (2007) Designing embedded courses to support international students' cultural and academic adjustment in the UK, *Journal of Further and Higher Education*, 31, 65–76.

Richard, L. (2007) Knowledge transfer in international education collaboration programme: the China perspective, *Journal of Technology Management in China*, 2, 84–97.

UKCISA (n.d.) *Higher Education Statistics*. http://www.ukcisa.org.uk/about/statistics_he.php.

Ward, C. Bochner, S. & Furnham, A. (2001) *The Psychology of Culture Shock* (2nd edn). Hove: Routledge.

Ward, C. & Kennedy, A. (1996) Crossing cultures: the relationship between psychological and sociocultural dimensions of cross-cultural adjustment. In J. Pandey, D. Sinha & D. P. S. Bhawuk (eds) *Asian Contributions to Cross-Cultural Psychology*. New Delhi: Sage, pp. 289–306.

Ward, C. & Kennedy, A. (1999) The measurement of sociocultural adaptation, *International Journal of Intercultural Relations*, 23, 659–677.

Yeh, C. J. & Inose, M. (2003) International students' reported English fluency, social support satisfaction, and social connectedness as predictors of acculturative stress, *Counselling Psychology Quarterly*, 16(1), 15–28.

Ying, Y.-W. & Liese, L. H. (1990) Initial adaptation of Taiwan foreign students to the US: the impact of pre-arrival variables, *American Journal of Community Psychology*, 18, 825–845.

Ying, Y.-W. & Liese, L. H. (1991) Emotional well-being of Taiwan students in the US: an examination of pre- to post-arrival differential, *International Journal of Intercultural Relations*, 15, 345–366.

Zhou, Y. (2006) Processes of cultural pedagogical shock and adaptation of Chinese postgraduate students in the UK. Doctoral dissertation, University of Dundee, Dundee, Scotland.

Zhou, Y., Jindal-Snape, D., Topping, K. J. & Todman, J. (2008) Theoretical models of culture shock and adaptation in international students in higher education, *Studies in Higher Education*, 33, 63–75.

Zhou, Y. & Todman, J. (2008) Chinese students in the UK: a two-way reciprocal adaptation, *Journal of International & Intercultural Communication*, 1(3), 221–243.

Zhou, Y. & Todman, J. (2009) Patterns of adaptation of Chinese students in the United Kingdom, *Journal of Studies in International Education*, 13(4), 467–486.

Zhou, Y., Topping, K. J. & Jindal-Snape, D. (2009) *Cultural and Educational Adaptation of Chinese Students in the UK*. Saarbrücken, Germany: VDM Verlag.

11
Intercultural Adaptation – It is a Two-Way Process: Examples from a British MBA Programme

Tianshu Zhao and Jill Bourne

11.1 Introduction

This chapter draws on a larger ethnographic study (Zhao, 2007) of the intercultural adaptation process between Mainland Chinese students and their British lecturers and fellow students in the UK. This study aims to extend Kim's (1988, 2001) model of cross-cultural adaptation and Jin's (1992; Jin & Cortazzi, 1993) cultural synergy model by providing qualitative data to demonstrate that the intercultural adaptation process is not simply one way, but essentially a two-way process. Participant observation, semi-structured interviews and web-based questionnaires were the main data-collection methods in the study, with episode analysis, transcript analysis and artificial 'dialogue' adopted as the main data-analysis methods.

The research findings of the study indicate that students from Mainland China and their British lecturers went through a three-stage adaptation process in their one-year intercultural encounters. In the first stage, both Chinese students and British lecturers encountered unfamiliarity and frustration. In the second stage, both encountered greater expectation gaps, intercultural academic identity conflicts and psychological struggles. In the third stage of their two-way adaptation process, students and staff experienced gradual adaptation and relaxation.

This chapter illustrates the findings by drawing on examples of classroom interaction between Chinese students and British lecturers at different stages of the adaptation process over the period of the students' study in the UK, showing how they tended to adopt different strategies in relation to the context. Two factors are identified as being important in relation to the ease or difficulty of integration: the pedagogical culture 'legitimated' by the lecturer, and the level of intercultural sensitivity, especially as shown in a sense of other-orientation and support.

11.2   Context and background to the research

In the research literature on learners from Mainland China, there are two contradictory orientations reported in discussions on their characteristics: they are held to be passive and quiet in class, lacking in critical thinking, adopting rote- or surface-learning strategies (Ballard & Clanchy, 1991; Carson, 1992; Jin & Cortazzi, 1993; Atkinson, 1997; Flowerdew, 1998; Liu, 1998; Ho, 2001), and, alternatively, as active, critical and adopting multiple and deep-learning strategies (Kember & Gow, 1991; Lee, 1996; Chan, 1997; Jones, 1999; Littlewood, 2000; Watkins & Biggs, 2001; Cheng, 2002; Jin & Cortazzi, 2006; Shi, 2006). Confusingly, Confucianism or Confucian Heritage Culture (CHC) (Biggs, 1999) is often suggested as the explanation both for Chinese students' perceived negative characteristics (Nelson, 1995; Oxford, 1995; Flowerdew, 1998; Hu, 2002) and for their positive features (Jin & Cortazzi, 2006; Shi, 2006; Watkins & Biggs, 2001).

We argue that the term 'Chinese learners' itself tends to be problematic, for the following reasons. Firstly, it presents Chinese students as a fixed and homogeneous group, and ignores the diversity within the category. Secondly, the influence of Chinese cultural values or CHC on Chinese learners tends to be overgeneralized and overemphasized. Rather, we need to consider the dynamics of cultural change and the 'situated contexts' (Clark & Gieve, 2006: 63) that influence how Chinese learners actively take up different learning strategies, student roles and academic identities.

Our main concern here is not to determine whether Chinese students fit into one or the other category, as active or passive learners, but rather to examine how they adapt to the new intercultural academic context they find themselves in when they start to study in the UK, and how they adapt their student identities to the demands made upon them by the British curriculum and assessment regime during their one-year adaptation period in the UK. In effect, this means they need to learn to respond to an interactive approach, which requires students to ask questions, express their own opinions and challenge their teachers (Littlewood, 1999; Broadfoot *et al.*, 2000), rather than to what is for them a more familiar transmission approach which involves more whole-class lecturing which generally dominates in Chinese education (Rao, 1996; Jin & Cortazzi, 1998).

We therefore adopt a qualitative or 'small culture' or ethnographic approach (Byram & Morgan, 1994; Samovar *et al.*, 1998), focusing on exploring the individual Chinese students' personal experiences and their intercultural adaptation processes in a particular cultural context – a British university. In doing this, we consider the interplay of many factors by exploring not only cultural and academic cultural reasons for adaptation, but also the contextual and personal factors that influence Chinese students' classroom interactions, with a particular focus on examining the influence of the British lecturers' classroom behaviour and talk on Chinese students' classroom behaviour and talk.

An integrated theoretical framework for the empirical study was developed based on the following intercultural adaptation models: Kim's (1988, 2001) cross-cultural adaptation model; Lysgaard's (1955) U-curve hypothesis (which is used to describe a sojourner's four periods in a new culture: excitement, frustration, improvement and satisfaction); Ward's (1996) acculturation model (which identifies two adaptation outcomes: socio-cultural (e.g. behavour) and psychological (e.g. emotional change)); Jin's (1992; Jin & Cortazzi, 1993) cultural synergy model; Lucas' (2003) intercultural learning model (which regards adaptation as a cyclical, dynamic and personal experiential process, involving an individual student's four stages of intercultural learning and adaptation process – arrival, uncertainty, gradual adjustment and re-entry stage); and Bochner *et al.*'s (1977) model of friendship network (which demonstrates overseas students' intercultural relationship with host teachers and students).

Our aim is to extend Kim's cross-cultural adaptation model (1988, 2001) and to provide qualitative data supporting Jin's cultural synergy model (1992; Jin & Cortazzi, 1993), by presenting the two-way intercultural adaptation process, rather than one-way adaptation process. Kim's model illustrates only the sojourners' adaptation to the host culture. We will explore both Chinese students' and British lecturers' adaptations to each other. Although Jin (1992; Jin & Cortazzi, 1993) and Casmir (1999) have addressed both native and sojourners' two-way cultural identity adaptation processes, their models still tend to lack ethnographic/qualitative data showing how both sides adapt to each other and develop intercultural academic identities in intercultural encounters over time. This study fills that gap.

The research questions we set out to answer in this chapter include:

- What are the expectation gaps and academic cultural identity conflicts between Chinese and British lecturers in the adaptation process?
- What strategies have been adopted by Chinese students and British lecturers in the intercultural adaptation process?

- What are the factors influencing the two-way intercultural adaptation process?
- What kind of a two-way intercultural adaptation model and a concept of intercultural adaptation competence can be developed from the findings?

11.3 Research methods

The context of the study was an MBA course in the Management School of 'Weston University' (a pseudonym). The participants of this study were 184 students (144 non-native speakers, average age 32) and 44 staff (32 lecturers plus 12 administrative staff).

Participant observation, semi-structured interview and web-based questionnaires were the main data-collection methods as discussed below (see Table 11.1). Episode analysis, transcript analysis and artificial 'dialogue' were the main analysis methods.

One academic year was spent in participant observation of the MBA programme over 2003/04. Nine months were spent regularly attending the main MBA's lectures and seminars, and three more months occasionally interviewing people or attending their social activities during their dissertation writing period in the field, in order to provide 'an insider's account', a 'thick description' and 'deeply rich' data (Brewer, 2000: 39). An observation checklist, including frequency of talk, length/duration of talk and types of talk, was designed in order to examine participants' classroom behaviour and academic identity change over time, with a particular attention to incidents involving expectation gaps and

Table 11.1 Methods and data information

Methods	Detailed information
Participant observation	There were 58 observations. The total recording time of classroom and group observation consists of 32.08 hours. Transcription: 50,981 words. 68xA4 pages of handwritten field notes. 11,494 words of research diary. 23xA4 pages of handwritten research diary.
Interview	91 participants were interviewed (36 Chinese, 18 British, 13 international students, plus 24 lecturers) out of 228 participants. There were 152 interviews in total. The transcription word length is 274,712.
Questionnaire	Total population is 228 (184 students, 44 staff). 66 returned responses (55 viable responses). Response rate is 29%.

intercultural academic identity conflicts during classroom discussions. Semi-structured interviews were conducted during break time or after class. Most Chinese students were interviewed 2–3 times at different stages). Web-based questionnaires were conducted as a supplementary instrument, accessible to all participants, to increase reliability.

As to data-analysis methods, transcript analysis was adopted to focus on both verbal and non-verbal languages in the incidents to provide a detailed description of what participants did in 'naturally occurring' situations (Hammersley & Atkinson, 1993), with a particular emphasis on the expectation gaps and academic identity conflicts in the particular contexts.

Episode analysis was the major method used to highlight 'key events' (Fetterman, 1998) or critical incidents and provide 'a lens through which to view a culture' (1998: 99). 'Episode' in this study refers to one incident or several similar incidents with the same theme, for the sake of triangulation and generalization of the analysis and findings. The title of the episode is the theme of each episode. Most episodes were based on observation field notes, together with follow-up interviews of relevant participants involved in the same episode (or in the same group), based on a 'snowball' strategy (Bryman, 2001).

Each episode consists of three parts: an introduction, including extracts of field notes and interview quotes; a discussion, exploring alternative interpretations of the episode, and followed with further interview quotes as necessary; then an artificial dialogue is developed as the theoretical theme of each episode; finally a summary is developed, giving a brief conclusion and relating the theme to the literature review.

An artificial 'dialogue' (Jin, 1992) was adopted as another representation method. In each episode, both British lecturers' and Chinese students' authentic quotes from interviews were put together, juxtaposed to form an artificial dialogue, in order to highlight the expectation gaps and cultural conflicts between two sides. In this study, two sides in one episode tended to have little interaction between each other. As the third person, the researcher presented their perspectives through these artificial dialogues. The aim of these dialogues is to help bridge the cultural gap between Chinese students and British lecturers, encouraging increased awareness of each other's expectations.

11.4 The findings

The research findings show that both British lecturers and Chinese students went through a three-stage intercultural adaptation process: from the initial unfamiliarity and frustration stage, via gradual adaptation and more frustration stage, to the final stage of adaptation and relaxation. Both sides tended to adopt more integration strategies over time.

11.4.1 The first stage in the adaptation process

In Stage 1, the participating Chinese students were found to exhibit less questioning and challenging behaviour than the British students in classroom interaction. Both Chinese students and British lecturers were found to adopt separation strategies in this stage. By separation strategies, we mean that Chinese students did not show motivation to adapt to the new academic identity wanted by the lecturers – questioning, challenging and independently learning; and at the same time, the lecturers did not show willingness to cater to international/Chinese students' needs by giving them more instructions and support. Chinese students were found to be unfamiliar with the subject knowledge, but they did not seek help by asking in class. Lecturers were either unaware or ignored Chinese students' initial academic difficulties and they were not observed to offer any extra support to Chinese students.

Episode 1 consists of three similar incidents (Extracts 1, 2 and 3) based on the field notes and interview transcripts. The extracts share the same theme: Chinese students did not ask lecturers questions directly in class, even though some lecturers did not provide adequate explanations of some acronyms (e.g. *JIT* in Extract 1, refers to the production or management concept of making things *just in time* rather than storing them which incurs inventory costs), culture-specific terminology (e.g. *white knight* in Extract 2, which refers to a saviour or rescuer) and sociocultural background knowledge of the case studies under discussion (e.g. ice-cream company, Gordon Brown in Extract 3).

Extract 1:

During break time, CS28 pointed to the sentence in the handout and asked CS7, '... I have no idea of JIT, what does it mean?' CS7 said, 'It means "Just In Time".' Some Chinese students gathered around CS7, 'Oh, JIT – just in time, I see.' ... I asked CS26 who sat beside me if he knew the meaning of JIT and why he did not ask. He said, 'I thought the lecturer would explain later'. (BT15, field note)

Similar incidents were found in other field notes and interviews. Below is another extract. Here, four idioms/metaphors were used in the handout without particular explanation. For example, 'death wish' refers to the merged company's final request before being merged; 'riding herd' refers to the strategy of a boss who keeps control over the companies and employees. These idioms were not quite familiar to many non-native students.

Extract 2:

> I found that there were four metaphors/idioms under the question title 'Why do mergers occur?' on BT14's handout: 'death wish' was used concerning the target company factors; 'white knights' in defence strategies; 'Halo' effects in methodological problems; 'riding herd' in practical issues. Chinese students might feel confused about these terms. No one asked questions about these terms during this session; the lecturer did not give particular explanations of them either. I asked CS16 who sat beside me, 'Do you know what "white knights" means?', she said, 'No'. 'Why not ask?', 'Don't want to look silly.' (BT14, field note)

Another example can be found in a British student's interview excerpt, which shows that Chinese students were not familiar with the socio-economic and cultural contexts of the case studies, yet they did not ask in class, nor did the lecturer explain.

Extract 3:

> BT4 talked about a case of a German ice-cream company. Most of Chinese students didn't know about this case ... The lecturers should give a little bit more information about the case ... In the Course D module, BT14 once referenced Gordon Brown, this is what Gordon Brown said, this is what Gordon Brown said, at the end of his lecture, CS6 asked me, 'Who's Gordon Brown?' [Then Chancellor of the Exchequer, later UK Prime Minister] (BS1)

11.4.1.1 Discussion

Episode 1 above (including Extracts 1–3) demonstrates Chinese students' initial academic difficulties in the first stage. They could not follow lectures fully, since they tended to lack familiarity with some 'new' Western business terminology and concepts (e.g. JIT, motivation, reward system, leadership, delegation, trade union, core-competence). Meanwhile, they tended to lack familiarity with British/European business theories and practice and socio-cultural knowledge of the target culture. Lecturers did not provide any support for these students; they simply assumed Chinese students already had the background knowledge.

Episode 1 shows an expectation gap between Chinese students and British lecturers on the social aspect of the teacher's role – to be sensitive and caring to students' concerns and to provide social/moral support. Questionnaire responses show that 78% of Chinese respondents regarded 'empathy' as being an important part of a teacher's role; whereas only 17% of lecturers thought it important. Many Chinese students also expressed disappointment about some lecturers' lack of awareness of their language/academic difficulties, and they thought lecturers 'did not care' (CS36) about 'slow' international students, since they kept 'fast-paced and less-structured discussions' (CS12), 'not giving hand-outs' (CS6), not showing much 'empathy and care' (CS16), not providing students with 'more opportunities' (CS14) and support in order to involve international students more in classroom discussions. Some students complained that many lecturers did not use international materials and 'international students' experiences' (CS14) in class, instead relying on UK or European-based case studies.

This episode also illustrates the gap in expectations between Chinese students and British lecturers on the role of a student. Interviews and questionnaires show that Chinese students tended to regard a 'good listener' as the top student role (83%), together with another highly rated role 'preparation'. By contrast, lecturers thought the student's role was to 'ask', 'actively participate' (BT2), 'disagree' (BT1), 'challenge' (BT5) and 'take responsibility' for their own learning (BT4). For the lecturers, being a 'good listener' was only the fourth important role of a student, after the top three roles – subject knowledge, challenging theories and challenging the lecturer.

Many episodes and interviews show that the British lecturers were generally dissatisfied with the Chinese students' classroom behaviour in stage one; they thought Chinese students were 'quieter' and 'difficult to teach' and they complained that they 'had to explain, it is tedious' (BT1), 'it's hard work' (BT4), 'you can't do anything about it' (BT29):

They are lovely, they are very easy to teach in a way, or superficially very easy to teach, they listen to what you are saying, but on the other hand, they are difficult to teach, because you don't know how much they understood, because even though you say 'is that all right' or 'do you understand', they are so busy trying to please you, they go 'yes', and you think 'no', but *you can't do anything about it.* (BT29)

They should be prepared to participate ... They should be prepared to disagree, but also they should be prepared to put their own ideas forward ... so I think students should take responsibility. (BT4)

By contrast, many interviews show that the Chinese students felt disappointed with what they perceived as the lecturers' inadequate explanations on the background to the theories presented, and they thought they were disadvantaged in less-structured and fast-paced classroom discussions. They thought they 'benefit less' and 'learned little'.

> I really hate when the lecturer says at 9:30am, 'now I give you a case, I give you 30 minutes to read and discuss, and we meet at 10 o'clock'. We paid so much tuition, we want the lecturer to teach, rather than read and discuss by ourselves. (CS27)

> *I've learned nothing from lecturers.* Most of the time lecturers just simply asked us to read and discuss cases, rather than give lectures. I have to say I taught myself by reading rather than learning from lecturers through the year. (CS10)

In sum, the above expectation gaps between Chinese students and British lecturers can be formed as a 'dialogue' below:

Chinese student	**British lecturer**
Why don't you teach us more?	Why don't you ask if you are unclear?
I've learned nothing from you.	If you don't, I can't do anything about it.
('They are not caring')	('They are not independent')

Dialogue 1: Teaching and asking

The above dialogue highlights the theme identified in this episode: Chinese students expected more academic (e.g. clearer instruction and sufficient knowledge input) and social/psychological support (e.g. empathy and care) from lecturers, due to their initial uncertain and unfamiliar experience in the first stage of adaptation. These Chinese students' preference for clear instruction and knowledge input is in line with Cortazzi and Jin's (1996) finding, based on a study of 135 university students' essay writing on the perception of a good teacher in China. While the Chinese students on the MBA course were supportive of each other and fond of working in groups outside class, when they were in class they expected to be taught. By contrast, the lecturers expected Chinese students to take the initiative in asking any clarificatory questions in class, to participate actively in in-class group work, and have the basic and necessary English and cultural background knowledge and skills.

We believe it is fair to conclude that it was not only the Chinese students who were in need of cultural orientation, but, if they were to teach effectively, the lecturers, too, needed support in developing intercultural sensitivity, in order to provide adequate teaching strategies to mitigate the Chinese students' initial academic difficulties.

The research finding shows that some British lecturers found it tedious to undertake the additional explanations necessary for newly arrived Chinese learners, and to take a more active teaching role for them. This confirms Bradley and Bradley's (1984) finding that although lecturers tended to do more talking in international classes, there remained a tendency to lack awareness of international students' initial language/academic and cultural difficulties/distances, as well as a lack of willingness to support them. This may however signal a wider issue of lecturer unawareness of students' needs, as Burns (1991) also found that most students at an Australian university, overseas and local, felt staff were hardly aware of their problems, whether academic, social, emotional or health-related, and lacked an interest in helping them. There is clearly work remaining to do in relation to the pedagogical training of university lecturers – a strong background in subject knowledge is clearly not enough.

11.4.1.2 *Summary of Stage 1*

Episode 1 shows an expectation gap between Chinese students and British lecturers. It also shows some of the initial academic difficulties that Chinese students encountered in the early stage of study, when they maintained their already established academic identities as good listeners in class. British lecturers were found to lack an awareness of and sensitivity to students' difficulties and expectations, and they tended to lack support for these students in the first stage. Therefore, both these Chinese students and British lecturers were found to be frustrated and unhappy with their classroom interactions in the initial adaptation process. The next section will illustrate the way in which expectation gaps and intercultural academic conflicts remained in evidence in the second stage on both sides, leading to further frustration. The strategies adopted by both sides are discussed, and the underlying reasons for these are explored.

11.4.2 The second stage in the intercultural adaptation process

As in the previous section, an episode extract will be given first, followed by interpretation and further discussion, and finally an artificial dialogue will be developed from the quotes and discussion.

Episode 2 (see Extract 4 below) took place in the second part of a classroom exchange between the lecturer and students. The first part involved two Chinese students taking active roles in sharing their experience of working in different types of teams, including a virtual team, in their previous companies. The discussion moved on to business communication by emails between and within companies. Then a British student suddenly interrupted by asking whether emails might replace meetings with someone in the same office. This led to some joking between the British students and the lecturer.

Extract 4:

> **BS15:** xxx I just think can we send an email to someone sitting next to you// [*some students laugh*]
>
> **BT11:** //How dare you? Oh no, how sad is that! [*BT11 said in a very high pitch with a smile, some people laugh*] How dare you? No! [*BT11 laughs along with students*]
>
> **BS2:** I would accept this.
>
> **BT11:** Really! Because I can't be bothered to go up a flight of stairs and talk to Julia! I need to send an email to remind her to do something for me//
>
> **CS2:** //I don't think//
>
> **BT11:** //but that's different from 'hello I am here, just give me ...'.// [*BT11 laughs*]
>
> **CS2** [*with a serious tone*]: //I don't think it is necessary to send an email to the person next to you. That costs money. I was in a company (0.1). The good thing is if you write through email, and obviously later when you read the email and you can just simply forward the email to the other person. We are a bureaucratic country//.
>
> **BT11** [*with a low and serious voice, and looking discomforted by this unexpected serious interruption*]: //I am supposing it depends on the nature of why you send an email to the one next to you. I think BS15 is just saying he was just doing it as a personal thing, rather than for a task-related reason, would you, BS15?
>
> **BS15:** xxx
>
> **BT11:** Yeah [*with a low voice, looking discomforted*] [*BS12 cleared his/her throat*]
>
> **CS7:** Sometimes, we send emails just because my boss forward to others, you can copy to others//
>
> **BT11:** //Yeah, but if that's to do with the task or to do with the team or project you are working on, and you need it for (0.1). Eh, you know, you need to use it for later information, I can understand it.

I thought it was just like 'Hi, how are you', a sort of personal thing when you send it to the person next to you.

International student 6: Anyway talking about something personal should not use the company's facility.

BT11: No, you shouldn't [*some people applauded and laughed*]

BT11 [*laughing and speaking with a high-pitched voice*]: No, very good.
[*BS12 raised his hand*]

BT11: Yeah, BS12.

[*BS12 continued his/her comment on appropriate communication for personal reasons*] (BT11, field note)

11.4.2.1   Interpretation

Episode 2 shows that lecturer BT11 was happily discussing an interesting issue raised by BS15, 'Can we send an email to someone sitting next to you?' CS2 interrupted by disagreeing, 'I don't think …'. His/her interruption was ignored by the lecturer the first time, since it seemed not to be at a suitable time – the lecturer and British students were still enjoying a jokey conversation about BS15's interesting point. CS2 made his/her second turn-taking attempt, 'I don't think it is necessary to send an email to the person next to you,' then he/she tried to argue that 'the good thing is …'.

CS2's solemn intervention appears unwelcome in this situation. One British student, BS12, cleared his/her throat. The atmosphere of the classroom became tense and serious. The lecturer appeared discomforted by CS2's serious tones and comments, and the lecturer's voice became low and serious. The lecturer tried to explain the British student's light-hearted comment, 'I think BS15 is just saying …' and invited the British student to continue.

At this point, another Chinese student (CS7) attempted to support CS2 and his/her argument by giving a task-based reason for sending emails through an example of his/her own company. This is a further example of the Chinese students' failure to gauge the situation, which they are turning from a light-hearted discussion of laziness in communication into a serious discussion on how to use emails at work. Again, the lecturer interrupted CS7's comment and told him/her directly by starting with a 'but' – 'but if that's to do with the task …'. The British and Chinese participants' discussion is running on parallel lines here.

Another international student chips in at this point, making a rather banal professional judgement – no one should be using company emails for making personal communications. The British lecturer and students can only agree with this, although one senses through their laughter and applause that for them a light-hearted event had apparently been turned into tediousness, the point of the discussion lost.

11.4.2.2   Discussion

Episode 2 shows how two Chinese students now, more established in the British academic context, tried to intervene and engage in the classroom interaction as they had seen the other students do. They were trying to adapt to the new academic identity – which required participating, asking, challenging and showing independent judgement. It also shows how the lecturer failed to appreciate their efforts and the very different style of thinking and of classroom discourse they brought to the interaction.

This episode shows that the Chinese students took a task-related perspective to the interaction, whereas the lecturer was engaged in a personal and informal interaction with the British students. They misjudged the context. The lecturer was insensitive to this attempt to participate. The two Chinese students' classroom talk appeared 'deviant' and out of context, and was not welcomed by the lecturer or other students. CS2, however, expected some encouragement for his/her contribution, by being given an opening to extend his/her idea. The lecturer did not permit the Chinese students' perspective on the point under discussion to be aired. Thus the two Chinese students were silenced, and reported that they felt demotivated and disappointed by what they perceived as the lecturer's discouraging attitude towards their own contributions to class discussions.

We turn now to examine the strategies adopted by the Chinese students and British lecturers in the second stage of the intercultural adaptation process. Both Chinese students were adopting integration strategies, participating in classroom discussions and expressing disagreement, in the way in which they thought they had seen the British students do. Interestingly, the second Chinese student, CS7, appeared to be trying to support CS2 by furthering his/her intervention point through offering a practical example. However, the lecturer appeared to adopt separation strategies – he/she seemed to discourage what was then perceived as deviant answers from two Chinese students. He/she interrupted the first Chinese student CS2 by defending the British student BS15's point. His/her interruption implied that CS2's contribution was misjudged. When the second Chinese student CS7 tried to support CS2, the lecturer, without hesitation, made a second attempt to pull the conversation back to the 'expected' point. Consequently, the atmosphere in the classroom was not encouraging to the Chinese students' perspectives and interventions.

There are several possible reasons for two Chinese students' unsuccessful interchange. Firstly, CS2 appeared inadequate in communication skills, especially in turn-taking skills. He/she seemed to interrupt at an unsuitable time – the lecturer and some British students were still joking. Instead of sharing their light-hearted discussion, CS2 interrupted abruptly in a serious tone, by saying, 'I don't think it is necessary.' At this point, CS2 appears inexperienced in this intercultural communication context.

Secondly, the lecturer appeared culturally insensitive and inexperienced in handling different opinions and approaches to conversation due to different speaking and thinking styles. Instead of trying to explore why the two Chinese students had made an unexpected turn in the conversation, returning the topic to the professional sphere, the lecturer remained more interested in following up the British student's more personal comment. His/her reaction in effect told the two Chinese students that their points were irrelevant. Consequently, the lecturer's lack of support or cooperation impacted negatively on the Chinese students' motivation and confidence towards intervening in future discussions.

CS2 felt very 'disappointed' about the lecturer's 'not quite encouraging' attitude. He/she thought he/she was 'not given an opportunity to speak more' on how emails were used in a bureaucratic business environment.

> My intention was to bring up the argument that email communication is indeed necessary in a bureaucratic business environment ... I felt disappointed that my argument was not rolled out. *I was not given an opportunity to speak more.* Discussion on this topic could be a good contribution for that international class ... he/she stifled the argument ... the lecturer's response was not quite encouraging. (CS2)

If the lecturer had been patient enough to give him/her an opportunity to continue his/her contribution, the classroom discussion might have led to a much wider topic – emails used in a bureaucratic business environment. As CS2 wrote in his/her email, it might be 'a good contribution for that international class', rather than a chatty and informal talk between the lecturer and British students about how emails were adopted for informal use in the subsequent five minutes. As one British student commented on rehearing the tape-recorded episode: it 'is more like a chat in the pub between mates' (BS1). These informal types of discussion may exclude Chinese students and other international students, since many of them felt it difficult to follow native speakers' informal conversations, which often involved contextual background knowledge and slang. Indeed, some Chinese students reported feeling that they were unhappy with the way British lecturers and students shared jokes in class:

> Some Western students sometimes spoke loudly and made nasty jokes in class, it was very annoying ... it is wasting our time ... and I feel not happy with some lecturers' attitude to us. (CS7)

CS7's quote reflects different intercultural academic expectations for the classroom. Chinese students tended to expect more formal talk in class, perhaps due to a Chinese view of learning as a serious and effortful process, with classroom talk and the teacher–student relationship which tended towards formality. In contrast, the use of colloquial language in the Western classroom is analysed as having the purpose of building solidarity between teachers and students (Scollon & Scollon, 1981). Yet in multiethnic classrooms it often reveals 'an appreciable asymmetry of power' (Jones, 1999: 251) between the native and non-native participants.

Episode 2 above confirms the complaint made by Chinese students in a letter to the university in the first stage. They argued that they expected 'tolerance' and 'understanding' from lecturers. They complained that some lecturers tended to ignore Chinese/international students, and failed to give clear instructions. They complained of being interrupted by lecturers and British students and not being given enough opportunities to contribute to the class.

We suggest that this episode reveals the taken-for-granted 'legitimate' pedagogical culture and power relations between the British lecturer and students contrasted with that of the international students in the multicultural classroom. This extract shows that the British lecturer controlled the classroom discourse. The lecturer regarded his/her talk with several British students as the legitimate discourse, whereas the two Chinese students' thoughts were perceived as irrelevant, marginal and deviant, based on the lecturer's own frame of reference and his/her own *habitus* (Bourdieu, 1977). *Habitus* refers to those aspects of culture that are anchored in the body or daily practices of individuals, groups, societies and nations. Those learned habits and beliefs have become unconscious and might be said to 'go without saying' for a specific cultural group, but may not be easily accepted by another group. This follows Bourne's (1992) discussion of the way in which the teacher controls and constructs the legitimate pedagogic culture, creating a classroom pedagogy which legitimates the contribution of one group, while constructing the contributions of another student as illegitimate, in this case the Chinese students' contributions.

In summary, Episode 2 shows that two Chinese students (CS2 and CS7) tried to adapt to the new academic identity in classroom talk, but they had an unsuccessful experience. It is partly due to their lack of communication skills (e.g. turn-taking) and unfamiliarity with the Western classroom discourse. But additionally, it is due to the authority position adopted by the lecturer, and his/her lack of cultural sensitivity to different forms of classroom discourse and academic expectations which are more familiar to Chinese students. The expectation gaps and academic identity conflicts between the Chinese students and the British lecturers in this extract can be summarized as a 'dialogue' below:

Chinese student   **British lecturer**
My voice was not heard   Your point was not relevant
Dialogue 2: Legitimate pedagogical culture

This episode shows that the academic staff exercise their power unconsciously in their teaching, by employing their established pedagogical practices, which 'are perceived and recognized as legitimate' (Bourdieu, 1985: 724), in order to maintain their status in the field. Thus the interventions of Chinese and other international students risk being perceived as 'deviant' and excluded from the legitimate classroom discourse.

Through the episode we have revealed a tension between Chinese students and the lecturer who have different expectations of discourse patterns and academic interactions. This raises the question of whether minority learners' discourses are recognized by the mainstream teachers (Bernstein, 1990; Gee, 1996), whether lecturers simply expect these international students to adopt the legitimate discourse patterns or whether they accommodate themselves to alternative cultures of learning and discourse patterns. There is the possibility of a lecturer seeing this 'otherness' as an opportunity to challenge their own behaviour and norms instead of as seeing different behaviour as a threat to their own academic identity or pedagogical authority position.

Both Chinese students and British lecturers in this study encountered more psychological struggles, more expectation gaps and intercultural academic identity conflicts in the second stage of the intercultural adaptation process (between the second and fourth months). Therefore, the second stage was found to be the crucial stage in the three-stage intercultural adaptation process. During this time, both Chinese students and British lecturers appeared to encounter the biggest psychological difficulty (emotional and affective struggles).

11.4.3 A discussion of the two-way intercultural adaptation process

The research findings indicate that the two-way adaptation process between Chinese students and British lecturers follows a positive socio-cultural adaptation curve: from initial unfamiliarity, via gradual adaptation, to the final stage of adaptation. In the third stage, both Chinese students and British lecturers were found to adopt more integration strategies in their interactions, and they felt more relaxed and satisfied with their interactions as well (see Figure 11.1).

However, both the Chinese students' and British lecturers' psychological adaptation curve tends to fluctuate over time and it follows a different pattern: from a frustration stage, to a greater frustration stage, to the final relaxation stage. Thus it tends to follow a reverse U-curve. This demonstrates that they encountered adaptation difficulties soon after the MBA programmes started, due to their unfamiliarity with each other's academic expectations; then both sides encountered more academic and cultural identity conflicts and psychological struggles in the second stage due to more complicated reasons. Two important factors in this greater struggle have been identified: the role of legitimate pedagogical culture and of intercultural adaptation sensitivity (especially a sense of other-orientation and a supportive attitude).

This finding is contrary to Lysgaard's (1955) U-curve hypothesis, which assumes that international students/sojourners have a honeymoon period in their initial stage of sojourning, but is consistent with Ward's

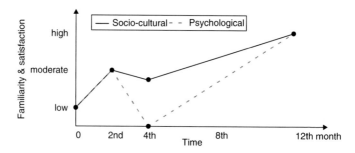

Figure 11.1 Socio-cultural and psychological adaptation curves
(Chinese students and British lecturers)

(1996) findings that Chinese students had a positive socio-cultural adaptation curve, but a reverse U-curve pattern in their psychological adaptation. Therefore, it is very important to facilitate and enhance Chinese/international students' initial- and middle-stage adaptation experience in the target culture.

11.5 Intercultural adaptation competence

In this section, the concept of intercultural adaptation competence (IAC) and an integrated model of the two-way intercultural adaptation process will be presented. The research findings show that two important factors influence a two-way intercultural adaptation process: legitimate pedagogical culture (see the upper rectangle in Figure 11.2) as the external factor, and intercultural sensitivity, with IAC as the main component (see IAC in the middle of the big oval), as the internal factor. The main components of IAC were identified: a sense of other-orientation and a willingness to offer support.

The concept of IAC refers to an individual's ability to manage one's intrapersonal factors, especially one's affective factor as the deep structure in the intercultural adaptation process. The concept also entails one's sense of other-orientation and willingness to support others. It identifies the affective factor as the deep structure, and behavioural and cognitive factors as the surface level of one's intercultural adaptation competence

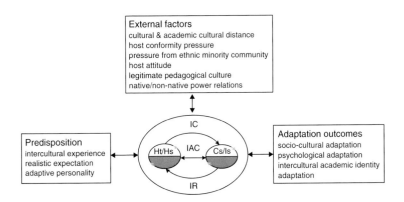

Figure 11.2 A model of the two-way intercultural adaptation process
Ht/Hs: Host teachers/Host students; Cs/Is: Chinese students/International students; IC: Intercultural Communication; IR: Intercultural Relationship; IAC: Intercultural Adaptation Competence.

(see the shaded areas in the two small ovals). The shaded areas in the two small ovals represent both Chinese/intercultural students' and the Host teachers/students' individual affective factors, which were identified as the deep structure of their IAC, based on the findings in this study, since both parties encountered great psychological struggles in their adaptation process. This concept extends the existing concept of ICC and Kim's (1988, 2001) concept of HCC.

This integrated theoretical model of a two-way intercultural adaptation process has been grounded and developed from the empirical research. The central big oval refers to an intercultural adaptation process in a particular intercultural context. In this intercultural adaptation process, both the Chinese/international students (Cs/Is) and the Host teachers/ students (Ht/Hs) communicate and adapt to each other in their adaptation process (see double arrows between Chinese/international students and Host teachers/students).

This model emphasizes both the host's and a sojourner's two-way communication and adaptation to each other, rather than simply a sojourner's one-way adaptation to the host culture, as is the focus of previous models, for example Kim's (1988, 2001) cross-cultural adaptation model. Thus this model is an extension of Kim's (1988, 2001) cross-cultural adaptation model and Jin's (1992; Jin & Cortazzi, 1993) cultural synergy model, since it has provided rich qualitative research evidence, with a particular emphasis on an individual's affective and psychological change in the intercultural adaptation process. It implies that one's intercultural sensitivity (e.g. other-orientation and mutual support) and external factor – legitimate pedagogical culture, play an important role in an effective intercultural adaptation process.

11.6   Implications and conclusions

These research findings show that the legitimate pedagogical culture and the lecturer's intercultural sensitivity play an important role in Chinese students'/international students' classroom participation. Therefore, some pedagogical suggestions are now proposed in this section, based on the above discussions and research findings.

Two pedagogical recommendations are proposed to both Chinese and British higher education institutions (HEIs) concerning the following two aspects: (1) The need to support international students by establishing an unbiased pedagogical culture and assessment system: such support should be different in different stages. (2) The need to develop Chinese students' and British lecturers' intercultural sensitivity and

IAC, especially a sense of other-orientation and support. Both Chinese students and British lecturers are encouraged to improve three intrapersonal factors – improving knowledge of both home and target culture; developing a sense of other-orientation/support; developing communication and interpersonal skills.

The research finding shows that lecturers tended to have the power to determine legitimate patterns of classroom discourse, and international students were more likely than British students to be excluded from the legitimate pedagogical culture. Meanwhile, further factors, such as wide variations in the marking criteria (e.g. different degree of stress on linguistic aspects) for postgraduates' written assignments, oral presentations and exams tend to be biased against international students, who are more likely to be unaware of the British assessment system. This can be seen as poor educational practice (Bush, 1994).

This suggests that a more equal and unbiased pedagogical culture and internationalized assessment system (rather than UK-centred or non-native-speaker-oriented) needs to be established where courses aim to attract international students. Firstly, lecturers should be expected to develop in their professional competence, individual habitus and 'pedagogic habitus' (Grenfell, 1998), a stance which takes account of students' dispositions in their pedagogical practice. They need to be encouraged to increase their awareness of international pedagogical philosophy with 'no ideological, national and cultural boundaries' (Calleja, 1995: 41), with an 'intercultural understanding' of an 'international context' (UNESCO, 1995: 7–10), to help enhance international students' intercultural adaptation process.

Secondly, multicultural teaching materials and 'multiple literacies' (Cazden, 1992; Michaels *et al.*, 1994; Gee, 1996; Michaels & Sohmer, 2002: 171) should be adopted. Since minority (e.g. international students') literacy practices (ways of talking, reading, writing, valuing) tend to be different from the mainstream students (Gee, 1996), therefore multiple literacies can ensure minority students' full participation in the classroom discourse, ensure their voices are recognized, and ensure their equal access to the mainstream curriculum and equal opportunities of academic success in the British academic culture.

Thirdly, an open and safe learning environment should be created, for example, by moderating the pace of teaching, and providing international students with sufficient time and space to become involved in classroom/group discussions. For example, an informal question time might be provided at the end of lectures, where questions can be asked in a less threatening way than is required to interrupt the lecturer

(Turner & Acker, 2002), or groups could be formed to discuss and put forward group questions.

It is suggested that the host institutions and their lecturers need to recognize international students' diverse communication/discourse patterns and expectations; to hear and respect the multiple voices from different cultural backgrounds; to provide a safe learning environment for the growing international student population, and to encourage genuine communication between international students and host institutions/lecturers/students. This is also crucial for British HEIs' own internationalization process (Brennan, 1997; Lin, 2005), which must include local lecturers' awareness that their pedagogical practices and the expected discourses in classrooms may well be different from those familiar to international students.

As to suggestions for further research, this study is only focused on postgraduate students' intercultural experience in a one-year intensive course; further research might explore undergraduate students who study for three years in the UK. Further research might also be expanded to include students from other cultural backgrounds.

In conclusion, this study has extended Kim's (1988, 2001) and Jin's (1992; Jin & Cortazzi, 1993) models, with a particular emphasis on both Chinese students' and British lecturers' two-way intercultural adaptation process, based on a one-year ethnographic study. This study has contributed to the existing knowledge by developing a concept of intercultural adaptation competence (IAC) and a two-way intercultural adaptation model which is grounded from the empirical study. Legitimate pedagogical culture has been identified as one of the important external factors in the two-way adaptation process, and the internal sensitivity, especially one's sense of other-orientation and willingness to support others, has been identified as the domain of the concept of IAC. It is hoped that the concept and model developed from this study can be applied in other intercultural contexts.

References

Atkinson, D. (1997) A critical approach to critical thinking in TESOL, *TESOL Quarterly*, 31(1), 71–94.
Ballard, B. & Clanchy, J. (1991) *Teaching Students from Overseas: A Brief Guide for Lecturers and Supervisors*. Melbourne: Longman Cheshire.
Bernstein, B. (1990) *The Structuring of Pedagogic Discourse*. London: Routledge.
Biggs, J. B. (1996) Western misperceptions of the Confucian-heritage learning culture. In D. A. Watkins & J. B. Biggs (eds) *The Chinese Learner: Cultural, Psychological, and Contextual Influences*. Hong Kong and Melbourne: Comparative

Education Research Centre, The University of Hong Kong/Australian Council for Educational Research (CERC and ACER), pp. 45–68.

Bochner, S., McLeod, B. M. & Lin, A. (1977) Friendship patterns of overseas students: a functional model, *International Journal of Psychology*, 12, 277–297.

Bourdieu, P. (1977) *Outline of a Theory of Practice*, trans. R. Nice. Cambridge: Cambridge University Press.

Bourdieu, P. (1985) Social space and the genesis of groups, trans. R. Nice, *Theory and Society*, 14, 723–44.

Bourne, J. (1992) Inside a multilingual classroom: a teacher, children and theories at work. PhD thesis, University of Southampton.

Bradley, D. & Bradley, M. (1984) *Problems of Asian Students in Australia: Language, Culture and Education*. Canberra: Australian Government Publishing Service.

Brennan, J. (1997) Studying in Europe. In D. McNamara & R. Harris (eds) *Overseas Students in Higher Education: Issues in Teaching and Learning*. London: Routledge.

Brewer, J. D. (2000) *Ethnography*. Buckingham: Open University Press.

Broadfoot, P., Osborn, M., Planel, C. & Sharpe, K. (2000) *Promoting Quality in Learning: Does England have the Answer?* London: Cassell.

Bryman, A. (2001) *Social Research Methods*. Oxford: Oxford University Press.

Burns, R. (1991) Study and stress among first year overseas students in an Australian university, *Higher Education Research and Development*, 10(1), 61–77.

Bush, D. (1994) Academic writing: faculty expectations and overseas student performance. Paper presented at the National Australian Council of TESOL Associations Conference, Western Australia.

Byram, M. & Morgan, C. (1994) *Teaching and Learning Language and Culture*. Clevedon: Multilingual Matters.

Calleja, J. (1995) International education: a common direction for your future. In J. Calleja (ed.) *International Education and the University*. London: UNESCO and Jessica Kingsley.

Carson, J. (1992) Becoming biliterate: first language influences, *Journal of Second Language Writing*, 1(1), 37–60.

Casmir, F. L. (1999) Foundations for the study of intercultural communication based on a third-culture building model, *International Journal of Intercultural Relations*, 23(1), 91–116.

Cazden, C. (1992) Performing expository texts in the foreign language classroom. In C. Kramsch & S. McConnell-Ginet (eds) *Text and Context: Cross-Disciplinary Perspectives on Language Study*. Lexington, MA: D. C. Heath, pp. 67–78.

Chan, P. (1997) *Same or Different: A Comparison of the Beliefs Australian and Chinese*. http://www.swin.edu.au/aare/97pap/CHANP97058.html.

Cheng, X. (2002) Chinese EFL students' cultures of learning. In C. Lee & W. Littlewood (eds) *Culture, Communication and Language Pedagogy*. Hong Kong: Hong Kong Baptist University Press, pp. 103–116.

Clark, R. & Gieve, S. N. (2006) On the discursive construction of 'the Chinese learner', *Language, Culture and Curriculum*, 19(1), 54–73.

Cortazzi, M. & Jin, L. (1996) Cultures of learning: language classrooms in China. In H. Coleman (ed.) *Society and the Language Classroom*. Cambridge: Cambridge University Press, pp. 169–206.

Fetterman, D. M. (1998) *Ethnography: Step by Step* (2nd edn). Thousand Oaks, CA: Sage.

Flowerdew, L. (1998) A cultural perspective on group work, *ELT Journal*, 52(4), 323–328.

Gee, J. P. (1996) *Social Linguistics and Literacies: Ideology in Discourse* (2nd edn). London: Taylor and Francis.

Grenfell, M. (1998) Language and the classroom. In M. Grenfell & D. James (eds) *Bourdieu and Education: Acts of Practical Theory*. London: Falmer Press, pp. 72–88.

Hammersley, M. & Atkinson, P. (1993) *Ethnography: Principles in Practice* (2nd edn). London: Routledge.

Ho, I. T. (2001) Are Chinese teachers authoritarian? In D. A. Watkins & J. B. Biggs (eds) *Teaching the Chinese Learner: Psychological and Pedagogical Perspectives*. Hong Kong: CERC and ACER.

Hu, G. (2002) Potential cultural resistence to pedagogical imports: the case of communicative language teaching in China, *Language, Culture and Curriculum*, 15(2), 93–105.

Jin, L. (1992) Academic cultural expectations and second language use: Chinese postgraduate students in the UK: a cultural synergy model. PhD thesis, University of Leicester.

Jin, L. & Cortazzi, M. (1993) Cultural orientation and academic language use. In D. Graddol, L. Thompson & M. Byram (eds) *Language and Culture*. Clevedon: BAAL and Multilingual Matters, pp. 84–97.

Jin, L. & Cortazzi, M. (1998) The culture the learner brings: a bridge or a barrier? In M. Byram & M. Fleming (eds) *Language Learning in Intercultural Perspective: Approaches through Drama and Ethnography*. Cambridge: Cambridge University Press, pp. 98–118.

Jin, L. & Cortazzi, M. (2006) Changing practices in Chinese cultures of learning, *Language, Culture and Curriculum*, 19(1), 5–20.

Jones, J. F. (1999) From silence to talk: cross-cultural ideas on students' participation in academic group discussion, *English for Specific Purposes*, 18(3), 243–259.

Kember, D. & Gow, L. (1991) A challenge to the anecdotal stereotype of the Asian student, *Studies in Higher Education*, 16(2), 117–127.

Kim, Y. Y. (1988) *Communication and Cross-Cultural Adaptation: An Integrative Theory*. Clevedon: Multilingual Matters.

Kim, Y. Y. (2001) *Becoming Intercultural: An Integrative Theory of Communication and Cross-Cultural Adaptation*. Thousand Oaks, CA: Sage.

Lee, W. O. (1996) The cultural context for Chinese learners: conceptions of learning in the Confucian tradition. In D.A. Watkins & J. Biggs (eds) *The Chinese Learner: Cultural, Psychological and Contextual Influences*. Hong Kong and Melbourne: CERC and ACER, pp. 25–41.

Lin, Y. ([1935] 2005) *My Country and my People (wuguo yu wumin)*. Beijing: Foreign Language Teaching and Research Press.

Littlewood, W. (1999) Defining and developing autonomy in East Asian contexts, *Applied Linguistics*, 20(1), 71–94.

Littlewood, W. (2000) Do Asian students really want to listen and obey?, *ELT Journal*, 54(1), 31–35.

Liu, D. (1998) Ethnocentrism in TESOL: teacher education and the neglected needs of international TESOL students, *ELT Journal*, 52(1), 3–10.

Lucas, J. S. (2003) Intercultural communication for international programs: an experientially-based course design, *Journal of Research in International Education*, 2(3), 301–314.

Lysgaard, S. (1955) Adjustment in a foreign society: Norwegian Fulbright grantees visiting the United States, *International Social Science Bulletin*, 7, 45–51.

Michaels, S., O'Connor, M.C. & Richards, J. (1994) Literacy as reasoning within multiple discourses: implications for policy and educational reform, *Proceedings of the Council of Chief State School Officers*. Summer institute on 'restructuring learning', 107–121.

Michaels, S. & Sohmer, R. (2002) 'Discourses' that promote new academic identities. In D. C. S. Li (ed.) *Discourses in Search of Members: In Honor of Ron Scollon*. Lanham, MD: University Press of America, pp. 171–213.

Nelson, G. (1995) Cultural differences in learning styles. In J. Reid (ed.) *Learning Styles in the ESL/EFL Classroom*. Boston: Heinle, pp. 13–18.

Oxford, R. (1995) A cross-cultural view of learning styles, *Language Teaching*, 28, 201–215.

Rao, Z. H. (1996) Reconciling communicative approaches to the teaching of English with traditional Chinese methods, *Research in the Teaching of English*, 30(4), 458–471.

Samovar, L. A., Porter, R. E. & Stefani, L. A. (1998) *Communication between Cultures* (3rd edn). Belmont, CA: Wadsworth Publishing Company.

Scollon, R. & Scollon, S. (1981) *Narrative, Literacy, and Face in Interethnic Communication*. Norwood, NJ: Ablex.

Shi, L. (2006) The successors to Confucianism or a new generation? A questionnaire study on Chinese students' culture of learning English, *Language, Culture and Curriculum*, 19(1), 122–147.

Turner, Y. & Acker, A. (2002) *Education in the New China: Shaping Ideas at Work*. Aldershot: Ashgate.

UNESCO (1995) *Policy Paper for Change and Development in Higher Education*. Paris: United Nations Educational, Scientific and Cultural Organisation.

Ward, C. (1996) Acculturation. In D. Landis & R. S. Bhagat (eds) *Handbook of Intercultural Training* (2nd edn). Thousand Oaks, CA: Sage, pp. 124–147.

Watkins, D. A. & Biggs, J. B. (2001) The paradox of the Chinese learner and beyond. In D. A. Watkins & J. B. Biggs (eds) *Teaching the Chinese Learner: Psychological and Pedagogical Perspectives*. Hong Kong and Melbourne: CERC and ACER.

Zhao, T. (2007) An ethnographic study of the intercultural adaptation process between Chinese students and their British lecturers and fellow students in the UK. PhD thesis, University of Southampton.

12
Adapting to Western Norms of Critical Argumentation and Debate

Kathy Durkin

12.1 Introduction

The number of Chinese students coming to the UK to undertake postgraduate courses has been steadily growing over the past decades and comprises a large proportion of the international students at master's level in the UK. Given their importance to the income and culture of UK universities, it is important to research the difficulties and challenges many students encounter in adapting to Western-style critical argumentation and debate. Critical debate is a defining concept in Western universities, and is rooted in the Socratic/Aristotelian pursuit and discovery of 'truth' through the disciplined process of critical thinking. Critical-thinking theorists, such as Paul (1993), Ennis (1996) and Siegel (1988), advocate this type of thinking as the highest form of reasoning for all human beings, though critics argue that this is an ethnocentric view, and that different cultures employ and value different styles of reasoning (Gee, 1994; Street, 1994).

Many believe that universities should be places where ideas can be turned inside out, thoroughly scrutinized and looked at from all angles, and where contradictory or alternative viewpoints can be evaluated and debated fair-mindedly. It is argued that such a robust approach to the pursuit of learning and to thinking should be the ultimate aim of higher education, where students are encouraged to problematize knowledge, and to challenge traditional assumptions about knowledge and its application (Facione *et al.*, 1995; Schwartzman, 1995; Barnett, 1997; Caproni & Arias, 1997; Mingers, 2000; Hutton, 2001). The question arises, however, as to whether Western-style critical thinking neglects the cultural and academic norms of international students where they are different from Western norms, and so fails to address possible mismatches of expectations. In an attempt to address this issue, the research project described in this chapter had two aims:

1 **To explore differences between the academic discourse expectations of UK lecturers and Chinese master's students regarding critical thinking and argumentation.** What do Chinese students understand by the term 'critically evaluate'? This is a term frequently used by lecturers to denote critical thinking and analysis, and it contains bedrock assumptions that underpin academic writing practices in the West.

2 **To explore how Chinese cultural values and norms can influence the understanding of, and attitude towards, Western-style critical thinking and argumentation.** What aspects of academic study in the UK do Chinese students identify as causing them the most cross-cultural challenges in relation to critical argumentation, and what are their lecturers' perceptions of the difficulties they face?

This chapter first provides a literature review that gives the background to this research, followed by a brief description of the methodology used, a summary of the key findings and a discussion of their implications for higher education. In line with many cross-cultural scholars (e.g. Trompenaars, 1993; Lim, 2002; Woodward, 2002), the term 'West' is used throughout the chapter to include Europe, North America, Australia and New Zealand, as referring to traditions of thought and practice and a historical trajectory. In this paper, British and Chinese cultures are not viewed as monolithically describing all individuals within those cultures, but as representing the general tendencies of large numbers of people conditioned by similar background, education and life experiences (Doney *et al.*, 1998). For similar reasons, the term 'Chinese cultures' will be used in this chapter.

12.2 Literature review

The development of critical thinking is a stated aim of higher education in Britain, seen in the calls for 'rigorous arguments' and 'critical analysis' in the Quality Assurance Agency's assessment criteria and demonstrable skills at master's level:

> [Students should be] able to think critically and be creative ... organise thoughts, analyse, synthesise and critically appraise. This includes the capability to identify assumptions, evaluate statements in terms

of evidence, detect false logic or reasoning, [and] identify implicit values. (QAA, 2007: section 3.10)

In Western higher education, academic argumentation and debate are rooted in Socratic/Aristotelian practice of rigorous debate, an aggressive search for truth and a discerning of error, bias and contradiction (Siegel, 1988; Paul, 1993; Ennis, 1996). Andrews (2007: 11) describes Western-style criticality as 'assuming scepticism towards given truth, and weighing up different claims to the truth against the evidence'. This traditional view of Western critical thinking has been described by Thayer-Bacon (1992, 1993) as 'the battlefield mentality' which results in polarized critiques, with theories and ideas rejected or accepted on the basis of supporting evidence and logical argument. It is based on the premise that evidence should be held in doubt and subject to scrutiny until it can be proved legitimate and truthful. Indeed, this is reflected in the notion of the 'Null Hypothesis' used in quantitative data analysis:

> The spirit of critical thinking is that we take nothing for granted or as being beyond question. In academic debate, arguments are analysed to find inconsistencies, logical flaws or evidence to the contrary. (Walkner & Finney, 1999: 532)

So all viewpoints need to be considered and critiqued in a fair-minded manner, and for this a critical thinker has to be prepared to recognize the weaknesses and limitations in his or her own position:

> When one becomes aware that there are many legitimate points of view, each of which – when deeply thought through – yields some level of insight, then one becomes keenly aware that one's own thinking, however rich and insightful it may be, however carefully constructed, will not capture everything worth knowing and seeing. (Paul 1993: 23)

Paul's main argument is that critical thinking is a universal skill, ideally to be pursued by all human beings regardless of culture and gender; that it is superior to all other forms of thinking, demanding fairness, discipline and creativity; and that it is the key to full personhood and self-realization. Such thinking demands a deliberate and conscious examination of assumptions and beliefs, which can be an uncomfortable exercise:

> Critical thinking is complex because it involves overcoming not only intellectual barriers to progress, but psychological barriers as well. We

are comfortable, as a rule, with our ideas, our belief structures, our view of the world. Certainly, if we thought our ideas were flawed, irrational, shallow, or biased in an unfair way, we would have already changed them. When questioned about the validity of our ideas or beliefs, particularly the foundational ones, we typically interpret the question to be a challenge to our integrity, often even to our identity. (Paul, 1993: ii)

While many opponents of Paul argue that these notions are culturally biased, they nevertheless agree on one point: that all humans are capable of higher-order cognitive skills. What they disagree on is how thoughts are *expressed* in the context of a diversity of cultures and across gender:

> All humans who are acculturated and socialized are already in possession of higher order cognitive skills, though their expression and the practices they are embedded in will differ across cultures. (Gee, 1994: 189)

Street (1994) and Gee (1994) argue that the type of thinking advocated by the Critical Thinking Movement is narrow and ethnocentric and that it represents male-oriented, Western logic. In Hofstede's (2001) terms, it reflects the 'masculinity' and 'individualism' of Western cultures. Hofstede's dimension of masculinity versus femininity refers to the distribution of roles between the genders, ranging from very assertive and competitive male values, to modest and caring feminine values. Street and Gee believe that 'nurture', that is, the social and cultural context, rather than innate 'nature', determines how these higher-order cognitive skills are expressed. In other words, cognitive expression is integrally linked to culture and social communication, and in some cultures the type of logical, explicit reasoning used in the West is not culturally acceptable. It is not that some cultures are incapable of using certain patterns of reasoning, but that they prefer particular patterns above others, such as diffuse thinking above specificity (Hampden-Turner & Trompenaars, 2000). If Street and Gee are correct, and if Chinese academic discourse patterns fall predominantly outside the dominant Western patterns, then Chinese students can be expected to have different notions from Western academics of how argumentation and debate should operate. As a result, they will employ different communication strategies when expressing disagreement or criticism, or when arguing a point, especially in public discourses.

Western-style public disagreement assumes a separation of a person's ideas from the person themselves, separating knowledge from the knower. Siegel (1988: 41) argues that strong critical thinkers are 'capable of distinguishing between having faulty beliefs and having a faulty character', and are able therefore to be 'emotionally secure' in their response to personal academic criticism. Consequently, Western debate assumes that another's view can be refuted and critiqued without involving psychological and emotional implications for those whose arguments receive critiques. Critical thinking is seen as detached, impersonal and transcending social interactions. This, however, is a very 'masculine' and individualistic perspective towards enquiry. The West tends not to view academic enquiry as a social activity but instead elevates isolation, separateness from others and individualistic speculation 'at the expense of the collective wisdom of the community' (Hird, 1999: 39).

In contrast to this, in collectivist cultures an interdependent relationship is developed between speaker and listener. This is because in collectivist societies, such as Chinese cultures, people from birth are integrated into strong, cohesive in-groups, often extended families, which continue protecting them in exchange for unquestioning loyalty. In individualist societies we find ties between individuals are far looser, with everyone expected primarily to look after him/herself and his/her immediate family (Hofstede, 2001). Thus the reactions of both speaker and listener are closely monitored by the other. In oral debates Chinese students will tend to empathize with the other participants, and to reject or challenge ideas is to risk a personal insult to the originators of these ideas. The notion of adopting an identity of individualism is 'quite foreign to his/her notion of a collective, relational sense of self-identity, and involves a reversal of acceptance, "face" and politeness behaviour' (Hird, 1999: 33). As Doi writes, students from collectivist cultures tend to demonstrate 'a reluctance to carry rationalism to the point where it will make the individual too aware of his separateness in relation to people and things about him' (1981: 9).

According to Hofstede and Bond (1984), maintaining harmony and avoiding offence or confrontation in China appear to be of greater value and importance than any search for absolute truth that might result in giving unnecessary offence. Hence, any evaluation of ideas would be based on the premise of first accepting all contributions with a view to conciliatory accommodation and dialogue. Whereas China is a high-context culture (Hall, 1976), where inference, indirect speech and an avoidance of public disagreement are the norm,

British culture has been described as low-context (Hall, 1976), where explicitness and directness in speech are valued, and where more open disagreement and free expression of one's beliefs and thoughts are acceptable. Teamwork for British students involves brainstorming of ideas, with a readiness to reject any contributions that do not stand up to critical analysis. Teamwork in China, on the other hand, lays an emphasis on listening to others, exposition of accepted fact and restraint in expressing personal opinions, especially when these are contrary to the common consensus or to those in positions of authority. Likewise, relationships among team members are more important than task completion, and critical evaluation of team members' ideas to achieve the best solution carries less weight than maintaining harmony.

To add to the complexity of these issues, feminist opponents of the Critical Thinking Movement (such as Belenky *et al.*, 1986; Orr, 1989; Nye, 1990; Thayer-Bacon, 1992, 1993; Bailin, 1995), and other writers such as Tannen (1990, 1998), argue that formal logic is dominated by masculine preference for polarized argumentation: 'The west's conception of mind and rationality are overwhelmingly male' (Orr, 1989: 2). Bailin (1995) claims that formal logic was developed by white Western males to reflect masculine styles of interacting, and that those in power have promoted the masculine style as universal and as the only legitimate mode of understanding. This mode can be characterized by aggression and confrontation, individualism, logic and a lack of emotion – the 'battlefield' mentality. Orr (1989) contends that women prefer conciliatory, intuitive reasoning (informal logic), where experience, emotion and feeling are valid sources of evidence, and are useful tools in reasoning. Chinese students, coming from a culture that scores higher than the UK in Hofstede's (1991, 2001) femininity dimension, may therefore be disadvantaged by the educational practice in the West, as they may find it more natural and culturally acceptable to engage in conciliatory and sensitive dialogue than in the 'wrestling debate' advocated in the West.

Moreover, Thayer-Bacon argues that dialogical or critical thinking is best developed through a more feminine, relational and social process and not through individualistic endeavour:

> We develop our thinking skills as we develop our communication skills and our social skills, by being in relation to others. Our thinking improves the more we are able to relate to others and discuss our thoughts with them. (Thayer-Bacon, 1993: 337)

A relational model of thinking emphasizes people working together – solving problems through conversing, listening and debating together, valuing all opinions and suspending judgement. Vygotsky (1962, 1994) and educational linguists (e.g. Bruner, 1973; Graves, 1978; Bakhtin, 1984) stress social contexts and the interactional construction of knowledge and understanding and, crucially, the role of talk in this social exchange for learning. In line with this, Thayer-Bacon believes that 'our thinking improves the more we are able to relate to others and discuss our thoughts with them' (1993: 338). Conversation can therefore promote the growth of thinking, especially when 'controversial partners holding different opinions strive to reach a mutually agreeable position, and in the process advance beyond the level of understanding that either partner possessed at the beginning' (Scardamalia & Bereiter, 1994: 297). Such endeavours to fair-mindedly consider and understand people's ideas in order to find the best solutions to problems is described as *constructive thinking* by Thayer-Bacon (1993). She argues that one cannot separate the self from the object, the knower from the known, personal knowledge from expert knowledge (1993: 324). In other words, reflective problem-solving, which requires judgements, decisions and choices, must involve the whole person and not just the mind. Sensitivity, she argues, is essential if one is to be truly open-minded and 'fair' to others' arguments. True critical thinking, Thayer-Bacon claims, requires one to know oneself and what one contributes to the knowing – in other words to be self-reflective and constructive, and for this relational skills are necessary to help open, not just one's mind, but one's heart:

> A constructive thinker attempts to believe the other(s) to make sure understanding has taken place, before she uses her critical thinking skills to doubt and critique. Judging and assessing are vital parts of constructive thinking, but so are caring and awareness of one's own personal voice. Caring is value-giving, whereas blind justice tends to be absolutistic and silencing. (Thayer-Bacon, 1993: 327–328)

In other words, one gives value and worth to the other person when one respects them enough to listen and try to understand their meaning, deeming what they say to be of value and worthy of close inspection, before opposing, dismissing or trying to silence their viewpoint. Caring is thus seen as an essential ingredient in critical thinking: 'Without caring, one cannot hope to be a good / constructive thinker. Caring is necessary to be sure ideas have been fairly considered and understood' (Thayer-Bacon, 1993: 323). The notion of caring as an integral aspect of education is found in the Confucian heritage, which advocates that a person cannot be educated in the absence of strong, caring relations, and without developing the heart (*jiao ren*) as much as the mind (Elliot & Martin, 2007). It also relates closely to the notion of 'face' (Gao & Ting-Toomey, 1998; Ting-Toomey, 1999), and to Ting-Toomey's notion of 'mindfulness' (Ting-Toomey & Kurogi, 1998), where participants in an interactive discourse take conscious care and are mindful of the other(s') face.

This discussion has highlighted aspects of Western-style critical argumentation that may cause adaptation challenges for Chinese students in the UK. It has also shown that some recent strands in Western thinking about argumentation stress the value of relationships and a more caring, holistic approach. The project, on which this chapter is based, sought to explore these challenges in more depth.

12.3 Methodology

A cultural, interpretive approach to investigate Chinese students' adaptations to Western norms of argumentation was followed as being the most appropriate for the research topic, and a qualitative, inductive methodology was employed. Two universities in the UK were selected as case sites, and a third case site was a university in China. The choice of subject disciplines for the case sites depended on three criteria: that large numbers of Chinese students are recruited onto their master's programmes; that the course assignments demand a high level of critical thinking and evaluative writing; and that the sites offered researcher access. Postgraduate students were targeted because master's courses are only one year long in the UK, making it essential for international students to adapt very quickly to the new norms of academia if they are to succeed in their studies. It was therefore judged that such rapid adaptation would be easier to reflect on, for both student and lecturer participants. The Chinese students were asked about their perceptions of Western-style critical thinking and argumentation, and these were contrasted with lecturers' perceptions of Chinese students' understanding of Western expectations regarding academic critical thinking.

The China case site was a prestigious foreign language university where final-year undergraduate students intending to study in the UK for a master's degree the following year were interviewed. The aim here was to explore their notions of critical thinking and argumentation immediately prior to their study abroad. The language of instruction at this university is English, and so the second language competency of this sample was good. In-depth interviews were conducted in English with 50 students: 24 master's Chinese students in the UK; 18 Chinese students in the Chinese university; and 8 British students in the UK universities, for comparison and triangulation purposes. In addition, 16 in-depth interviews were conducted with lecturers at the three sites (5 Chinese and 11 British). The researcher conducted and transcribed all the interviews, so the participants needed to have sufficient competency in English oracy in order to express their thoughts clearly. The sample was restricted therefore to those with a minimum of IELTS 6.5 (International English language testing system). Although interviewing the Chinese participants in their second language may be seen as problematic, this is arguably a suitable research medium for this study as English is the medium of study in UK universities, and it was also the medium in the Chinese university. All the interviews were tape-recorded, and analysed using open coding (Corbin & Strauss, 1990), emerging themes and categories were identified using the Constant Comparative Method (Glaser & Strauss, 1967), and findings were member checked throughout the data-analysis process to ensure trustworthiness (Daymon & Holloway, 2002: 93). The data were then interpreted to generate the theoretical concept of 'The Middle Way' (see Figure 12.1). The next section distils the main findings. All quotes are from the Chinese student participants unless identified as lecturers or as British students.

12.4 Findings and discussion

The research found that by the end of their master's courses many of the interviewed Chinese students had rejected aspects of Western-style debate, and they had no desire to leave aside their traditional, encultured ways so as to embrace the new mindset. There were four main reasons for this: a genuine dislike of the abrasive, polarized style of much of Western argumentation; discomfort with the risk and uncertainty associated with it; pressure from members of their collectivistic culture to conform; and a pragmatic decision based on their view of the usefulness of such skills once they returned home to China. In discussing the findings, quotes from the data are coded CS for Chinese students, BS for British students, and CL and BL for Chinese and British lecturers.

The key finding was that many of the Chinese participants perceived Western academic critique as being insensitive and unnecessarily offensive, one Chinese student remarking that 'British students have been encouraged to challenge too much. They are rebellious!' The British

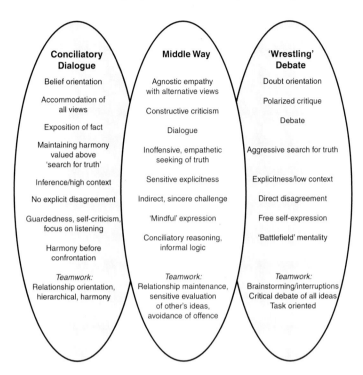

Figure 12.1 The Middle Way

students, on the other hand, thought that 'the whole educational environment and society in the UK encourages one to ask questions and query things', and that they had been 'institutionalized into the argument culture' before starting their master's course. They were also aware of the very different expectations that some of their Chinese peers had, for instance that students 'should think more and talk less'. The British students were surprised that their habit of interrupting others mid-speech was viewed by Chinese students as being 'rude, strange and a bit arrogant' (BS).

In a class debate, direct disagreement or challenge by British and other students was often seen as threatening and inconsiderate, and caused Chinese students to feel 'very embarrassed and scared'; they thought students 'should listen, at least until people have finished talking'. The Chinese students were more concerned with preserving the 'face' of others, and not embarrassing or offending them by disagreeing with them in public, which 'can be taken personally', especially if speaking to one's superior. Similarly, another's mistakes should not be pointed out in a direct manner (as British students tend to do), but 'secretly and indirectly, so as to avoid embarrassment' (CL).

In low-context Western cultures, emphasis in academic writing is laid on explicitness, where everything is stated very clearly and in a logical sequence. The Chinese students contrasted this with the indirect, inferential speech of Chinese cultures which is seen as more sensitive, and representing 'a higher level of communication' where 'everything is implicit', the hidden message is 'behind the language', and where the responsibility lies with the reader or listener to accurately interpret any ambiguities (CL).

These perceptions are in agreement with Tannen's (1998: 6) claim that 'the scale is off balance' in Western debate, with 'conflict and opposition over-weighted' in Western debate. The consequence of all this is that contributing to class debates may appear alien at first to many Chinese students, and they may see Western argumentation as being unattractive in the light of their own cultural values. Some may choose to remain silent and prefer just to listen to others contributing, for fear of making mistakes, of looking unintelligent or of offending others:

> The majority of Chinese tend to watch and evaluate many things before they speak, such as 'Will the teacher accept what I say?', 'What will the authority think?', 'What will be the danger if I speak out?', 'What will the other students think?', 'Will I lose face?' It's a very big struggle for us. (CS 1)

Disapproval from one's own cultural group can act as another inhibitor to critical thinking and debate. A Chinese student described vividly how other Chinese students in her class criticized her for being too outspoken in the first few weeks of the master's course. She began the course as an outspoken student, actively engaging in class discussions, exhibiting individualistic tendencies even though she was from a collectivist culture (Triandis, 1995). The lecturers all appreciated her openness in expressing her opinions in class, especially as the majority of Chinese students were very quiet during those first weeks, and this student had a rich working experience which added value to her contributions. However, she quickly discovered that although the British lecturers and British students were very comfortable with her outspokenness, some of her Chinese peers were not: 'They did not want me to stand out in class. Some stared at me, black-mouthed me afterwards, and said I was ambitious. So when I realized that, I reserved my opinion' (CS 2).

She felt hurt and upset, so much so that she made a conscious decision to be quiet in class unless directly addressed by a lecturer. This frustrated her because 'the purpose of me coming here was not to keep silent all the time'. She used a Chinese proverb to explain this phenomenon: 'The bird which flies higher can easily be shot by the hunter,' so 'one should not fly higher than the others. You should be the same.'

Thus, while British lecturers may encourage a student to engage in critical debate and discussions in class, there may at the same time be a counter-influence from the student's cultural-group peers suppressing individualist public expression, exerting pressure to conform and not tolerating Westernization of behaviour. In this way, students from collectivist cultures may demonstrate 'an unwillingness to be cast into a world of objective reality' if that world isolates them from the collective consensus and mind (Matsumoto, 1988: 407).

A third reason for some Chinese students not wanting to exercise critical skills was their aversion to risk-taking: 'The traditional mentality of the Chinese is to be safe and be stable, to conform and not take risks; to take the middle way and not go to extremes' (CL). Some thought that being 'critical all the time about everything and everyone, just makes you upset, since you see the "truth" about things, and how the world really is, clearly' (CS). One student described the inner struggle she faced when learning to think more critically:

> It is very hard to confront with ourselves, it is a struggle to write. Thinking in English is like arguing with another person. I am not allowed to confront or to conflict with myself in Chinese. (CS 3)

Finally, students may draw back from developing Western-style critical skills believing that, pragmatically, there is no long-term purpose for them in pursuing these skills. They may make the conscious decision that as they are only transient sojourners in the host culture, and will be returning home where critical skills may not be so acceptable, it would be a futile, and even detrimental exercise to pursue their critical development. They may, on the other hand, recognize that they do not have the time in one year to fully adapt, and that further experimentation would not further their main goal of achieving the degree award.

Having briefly discussed some of the reasons why Chinese students may be reluctant to take on board the style of critical argumentation encouraged in universities in the UK, the research findings also reveal that most students appreciated some aspects of Western-style critical thinking, and that they endeavoured to combine the best elements of this approach with their own traditional values. What they appear to be rejecting is the confrontational, battlefield approach, which is doubt-orientated, and which emphasizes an aggressive search for truth. Instead, they favour the more empathetic, 'constructive' thinking advocated by Thayer-Bacon (1993), and the conciliatory reasoning which values maintenance of relationship above the need to push forward one's own opinion on others (Orr, 1989). This may suggest that a more nurturing, less aggressive approach to debate may be more appealing to Chinese students. Many, however, did appreciate the value of Western explicitness in communication and in expressing one's opinions openly, one Chinese student admitting that always having to infer meaning can 'be very tiring and difficult'.

The overwhelming preference of Chinese students in this research study was to opt for what I term 'The Middle Way', which was theorized and inducted from the data findings, as a means for students to retain those elements of the Western mindset which they accept, and believe can be accommodated with relative ease within their traditional cultural boundaries, and which pose less risk and uncertainty on return home.

12.5 The Middle Way

Many of the interviewed students chose a pragmatic third alternative to either fully embracing the Western approach, or rejecting it as incompatible with their own culture. This third way was frequently described as 'the Middle Way' by the interviewees, which synergizes Western and Eastern approaches to critical thinking.

Because Chinese cultures place much value on maintaining harmony and not taking an extreme or polarized position in any discussion, the idea of a 'middle way', what Thayer-Bacon (1993) calls 'constructive thinking', may be a more acceptable approach to academic debate. In this model, alternative views would be accorded equal validity and neither position would be rejected outright, as happens in Aristotelian debate. Many students, when faced with two opposing views, think: 'This is right and this is also right. They are equal. This happens a lot in China – the middle way. We are encouraged to think this way' (CL).

In China, the expression 'Middle Way' signifies moderation and shunning extremes. Discussing the way to remove the cause of suffering, in Buddhist terms, Humphreys (1951: 21–22) comments, 'This way is the Middle Way between extremes, for its manifestation is based on the "pairs of opposites"; the way to the Unity from which they sprang must be between them and above them and beyond.' Similarly,

David-Neel (1979: 118) quotes the Buddha himself, 'There are two extremes which he who would live a spiritual life should avoid ... the Tathagata [Buddha] has kept aloof from these two extremes; he has found the middle path which unseals the eyes and the mind, which leads to wisdom, to tranquillity, to enlightenment.' For Confucians and referring to the Confucian classic of *The Doctrine of the Mean*, Yao (2000: 65) remarks: 'This way is called The Middle Way, the way of centrality and harmony. The Middle Way does not simply mean pursuing a middle course. It is said to be a course following the harmonious course of the universe.'

In academic terms, in 'The Middle Way' traditional basic values such as maintaining harmony are apparently retained, basically intact, and are not deconstructed at all. Synthesized into them, however, are aspects of the Western mindset which expand or complement their own cultural values. Thus, the 'Middle Way' synthesizes the two different approaches of 'conciliatory dialogue' and 'wrestling debate' (see my theoretical model: Figure 12.1).

Although characterized by constructive dialogue (Thayer-Bacon, 1993), which is inoffensive and which involves empathetic listening to the other's viewpoint, the Middle Way nevertheless does allow some challenge. This, however, is indirect and the focus is on reasoning which aims to bring together, rather than separate. Participants are therefore very 'mindful' (Ting-Toomey, 1999) of their use of language and are sensitive and circumspect in their use of explicitness in positing an idea. The aim is not to battle between two polarized positions, as in the Western adversarial approach to debate, but to sustain a more conciliatory approach which allows ample space for diversity of opinions. In this 'gentler' approach to critical debate, one of the top priorities is to maintain relationships and preserve the dignity and integrity of all participants. The Middle Way thus begins the search for truth with an 'agnostic empathy' towards all views presented. The term 'empathy' here is used in line with Thayer Bacon's (1993) definition of it, to describe a sensitive 'openness' to another's viewpoint, a determination to listen fair-mindedly and delay judgement and critical evaluation until the other's position is fully understood and 'entered into' in a sympathetic fashion.

The Middle Way also synergizes the UK's stress on low-context explicitness with China's preference for high-context inference, resulting in what I am terming 'sensitive explicitness'. This kind of sensitivity towards others' feelings and 'face' merges with a search for truth in the Middle Way, so that one can be true to oneself and honest, without

288 Kathy Durkin

being offensive. This would also mean a moving away from having to always infer or guess at what people are really thinking.

Is this Middle Way, then, a more creative and caring, more ennobling and humane way of managing opposition and disagreement, and in the search for 'truth'? Or does it go too far for Western educational goals in attempting to avoid conflict and in emphasizing harmony and conciliatory dialogue? Tannen (1998: 12) argues that truth is often 'a crystal of many sides', a complex overlapping of different perspectives, all of which are legitimate and are to be respected. On the other hand, Hellenistic thinking, which underpins much of Western critical thinking, advocates that there are absolutes to the truth and that it cannot, and should not, accommodate all perspectives. It follows that if indecisive and unacceptable compromise is to be avoided, then conflict and polarization of views are inevitable (Tarnas, 1991). The question arises, then, as to whether this Middle Way approach can work in practice and whether it could have a place in Western higher education. Is it possible, appropriate or even desirable for universities in the West to adopt such a constructivist approach to critical thinking and debate? As shown, some Western academics have been advocating this for some time. So is it now the time for lecturers in the West to develop their own 'Middle Way', which would integrate the caring, more holistic and empathetic emphasis of Chinese cultures, without losing the rigorous 'quest for truth'? This would soften the masculine, linear logic of the Socratic dialectic tradition, and bring more conciliatory reasoning into the often cynical scepticism of post-modernist thinking in the West. This need not lead to what I call 'agnostic empathy', however, where no firm convictions or convincing evidence underpin and drive an argument, and where direct challenge is avoided.

This 'Middle Way' for Western lecturers would therefore be a merging of the best of both conciliatory dialogue and 'wrestling' debate, while leaning more on the heritage of the West – even as the 'Middle Way' of Chinese students leans more towards Chinese traditions and belief systems. In this way, UK lecturers and Chinese students could move closer to each other in their expectations and thinking, without either group abnegating their unique cultural identities and beliefs, a proposition also advocated as a 'cultural synergy' model by Jin and Cortazzi (1993, 1998).

As more UK lecturers enter into dialogue with each other, and with their students, regarding these issues, a way may be brokered for university educators to develop a new 'Middle Way' which need not result in reducing the rigour of academic critical thinking, but rather, one could argue, in enhancing it by making it more humane and holistic.

References

Andrews, R. (2007) Argumentation, critical thinking and the postgraduate dissertation, *Educational Review*, 59(1), 1–18.

Bailin, S. (1995) Is critical thinking biased? Clarifications and implications. *Educational Theory*, 45(2), 191–197.

Bakhtin, M. M. (1984) *Problems of Dostoevsky's Poetics*, ed. and trans. Carl Emerson. Manchester: Manchester University Press.

Barnett, R. (1997) *Higher Education: A Critical Business*. Buckingham: Society for Research into Higher Education and Open University Press.

Belenky, M. B., Clinchy, B. M., Goldberger, N. R. & Tarule, J. R. (1986) *Women's Ways of Knowing*. New York: Basic Books.

Bruner, J. (1973) *The Relevance of Education*. New York: Vintage Press.

Caprioni, P. & Arias, M. E. (1997) Managerial skills training from a critical perspective, *Journal of Management Education*, 21(3), 292–308.

Corbin, J. & Strauss, A. L. (1990) Grounded theory research: procedures, canons and evaluative criteria, *Qualitative Sociology*, 13(1), 3–21.

David-Neel, A. (1979) *Buddhism, its Doctrines and its Methods*. New York: Avon Books.

Daymon, C. & Holloway, I. (2002) *Qualitative Research Methods in Public Relations and Marketing Communications*. London: Routledge.

Doi, T. (1981) *The Anatomy of Dependence*. New York: Kodansha International.

Doney, P. M., Cannon, J. P. & Mullen, M. R. (1998) Understanding the influence of national culture on the development of trust, *The Academy of Management Review*, 23(3), 601–620.

Elliot, J. & Martin, J. (2007) Confucian philosophy for teaching twenty first values in Australian schools, *International Journal of Humanities*, 7(5), 145–156.

Ennis, R. H. (1996) *Critical Thinking*. London: Prentice Hall.

Facione, P. A., Sanchez, C. A., Facione, N. C. & Gainen, J. (1995) The disposition toward critical thinking, *Journal of General Education*, 44(1), 1–25.

Gao, G. & Ting-Toomey, S. (1998) *Communicating Effectively with the Chinese*, vol. 5 of *Communicating Effectively in Multicultural Contexts*. Thousand Oaks, CA and London: Sage.

Gee, J. P. (1994) From 'the savage mind' to 'ways with words'. In J. Maybin (ed.) *Language and Literacy in Social Practice*. Clevedon: Multilingual Matters and The Open University, pp. 168–192.

Glaser, B. G. & Strauss, A. L. (1967) *The Discovery of Grounded Theory: Strategies for Qualitative Research*. New York: Aldine de Gruyter.

Graves, D. H. (1978) *Balance the Basics: Let them Write*. New York: Ford Foundation.

Hall, E. T. (1976) *Beyond Culture*. New York: Doubleday.

Hampden-Turner, C. & Trompenaars, F. (2000) *Building Cross-Cultural Competence*. Chichester: Wiley.

Hird, B. (1999) English for academic purposes: cultural impediments to academic objectivity, *Prospect*, 14(1), 28–43.

Hofstede, G. (1991) *Cultures and Organizations: Software of the Mind*. London: McGraw-Hill.

Hofstede, G. (2001) *Culture's Consequences* (2nd edn). Thousand Oaks, CA: Sage.

290   *Kathy Durkin*

Hofstede, G. & Bond, M. H. (1984) Hofstede's culture dimensions: an independent validation using Rokeach's value survey, *Journal of Cross-Cultural Psychology*, 15(4), 417–433.
Humphreys, C. (1951) *Buddhism*. Harmondsworth: Penguin.
Hutton, J. (2001) Narrowing the concept of marketing. In M. T. Ewing (ed.) *Social Marketing*. New York: Best Business Books.
Jin, L. & Cortazzi, M. (1993) Cultural orientation and academic language use. In D. Graddol, L. Thompson & M. Byram (eds) *Language and Culture*. Clevedon: Multilingual Matters.
Jin, L. & Cortazzi, M. (1998) The culture the learner brings: a bridge or a barrier? In M. Byram & M. Fleming (eds) *Language Learning in Intercultural Perspective*. Cambridge: Cambridge University Press.
Lim, Tae-Seop (2002) Language and verbal communication across cultures. In W. B. Gudykunst & B. Mody (eds) *Handbook of International and Intercultural Communication* (2nd edn). Thousand Oaks, CA: Sage, pp. 69–87.
Matsumoto, Y. (1988) Re-examination of the universality of face: politeness phenomena in Japanese, *Journal of Pragmatics*, 12, 403–426.
Mingers, J. (2000) What is it to be critical? Teaching a critical approach to management undergraduates, *Management Learning*, 31(2), 219–237.
Nye, Andrea (1990) *Words of Power: A Feminist Reading of the History of Logic*. New York: Routledge.
Orr, Deborah (1989) Just the facts ma'am: informal logic, gender and pedagogy, *Informal Logic*, 11(1), Winter, 1–10.
Paul, R. (1993) *Critical Thinking: What Every Person Needs to Survive in a Rapidly Changing World* (3rd edn). Robert Park, CA: The Center for Critical Thinking and Moral Critique, Sonoma State University.
Quality Assurance Agency (QAA) (2007) *Subject Benchmark Statements: Master's Degrees in Business Management*. QAA 158 02/07. Section 3:10. http://www.qaa.ac.uk/academicinfrastructure/benchmark/statements/BusinessManagementMasters.asp.
Scardamalia, Marlene & Bereiter, Carl (1994) Development of dialectical processes in composition. In B. Stierer & J. Maybin (eds) *Language, Literacy and Learning in Educational Practice*. Clevedon: Multilingual Matters and The Open University, pp. 295–309.
Schwartzman, R. (1995) Students as customers: a mangled managerial metaphor. Paper presented at the Carolinas Speech Communication Association Convention, October, Charlotte, North Carolina.
Siegel, H. (1988) *Educating Reason: Rationality, Critical Thinking and Education*. New York: Routledge.
Street, B. V. (1994) Cross cultural perspectives on literacy. In J. Maybin (ed.) *Language and Literacy in Social Practice*. Clevedon: Multilingual Matters and The Open University, pp. 139–150.
Tannen, D. (1990) *You Just Don't Understand: Women and Men in Conversation*. New York: William Morrow.
Tannen, D. (1998) *The Argument Culture*. London: Virago.
Tarnas, R. (1991) *The Passion of the Western Mind*. London: Pimlico.
Thayer-Bacon, B. (1992) Is modern critical thinking sexist?, *Inquiry: Critical Thinking Across the Disciplines*, September, 323–340.
Thayer-Bacon, B. (1993) Caring and its relationship to critical thinking, *Educational Theory*, 43(3), Summer, 322–340.

Ting-Toomey, S. (1999) *Communicating Across Cultures*. New York: Guildford Press.

Ting-Toomey, S. & Kurogi, A. (1998) Facework competence in intercultural conflict: an updated face-negotiation theory, *International Journal of Intercultural Relations*, 22, 187–225.

Triandis, H. C. (1995) *Individualism and Collectivism*. Boulder, CO: Westview Press.

Trompenaars, Fons (1993) *Riding the Waves of Culture*. London: Nicholas Brealey.

Vygotsky, L. S. (1962) *Thought and Language*. Cambridge, MA: MIT Press.

Vygotsky, L. S. (1994) Extracts from 'Thought and Language' and 'Mind and Society'. In B. Stierer & J. Maybin (eds) *Language, Literacy and Learning in Educational Practice*. Clevedon: Multilingual Matters and The Open University, pp. 45–58.

Walkner, P. & Finney, N. (1999) Skill development and critical thinking in higher education, *Teaching in Higher Education*, 4(4), 531–544.

Woodward, K. (2002) *Understanding Identity*. London: Arnold.

Yao, Z. (2000) *An Introduction to Confucianism*. Cambridge: Cambridge University Press.

13
Different Waves Crashing into Different Coastlines? Mainland Chinese Learners doing Postgraduate Dissertations in the UK

Nick Pilcher, Martin Cortazzi and Lixian Jin

13.1 Introduction

This chapter focuses on the process of learners from China completing their postgraduate master's dissertations in Britain and on the accounts given by the students and their supervisors of change during this process. This is an important topic as the dissertation is the culmination of their programme and a very high-stakes assessment; it means the difference between receiving an MSc or a Diploma. The answers to research questions here could help future learners and supervisors. To explain the analogy used in the title of the chapter, the 45 learners in the study are described as 'different waves' because despite having many common experiences and backgrounds, there was much variation in their dissertation processes: the processes differ in 'size, shape and movement' as waves differ. The waves 'crash' into 'different coastlines'; this is an analogy to describe their meetings with their supervisors in the study and the individual nature of the process of completing their dissertations. Most supervisors were British but others could be considered international, that is, they came from different countries originally: this is one marker of the internationalization of UK universities. The act of 'crashing into' is a metaphor for a synergy of learning since the 'different waves' move into and adapt to, and are finally shaped by, the 'different coastlines' they crash into. In the same way, this group of learners from China adapted to the dissertation process, rationales of study, and to the study topics and supervision they experienced. This was borne out over the course of four interviews conducted with each of the learners during their dissertation. Furthermore, over time, the waves themselves can mould and shape the coastlines they crash into: the supervisors showed signs of being shaped by the learners, although, as the analogy would suggest, their changes were often much slower than student changes, and changes depended upon how different supervisors reacted to the waves (whether, for example, the coastlines were 'chalk' or 'granite'). The metaphor provides a simple visualization of this research into an extremely complex process of adaptation to educational practices, but it adds to our picture of learners from China through expanding and drawing upon past research findings and paradigms.

Previous research concerning 'Chinese learners' is conceptualized here as orbiting around two 'hubs': one that identifies key traits or common 'core' characteristics and another that emphasizes variation, exceptions and individual differences to these 'cores'. On the one hand, researchers isolate and identify core characteristics, based on student experiences (Liu, 1986) and/or on culturally developed learning processes which are said to be common to Chinese learners (Nisbett, 2003). The label 'Chinese' need not reflect any stereotype and the core need not be exclusively Chinese but can simply be a general summary of some common characteristics found in research which seem to apply to the significant group of Chinese learners. On the other hand, researchers isolate and identify instances where core characteristics are not essential to learners from China, either in terms of transferability to other members in a group of Chinese (Clark & Gieve, 2006), or among Chinese across periods of time (Jin & Cortazzi, 2006). This hub of variation may stress local cultures, changes and individual differences or agency among Chinese learners. Indeed, the idea of a common core may be criticized from the viewpoint of the second hub as an essentializing or reductionist conception, but stressing the hub of variation does necessarily mean an absence of some influence of core characteristics. The present study does not look only at one hub, but tries to take account of – and investigate – both hubs, in order to help learners.

This analogy of 'hubs' can also be applied to research into education in the UK: in the present case, research into processes of completing postgraduate dissertations in the UK can be interpreted as orbiting around similar 'hubs'. Around one hub, 'core' features of dissertations are teased out to identify common characteristics (Clark, 2007), and around the other hub, variations and exceptions are noted (Naoum, 1998). Tables 13.1 and 13.2 are organized around the two hubs of these characteristics: core areas of dissertations and exceptions, both as recounted in students' experience (Table 13.1) and that of their supervisors (Table 13.2). Again, the aims of this study are not aligned exclusively with either

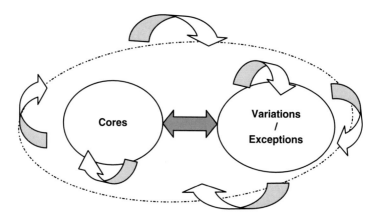

Figure 13.1 Conceptualizing research about Chinese learners and their dissertation writing around two hubs

orientation; we believe both hubs are necessary in a conceptualization which will benefit learners (see Figure 13.1).

This chapter now describes the research questions and methodology used in the study. Following this, it presents the focus and the outcome of the study, namely, two models of supervision experiences from two different perspectives: a learner perspective and a supervisor perspective. These models show the 'core' experiences, and exceptions. The models also show changes over the course of the dissertation for the learners and over the course of two years of interviews for the supervisors. These models provide a structure and focus for the rest of the chapter, which is organized according to the categories in the models. These categories are related to the dissertation and are: knowledge and process of doing the dissertation; rationale for doing the dissertation; qualities of dissertations; difficulties with doing the dissertation; help and supervision for the dissertation. A large number of learner and supervisor quotes (cited verbatim in order to retain authenticity) are used to provide immediacy and genuine examples of the findings. These findings are then discussed and placed within a larger context of other research into learners from China, before the chapter concludes.

13.2 Research focus and method

The research focus of this study is on learner and supervisor perspectives of the dissertation process. The context of this study was a School of Mathematics and Computer Science in a UK university. Its specific context was the experiences and perceptions of doing postgraduate master's dissertations of a group of 45 learners from China, and their supervisors. There were a number of key questions for this research, from both a supervisor and a learner perspective. To investigate a learner perspective, key questions were:

- Were experiences of supervision and help which learners received different between the UK and China?
- What difficulties did learners experience with the dissertation in the UK?
- Did learners change during the course of the dissertation in their outlook and/or approaches to learning?

To investigate a UK university supervisor perspective there were also a number of key questions:

- How did the supervisors perceive these postgraduate learners from China?
- What difficulties did the supervisors feel the learners had?
- How did they approach help and supervision?
- To what extent did they help?

These were important questions as the answers to them could show, for example, potential mismatches between student expectations and educational practices, and they could show the degree to which supervisors were adapting to help the learners. In a broader sense, through the lens of the supervisor–learner relationship, the answers to the questions show:

- The extent of any learner and supervisor adaptation.
- The extent of any clashes and difficulties in adaptation.
- Any fundamental differences in approaches to learning between more Confucian-type approaches and Western-type approaches.

The approach to the data was broadly qualitative. Data were collected through a total of 260 semi-structured interviews (four with each student plus two interviews with their supervisors). Learners were offered help with proofreading drafts of their dissertations in return for their time, and supervisors were told they would receive the results from the study in return for their time: the interviews were 'participatory' in Fontana and Frey's (2005) terms. Both learners and supervisors were asked if they had felt relaxed or nervous, if the room had been satisfactory and whether the interview length had been appropriate: the interviews were 'reflexive' in Jia's (2001) terms. Learners and supervisors were also asked if the interviews could be improved by adding/changing or removing any questions; in this sense the interviews were 'constructivist' (Denzin & Lincoln, 2005). The semi-structured interview format allowed for negotiation of meaning between researcher and participant – an 'active' interview (Holstein & Gubrium, 1999) – and all participants were asked if they wanted to know what others had said – thus the interviews followed a quasi-delphi technique (Cogswell & Stubblefield, 1988). The interviews were 'iterative' in that in the subsequent interview students and supervisors were read the interview transcript of their previous interview and asked if they felt the same. Regarding the number of interviews for each group of participants, the learners were interviewed at four key points over the course of the dissertation (at the start, at the stages of reading, writing up and after submission) and 31 of the total number of 45 supervisors were interviewed twice (once in 2005 and once in 2006) to investigate any changes. Regarding ethics, the interviews were all approved by the appropriate university bodies and followed a 'feminist communitarian approach' (Lincoln, 1995) for the above reasons of participatoriness, constructiveness, anonymity and protection of the individuals involved in the project. Interviews were conducted in the medium of English. However, 'shadow' interviews in Chinese were also conducted to investigate whether any major differences occurred in content as a result of the language choice of the interview. Some contrasts between the two sets of interviews are being analysed elsewhere. The interviews were then author-transcribed using a self-generated system (Poland, 2002) and were returned to each participant for verification or modification. The transcripts were analysed by identifying key areas – 'phenomenologically' (Hycner, 1999) – using an approach where key patterns and interpretations emerged as data coding took place, which is a recognized constructivist grounded-theory approach (Charmaz, 2008).

With such an open approach to data collection, a number of interpretations could be expected, and these could be multiplied when coupled with the individual nature of the dissertation. However, it could also be expected that despite differences in the content of dissertations being studied, there would be 'cores' to the process of producing the dissertation.

13.3   Key models of dissertation experience

It is unorthodox to present the results and findings of the research first. Here, this is done to focus on the models – a product of the study – which give an overview of the students' and supervisors' perceptions and experiences before we discuss categories of perceptions of the process, and then discuss the results in the wider context of other research with learners from China.

Tables 13.1 and 13.2 organize the research findings around the two hubs discussed briefly above: the horizontal row of 'core' areas of dissertation processes and another row of 'variations and exceptions' which express individual variation. The results summarized in the vertical columns will be discussed and illustrated with representative quotations

Table 13.1   Representation of the student experience of completing the postgraduate dissertation

Student model

CORE AREAS

PROCESS	RATIONALE	QUALITIES	DIFFICULTIES	HELP
• Read then write • Start early • Use supervisor	• Knowledge • Job • MSc • Chosen for supervisor	• Content • Structure • Coherence • Language	• Content • Language • MAY be specific to Chinese • May NOT be specific to Chinese	• Supervisor • Peers • Sources • Self – ask more • Good supervisor = patient, responsible, available

EXCEPTIONS

• Write then read • Referencing styles vary	• PhD preparation	• Originality	• Language not difficult for all • Dissertations not equally difficult	• Could be same or different to China

CHANGE OVER THE COURSE OF THE DISSERTATION

• Knowledge increases • Individuality increases	• Educational rationale increases	• More in line with Department aim	• Content replaces language as main difficulty	• Little change

Table 13.2 Representation of the supervisor experience of the dissertation

Supervisor model

CORE AREAS

PROCESS	RATIONALE	QUALITIES	DIFFICULTIES	HELP
• Read then write • Read a lot for some • Read little for some	• For students – • Job • Ease • Interest • For department – • Money • Research	• Structure • Coherence • Difference between good and excellent • Very difficult to judge • Students cannot judge	• English language • Language of Mathematics • Writing up • Chinese students MAY have specific difficulties • Chinese students do not have specific difficulties	• Supervisor • Peers • Sources • Prep. Courses • Self – ask more • Good supervisor is: • Patient • Responsible • Available • Help levels are student, project and supervisor dependent

EXCEPTIONS

PROCESS	RATIONALE	QUALITIES	DIFFICULTIES	HELP
• Some write then read • Student ability is institution dependent	• For PhD preparation	• In computing students underestimate write-up • Originality may be important	• Language difficult for Native speakers • Independence can be defined differently	• Unsure of how much to help with English • Unsure of value of Prep. Courses

CHANGE OVER THE COURSE OF THE DISSERTATION

PROCESS	RATIONALE	QUALITIES	DIFFICULTIES	HELP
• Student knowledge increases • Very little at first – especially overseas	• No change	• Students can judge better over time	• Over time, changes in departmental procedures can affect students	• Supervisor help changed over time – less help with language, and reduced levels of guidance

below, with some emphasis on the process of change and developing synergy between learners and supervisors.

13.4 Knowledge and process of doing the dissertation

The learners' knowledge of the dissertation increased as they completed it, and they usually met their supervisors once a week. The supervisors mostly felt the learners would have little knowledge about the dissertation but would learn more throughout the course of the dissertation. This is probably because students met their supervisors weekly, but also because supervisors themselves directed the dissertation. Indeed, the supervisors not only told the learners what to do, but also created content structure for them. For example, one supervisor said the steps for the dissertation were 'laid down by the supervisor' and another that they created a 'table of contents' with the learners. Despite this, exceptions existed: one learner did very little work to complete the dissertation, despite meeting their supervisor every week, and had a low opinion of it as a piece of work, saying that:

> I just used four days to complete my paper ... it really surprised me ... I think it's too short. (CS)

Other learners found that there were obstacles to acquiring knowledge that dictated where they were able to work, for example in not being able to work at the university due to a lack of software. This was not viewed positively by the learner, who said:

> I found out that I can't do the test on school's network ... I have to do it at home: that's pretty bad surprise actually. (CS)

The process of tasks involved in completing the dissertation (see Tables 13.1 and 13.2) was generally similar: there was a 'core' process of learners reading first, then collecting data and then writing, as perhaps could be anticipated. However, and surprisingly, some of the dissertations in computing required the exact opposite procedure of tasks. For some dissertations, learners had to experiment with software first, and later read about the software, so they were doing the exact inverse of this core. In the words of one supervisor, this effectively meant that the task of completing the dissertation for some learners meant 'doing it back to front'. In addition, the individuality of the supervision process was stressed by many supervisors, meaning it was impossible to structure.

For example, in the words of one supervisor: 'I never try to structure it because it's so individual' (BT). This individuality was also viewed as being positive by some supervisors; one noted that:

> there's as much variation in supervision as there is in personal characters and quite rightly too. (BT)

Perhaps such variety is due to the fact that the learners themselves had had greatly varying previous experiences of study. A number had come to study straight from China, yet a number of others had done undergraduate degrees in Western academic environments. In terms of the supervisors, too, there was a wide range of experience; some were novices, others had many years of experience.

Thus, despite a core of similarities to the process of completing the dissertation, and of the accumulation of knowledge for it, many exceptions existed, and here the 'waves' (the learners) and the 'coastlines' (the supervisors) were often different. The 'coastlines' often greatly determined the shape and direction the 'waves' took when they met, through very guided and direct supervision. This may have been due to the mathematical and scientific nature of the subjects of the dissertations, although it nevertheless contrasts with much of the assumed models that supervision is very 'hands off' in the 'West' but very 'directed' in 'China' (Cortazzi & Jin, 1997; Spencer-Oatey, 1997). Yet in many ways, rather than being separate, 'wave' (learner) and 'coastline' (supervisor) had synergy. This is shown by the change in rationale for doing the dissertation.

13.5   Rationale for doing the master's dissertation

Rationale is defined here as perception of value and motivation for doing the dissertation. The continual meetings between learner and supervisor had the effect of changing the 'waves': learners changed from having utilitarian rationales such as doing the dissertation 'for a job', or 'for the MSc' in the first interviews, to more educational rationales of studying independently and working by themselves in later interviews (see Table 13.1). These were often perceived beneficially. For example, one student noted in a later interview that:

> I think independent study is important ... it's very good for me to ... develop the ability to study independently. (CS)

Here, then, if the rationale is placed in the context of the close direction given above, the learners were being very strictly directed to learn for themselves, or, to keep with the analogy of the title, the 'waves' were being closely shaped by the 'coastlines'. Indeed, supervisors themselves often remarked that learner and departmental rationale differed, although most supervisors believed students followed the dissertation out of interest.

Ultimately, the question arises as to whose rationale was being shown: that of the learners, of the supervisors, or both? The more students met their supervisors, the more they noted educational aims. The learners were thus encountering 'different coastlines', and adapting to these as they encountered them. This represents a true synergy of learning, with the 'waves' of the learners being shaped by the 'coastlines' of the supervisors they are crashing into. This is further illustrated by the learners' ideas of the qualities of a dissertation.

13.6 Qualities of a dissertation

The qualities of a dissertation are understood to be what learners and supervisors believed constituted a dissertation of high quality, and how it would be judged (see Tables 13.1 and 13.2). Regarding what should constitute the core of a good dissertation, this was generally related to language, clarity and structure; however, there were differing opinions regarding whether originality was important, some supervisors believing it was, others believing it was not necessary at MSc level. Regarding learners' ability to judge how their dissertation was progressing, many supervisors noted that learners would judge the standard of their work based on supervisor feedback, often in face-to-face meetings. For example, one supervisor said directly that 'they probably always judge based on the feedback they get from me' (BT) and another said that students would judge their dissertation 'from the look on my face when I read it' (BT). This example shows learners developing a sense of quality through face-to-face interaction. The process of this can be regarded as intentional 'scaffolding' by the supervisor, since there was often strong initial guidance, but this diminished systematically, thereby increasing learner independence and confidence (Forman *et al.*, 1993; Kozulin *et al.*, 2003), combined with a less deliberate or unintentional 'leaking' of feedback through facial expression. The learners confirmed that they judged the dissertation from supervisors' feedback; for example, one learner said that:

> I think I've got 85% probability of getting a distinction, I know the grade of the last draft the supervisor had seen, and this was a distinction. (CS)

Nevertheless, what constituted a high grade was often more difficult to ascertain. Supervisors noted varieties in marking and the difficulty of grading and writing guidelines for dissertations. For example, one supervisor noted these varied greatly according to institutions; this personally confused them, and would be extremely confusing for learners:

> we try to give them guidelines as to what's expected of them ... quite frankly I've seen so many of these in different universities now that they confuse me so I don't know how the students can cope. (BT)

Such differences also resulted in wide intra-departmental marking variations, with differences of up to 25%; one supervisor said that:

> there was a difference between my assessment: I gave the student 75 marks and ... there was an internal examiner's report giving it ... 50 so there was a big difference. (BT)

Learners were also aware of these variations; they were confident their supervisor would award their dissertation a good grade, but were unsure how others would judge it, due to different ideas in the department:

> I think my supervisor's is good one but I don't know what the department says; there's like different idea. (CS)

Thus, despite core areas of language, structure and clarity, a huge range of experiences existed, and there was a perception of variation in judging dissertations, even if this stressed the complexities of judging. There was also uncertainty as to what a good, or high-quality, dissertation was. Indeed, the individuality of the dissertation was firmly prominent within these core areas. In this sense, if the dissertation is such an individual exercise, it is undoubtedly the case that the learners were encountering very different 'coastlines', although this would be content-related, rather than both content- and process-related. Over time, regarding the qualities of dissertations, the learners again came more in line with the department as the dissertation progressed, and again because of a synergy of learning.

13.7 Difficulties

For the learners, there were two core difficulties of language and content, with content replacing language as the greatest difficulty as the dissertation progressed (see Tables 13.1 and 13.2). Regarding whether the students felt learners from China had specific difficulties, there were a range of differing opinions. Some students noted difficulties all Chinese learners faced, and that this could be language, for example 'language in writing is quite difficult' (CS). In contrast, others felt Chinese learners did not share common difficulties, and that these varied, for example 'no, different person have different difficulties' (CS). Some learners were also unsure: 'maybe ... there are some difficulties for the Chinese student to find something new, but I'm not sure' (CS). Students also emphasized distinctions in 'types' of Chinese learner, contrasting learners who had recently arrived from overseas with others who had been in the UK or another country outside China for a number of years. For example:

> no, we're in a different level ... some Chinese student have stay you know in this country or other oversea countries for a long time, three, four, you know five, six years ... [whereas] ... somebody just come have just been here for one year everything's new. (CS)

Supervisors also had very similar views to the learners. Some believed that Chinese learners did have key traits which could, say, hinder the ability to criticize and analyse. Such traits included a desire to reproduce and memorize, which could be connected with educational cultures. For example:

> I think a characteristic of the Chinese students that I meet is that they are very good at memorizing things and it may be a feature of the way they've been educated ... they like to remember things and then reproduce them. (BT)

Similarly to the students, some supervisors stressed that dealing with learners from China was the same as dealing with anyone else, and that Chinese learners could be extremely independent and demanding, which was a good thing. For example, that dealing with Chinese students was

> no different to dealing with foreigners in everyday walks of life ... I think Chinese students are actually quite independent in a way ... they tend to be able to go off and do stuff on their own ... come and see you quite a lot ... and some of them are quite demanding. I find that's good because they're actually asking good questions. (BT)

Also similar to the students, other supervisors had a somewhat less hardened view that although Chinese learners generally lacked independence and liked to be directed, this did not apply to all learners from China:

> they do have specific difficulties; they like to be told what to do quite a lot. This is not unique to Chinese students of course but maybe a higher proportion of them like to be told what to do. (BT)

And again, like the students, supervisors emphasized the different types of learners from China, contrasting learners who had been here for some time with those who had just come for their MSc. Some learners from China:

> did finish their undergraduate in UK ... and some of them just came for studying ... their MSc ... of course those two groups of students ... have different experience. (BT)

In addition, other supervisors emphasized an increased variety of learners from China, ranging from the extremely good to the very poor:

> the trend is ... they're getting more variable ... and ... this was confirmed by coffee conversations: 'so how's your Chinese student?' 'Oh mine's alright' and so on but now the conversations are: 'Oh I've got a really, really terrible ...', 'Oh well, I've got a great one.' (BT)

Conversely, others believed that the nature of Chinese learners was fixed. Whether the students completed foundation courses prior to their studies made little difference, as their education system was said to be so embedded:

> [a foundation course] doesn't actually change what they end up doing in the project ... I think their education system is quite deeply ingrained. (BT)

Thus, as students do, supervisors present a very complex picture of Chinese learners' difficulties. A specific subject complexity was also noted by some mathematics supervisors, who commented upon the complexity of having to write about mathematics, as mathematics has its own grammar, which is different to English grammar, making dissertation writing even more difficult for the learners:

> mathematics itself has a grammar ... and so that has to get blended in with English language which also has a grammar and the two grammars are not necessarily the same so how you switch in and out of for a mathematical argument ... it's actually a very difficult thing to do that for a student. (BT)

Here, then, much of the data shows the perception of different 'waves' of learners by *both* the learners from China and their supervisors. This in itself is an example of synergy, in that all the same views about the learners were present in the views of the supervisors. In other words, the 'waves' had clearly crashed into the 'coastlines'.

13.8 Help and supervision

For the learners, core good supervisor qualities were personal ones of patience, empathy and responsibility, particularly with overseas students (see Table 13.1). For example:

> [supervisors should be] patient especially ... for foreign students; sometimes we don't understand; never do .... English dissertation before don't know the system. (CS)

Surprisingly though, although knowledge was of importance, these personal qualities were accorded far greater priority. Nevertheless, some learners believed knowledge was critical, and expressed surprise that supervisors could supervise dissertations if they seemed to lack content-area knowledge. For example:

> I found it a little bit strange ... many friend ... has a supervisor and some of them know nothing about the research field and nothing about programming ... that confuse me ... how could them supervise a master's student? (CS)

Regarding guidance, some learners believed the supervisor should be traditionally 'Western' and guide rather than direct; this was often cited as preferable to 'Chinese' directive supervision. For example:

> in China headache ... the teachers have different culture to teach ... when I did dissertation in China I also had a very good supervisor

> but when I finish my first draft it seemed he did not give me the
> guidance but he amend everything for me ... at that time when I was
> in China I think I always recognize he's a very good supervisor but
> right now I think I prefer my supervisor here ... he just give me guid-
> ance I should do everything by myself, I prefer this way. (CS)

Nevertheless, not all learners experienced supervision this way; surprisingly, some had experienced much greater direction in the UK (the 'Chinese'
way) and much more independence in China (the 'Western' way):

> No, it's totally different ... here the supervisor he gives me the mate-
> rials information whatever you need and he help me a lot ... but in
> China I have to do the dissertation by myself. (CS)

This could be due to the huge pressures on teachers in China after the
rapid expansion in numbers in Chinese higher education (Jin & Cortazzi,
2006) which has arguably provoked changes in supervision practices, or
it may simply indicate that there are a range of supervision styles both
in China and in the West, and both include some that run counter to
common perceptions.

Supervisors had similar core ideas as learners regarding a 'good' supervisor; that is, that they should be patient, responsible and available (see
Table 13.2). One area of tension was regarding English language help.
Some supervisors were very reluctant to help with English, emphasizing
it was outside their remit:

> I don't want to hear 'Could you make this read better?' I'm not inter-
> ested in dealing with English language issues. (BT)

Conversely, others felt an obligation to help learners, particularly non-
native speakers; for example:

> I feel supervisors have an obligation to, particularly to assist people
> whose native language isn't English ... in writing a dissertation in
> English but not all my colleagues take the same view. (BT)

Moreover, some supervisors noted that they considered assumed
cultural characteristics of learners from China, and that they were
therefore more directive:

> I would suggest Chinese student is a wonderful example do work
> better under a structured process ... someone that tells them what to
> do what's required at each stage. (BT)

One supervisor even noted how they were changing after encountering the different 'waves' of the learners, and were now far more appreciative and accommodating of a Chinese writing style:

> I used to be more worried about the English but now I'm not 'cos I mean in Chinese writing you often ... see superlatives and flowery statements all the time and I think that's fine now, it's an interesting way of seeing the world. (BT)

Thus, there were changes in supervision. This was partly to support the need for students to move towards the university expectations and partly of the need for the university to move towards the students. There were also changes of ideas regarding the acceptability of different written styles, and an appreciation of a wider diversity of styles. These are arguably effects of the different 'waves' of learners upon the different 'coastlines' they were crashing into.

There is an interesting paradox here. On the one hand, the UK university supervisors are clearly trying to help the learners from China by adapting how they supervise in order to meet their perceptions of students' expectations and needs, and this partly reflects their received ideas of how supervision is done in China. On the other hand, by doing this, the learners from China may have a similar experience in Britain to that of many students who remain in China. Yet the learners from China are unlikely to expect the processes of the master's programme in the UK to be the same as they are in China; surely perceptions of benefits include ideas about acculturating to different learning processes. If things were not different, at least in some key aspects, then there would be little point in the learners studying in Britain, unless the students' focus is solely and specifically upon the content delivered. Some of this paradox might be explained by differences between undergraduate and postgraduate supervision styles in the UK and in China, but none of the supervisors mentioned this. It is perhaps the case that things are quite simple in fact: the students from China could have been learners from anywhere, and they were simply working their way through the dissertation, with help from the supervisors, and that the process was a synergetic one. This chapter now discusses the relationship of these results to past and recent literature about learners from China.

13.9 Discussion

This chapter has conceptualized research into Chinese learners as an orbit around two 'hubs': one hub seeks to establish key traits or commonalities among learners designated as 'Chinese'; and a second hub emphasizes variations and individual differences among such groups. The idea of a hub of key traits and another of variations provides a useful framework with which to discuss the results of this research. First, it is claimed that some key traits of 'Chineseness' apply to all or many Chinese learners (Watkins & Biggs, 2001; Nisbett, 2003; Ouyang, 2004, 2006). Consequently, knowledge of these key traits can help tutors of Chinese learners identify and anticipate students' needs, and thus the students can be more successful in British (or other) academic circles. These 'key' traits may be different ways of viewing general concepts of the world as 'either–or' binary choices in the West or as 'both' aspects in a more holistic view which characterizes influential traditions in China (Moore, 1967: 6) or that the processing of mathematical concepts differs between China and the West (Nisbett, 2003). Furthermore, certain issues are widely recognized as more important in China than elsewhere, such as preserving and maintaining public image, or 'face' (Pan, 2000; Jia, 2001). Regarding supervision and teaching, it is often emphasized that in China a Confucian approach notes the importance and reverence given to the teacher (Spencer Oatey, 1997). Such Confucian approaches are also integrated with social and family structures (Bond & Hwang, 1986: 263).

However, the possibility or appropriateness of assuming key traits which are thought to apply to all learners from China is questionable. Clearly, defining 'the Chinese learner' (Clark & Gieve, 2006) is complex, and different 'waves' of Chinese learners exist (Jin & Cortazzi, 2006); previous learners would have been 'first-rank' government-scholarship winners, but many 'other ranks' of learners are now coming to the UK in the wake of the Chinese economic boom. Notably, the notion of variation and exceptions within groups of learners exists in earlier and more recent literature. For example, regarding training and disciplinary techniques used by Chinese parents, 'evidence does not allow unequivocal generalizations to be made about a single Chinese pattern of disciplining children' (Ho, 1986: 16). Further, core statements are often couched in modal terms that imply cautions and caveats: for instance, that for Chinese students to see British students being 'active in schools in Britain *is likely* to be a shock' (Jin, 1992: 70) and that Chinese students *will often* ask questions after class rather than during a class (Jin & Cortazzi, 1998; our italics). Reviews of literature on Chinese learners have also noted key elements and tendencies rather than essential characteristics, and championed this approach as being one to use when working with learners from China (Crooke & Windrum, 2006). As with the 'key trait focused sources' above, these 'exception'-type sources are also both recent and old, and also show continuous rather than absolute paradigms.

Indeed, the dates of the sources cited in this section show that the notion of 'key trait focused' research and 'variation type' research both work within long-standing paradigms. Thus, rather than show a *teleological* picture of research, they show the existence of both these paradigms *over time*; it is not the case that research is 'progressing' towards a goal (*telos*) of, say, one hub predominating over another, but that researchers structure and view their research in a specific way. Moreover, many who read the sources may themselves view them *through* such paradigms, that is, of being able to identify generalized 'key traits', or to look for 'variations' and exceptions. Arguably, paying attention to research from both hubs can help participants to predict or manage different futures. To say what core issues and characteristic experiences some (or many, but not all) students from China will (or may) have needs to be offset by statements of variation and allowance for local contexts. There will always be variation, since general statements in this area are not intended to be rules. However, looking only at individual differences and local variation may lose some of the power of generalization, where general statements are warranted.

Clearly, the data in this chapter show that the 'sea' in this case was one of uncertainty and of 'exceptions', yet with 'core' experiences. Although many learners and supervisors believed there were key traits to experiences and approaches, others did not. This group of 45 learners from China experienced many types of supervision from their supervisors; they had a range of views, and these changed to be more in line with what their department (or rather, their supervisor) was advising. The learners had had greatly differing previous experiences of study, as had their supervisors. Yet, just as the 'key trait' paradigm can provide researchers with a firm hold in a sea of uncertainty, it also clearly did so here for many of the students from China and their supervisors who operated successfully under such paradigms.

Nevertheless, this chapter shows a great variety in this group of learners and in their experiences in terms of: previous supervisory experiences, their difficulties, and their experiences of help and supervision. A major reason for such differences was the very fact that they were following an individual assessment exercise. The dissertation is by definition an individual piece of work, and consequently experiences of it would be different. Yet it is worthwhile to briefly consider whether it is possible to pin down the master's dissertation itself as being a fixed entity.

Many courses in different disciplines refer to the fact that students need to do a 'dissertation', but it can be a very varied object. Student advice for master's dissertations varies greatly: it can be general (Clark, 2007), subject-specific (e.g. Naoum, 1998), specific to a university department (e.g. Steven, 2008) and specific to Mainland Chinese students (Pilcher, 2008). For dissertations (as with learners from particular backgrounds), some researchers find 'key traits' that can be described (e.g. Clark, 2007), yet for others, there are 'exceptions' (e.g. Naoum, 1998). Arguably, the individual 'core' of the master's dissertation highlights a paradox in the assumption of the 'key traits' aspect to a dissertation. At the master's level Scottish Credit and Qualifications Framework Level 11 (SCQF, n.d.) and at UK master's level in general, the dissertation is expected to be an individual piece of work (e.g. Seymour, 2005). This individuality means *by implication* that the content of the work cannot have key characteristics, unless this individuality is considered an essential characteristic, which is paradoxical. Nevertheless, in terms of the process of completing the dissertation, it is possible or likely that 'key traits' exist. This chapter shows that this is so in this case, both regarding how judgement was arrived at, and regarding the steps for completing the dissertation (allowing for the 'exceptions' of how the dissertation was completed in computing).

To summarize: all these learners from China completed an MSc dissertation; there was great variety in the completion process and in the dissertations. Inevitably, if the content of the dissertation is individual, the learners will have individual experiences and rightly show differing perceptions. Furthermore, the learners were clearly coming to do the dissertation with very different backgrounds and experiences. Nevertheless, in terms of the process, there were 'core' areas and experiences, and also synergies of learning. While it is natural in research to seek generalizations and perhaps 'key traits', we cannot assume these apply to all cases and we should guard against overgeneralizations or stereotypes. Yet, this chapter shows that, even despite this, many learners from China, and many supervisors they encountered, operated perfectly successfully using these 'key traits' in their academic worldviews.

13.10   Conclusion

Through the consideration of 45 learners from China and their supervisors' experiences and perceptions of completing MSc dissertations a number of conclusions can be drawn. The learners were described as being different 'waves' as their previous educational experiences varied greatly, and they had differing views and experiences of the dissertation. Their supervisors were described as different 'coastlines' to represent the different experiences of the learners, as 'waves', when they met them. Nevertheless, there were a number of core ideas and experiences, and learners did indeed adapt to their department over the course of the dissertation. Many supervisors also changed through encountering these different 'waves' of learners; their views and perceptions varied, and changed over time, although not as greatly as those of the students. This chapter invites teachers and tutors to consider their own academic topography, and to encourage their students either directly or indirectly to consider the nature of their own individual 'wave'. The metaphor in the title can be extended in that 'currents' (cohorts of learners) can influence the nature of the waves, and 'sea breezes' (local institutional or international climates) can smooth the encounter of the waves or make it choppier.

The case studied in this research and the qualitative nature of the data collection used arguably amplifies the generation of individual and non-essential experiences shown. Nevertheless, they do show the variation in learners from China, and in how they are perceived and supervised in the UK. Other learners from China going to study elsewhere will be similarly varied, and can arguably expect to encounter a different experience of education. Having concluded that different 'waves' crash into different 'coastlines', an obvious practical application of the findings of this chapter is to give a blank copy of the model to students in initial supervisory meetings and ask them to complete it (or to supervisors in in-house training sessions). This blank model, once completed, can be compared to those presented here and discussed. Whether the dissertation process and product have universal qualities is debatable, but the use of the models shown here will provide a reflective focal point for both students and supervisors to discuss their specific dissertation.

References

Bond, M. H. & Hwang, K. K. (1986) The social psychology of Chinese people. In M. H. Bond (ed.) *The Psychology of the Chinese People.* Hong Kong: Oxford University Press.

Charmaz, K. (2008) Advancing qualitative research through grounded theory. Keynote presentation at the 7th Biannual Qualitative Research Conference, Bournemouth University, UK, 8–10 September.

Clark, I. L. (2007) *Writing the Successful Thesis and Dissertation: Entering the Conversation.* Princeton: Pearson.

Clark, R. & Gieve, S. N. (2006) On the discursive construction of 'the Chinese learner', *Language, Culture and Curriculum*, 19(1), 54–73.

Cogswell, D. & Stubblefield, H. (1988) Assessing the training and staff development needs of mental health professionals, *Administration and Policy in Mental Health*, 16(1), 14–24.

Cortazzi, M. & Jin, L. (1997) Communication for learning across cultures. In D. McNamara & R. Harris (eds) *Overseas Students in Higher Education*. London: Routledge.

Crooke, C. & Windrum, W. (2006) *The 'Chinese Learner': A Literature Review: University of Nottingham in Collaboration with Beijing Foreign Studies University*. http://www.echinaprogramme.org/papers/reports/reports.php.

Denzin, N. K. & Lincoln, Y. S. (2005) Introduction: the discipline and practice of qualitative research. In N. K. Denzin & Y. S. Lincoln, *The SAGE Handbook of Qualitative Research*. Thousand Oaks, CA: Sage.

Fontana, A. & Frey, J. H. (2005) The interview: from neutral stance to political involvement. In N. K. Denzin & Y. S. Lincoln, *The SAGE Handbook of Qualitative Research*. Thousand Oaks, CA: Sage.

Forman, E., Minick, N. & Stone, C. (eds) (1993) *Contexts for Learning: Sociocultural Dynamics in Children's Development*. Oxford: Oxford University Press.

Ho, D. Y. F. (1986) Chinese patterns of socialization. In M. H. Bond (ed.) *The Psychology of the Chinese People*. Hong Kong: Oxford University Press.

Holstein, J. A. & Gubrium, J. F. (1999) Active interviewing. In A. Bryman & R. G. Burgess (eds) *Qualitative Research*, vol. 2. Thousand Oaks, CA: Sage.

Hycner, R. H. (1999) Some guidelines for the phenomenological analysis of interview data. In A. Bryman & R. G. Burgess (eds) *Qualitative Research*, vol. 3. Thousand Oaks, CA: Sage.

Jia, W. (2001) *The Remaking of the Chinese Character and Identity in the 21st Century: The Chinese Face Practices*. Westport. CT: Ablex Publishing.

Jin, L. (1992) Academic cultural expectations and second language use: Chinese postgraduate students in the UK: a cultural synergy model. PhD thesis, University of Leicester.

Jin, L. & Cortazzi, M. (1998) The culture the learner brings: a bridge or a barrier. In M. Byram & M. Fleming (eds) *Language Learning in Intercultural Perspective: Approaches through Drama and Ethnography*. Cambridge: Cambridge University Press.

Jin, L. & Cortazzi, M. (2006) Changing practices in Chinese cultures of learning, *Language, Culture and Curriculum*, 19(1), 5–20.

Kozulin, A., Gindis, B., Ageyev, V. & Miller, S. (eds) (2003) *Vygotsky's Educational Theory in Cultural Context*. Cambridge: Cambridge University Press.

Lincoln, Y. S. (1995) Emerging criteria for quality in qualitative and interpretive inquiry, *Qualitative Inquiry*, 1, 275–289.

Liu, I.-M. (1986) Chinese cognition. In M. H. Bond (ed.) *The Psychology of the Chinese People*. Hong Kong: Oxford University Press.

Moore, C. A. (1967) *The Chinese Mind: Essentials of Chinese Philosophy and Culture*. Honolulu: The University Press of Hawaii.

Naoum, S. G. (1998) *Dissertation Research and Writing for Construction Students*. Oxford: Elsevier Butterworth-Heinemann.

Nisbett, R. (2003) *The Geography of Thought: How Asians and Westerners Think Differently and Why*. New York: Free Press.

Ouyang, H. (2004) *Remaking of Face and Community of Practices: An Ethnography of Local and Expatriate English Teachers' Reform Stories in Today's China.* Beijing: Peking University Press.

Ouyang, H. (2006) Understanding the Chinese learners' community of practices: an insider–outsider's view. Plenary presentation at the Conference Responding to the Needs of the Chinese Learner: Internationalising the University. The University of Portsmouth, UK.

Pan, Y. (2000) *Politeness in Chinese Face-to-Face Interaction.* Westport, CT: Ablex Publishing.

Pilcher, N. (2008) Mainland Chinese student suggestions for producing good masters dissertations. In B. Beaven (ed.) *IATEFL 2007 Conference Selections.* Canterbury: IATEFL.

Poland, B. D. (2002) Transcription quality. In J. F. Gubrium & J. A. Holstein (eds) *Handbook of Interview Research: Context and Method.* Thousand Oaks, CA: Sage.

SCQF (n.d.) *Scottish Credit and Qualifications Framework Level Descriptors.* http://www.scqf.org.uk.

Seymour, D. (2005) Learning outcomes and assessment: developing assessment criteria for masters-level dissertations, *Brookes eJournal of Learning and Teaching.* http://www.brookes.ac.uk/publications/beltj/volume1issue2/academic/seymour.html.

Spencer-Oatey, H. (1997) Unequal relationships in high and low power-distance societies, *Journal of Cross-Cultural Psychology,* 28(3), 284–302.

Steven, G. (2008) Edinburgh Napier University. School of Accounting, Economics and Statistics Honours Dissertation: Student Guide. Unpublished dissertation guide, Edinburgh Napier University.

Watkins, D. A. & Biggs, J. B. (eds) (2001) *Teaching the Chinese Learner: Psychological and Pedagogical Perspectives.* Hong Kong: Comparative Education Research Centre, the University of Hong Kong.

Conclusions: What are We Learning from Research about Chinese Learners?

Martin Cortazzi and Lixian Jin

These conclusions briefly pick up several issues which emerge from the chapters presented here and point to some directions for further research, mainly in the form of questions. Arguably, the main outcome from the research presented here is, in fact, a series of further questions: any good research is based on questions, the answers to which lead to further questions.

'Chinese learners'

The term 'Chinese learners' is a trade-off between generalization and diversity. There is always a need for some level of generalization in research, and related to Chinese learners there is a need to take account of Chinese perceptions and self-identification with linguistic, ethnic and cultural aspects of being recognized as 'Chinese'. However, there is another need to recognize the clear diversity and differences between individuals, groups, local communities and the geographic, economic, social and cultural diversity that must characterize Chinese learners. Those who make generalizations need to avoid reduction and over-simplification through labelling as 'Chinese' or a false sense of sameness and homogeneity. In one sense, at least, the group of Chinese learners cannot be fixed, static or reified into a supposed object of study: apart from changing contexts, learners by definition should be changing and developing over time precisely because they are learning, since this must imply some cognitive and maybe social change. On the other hand, those who investigate local cases of learning and contexts of Chinese learners, whether in China or internationally around the world, will likely concentrate on particular details and specific, perhaps local, issues but they would be unwise not to consider generalizations that probably apply to many other Chinese contexts or to Chinese learners as a whole or, as we might prefer to say, to learners who happen to come from China or who have a Chinese heritage. In considering learners from China, some aspects may well prove to be specifically Chinese but others will surely relate to commonality or to achievements, developments and issues that are worldwide and which apply to humanity as a whole. In this sense, research with Chinese learners needs to be humane in general or, to take a Chinese term, it may be seen as having a dimension of the Chinese traditional value of *ren*, a concept which is variously translated as humaneness, kindness, benevolence or love, with overtones of being good-hearted and having a sense of connectedness and reciprocal relations with others.

Some research issues and topics for further investigation

From the studies in this book, the topic of researching Chinese learners is clearly highly significant, both in China and internationally. This topic is both open-ended and dynamic since educational contexts and learners are visibly changing and because our understanding of the complexity of relevant issues is, we hope, somewhat deeper and broader than was previously the case. The contributors here have shown a wide range of focus on interesting and useful areas for further research and in the range of methods used in the various projects. These uses of the methods reveal that researchers can use established methods in new ways for a variety of contexts for Chinese learners. Researchers here also use innovative methods to investigate established topics with intriguing outcomes. Methods which have been discussed here and which can be further developed and applied include: iterative interviewing and combinations of research approaches in longitudinal studies; the further application of metaphor research to educational values and beliefs; and the investigations of students' personal experiences of learning using narrative inquiry, and visual representations of student learning using pictures, maps, diagrams and storylines.

From the work represented here, topics for further investigation include the following lines of inquiry. There are the questions of exactly how Chinese learners use *memorization* and develop *creativity* in different skills and disciplines – the former has been seen as a strength and the latter as a weakness in China and probably both have been misrepresented in many Western discussions. There are further questions about the development of *language skills*: how can teachers find further ways to overcome reticence and develop confident speaking in classrooms, especially in large classes? How can teachers develop students' specific academic skills required in writing, especially those written skills which are intertwined with *thinking skills*? This includes investigating further ways to develop learners' awareness and competence in argumentation, critical thinking and evaluation and the kinds of *research skills* required, for instance, for postgraduate education. There are a further set of questions about challenges for Chinese *teachers as learners*: how or how much do teachers develop their knowledge of and learning about world Englishes, about English-speaking cultures worldwide and, of course, about other cultures around the world? How can or how do Chinese teachers develop professional and pedagogic skills to meet the demands of internationalization, and develop their *ability to help Chinese learners* to know about, reflect on and prepare for these areas in relation to their identities, Chinese cultures and students' professional futures?

Intercultural adaptation and cultures of learning

There are many further research questions about the *intercultural adaptation* of Chinese learners in international contexts. This adaptation may feature important aspects *linguistically, socially, academically* and (recognizing that many learners are already, or will shortly be, professionals) *professionally* in both study and workplace contexts. Recognizing that cultural adaptation is a two-way – or multiple – concern, we should ask how other international students or teachers adapt to Chinese learners. We can, therefore, still ask: who adapts to what, exactly, and at what stages of what kinds of pedagogic or social relationships, how or to what extent, and under what circumstances? The question of learners' *agency* is crucial: to what extent, and at what points of the period of being a sojourner, do learners feel they have adequate knowledge, choice and control over key aspects of adaptation on the dimensions indicated above?

When Jin and Cortazzi introduced the term *cultures of learning* into language teaching and applied linguistics discussions in the early 1990s (see references in the Introduction and Chapters 3, 4, 7, 10, 11 and 13), they had three intentions: first, to draw attention to cultural features of learning which at the time were largely overlooked; second, to analyse in some detail the cultural features of how Chinese learners said they were learning, which at the time gave significant insights to language teachers and others teaching Chinese students; third, to propose the strong need to learn about learners' ideas of learning and to see this in terms of synergy. 'Synergy' suggests working together coherently so that the whole is more than a sum of the separate elements. This third idea was that while Chinese learners, studying internationally, had a necessity to learn about Western ideas of learning and teaching, there was a complementary obligation for Western teachers to learn about Chinese ways of learning: cultural synergy is thus reciprocal learning, not just about culture and intercultural communication but specifically about learning. Teachers and students, it was argued, need to learn about each other's values, conceptions and experiences of teaching and learning. For students, this would be a metacognitive awareness of learning across cultures; for teachers, it would be the professional and humane development of learning about cultural ideas of learning. Further research questions which can be asked about this include: what are the processes and stages of the development of cultural synergy; how do academics and professionals in the West interpret and draw on cultural synergy; and how do students returning to China use the social cultural values that they have learned internationally in their professional work to benefit China?

The Confucian heritage

While the concepts of intercultural adaptation and cultural synergy look forward from the present to likely future practice, many writers about Chinese learners have looked back at the cultural heritages of East Asia in the search for explanations about current learning. Special mention is often made of Confucian ideas in this regard. Given the long educational history of Confucian influence in China – one only has to think of the thousand or so years of Confucian-based examinations in China between the Sung dynasty and the early twentieth century – this leads to understandable questions about what this influence might be for contemporary learning among Chinese students. Researchable angles here include: what exactly do the writings of Confucian scholars over the centuries say about teaching and learning; how do Confucian traditions blend with other important streams of historical influences on Chinese thinking and practices of learning, notably those of Buddhist, Taoist and contemporary 'socialist' ways of thinking? Does the Confucian tradition simply reduce to a high evaluation of education, determined efforts to learn and a drive to succeed in educational examinations, to conform to parental wishes for educational success, and, usually, evince a respect for teachers and knowledge, or are there other Confucian values (such as *ren*, mentioned earlier) which are highly relevant to modern living and learning? Like the term 'Chinese learners', the expression 'Confucian heritage' should not be used simplistically nor reduced to a few social values: the heritage, after all, clearly has multiple strands, is heterogeneous and dynamic, and, like many features of Chinese culture, is not just a historical artefact. It is thought by many to be relevant today: witness the huge popularity in China of recent TV programmes and books about Confucian teachings.

For researchers into Chinese learners – or those who are interested in learning in general or who investigate other kinds of learning – the Confucian tradition has many gems which offer insights, including the following verses from the *Li Ji*, the Book of Rites, one of the Chinese classics which has been circulated in education since the second century BC if not far earlier:

Learn avidly! Question what you have learned repeatedly!

And this advice to a student, surely advice for every student and researcher, from the *Li Ji* and widely known in the smaller much-studied book of the *Da Xue*, The Great Learning:

He should not stop questioning until he has known all, neither should he stop asking until he has exhausted his questions, nor should he stop thinking until he has found all the answers, nor should he stop distinguishing until he has made the differences clear, nor should he stop acting until he has done his sincere best.

Index